FIRST EDITION

D1430376

EMPIRE OF FUNK

HIP HOP AND REPRESENTATION IN

FILIPINA/O AMERICA

Edited by
**Mark R. Villegas, Kuttin' Kandi,
and Roderick N. Labrador**
with Foreword by Jeff Chang

Bassim Hamadeh, CEO and Publisher
Michael Simpson, Vice President of Acquisitions
Jamie Giganti, Managing Editor
Jess Busch, Graphic Design Supervisor
Becky Smith, Acquisitions Editor
Monika Dziamka, Project Editor
Natalie Lakosil, Licensing Manager
Miguel Macias, Interior Designer

First published in the United States of America in 2014 by Cognella, Inc.

Images found on cover and interior, adapted from the original:
Copyright © 2012 Depositphotos Inc./Blinkblink
Cover photo by Mike Dream
Cover photo by Jonathan "Took" Evangelista
Copyright © 2013 Allan Aquino

Printed in the United States of America

ISBN: 978-1-62661-283-9 (pbk)/ 978-1-62661-284-6 (br)

www.cognella.com   800-200-3908

Reviews of *Empire of Funk: Hip Hop and Representation in Filipina/o America*:

"Hiphop has long been a culture that has brought together different types of people. We know its creators were African American, Latino/a, and West Indian. But what many do not know is the incredible and powerful contributions of the Asian community to hiphop, the most dominant youth culture on the planet since the late 1970s. *Empire of Funk: Hip Hop and Representation in Filipina/o America* is a very necessary and spectacular contribution to correcting that great omission. And it is my sincere hope that scholars, the media, and hiphop heads will all make Empire of Funk a necessary reference point in our understanding of who we are, the multi-cultural and multi-generational hiphop nation."

—KEVIN POWELL, President/CoFounder, BK Nation

"You have to marvel at the evolution of Hip Hop. The music and culture that started off in the Bronx by disenfranchised and overlooked kids from the ravages of the South Bronx, one of the poorest, most desolate places in the country, is now 40 years old and global. During its evolution, we've seen folks of all shapes and ethnic stripes and from a variety of different regions step up and represent in the Global Cipher. We've seen folks rap, dance, show off their turntable skills and get busy with the spray can. Now folks are stepping forth and repping in the knowledge cipher. That means we are looking at history, contributions, cultural aesthetics, socialization, political and economic impact, etc.

Stepping up to the proverbial mic and throwing down is Kuttin Kandi, Mark R. Villegas and Roderick N. Labrador. They are bringing serious scholarship and "dropping mad science" in this new, fascinating book called *Empire of Funk*, which chronicles the [influence] and contributions Filipinos throughout the diaspora have had on Hip Hop.

From the early days of mobile deejays on the West Coast, to the first rap record via Joe Bataan, to one of the first Hip Hop radio shows via Nasty Nes, to the domination of turntablism with folks like DJ QBert, to indepth conversations around the challenges of identity, navigating America, and fitting into a culture dominated by African Americans and Latinos, no stone is left unturned as this trio and their array of contributors do what Hop has always done and needs to do—Show and Prove—and, in this case, take the game and culture to higher levels. This is a must-read book."

—DAVE "DAVEY D" COOK, journalist, adjunct professor at SF State, host of Hard Knock radio

"In *Empire of Funk: Hip Hop and Representation in Filipina/o America*, we have a new Hip Hop classic! Kuttin Kandi, Roderick N. Labrador, and Mark R. Villegas bring wisdom, awareness, and acknowledgment of Hip Hop's global tribe through the eyes of the Filipina/o community. Moving, historical, and powerful, the stories, the rhymes, the beats, the moves, the politics, the language, and the love all shine through and give voice to a critical part of Hip Hop's history. A must-read!"

—JLOVE CALDERÓN, activist, social entrepreneur, and transmedia producer

TABLE OF CONTENTS

III.

THE STREETS IS EVERYWHERE: GEOGRAPHY AND HIP HOP IN FILIPINA/O AMERICA

IV.

MASCULINITIES, POWER, AND HIP HOP PINAYISM

V.

VISUALIZING FILIPINA/O AMERICAN YOUTH CULTURE

VI.

ACTIVISTAS ON THE DOWN BEAT: HIP HOP AS PRAXIS

VII.

PESOS AND CENTS: SURVIVING INDUSTRIES

A NOTE ON TERMINOLOGY

Throughout the book, authors use a variety of terms to refer to people whose ancestry can be traced to the Philippines. In Filipino American Studies, there has been healthy debate about what label should be used for the identity formation. Are we "Pilipino" or "Filipino" (i.e. the P/F debates),[1] "U.S. Pinoys" instead of "Filipino American" (to mark the exilic and diasporic condition of Filipinos as result of Spanish and American colonialism and the contemporary operations of global capitalism), Pin@y or Pinay/Pinoy? We acknowledge that identity nomenclature is politically fraught; what we call ourselves and how we and others label us says a lot about power, representation, language, and naming. In the book, authors use a variety of terms because of intentional political choices and/or convenience. For example, in her introduction Kuttin Kandi uses a range of terms, "Pilipina," "Filipina," and "Pinay" to mark specific types of identities and politics (i.e. these terms center the experiences of women, much like the term "womyn," and a term like "Pin@y" also extends the traditional fe/male gender binary). What is seemingly an inconsistent usage of terms is in fact a reflection of the diversity of identity politics and community dynamics.

Authors will also spell, hyphenate, and capitalize "hip hop/Hip Hop/hip-hop/Hiphop" in a variety of ways. Without a widely-agreed upon format, writers use the style with which they are most comfortable, often deploying their choice with political intention. For example, the capitalized "Hip Hop" is usually the preference of the Universal Zulu Nation, Hip Hop's first cultural organization that holds historical authority.

You will also encounter different spellings of "cipher/cypher." This term simply means a circle of improvisation, whether through dance, lyricism/emceeing, or knowledge-sharing.

---

1   See Sarita Eschavez See's *The Decolonized Eye: Filipino American Art and Performance* (Minneapolis, MN: University of Minnesota Press, 2009) for further discussion around the politics of identity naming and the role of decolonization in the P/F debates.

FOREWORD

FOR THE MOMENT

By Jeff Chang

It might have happened in any of a million moments.

Perhaps it came in 1979 when you learned that the guy rapping on the disco record that wasn't "Rapper's Delight" called himself Joe *Bataan*. Or maybe it was 1988, when you found out that the penultimate voice on Eazy-E's "Radio" was a DJ named Nasty *Nes*.

It might have come in 1992, when you saw a snowy VHS copy of the Rocksteady DJs burying the World DMC competition. Or 2000, when Gene Cajayon's indie film *The Debut* broke out into a full-scale, old-school style battle scene. Or also in 2000, when you saw a photo of a Psycho City DREAM piece alongside a memorial to the slain spraycan master.

Maybe it was 2007, when Krishtine De Leon walked her smarts and swag into the *Rolling Stone* offices or 2008, when JabbaWockeeZ (and Kaba Modern) dropped jaws from the stage of America's Best Dance Crew. It might have been a moment in any of a million cyphers—rhyme, dance, or knowledge—before, in-between, or since.

In that moment you felt that tremor of recognition. You had the feeling that you were not alone. And you thought that maybe everyone around you *recognized* too, and you could say to yourself, "We're here. This is us and no one can ignore it." This Empire of Funk began in that moment, whenever and wherever it happened.

As hip-hop moves into its fifth decade, the empire has become visible—whether in the historic Pacific hubs of the San Francisco Bay Area (The City's SOMA, Excelsior, and Sunset Districts, Vallejo, Daly City, Oakland, Richmond, Hercules/Pinole, Fremont, San Jose), Central California (Fresno, Stockton), Southern California (L.A. Filipinotown, Cerritos, West Covina, Irvine, San Diego/Chula Vista/National City), and Honolulu, or across the Filipino-American diaspora, from Chicago to Jacksonville, Virginia Beach to New York City. It stands now, visible, tangible, but not yet fully legible.

Many who dabble in hip-hop or sociology or both explain the presence of Pin@ys in hip-hop using what might be called "the Puerto Rican analogy." They may say, "Filipinos are the Puerto Ricans of the West Coast."

Certainly Filipinos and Puerto Ricans share a common history of American imperialism, with all of its consequential impacts on language and vernacular culture (a history that also holds, sans the Spanish experience, for most Pacific Islanders and Locals from Hawai'i). More serious studies in the future may unpack this idea. But for now it's important to note that Filipino Americans complicate the hip-hop narrative from the beginning.

Joe Bataan came to pop prominence in a Puerto Rican and North American Latino context. He gave the famous Salsoul label its punning name. But he also proudly called himself "Afrofilipino." His pioneering single, "Rap-O Clap-O," is important not only because its release preceded "Rapper's Delight" by several weeks, but because its international success was equally remarkable. What does it mean that one of the first big-selling global rap records was recorded by a Black Pinoy known primarily as a Latin artist?

And what does it mean that West Coast hip-hop owes much to a DJ who calls himself "the Crazy Pinoy"? If there is a godfather to this Empire of Funk, it is Nestor "Nasty Nes" Rodriguez, who started the West Coast's first hip-hop radio show on a Sunday night in Seattle back in 1980. From a modest Sunday night slot on an AM station KFOX 1250, his "Fresh Tracks" mixshow was expanded into a nightly weekday event that topped the Arbitron ratings and helped launch the West Coast rap scene.

Born in the Philippines, he had spent part of his childhood in Okinawa. At the age of 10 he immigrated to Seattle with his mother and older sister. Like Kool Herc and Cindy Campbell's mother, Nes's mom eventually found work as a hospital nurse. On his first trip through Honolulu airport heading to Seattle, he bought his first record, The Jackson 5's "ABC."

In his teens he took up bodybuilding and studied Bruce Lee's Jun Fan Gung Fu with Taky Kimura, but radio became his core passion. When visiting his sister in New York City, he was introduced to her clique of WKTU DJs and on-air personalities. He returned to study radio at Bellevue College, and by the age of 20, he had become a weekend on-air host on KFOX, breaking new R&B and rap releases.

He convinced station heads to allow him to try out WKTU's mix format, lugging in his turntables and mixer to perform custom "Master Mixes." Phone lines lit up and ratings soared. The show naturally evolved towards a nearly all-rap playlist. "For a while I kept getting negative feedback—'Rap is just a fad and it will not last.' I believed that in 10 to 20 years it would be the biggest thing out," he recalled. "I was right."

As time went on, his playlist changed from one largely filled with singles he had brought back from New York to one more balanced with songs by West Coast artists. Getting spins on his show became crucial for young rappers from Los Angeles and the Bay Area. When someone finally writes the definitive history of West Coast rap, they'll have to note that, if not for Nasty Nes, Ice-T and Eazy-E might have remained just the strange nicknames of musicians nobody remembered.

Nes was a big dude, six feet tall, eyes covered by large wrap-around shades, yoked like Brian Bosworth with an awesome mullet to match. He was a walking statement. "In the beginning my audience was 90% Black," he said. "As I started making public appearances my audience started expanding to also whites and Asians."

In 1985, Nes formed Nastymix Records with a Chinese-American promoter Ed Locke and a local rapper named Anthony Ray, who called himself Sir Mix-A-Lot. Soon the three had secured two of West Coast rap's first platinum albums. The label exemplified the emergence of a multiracial West Coast scene and hinted at hip-hop's future global hegemony. As the rap underground matured, Nes became a key player in a national network of college and community radio DJs and hip-hop journalists, and kind of a *kuya* figure for a hungry generation of young Asian and Filipino American heads.

That generation—who, especially in Cali's hothouse scene, had already been establishing their place in proliferating dance cyphers, graf walls, DJ showcases, and hip-hop activist campaigns—would break through to international prominence. From the mid-1990s into the new millennium, these DJs, dancers, artists, rappers, promoters, poets, writers, actors, activists, and cultural organizers would rock the performances, forge the narratives, and build the institutions that would transform hip-hop, pop culture, and North American youth movements.

The Pin@y presence was always there. There is no need for an analogy.

Instead we can begin to *recognize* how history looks from multiple (b-boy and b-girl) stances. Hip-hop comes from the specificity of the urban U.S. version of Afrodiasporic Blackness—that is undeniable—but it has also always been open to the presence of multiraciality and polyculturalism. Our question should not be how to privilege one of these facts over the other, but how to understand their co-evolution, and their implications for cultural strategies to eradicate racism and anti-Blackness.

If this latter point about racism and anti-Blackness sounds redundant, well, I agree. But then there was a Youtube video featuring members of a UC Irvine Asian-American fraternity lip-syncing to a Justin Timberlake song…and let's just say that if we still must confront the spectacle of Asian American blackface, especially performed by those whose genealogy traces back directly to those who engaged hip-hop in the 1990s and early 2000s as an act of social engagement and liberation, redundancy is the least of our worries.

Hip-hop, the cultural thinker Johan Kugelberg has said, never focused much on documentation in its early days because its practitioners were kids caught up in the fullness of their own genesis. They were not art school students. They had no time to worry about their place in history because they were too busy getting their game up for the next weekend, when the fruits of their creative labor would be up for judgment again, making of them instant legends or fools. That was especially true for dance and DJing, forms of embodied hip-hop knowledge that mainly demanded being in the moment and being ready for the moment.

What has been true of hip-hop as a whole has also been true for Pin@ys.

It was not until the late 1990s that pioneering scholarship on Filipino Americans in hip-hop began to appear. What we have not yet documented could fill volumes.

But this book is a moment, like any of those million moments. It's a beginning. It starts with the tremor of recognition. And hopefully that tremor sparks something deeper—passion that leads to creativity, empathy that leads to community, culture that leads to transformation.

INTRODUCTION

A HIP HOP STORY TO TELL:
IT'S JUST BEGUN

By DJ Kuttin Kandi

i do this
for the love of Hip Hop
i do this whether
i make it or flop
i do this so i can one day
open a record shop

nod my head
to a funky be-bop
hands in the air

nothing

can't ever make me stop
playin a good beat drop
can't break me up
cause i can't seem to get enough
of a love more than just Hip Hop
—"A Love More Than Just Hip Hop," Kuttin Kandi

t was a cold night in Pomonock, Queens. Kissena Boulevard was quite a few blocks away, but through the wide-open windows, you could almost hear the regulars hanging out at the corner by the neighborhood deli chuggin' on an OE. Further down the street, between the supermarket Kissena Farms and McDonald's, a bustle of leaves whirled through the wind and curled up at its doors, seeking any kind of warmth. Not too far away, stood the small-like city of Pomonock Housing that towered over much of Pomonock, South Flushing, and Kew Garden Hills. The whistle of its loneliness flew through the gaping curtains and sat amongst the chattering voices of an antsy audience who were waiting for a performance that would change the life of one nine-year-old girl.

In the auditorium, the seats were all filled and the aisles were jam-packed with parents, grandparents, aunts, and uncles. They fanned their programs, hoping that the little air that it provided would keep them from sweating from the overly crowded room. In the front rows sat the students of 4th, 5th, and 6th graders of P.S. 154 all excited to see some of their classmates perform for the yearly talent show "Encore."

"Fresh" by Kool & the Gang burst from the speakers. The crowd, young and old, started screaming as soon as two Pilipina American girls dressed in red hooded sweatshirts and swishy pants came from behind the curtains and started poppin' to the beat of the song. They moonwalked across the stage, busted waves, and locked on rhythm. The audience stood from their seats, and jumped wildly as they cheered them on, for they were amazed that the two sisters could dance with the confidence of seasoned professional dancers.

Then it happened. The most ultimate dance move ever was experienced right before everyone's eyes. It was the move that only a few were lucky to see live if they were given the chance. The girls simultaneously flipped onto the floor and spun on their backs continuously. Each turn of their spin caused loud of cries and cheers, creating the most exhilarating encounter for those who had just witnessed what b-boys and b-girls (breakdancers) from all around the world called the backspin.

It was 1984. Hooded sweatshirts, Adidas, Pumas, and doorknocker earrings were in fashion. It was the year the movie "Beat Street" by Harry Belafonte featuring Kool Herc, Rocksteady Crew, NYC Breakers, and Doug E. Fresh was released. The movie "Breakin" was also released, which presented a West Coast line-up of poppers, lockers, and b-boys. In that same year, rap group UFTO released "Roxanne Roxanne" and Marley Marl & Roxanne Shante released a response called "Roxanne's Revenge." It was also the year that "Graffiti Rock" the first Hip Hop Dance Show aired on television, Rick Rubin and Russell Simmons formed Def Jam, Queens-based Run DMC put out their self-titled debut LP, and Michael Jackson performed the moonwalk (which he learned from LA poppers) at the Grammys.

In 1984 Madonna's "Like a Virgin" and the "GhostBusters" song blasted on everyone's radio, India's Prime Minister Indira Gandhi was assassinated, 22 Americans were freed when Jesse Jackson met with Castro, the British agreed to leave Hong Kong by the year 1997, and the movie *The Killing Fields* shocked the world with the atrocities endured in Cambodia.

In 1984, I was a quiet, shy little girl in the fourth grade. It was the year that I, a Pilipina American who was still confused what that meant, sat with an audience of classmates and parents who were predominantly Black and Latino, denying I was a brown-shaded Pinay, so ashamed I was not the same as those around me. In fact, I remember telling one of the girls Johanna long before the "Encore" event that I was not Pilipina when she asked me. It was on that night that I sat alone in those auditorium seats wishing I had the same confidence that popular Pilipina classmate Johanna and her older 6th grade sister Jeanette had on stage, as they made me proud to be Pilipina and gave birth to my first Hip Hop experience.

It is no coincidence that my first Hip Hop experience paralleled my early sense of Pilipina identity. Just like me, I'm sure there were many Pilipina/o American kids who were swept up by the whirlwind of Hip Hop culture that would soon engulf the nation. And I'm sure there were many Pilipina/o American kids like Johanna and Jeanette who took to their school stages to inspire a gawking group of young onlookers. It became evident to me many years later after discovering a broader community of Pilipina/o American Hip Hop participants and fans that Hip

Hop had become a strong fixture in the lives of many young Pilipina/o Americans who at some point were like me in the fourth grade navigating the tumultuous American cultural landscape and exploring ways of growing up as a young Pilipina/o American.

Granted, living in Queens gave me special access to Hip Hop as it developed early on in New York's urban epicenter. An argument can be made that almost every young person in New York had become enamored with this new "fad," including Johanna and Jeanette. Hip Hop in New York in the early 1980s, it can be said, had no unique resonance for young Pilipina/o Americans because, quite frankly, who wasn't popping, waving, and bustin' back-spins at that time? Even though Hip Hop did in fact make an imprint on the lives of youth in New York and even on broader culture of New York, something else was happening. Years later, I would learn that indeed Pilipina/o Americans in other parts of New York and around the nation were taking part in a larger cultural phenomenon that would shape the way they move, speak, pray, consume goods, and think. As Hip Hop forever changed my outlook on life in my school auditorium in 1984, I learned that for many Pilipina/o Americans it became a common form of cultural identification. No matter if you grew up in a white suburb, in the mixed environment of a military town, or the black and brown surroundings of the inner city, young Pilipina/o Americans were for some reason committing themselves to a culture that emerged out of the passion, anger, angst, creativity, and the hearts of African American and Afro-Caribbean youth in New York.

True, living in the birthplace of Hip Hop immediately connected me to Hip Hop but it was still a gradual process before I even fully understood the power of Hip Hop culture. It took me a while before I even realized my own agency to live the famous words of KRS One's "I AM HIP HOP." Similarly, it took a journey for me to understand and fully embrace my Pilipina identity and culture. Little did I know that as I traveled on a Hip Hop groove, Hip Hop was getting me in touch with not just my own Pilipina self, but also my whole being.

It was a journey of getting out of being around the "wrong crowds" to finding good mentors in my life. It was a path of non-stop partying and drinking to a path of finding substance through music and community. It also meant having to go through many mistakes, heartbreaks, losses, and so much pain to get to a place of enlightenment to fully see how Hip Hop had been right there, embracing me the whole time.

> *"Now, i've been roamin/searchin for a home and/i found it in my*
> *soul when/i opened myself/to the truth before me/i thought i came*
> *so far but i just started my journey …"*
>
> —"Come Back," Knowa Lazarus

It was my journey with Hip Hop that helped me realize my own passion, anger, angst, creativity, and heart. It got me through some of the toughest times of my life. Like many people around the world so often say, I too, find myself saying "Hip Hop saved my life." I was a confused soul, unaware of who I was and lost between the violence in my home and environment. I grew up in the intersections of South Flushing, Queens where to my left lived predominantly Hasidic Jews and to the right of me Black and Brown people, while living in a home of 26 family members, most of whom were strangers who came from the Philippines after the Immigration Act of 1990. Being one of the only 3 Asian families in my neighborhood, we definitely experienced much racism but it was no different from the internalized racism that happened in my own home. I had a hard-working mother who didn't want me to get dark in the sun nor did she want me to speak Tagalog or her Bikol language because she didn't want me to grow up with an accent. I had a father who battled with his own rage and anger while battling with cancer his whole life. I also had a sister and young little cousins I felt extremely responsible for protecting from all the chaotic family drama. At the same time, I was struggling with depression, an eating disorder, and my violent ways. All this was happening while experiencing not just assimilation and colonial mentality but also sexual abuse, violence, lies, deceit, and tons of other family secrecy. It is not a wonder that, as I had often run away from home, I was also running from my own identity, trying to deny and escape the parts of me that had any connections to my family, even if it meant denying my own roots.

Yet somehow, even with all the denial, I found myself thirsting for knowledge. At the time I wasn't sure what I was in search of but I knew I was curious and was constantly exploring new friendships, people, and places. I didn't realize this then but considering the dynamics of my household, I was longing for community, culture, and home. I was longing for a place to fill my heart with joy and something to help me express all this rage and passion inside of me. I didn't know it was going to be Hip Hop nor did I envision it would take me through a whirlwind of drunken and drugged-up party nights to celebrity friendships to championship titles to being a radical activist and now writer.

It was my senior year in high school when I moved from sophomore partying at hooky jams and house parties to the New York City club scenes and nightlife of VIP guest lists. Long before Mayor Rudy Giuliani's zero-tolerance policing, "quality of life" initiatives, and "broken window" theory existed, there were still 18-and-over clubs and teen nights at many venues. So, I was pretty lucky to experience the club scenes at such a young age. Thus, I began my venture into club promoting and organizing parties. As I danced my night away in many of these clubs, I was also seeking out more Pilipina/o American friends. My non-Pilipina/o friends didn't understand this, nor did I care if they "got it." All I knew was I wanted to know more. Consequently, I met a Pilipina/o American DJ crew, 3DS, who DJed for a party my best friend and I organized. DJ Sonny D-Lite of 3DS, who was about 4 years younger than my 17-year-old self, became my first DJ teacher.

Ironically, it wasn't through any of the party or club scenes but through a teen youth group from one of my mother's Charismatic Church events that I met a few Pilipina/o teens who gave me a flier to my very first Pilipina/o American party at a club called the Village Gate. The party was organized by the legendary Pilipina/o American promoters called Bunz Culture. Just witnessing the way the long line full of young brown people like me went around the block to get into the club just to dance to Hip Hop had me excited and taken aback. I had no idea that this many Pilipina/o Americans existed in New York City nor did I know there were any Pilipina/o Americans who were just like me, who loved Hip Hop.

From that point on, I was drawn in and I began getting connected. This was where I met DJ Roli Rho, my then-boyfriend, who became a major influence in my DJ career. At the time, he was also part of the predominantly Pilipina/o American mobile DJ crew, IntroBass Productions, which I later joined in 1997. Throughout those years, I gained a whole lot of mentors and made some of the best friendships I ever had with other notable Fil-Am DJs, crews, and promoters like DJ Krazie Charlez and All Mixed Up (AMU), DJ Rob Non-Stop, CL Slick, JSwift, DJ Conrad, DJ Halo-Halo, DJ Bula, 2Krew, Kuya Tribe, DJ Kuya Derrick, DJ DDC, DJ ShoNuff, DJ Macapuno, DJ CamOne, DJ Rich "The Riddler," Treble & Bass, Xen Tech, DJ Boo, Clubhouse, DJ EdSwift, DJ Fish, Fat Mark, 201 Crew, DJ Yoshi, Flip Da Lid, 169 Crew, AIC, FlipCyde Entertainment, 5 Star Original, Benjapol & Rob Koda, Euphoria Entertainment, Elite Entertainment, Dennis Zaide (Side A), Mark Anthony, Manny Lorenzo, Al Lee, Ron Rae, Mike Varias, Sarah Corpus, Tommy & Larissa Ovejas, Joey Cassanova, Boom Bass, F.A.T. Productions, Homer, Apple, RJ Corporation, Jay Zuno, QCC Flip Club, Jonathan Santos, NYCircus, and so many more.

From clubs to rental halls, us Pilipina/o Americans were doing whatever we could to throw historical parties just like the "Village Gate" days like "Gonzalez & Gonzalez," "Malacañang," Makati Ave, Philippine Village, Neolounge, Demerara Club, Coney Island High, Silverado's, Ukrainian "Box" and the Armenian hall parties, Lutheran Churches on Goethals Avenue, and yes, my annual free birthday parties at YIPs and Club Speed that are still talked about today. These party scenes forged friendships that also forged other friendships and connected us to even larger communities such as our overall Asian American party scenes like A. Integration, 330° Entertainment, KM Productions, Digital Explosion, Xtreme Entertainment, Ultimate Bass Int'l, CK, and Legendary. Over time, I eventually learned that our mobile DJ movement and party scenes had a long history, dating back to the 1970s much like the San Francisco mobile DJ scene (see Oliver Wang's chapter in this collection).

Of course, the DJs at our parties played more than just Hip Hop music and not every DJ claimed themselves as Hip Hop either. Any real DJ would know that a real DJ can and should play every genre, for it is not necessarily *what* the DJ plays but *how* the DJ plays that rocks a crowd. After all, we were also the mobile DJs who played at your weddings, baptism parties, debutante balls, and sweet sixteens. But it was the spin of the turntables that brought in the very foundation of Hip Hop. Whether anyone realized it or not, Hip Hop was always at the core of our parties, for it was the DJ who brought everyone together. The day I fell in love with those turntables was the day I became captivated by the DJs who spun those records. I was fascinated by the way the DJ led the crowd and invoked a powerful energy into the room by the music they played. Interestingly, my father was the first real DJ in my life, for he had a huge collection of records along with his own record player where he often played his favorite selections from Motown to the Beatles. As a matter of fact, the times my father seemed more at peace and away from his internal rage was whenever he was listening to his records. Unbeknownst to me, I was getting my first real lesson on music: listen and appreciate. I was in awe of the way my father appreciated music just as I was fascinated by the DJs I met later in my life. Music became my salvation; a way to find peace through all the struggle. I became mesmerized by the sound of the scratch and with a set of my own two turntables I began itchin'.

Right around my father's death, I began questioning if I should take DJing not just as a passion but as a serious career. Growing up with a life full of instability and many uncertainties because of financial struggle, which included the loss of our home coupled with family illness and other traumatic experiences, I was very uncertain if I could live the "DJ life." Still, even with these fears, I pursued playing records anyway. As I played on, I ended up gaining so much more than a "career"; I found family.

When Roli and I started entering DJ competitions like the DMC (which is much like the Olympics for DJs) we didn't realize we were stepping into a worldwide turntablist community that existed far beyond the familiarity of our Fil-Am party scenes where we had grown accustomed to DJing and promoting. It was through the turntablist community that we learned just how widely our fellow Pilipina/o Americans were representing through musicianship, composition, competition, and Hip Hop. While there were super-battle DJs in our hometown of New York City like the X-ecutioners (formerly known as the X-men) who inspired and mentored us, there were Pilipina/o Americans who were making a mark on DJing and turntablism, especially on the West Coast. It was DJs like DJ Qbert, Shortkut, and DJ Symphony who captivated and motivated us simply by their representation. It was their stage presence, turntable brilliance, and courage to compete against some of the best, along with being one of the best that encouraged us to believe in ourselves. Not too long after, our crew, the 5th Platoon was born. Hence, we learned that our own 5th Platoon crew, who are predominantly Pilipina/o Americans, can rock a show and win international championship titles, too.

As our turntable wizardry grew, so did our knowledge of other Pilipina/o American DJs and other Fil-Am Hip Hop/Party scene movements in other cities. We later realized that these movements paralleled our own movements in New York/New Jersey. I was proud to learn that DJ Nasty Nes was the first DJ to bring an all-Hip Hop radio station to the West Coast with Seattle's KFOX in the early 1980s. In the 1970s–1980s in the Bay Area with groups like Sound Explosion and in Los Angeles with groups like Spectrum Entertainment, Pilipina/o American mobile DJs spun for Pilipina/o weddings, debuts, and fiestas. They were setting up a pre-Hip Hop scene that would eventually blossom into a tradition of Pilipina/o American turntablism that my crew would eventually inherit.

Thanks to the DJ scene I made friendships with Pilipina/o American DJs far and wide who I had looked up to: members of the Invisibl Skratch Piklz, The World Famous Beat Junkies, Supernatural Turntable Artists (STA), Immortal Fader Fyters (IF2), Interboro Rhythmik Turntablists (IRT), and so many more! Filipina/o cultural festivals across the country would soon honor this DJ tradition by having DJ exhibitions and competitions. For example, in 1995, a group who were originally party/entertainment promoters within the Pilipina/o American community organized the underground Hip Hop classic Rhythm Method DJ Battles. In the late 90s the only largest annual East Coast gathering of Pilipina/o Americans called the Filipino International Networking Dialogue (F.I.N.D.) Conference held a DJ battle that I entered and the Festival of Philippine Arts and Culture (FPAC) in Southern California would hold its annual DJ battle, inviting amateur performers, Filipina/o or not, to claim FPAC DJ supremacy. In 2008, I was fortunate enough to be honored along with DJ Nasty Nes, DJ Babu (Beat Junkies), and DJ Rhettmatic (Beat Junkies) in the FPAC Tribute to the Pilipina/o DJ. As the Pilipina/o American DJs were on the rise, so were the Pilipino music producers like !llmind and Chad Hugo of the Neptunes, graphic/web designers like Def Case, and filmmakers like Patricio Ginelsa and Rik Cordero. This brings to view the growth of our Pilipina/o American people as we began to cross over and expand beyond our own parties and into global view in many different elements and artistry.

When you're a DJ in the music industry, it's common to meet all kinds of people in the entertainment field. Throughout the years, I got to know and work with amazing artists from all over the world. I met not only famous DJs and rappers but I met photographers, writers, educators, activists, singers, poets, filmmakers, actors, and all kinds of musicians. Yet, as I met celebrities from all parts of the world, it always meant a lot to meet another Pilipina/o. I had the honor to meet and work with many Pilipina/o American performers and artists such as Jocelyn Enriquez, John Flor Sisante, Jay Legaspi, Emm Gryner, Nomi, !llmind, Kai, 6th Day, Drop N Harmony, Innerlude, Pinay, Regie Cabico, Paulskee, Kid Riz, DJ DDouble, Corinne Manabat, Alfie Numeric, Eighth Wonder, Members of the Rock Force Crew, Rowie of DNA, Rex Navarrete, The Pacifics, Dante Basco and the Basco Brothers, Patricio Ginelsa, Def Case, ABGirl, Baby Angles, Jay Perez, Kevin Nadal, Kilusan Bautista, Delrokz, Dannu of the Visionaries, Odessa Kane, Ree Obana, apl.De.ap of the Black Eyed Peas, and so many more. Every single one of them have inspired me and carried me through another day. Through their performance they told me I wasn't alone and that we were in this together. If I didn't tell them then, I am most certainly telling them now: "Thank you." Meeting another artist with my brown skin meant finding family to me. It meant joy, struggle, love, and home all at the same time. And somehow, whenever I met another Pilipina/o Artist, I always felt that they felt the same as I did—a sense of belonging and a shared feeling of respect and understanding that we both knew what we went through to get right here.

> "this is for the place of my mother's land/where i got my face and
> this browner hands/i used to be ashamed/and now i understand/
> cause this is who i am/i said it's who i am ..."
>
> —"Who I Am," Ruby Ibarra

In a tough city like New York it was hard to find venues willing to just rent out to us Pilipina/os trying to have a good time and celebrate together. It was especially hard as Pilipina/os to find each other unless you lived in Jackson Heights or already had friends and family members who socialized with the community. So, many of us depended on our church groups, youth groups or the Pilipina/o Clubs on college campuses to throw events like the yearly St John's University's Barrio Fiestas, which were filled with love song ballads, Pandanggo sa Ilaw and Tinikling performances. Unlike the West Coast, we didn't have Tagalog classes or Pilipino studies in high school or colleges to teach us about our culture. So, even if it was just once a year, we always looked forward to Barrio

Fiestas to catch a glimpse of ourselves on stage and a chance to learn a bit of our roots. Barrio Fiestas were also a moment for us to bridge both the generational and cultural gaps, for everyone brought their parents, siblings, and grandparents. It was that one time a year where young Pilipina/os had a moment to not only show that they were learning their history through cultural dances but they were also learning newer art forms to express their Pilipina/o American identity. This was where many of the Pilipina/o American dance crews from Queens, New York started to flourish. In the auditorium of St John's University I witnessed Hip Hop dance routines by dance crews like Flying Jalapeño Popper Stick Avengers, Menace Mindz, and Junior Freakz. Although I mostly performed as a DJ or as a poet at Barrio Fiestas, I also had co-formed my own dance crew called Rhythm Xstacy and Desire (RED) in the mid-90s. This was where I began to appreciate the groundbreaking contributions Pilipina/o Americans made in dance.

As I began to tour the world as a DJ and a speaker, I learned about other Pilipina/o American dance crews in other cities. For example, Kaba Modern, like the Beat Junkies, celebrated their 20-year anniversary in 2012. In 1992, Kaba Modern became the brainchild of South Bay youth Arnel Calvario, who was influenced by Pilipina/o American dance crews in Cerritos, such as Funki Junction and Johnny's Quest—crews that performed at house parties and family events. Today, Kaba Modern has helped create a worldwide street dance culture that has given Asian Americans more visibility and respect in Hip Hop and in American popular culture generally, most notably through the TV show *America's Best Dance Crew*. Soon enough, many more Asian American dance crews made appearances on similar dance competition shows, forever changing America's perception of Asian American youth and igniting an Asian American dance movement in cities across the country. Around the same time Kaba Modern began, another group that was respected for their dance moves was the Atban Klann. Made up of a multiracial group of dancers and emcees, with apl.de.ap eventually becoming the most recognizable Pilipina/o American member, the Atban Klann performed at Pilipina/o American parties and eventually grew into the pop megagroup the Black Eyed Peas. At a recent concert at the Hollywood Bowl, apl.de.ap credited the historic Los Angeles-based Pilipina/o American community organization Search to Involve Pilipino Americans for providing performance space that he believes helped launch the career of the Black Eyed Peas.

> *"So check the work ethic in the name*
> *The lessons might change,*
> *But the essence in the message is the same."*
> —"No Rest for the Weary," Blue Scholars

In the early 2000s, I was blessed to meet and eventually become close comrades with key figures in the rise of the Pilipina/o American emcee scene. The Pacifics, Geologic from the Blue Scholars, Bambu and Kiwi, who were to become the Native Guns, and so many others have made a lasting impression on the emcee game, all the while keeping a positive and uplifting message. By no coincidence, these emcees have also become a strong voice for Pilipina/o American political consciousness. Just as with our artistic expressions, Pilipina/o American performers have proven to be great intellectual leaders. Long-time friends of mine who were also Pilipina/o emcees from New York City and New Jersey were also making their own marks like Deep Foundation, Hydroponikz, JEncite, Kontrast, Organic Thoughts, Mike Swift, and long-time veteran Knowa Lazarus (who later moved to California and now resides in the Philippines). Watching them take the stage as they performed also tickled my own hidden passion of being an emcee. Although there were my teen days of writing raps at the school cafeteria and my freestyle moments with my old friend Knowa Lazarus while DJ FatFingaz would beatbox for us back in the day, I've always been more of a spoken word poet.

During the late 1990s and early 2000s, the Pilipina/o American and Asian American poetry scene were in full bloom and the worlds of Hip Hop and spoken word were crossing. This became truly sacred for me because after being influenced by the poetry works and performances of my friends Jessica Caremoore and Saul Williams in the mid-90s, I started performing my poetry, too. However, at the time I was still new to spoken word and I wasn't as confident that a young 19-year-old Pilipina like myself could voice myself as boldly as Jessica and Saul did on stage. As a DJ, it was like nothing for me to beat juggle in front of thousands, but poetry was different: it required a different kind of vulnerability. But I had been writing poetry since the age of 7 years, so I knew I had so much to say. I was also growing as a radical activist and feminist with so much inside of me that wanted to get out that I knew I couldn't give up.

A few years later, I became close friends with the Chicago-based poetry group I Was Born With Two Tongues, and I no longer felt alone. I heard and saw the voices of Asian-Americans on stage speaking truth to power. Their words gave me courage and their passion ignited my own passion. I finally began performing poetry again. In 2002 in Gainesville, Florida at an event organized by the Filipino Student Association, I first met the amazing poets and performers of the Isangmahal Arts Kollective. Based in Seattle and beginning in 1996, Isangmahal was foundational in helping grow the national Asian American spoken word scene. In 2001, they hosted the first national Asian Pacific Islander American Spoken Word Summit, which brought together a community of artists, including members of I Was Born With Two Tongues, Mango Tribe, Eighth Wonder, and Balagtasan Collective. This kind of nationwide artistic dialogue seemed unprecedented, and I am honored to be a part of it. Aside from DJing, I continue to write and perform poetry thanks to the seed planted in me from the amazing artists I have grown to love and proudly call my *kasamas*.

> *"The thing that's good about Hip-Hop is that it has experimented*
> *with a lot of different sounds and music."*
> —Godfather of Hip Hop, Afrika Bambaataa

In 2008, I participated in a round table discussion with other Pilipina/o American artists where I met the legendary Joe Bataan, an Afro-Pilipino singer and musician who became a worldwide hit beginning in the late 1960s and is credited for his Latin Soul sound. He is also known for his early rap record "Rap-O-Clap-O," which, pressed in 1979, was one of the first rap records ever made. A whole generation of young Pilipina/o Americans, including myself, are digging for Joe's music while they discover the contributions and impact of Pilipina/o American artists who have come before. Joe has embraced this growing fanbase and has made several appearances at FPAC and other Pilipina/o American gatherings. In fact, Joe made his first trip to the Philippines in 2012, where he met an adoring crowd who represent his father's birth country. For me, Joe has come to symbolize a long Pilipina/o musical tradition, including a Hip Hop tradition, which spans many generations here in the United States. When I met Joe Bataan, I felt just as starstruck as I did when I first became friends with the legendary Godfather of Hip Hop, Afrika Bambaataa. It was a drop-dead moment for me and it had me reflecting on the last 15 years of my music career.

I was at the crossroads where I moved 3,000 miles away from the birthplace of Hip Hop where I had established my name and built my accomplished resume to a city I knew nothing about: San Diego, CA. I left an industry that was my stomping ground, a community of folks who guided me for years, and the only place I ever called home. I was at a pivotal moment in my life where my self-awareness, Pinayism, and activism were evolving and I wanted to find newer ways to contribute my music that aligned with this growth. Living a non-stop, busy touring lifestyle for more than 15 years was wearing me down and I knew I needed to slow down. I knew I had much to do in my continuous work at inner healing and it was time for me to just breathe.

Still, stepping away from the only busy life I ever knew had been a lot harder than I thought it would be. It was hard for me to leave it all behind. But when I saw Joe Bataan on stage, performing at FPAC, he gave me hope. I came face to face with a piece of myself I never thought I'd find. I always felt so lost and the only time I ever felt "found" was whenever the music played. So, hearing Joe Bataan rap,

"We got a new thing out, gonna make you shout
Got rhythm, got heat, gonna move your feet
Got class, finesse, a whole lotta style
Gonna be around for a long, long while"

meant hearing my life story unfold before me. I had searched the ends of the earth for my identity but when I made the connection of meeting Joe and Bam, I realized that all I had been searching for was right there the whole time. It hit me right then. It didn't really matter where I lived. The music was always inside of me. Hip Hop was inside of me. My Pilipina was inside of me. And I was expressing it all along. It was in every table that I turned, every poem that I spoke, and rallies where I've chanted with fists up high in the air. It all made sense; it was like that old mix tape. No, not a CD or an MP3 but a real cassette mix tape where the mixes sounded so crisp and the blends were so smooth even as it sometimes got caught in a tape deck. Mmmm just like an ice cold halo-halo, right?

Alas, just as it is with Hip Hop, I will always be a student. There are still so many things I have to learn about Hip Hop, just as there is still so much to learn about myself. There is definitely a lot to be learned about Pilipina/o Americans in Hip Hop such as Pilipina/o Americans in areas who are not given much attention, such as those in Florida, Texas, Hawaiʻi, military bases in Japan, Puerto Rico, and many other cities. When this book project came about, it was just a mere idea that I brought up to Mark R. Villegas nearly five years ago after famed author, activist, and friend Jeff Chang and I created an "Asian-Americans in Hip Hop" timeline at the National Political Hip Hop Convention. I just never envisioned myself to be the one co-editing this book with Mark and Rod. I most certainly didn't imagine I'd be writing the introduction to the book either. I'm far from what any formally educated writer would call an "author." Yet, prior to this book I've already contributed to four published books and I am currently writing my autobiography. Go figure. Look at how far Hip Hop has taken me. Nonetheless, I knew this book was important and I knew our stories needed to be told. I learned from my mentors that it is important to document our story, to tell our own stories or someone else was going to do it for us. Sadly, Hip Hop is often co-opted by large corporations and the stories of our Hip Hop legends are often made "Hollywood" and at times not as genuine and authentic as it is when coming from the legends themselves who actually lived the Hip Hop experience. This is the reason that there is a need for an anthology, and not another book written by someone telling you someone else's story. Instead, we need our own stories written by our very own Pilipina/o Americans who lived their Hip Hop experience.

We recognize our privilege to be able to produce this book and fully acknowledge that we are in no way speaking as though we are the experts of Hip Hop and/or Pilipina/o-Americans in Hip Hop. We also recognize there are countless Pilipina/o Americans with a Hip Hop story to tell. In time, we are hopeful to meet you, hear your stories, and learn from all of you. We hope that this book will be a start of a bigger conversation about the role Hip Hop has played in the lives of Pilipina/o Americans. *It's just begun.* For many ethnic groups who became integral parts of Hip Hop, the culture was dismissed as a passing fad. But in reality, Hip Hop has decided to stay in Pilipina/o American communities, and actually has become for us a main mode of expression and a crucial method of organizing. Hip Hop has become our way of telling the world like the title of Deep Foundation's song, that we are the *children of the sun* and that, "we are here."

In the meantime, as thousands of us continue to write our dreams on walls or rhyme books, I hope that this book brings you joy, affirmation, comfort, release, pride, and a place of healing as it did for me to co-edit, write, and co-produce this book. As I am finishing up this introduction, I am realizing that I am still in awe of my own journey in Hip Hop just as I was in awe of Johanna doing the backspin all those years ago. As I read everyone's final submissions, I am (re)inspired by our people's brilliant minds, resiliency, and strength to continue on as a community with that Hip Hop instrumental as the heartbeat of our stories. Writing for this book has given me the chance to claim my Pilipina and dance with Johanna right by her side while listening to my father play his records once again. While nothing has ever been perfect in my life (as it shouldn't be), I now understand that it's more about the journey of *looking for that perfect beat* that brings substance to a song than it is ever about "figuring it all out." It's that "beautiful struggle" that Talib Kweli speaks of that helps me to find my narrative and my sense of purpose. It's about that *call and response* of my community, who continues to stay with me every step of the way, guiding me home.

Now, that's what I call Hip Hop.

I.

STYLES UPON STYLES UPON STYLES: EXPLORING A
FILIPINA/O AMERICAN HIP HOP AESTHETIC

FEEL THE FUNK

By Mark R. Villegas

Why "Empire of Funk"?

"Empire" because once upon a time in the seething cauldron of imperial USA, various people who worshipped their own gods were forged together. *Indios* wanted to prove their worth to self-governance, and Americans promised—with a smirk—that these so-called Filipinos could be free. Finally, a free Philippines, after three centuries of Spanish soul salvation before American democracy at the point of a Colt .45. From 1898 to 1992: The U.S. Navy Pacific fleet, an overstayed heir to the Manila Galleon. Let freedom ring.

> *When the colonizer came with the cross and the sword*
> *I threw the first spear and said "I declare war!"*
> *I'm a battle-scar wearing heir apparent*
> *A descendant of a long lineage of proletariat and peasant*
> —"No Rest for the Weary,"
> Geologic of the Blue Scholars

"Funk" because Filipinos are never what they seem to be. Never finished, always in process, a freestyle verse on top of unlimited bars. Tbd. Even after whites deemed these indigenous people dark, damned, deserving death by modern warfare, they survived with freedom remaining a question mark. The funk is the mess of war, the violence of colonial statecraft. The funk is rotting flesh.

Yet, the funk is the sunrise of America in the East. Funk is the flesh of birth to the children of Empire: Filipinos' debut to "modernity."

> *Call me a goddess, a devil*
> *I'm modern and I'm modest*
> *I'm evil but I'm honest*
> *At whatever you been sayin'*
> *I been that*
> — "Solar Systems," Hopie

Debut to exodus. Who are these survivors in the afterlife of Empire? Who are these who are always dancing, singing, praying, cursing? This is the funk band. The cross-dresser, the punk, the gangsta, the tattooed islander, the b-boy, the choreographer, the clubbing freak, the praise and worship leader, the born-again Muslim, the Catholic slut, the student body president, the Latin lover, the Japanophile geek, the model minority, the JROTC cadet, the lumpen pro hood, the illegal immigrant, the fob, the Magic Mic virtuoso, the YouTube narcissist, the raging activista...

> *But we be the children of the most high*
> *Ghosts of the colonized lost in the times*
> *Redesign, redefine what it meant to be divine*
> *Knowing that she meant for me to rhyme*
> — "Burnt Offering,"
> Geologic of the Blue Scholars

Soul salvation redux. For Filipinos of the American exodus, the funk has come from Hip Hop. Over heavy bass and crisp snares, Hip Hop invites the blended, contradictory. The ugly, beautiful, dangerous, dope. It disturbs complacency. It raises ghosts. It awakens.

It feels so good.

What is the Empire of Funk?

It's an old record sampled, scratched, flared, transformed, looped, hectic, dirty. It's the holler of the *indio*, *chino*, *moro*, *negrito*, *pagano*, *mestizo*, and the Fil Am who hollers back with a dap.

Out of exodus, the Filipino American Hip Hop scene expands and dominates, like any Empire. DJs, dancers, graffiti writers, and emcees tour the world and, sometimes, their ambiguous faces synonymous with Hip Hop. Out of local crews and fans, Filipino American Hip Hop scenes became an Empire of Funk.

Where will the Empire go from here?
How do we use it?
Will it promise freedom?

MIXIPINO

By Anna Alves

Jules Serrano wonders wants wishes as he plucks a linen-sleeved vinyl disc from a creaky crate, slides the 33 rpm record out, his fingers caressing the grooves, tiny striations smooth soft never scratched no not scratched until he did the scratching learned the scratches got the skillz to make music from the mess of song and screech and bass and brawn of lyrics and orchestra and gunshots and bravado, all the voices rapping who am I and who are you and fuck tha police and fight the power and Elvis being a hero to most but never meant shit to me mother fucker was racist, simple and plain, mutha fuck him and John Wayne.

His father loved John Wayne. The one thing he knows, which his mother told him. That's a lie. He knows two things. His father was Mexican. And he was gone, ever since Jules was born. Three things he knew then. John Wayne. Mexican. Gone. His mother, Petty, short for Petunia, was Pilipina. Too many Ps make you spit so he goes with Filipino instead. He's half Hispanic so he figures he's cool with that. He's down with the brown two times over. So what if he says "Hispanic" instead of "Latino" or "Chicano" like the hard-core guys from San Francisco State—he's thirteen years old and doesn't care. He likes the "Hissss" of Hispanic over the "Lat" and the "Chih."

Jules places the vinyl disc reverently on one of the waiting flat wheels on the turntable altar, reaches back, slides another vinyl disc out of the crate, slips it from its sleeve, sets that one down too, on the other. He yearns to do this right, like his heroes Mixmaster Mike and Qbert and the Skratch Piklz, hometown boys from Daly City who blew up the globe with soundscapes. Mixed and scratched all the way to London Bridge, to The Ultimate Competition. Conquered the world so often, they were blessedly retired. But Jules is just a beginner, bought the turntable and a crate of records last week, secondhand from his cousin Bong in San Jose, who was moving on to digital and monitor, who no longer wanted to lug around history in heavy crates, nostalgia expired. In the documentary film *Scratch*, Qbert said he always wondered what music would sound like on Mars, and that's what he listened for when he crafted his genius mixes. Reaching beyond turntable and bedroom, and home and town, state and country, and Earth. Headphones scattering DNA of humans amongst the stars. Jules believes that if everyone learned how to halo-halo the sounds, the world would be a better place. Maybe even better than Mars.

That's why he decided to be a DJ. His best friend Gabby Gonzales from next door—the girl of the snappy serenade, her voice a feisty sing-song—says, "It's because you watched Skratch and saw all the Filipinos and now you think it's cool." But that's not true. It was the movie *La Bamba* that did it. Lou Diamond Phillips—Filipino, Mexican, Indian, what?—playing Richie Valens, a Mexican-American rock star, making Latin sounds as American as apple pie. Or rather, making Mexican flan like apple pie. Which meant Philippine leche flan was fair game, too. It was the mix-it-up that got him. He marveled that Lou Diamond could be Mexican in *La Bamba* then Indian in *Young Guns*, then Filipino in that movie he wrote and directed himself, *Blind Ambition*, which no one saw or liked but he did—saw and liked it on DVD.

God said, in the beginning was the Word. But he had to say it first, that Word, so it could be heard. Jules is not good with words. When he meets someone, he listens. A voice has its own music, a timbre, a volume. His mother makes melodies, yet bites her words, sharp, cuts off the ends. Her Tagalog lisp softens the sharpness of the English truncating. Once, her sound embarrassed him. Now, he hears mash-up of countries, beats of the States over bass of old Filipinas, no rhyme, just reasons that extend beyond him and his mom and this house and San Francisco, even California. Reasons wrapped up in a series of sounds he would like to isolate and intermingle and intersperse at will, bridge cultures and countries, span oceans and universes. Somewhere in there was Mexico, too, and Jules yearns to find it, digs for salsa and mariachi alongside Tagalog ballads and OPM. "Besame Mucho" entwines enzymes with "Dahil Sayo."

Maybe he'll discover resurrection in the reverb; perhaps in sound, found.

"WE'RE UP THERE PERFORMING A CHARACTER"

By DJ Qbert and Roderick N. Labrador

RL: Where were you born?

Q: I was born in San Francisco and raised in San Francisco, in the Excelsior district near Mission. And then I moved out to Hawai'i when I was 22-ish.

RL: Isn't Excelsior a Filipina/o area?

Q: I think you're thinking more Daly City and Union City. Excelsior is more of a mixed district. There are Mexicans, Italians, other people.

RL: What about your parents?

Q: My parents were born in the Philippines. My mom is from Cebu and my dad is from Ilocos.

RL: Is that why you moved out to Hawai'i?

Q: My dad moved out to Hawai'i when he was 15. He was in Kaua'i then he moved to Honolulu after. He went out there at first because they were looking for "slave labor" for the plantations, or some shit like that and he said, "Yeah, I'm down. I'll go to Hawai'i." He ran away from home. He was kind of a rebel kind of guy, kinda gangster. He was 15 and he moved to Hawai'i.

RL: When did your parents meet?

Q: They met in SF when he was around 40. He moved out here to pursue construction and a master's in engineering. He built a lot of DJ sets for me and he knew how to build houses. He built houses in Hawai'i. Every time we go to Hawai'i, "Hey, that's the house I built." In the Kalihi area. He was also in the military during World War II. And then he was stationed in Okinawa.

RL: So when did he move to HI?

Q: Well, he was born around 1920 and he moved there when he was 15, so probably around 1935.

RL: So did he join the military when he was in Hawai'i during World War II?

Q: Yeah.

RL: So was he part of the First and Second Filipino Infantry Regiments?

Q: Yeah, I think, yeah, probably.

RL: Did he move to San Francisco after the war?

Q: Well, a little after. He was pretty much in Hawai'i for 25 years, so not until around 1960 or so.

RL: So your parents met there in SF?

Q: Yeah, after my mom moved out here when she was 30 and that's when they met.

* * * * * * * * * *

RL: So when does all the Hip Hop stuff come in?

Q: I'm about eight years old when I first hear "Rapper's Delight" in 1978. And then I start collecting those kinds of records and I started DJing when I was about 15, this is 1985, and I liked all of the dance music … and then whole underground culture. Then I started learning more about it when I was around that age. It was fun.

RL: Did you start as a DJ?

Q: Well, I started breaking but, DJing came in handy and I didn't have to move around or anything.

RL: So why did you choose Hip Hop?

Q: It was in all the dances and all the breaking. And all of the music I listened to was Hip Hop. That was the best type of music for that. So I starting finding the best beats, it was raw.

* * * * * * * * * *

RL: At what point did you decide this is what I want to do?

Q: I think I was around 18 years old. I was getting better, entering battles, winning more than I was losing. I was losing a lot more than I was winning in the beginning. And then as I turned around 18-19, I started getting a lot of trophies and then I entered the US World Competition for the very first time and the DMC Competition at 21 years old and then made it all the way up to the US finals. I was the US winner and I represented the United States in the World Championships and I went all to the end and I won second place in the world and I was like, "Holy crap!" And then the next year, I won first place. And I got the title for a couple of years after that and I really wanted to do this for the rest of my life. To use my talents, everything that had to do with my scratching abilities, I wanted to do that for the rest of my life.

RL: When did you meet the other members of the Invisbl Skratch Piklz?

Q: I met them all about a year after I started DJing. Actually, I met MixMaster Mike when I first started and he started a few months before I did. He was doing a bunch of scratching in the San Francisco area at that time … I was kinda like a tag-along. I was going to their shows to check them out. I followed Mike a lot. I would go kick it with him a lot. I couldn't believe I was kickin' it with him sometimes because he was so good: "Wow!   This guy is amazing, I can't even believe he wants to kick it." And years later, after I won the DMC competitions and all that … maybe 3 or 4 years after that we formed the crew … I went to the DMC competition solo first in 1991 and then in '92, that's when they had a team competition and I went, "Damn!" Me, MixMaster Mike, and Apollo had a team and we entered and took first place and we took the title until 1994.

* * * * * * * * * *

RL: Where do you think being Filipino has played a role in Hip Hop?

Q: Well, I think one of the very first crews in the Bay Area that was a DJ group was Electric Sounds. That's probably the very first. I can't think of another earlier Filipina/o group. In the 1970s, they started under the name Electric Sounds … Filipina/os, they just have that entertainment thing in their blood. If you look at all around Asia, in Japan, and you look around and say, "Why are the band members in this club all Filipina/o?" A lot of the best b-boys are Filipino. Although there are all nationalities that are great in music, Filipina/os just have this thing as musicians, entertainers, or what have you. It's just normal, I guess … .But there's a diverse crowd of Filipina/os. It's such a huge population that you got all kinds of Filipina/os, you got Filipina/os in other countries. You got Filipina/os who are mainstream, guys who are underground. It's such a huge population, I wouldn't say that Filipina/os are just one thing. You're just taking a piece of the pie that's huge.

RL: Why do you think there are so many Filipina/os who are DJs?

Q: A lot of DJs are Filipina/o. I always thought it was our tribal roots. And that stems from the original man. You know actually the first people here were black people. And in Filipina/o history we have Negritos, and they're rooted and they have a lot of earth spirits. We have a lot of spirituality in our ancestral lineage that flows still and you may be reborn again and not know you have thousands of little lives that are in you, in your spirit. It has all these ancient roots, from tribal drums and all that, is what Hip Hop is. We feel the beat, we're rooted. That's what Hip Hop is, what we're feeling. It's pretty natural to want to do that type of movement. That's the culture of Hip Hop. It's just coming from the heart. There's no rules, there's no formula or anything. It's just like, "Hey, I feel like dancing weird like this. I feel like playing beats like this. I feel like banging on the desk like this for some strange reason. I just feel like yapping at the mouth and rapping, you know. I feel like drawing like this." It's not the norm. It's just coming from the heart, which is of course, rooted in our ancestry.

* * * * * * * * * *

RL: Why do you think when people think Filipina/os in Hip Hop they usually think DJing?

Q: Well, I don't know. I think it's also because of back in the days when we were all DJing. We were competing and probably because we got to the world stage. You know, at the world competition, we got all that light. That maybe Filipina/os were like, "Oh shit! They're Filipina/o, then we could do it, too." And Filipina/os shouldn't feel like that. They should feel like they can *always* do stuff. When we were competing, we weren't thinking we were Filipina/o. We were just out there to beat everybody. And so if you have the mentality of doing something to make the world a better place, that's the only thing you need to have. Don't think you're that Filipina/o or that you're doing this for the culture, you gotta do it for the whole world. Everybody is one, really. We're all one with God, or with the universe or whatever. We're all one, God's children. We're all one race, really. So don't think you're doing it for one flag-waving type of people, you have to do it for humanity. When you have that mentality, you can do anything. We're working for humanity, that's how it should be.

RL: When you started, it wasn't about being Filipino? It was about DJing?

Q: Not at all. No way … When we were battling, it was about kicking everybody's ass. That's what it was about. Not saying that we were veterans, but we were trying to be the best as we could, that's all that mattered. Trying to elevate, to do something different that had never been done before, and everyone has that power because we have unique talents. And we were like, "Hey, why don't we use all those unique talents and push it all the way to the limits and further this thing?"

RL: So was it then much more about the art?

Q: Without a doubt, yeah. No doubt. It was *just* about the art. It was strictly about Hip Hop culture and pushing it forward, nothing about racism.

RL: How about how artists use Hip Hop to talk about their identity, whether it's about their race or ethnicity or gender or sexuality?

Q: Well, it's theater … If you want to be a character that is a Filipina/o character, that's fine. But make it the best you can be. If you want to be a clown up there, if you want to be a gay rapper, do whatever you want. If you want to be the naked rapper, that's fine but there needs to be some skills. It's all theater. People don't see it as that they're up there as an actor. We're up there performing a character. But if you're an actor, you need some skills, too. You can be whoever you want to be. It's your stage.

RL: So your 15-year-old self, what was your character?

Q: My character was … the root was having skills. Second, was kinda to look trippy up there so it was kinda entertaining. And that's about it really. That was my character. But if you watch my videos, I kinda wore beanies. I looked all weird. If you look at the DMC USA finals, the competition in 1991. I'm wearing a black tank top with a white beanie that my grandmother made and it's just flapping all over the place. I look like a chef on crack or something. But if you really listen close, it's like, "Whoa, this guy's got some skills." But at the same time, it's eye-catching, like "This guy looks retarded!" … I didn't know that we were supposed to look weird until after that competition. Later, I started getting into theatrics and they were like, "Look at all these young guys who got black eyeliner on and he wears women's clothing. It's like hilarious. He looks silly up there." But it's not gonna work unless you've covered category number one, which is skills. It'll work for a while but people will get sick of it if you don't have the main category covered … "He looks crazy and all that but he got skills." … If you have them both together, then that's entertainment.

RL: How did you decide to do the DMC to begin with?

Q: It was the biggest DJ battle in the world at the time and so I wanted to enter it … So the DMC boils down to the regional, which is the Bay Area. If you win that, you go to the West Coast finals. Then you move up to the US finals. And then you go through world eliminations and after that you go to the world finals. So all the countries go through that.

RL: How did you turn this into a career?

Q: That comes with notoriety. Because we won that world competition and we were on that world stage, we automatically had a lot of notoriety. So from there, whatever you do, people will follow you: "Hey, what are you doing next?" So you just gotta keep that going.

RL: How have you maintained your high level, from the first DMC competition to Thud Rumble to the Apple commercial to be seen as one of the DJ legends?

Q: I wouldn't say all that but I try to practice every day still. I treat my craft like a musician. And you see those old kung fu masters, with their white beards and white eyebrows and they're still practicing. You see these old musicians who are 70, 80 years old and they're still going off like they're in their teens or twenties. I guess that's what we're going to do with scratching. We're gonna keep elevating it forever … We're going to keep doing it to see how far it gets. Like you're watching all these old masters doing it, Picasso, Michelangelo painted until they died. Why not scratching? Who makes up the rules but you?

CREATING COMMUNITY, BELONGING, AND VOICE

MY HIP HOP CREATION STORY

By Janice Sapigao

with hip hop,
at least
i tried.

1.
i used to steal listens from my brother's CDs.

naughty by nature
 bone thugs 'n harmony
 tupac
 kriss kross
 voices too big for my boombox
 too backwards for my mom's liking
never made it past a public second spin
 at nine years old, i stayed listening
  spun ideas from sound
 words from musical riot
 took hip hop to my journal
 labeled it poetry to hide it

2.
MTV brought me imitation.

at breakfast every morning
 i ate cereal streets dancing
 i drank milk nas wu tang
 sat up full from remixes
i made bad mixtapes
 recorded fresh off the radio
 wrapped in cartoon covers
 called 'em hello kitty paper jams
made elbow room to read album covers
 with the attention of essays
 sketched myself platinum and gold
 the colors of easy dreams
 and false heights

3.
when i was a b-girl, everyone laughed.

i didn't get to battle anyone
 just my reflection
practiced with another pinay
 our upper body strength trembled
 our footwork nonsensical
 the joke was my six-step
 my head spun from outside circles
 wanted to jump in from the sidelines   still do
 wanted to make a name
out of dance routines
 spell success with signature freezes
laugh back at mistaken feelings

4.
we used to battle on AOL instant messenger.

 it wasn't a cypher at school
so we typed as fast as speech
 played to a mind's song on repeat
 occupied chatrooms
 reading for digital rhythm
 freestyling with our fingers
 each letter leading
 to learned lyricizing

5.
saw brown sugar on my first date.

hip hop held my hand
 tried to tickle skin
 under my tanktop thought
my body belonged to beats
 before i discovered
  it belonged to me
took the course of a movie
 to learn to love with scrutiny
hip hop lived to break
 it was too free to be mine
too wild to be tied
 they right when they say
 you never forget your first time

with hip hop,
at most
i tried.

FILIPINO AMERICAN DANCE CULTURE IN SUBURBIA

THE STORY OF FUNKI JUNCTION

By Cheryl Cambay

I grew up in Cerritos, CA during a time when it seemed there was a large population of second-generation Filipinos coming of age. It was 1989 and towards the end of my freshman year at St. Joseph High School in Lakewood, CA—an all-girls' high school—and the majority of my friends were Filipinos from in and around Cerritos. The annual school talent show was coming up and a group of us decided to get together and form a dance group to enter the competition. Queen Latifah had a hit song, "Ladies First," and being that we went to an all-girls' school, we thought this to be the perfect name for the crew. And in order to really be original, we changed up the spelling and "Ladyz First" was born. Along with the title, we added key songs from Janet Jackson's hit album of the year *Rhythm Nation* to our dance tape. We were inspired by the strong female energy both these artists displayed and this was the cornerstone of the creation of our crew and what we showcased through dance and movement. Protégé was a group of guys we grew up with from different high schools who also entered the talent show. They added 1 girl from our school to perform with them, as that was the only way to enter our all-girls school talent show. It was a natural comparison—girls vs. boys—2 crews performing in movement the songs that defined the era. I am happy to say we came in first place that night over our fellow homeboys in Protégé.

Most of the friends I had were Filipino American, and although we attended different high schools, there were plenty of opportunities to meet and hang out with those who didn't go to our school—Confirmation classes at St. Linus Parish was one of them. The Filipino association at this parish is also where a lot of our parents interacted with each other and socialized. Out of these outlets grew a group of us teenagers getting to know each other, sharing interests, listening to the same music, identifying with our upbringing. Most of us from both Ladyz First and Protégé were part of this parish and gave us the opportunity to get to know each other more and hang out with each other outside of church and school. The guys added Emil Soriano Jr. (who was in our confirmation class) to their group and began to perform under the name TRIBE, which stood for The Royal International Boogie Era. Being that we were such a close group of friends and we performed at a lot of the same venues it was a natural fit

19

to eventually merge the 2 groups so we could showcase the female group, then the males, then perform in a piece together. That was the beginning of Ladyz First featuring TRIBE. It was more powerful to join forces on stage. From the talent shows, lots of folks began to ask us to perform at debuts, garage/house parties, our parents' Filipino association balls, Kaibigan's Pilipino Cultural Night (PCN) at Whitney High School, Maharlika's PCN at Cerritos High School—by my junior year we began driving ourselves to gigs and began performing under the name Funki Junction. The name change grew out of the fact that we were now performing and identifying as one crew rather than two separate crews.

I remember rehearsals well—we'd end up at someone's house and practice in the garages, front yard or the street. At one of the girls' houses—without the mirrors like you see in dance studios—the way we viewed our progress was literally to video tape rehearsals on a camera that was propped up on a tripod and view the footage and make adjustments, corrections, blocking as needed. When we rehearsed at Emil's house, I remember his mother had a glass-mirrored wall that we used to rehearse in front of and it was small so you couldn't see the whole group in the reflection! Oh the joy of practices at our parents' houses after school! And whenever we needed to rehearse or perform at a gig we literally had to call each other at home (no cell phones or email) or page each other to make sure we scheduled rehearsals and made ourselves available for the gigs we were asked to perform at. We also went shopping for performance outfits, which consisted throughout the years of overalls, paisley shirts, timberland boots, embroidered hats, parachute pants—what we considered cool and hip at the time!

The annual St. Joseph talent show became one of our biggest shows of the year because it was also a competition with a large attendance from youth all over the areas of Cerritos, Long Beach, Lakewood, and South Bay LA. It was important for us to step up our styles and being that we were a coed crew, we took advantage of this and implemented boy/girl partner pieces to slow songs of the time to which the audience responded well. Today, fans of dance can view YouTube, attend dance showcases and classes, and be inspired by other dance crews from all over the world with worldwide access online. Back then, our inspiration didn't come from other crews (as we were one of the few crews we knew in our area), but from the music videos of our time. Playing the videos we taped and rewinding and pausing when we saw something dope that inspired a set of choreography. One year, we decided on a Hip Hop history theme and added a voice track where we got one of our homeboys to record a narration of Hip Hop dance history—disco to breakin' to New Jack to the present at that time 1990s—the Housin' era. The last year we did that talent show we added the *Boogie Unit* a duo of dancers—Chris Natalio and Dennis Calvero.

During the time there were a lot of DJs in the scene and they provided the party scene in high school. Some of them also created the dance mixes we used during performances. I remember there was always a concern in the back of our minds if the parties were going to be hit up by gang activity. A couple of folks in our crew may have been active in the gang culture and everyone knew someone who was "gang bangin." I remember knowing early on whenever someone asked "Where you from?" you always responded "Nowhere." Gang activity, although it was quite rampant with Fil Am youth where I grew up, was the antithesis of Hip Hop dance and the party scene we chose. Where gangs were involved in violence against rival gangs, we were battling other crews at parties, providing the polar opposite to violence by dancing in the name of peace and Hip Hop. In both cases, it was important to belong, to rep your crew, and always get your crew members' or gang members' backs.

From the point of view of the Filipino American experience, and knowing we came from first-generation Filipinos who immigrated to the US prior to raising their children—there are some clear observations. Most of our parents worked full-time, making us a group of latch-key kids. Adolescence already garners a sense of wanting to seek an identity outside of our nuclear families and make strong connections and friendships. Our parents worked hard to provide us a lifestyle most of them did not have back in the Philippines. Cerritos was a booming suburban area at the time we grew up. It went from being primarily a dairy land in the 1970s to new housing tracts and local

Filipino American dance crew in Cerritos, 1988. Copyright © by Jennifer Chandler

businesses by the 1990s. Most of us lived in large family homes and enjoyed the booming economy of the 1990s. To keep up with this, our parents worked hard and long hours. Our parents also wanted us to quickly assimilate so that we didn't feel left out or feel like we were different from other American youth growing up in the US. This may be a reason that most of our generation did not speak Tagalog or another Filipino language fluently. There were traditions passed down from our Filipino culture, but in order to define that identity growing up in the US,– we had to reach out to each other with similar backgrounds. Out of this home environment, we took to the streets to connect with others, find outlets of creativity, and explore our identities. As I mentioned earlier both Cerritos High School and Whitney High School had Filipino clubs where we participated (even though a few of us didn't attend the schools) in performing in traditional Filipino cultural dance during the annual PCN (Pilipino Cultural Night). Funki Junction performed as the "modern" portion of the dance performance—being the symbol of the Filipino American culture of dance. Keeping true to our roots as Filipinos, we learned and performed traditional dance but it was also important to express our Filipino American culture through dancing in Funki Junction.

Cerritos and the surrounding areas were large hubs of Filipinos in Hip Hop—from us dancers in Funki Junction to the DJs who threw the house parties we attended. Having these venues to attend, without having to be 18 or 21 years and older, gave us those opportunities to dance/battle, interact with others who were young and also huge fans of Hip Hop. Out of these roots came large influences in Hip Hop culture today. DJ Eman (Power 106), DJ Virman (Far East Movement), DJ Rhettmatic (Beat Junkies, Visionaries), DJ Icy Ice (Beat Junkies), Cerritos All

Stars, and many more DJs of our era are still making their mark on the Hip Hop culture in the industry. A local youth from the South Bay of LA named Arnel Calvario used to travel to Cerritos to watch Funki Junction perform and he also recruited me to dance in Kaba Modern when I entered the University of California, Irvine in 1992. Arnel is the founder of Kaba Modern—today one of the most influential dance crews with a legacy of over 20 years and members who have made huge names for themselves in the dance and music industry. He always tells me how inspired he was as a kid watching Funki Junction perform. Emil Soriano, Jr., Chris "Lewds" Natalio (R.I.P), and Dennis Calvero, with whom I had the honor of dancing with in Funki Junction, continued their influence and creative design in the fashion world creating Crooks & Castles, an urban clothing company whose products have been represented throughout urban and Hip Hop culture by many of the music artists of the genre and in addition they have also sponsored the Jabbawockeez.

There is one last existing VHS tape of the collection of Funki Junction footage that I am working on transferring onto DVD for our group. When I view the footage, it takes me back to a pivotal time in Hip Hop music history—on the eve of the gangsta rap era, where knowing different names of dance moves, attending house/garage parties, and the party and dance golden era of Hip Hop in the 1990s reigned supreme and where I identified myself as a proud Filipino American youth and die-hard Hip Hop head. I still keep in touch with the folks in our dance crew and recently asked the question—why did we do this? What drove our ambition to create? It seems an easy enough question, but much harder to answer than you would think. Most of them couldn't even express through words why—it was mostly because "we just did it." There was no specific rhyme or reason to what was behind what we did; it organically grew out of our similar backgrounds, family lives, interests in Hip Hop music and dance and overall, our sense and need of wanting to *belong*. With the gift of hindsight I can express that our experience falls directly in line with the history of Hip Hop. Utilizing our love of dance, music, and creativity as a way to be heard and seen. We were representatives of Filipino American youth of our time. It was never about the recognition we received from our friends and audiences—that was a sweet byproduct of our love of the Hip Hop culture, dance as a creative outlet, and lifelong friendships with people I will always consider my family. I can still hear our friends in the audience, hyping us up before every performance—screaming in unison at the top of their lungs: "Funki Junction's in the house and the house is PACKED!"

SOUL IN THE WHOLE

THE SUCCESSES AND CHALLENGES OF REPRESENTATION FROM KABA MODERN AND BEYOND

By Arnel Calvario

"**S**oul in the hole!" is what is often traditionally called out when my Kaba Modern family is huddling up for a performance as we link our hands together and throw positive energy into the circle that binds us. To this day, urban dance continues to be an important part of my Filipino-American experience. I was born in the early 70s when club and street dance styles were thriving in underground culture. Snippets of Waackin', Lockin', and Poppin' were seen on shows such as *Solid Gold* and *Soul Train*. It was the era of soul and funk music and I remember seeing the Original Lockers in their striped shirts, striped socks, knockers, and apple hats. At the time, I didn't know what their dance style was called, but I clearly saw that they were funky, soulful, powerful, and extremely entertaining. Dance was viewed as premier entertainment and I was definitely captivated. Even that early on, I knew that urban dance would have cultural significance and that I would pursue my dreams to be a part of its social movement.

Jumping into the 80s, movies such as *Beat Street* and *Breakin' 1* and *Breakin' 2* came out and the world was exposed to Hip Hop culture. Street and club styles were propelled into pop culture. The media called it "breakdancing" and "pop-locking," but all of us who went to underground/street events such as Radiotron and sessions in our parks knew that each of these three styles were breakin', poppin', and lockin'. I vividly remember some press describing breakin' as dangerous and violent, but this reputation faded as artists demonstrated that these dance styles were art forms created by and for the community. These dance art forms were outlets for communities all around the world to express themselves, to connect to the music, and/or to sit back and be entertained by something fresh, raw, and vibrant. The spirit of lockin' mirrored the celebration, freedom, and empowerment of the civil rights movement, while art forms such as breakin' served as a more positive alternative to gangs and violence when communities were facing economic and social challenges.

I remember admiring people from my neighborhood parks and street corners busting their moves on the concrete with only linoleum or cardboards as their dance surface. People were dancing to the sounds blasted through the ghetto blasters or in larger events to the beats and breaks of a live DJ. Some of my older cousins even formed poppin' crews. I was on the outside of the circles looking in—full of admiration and respect for their craft, but limited by my own shyness and insecurities. I would practice moves in the privacy of my room in hopes that maybe one day I would have the courage to perform or express myself as a dancer within the cipher. Seeing so many of my cousins as well as many other Filipino-Americans in my community thrive as dancers inspired a vision that being a dope dancer was possible for anyone who put in the hard work and surrounded themselves with the right people. I also noticed that much of the energy and drive of the dance crews in my community replaced that inherent in local gangs. Dance became a healthier, safer outlet for our community. It was more than just entertainment; it was a vehicle for camaraderie and artistic expression of shared life experiences.

In reflecting back on those dance ciphers, I now see how it truly reflects the power of dance circles even in our traditional Filipino cultural dances. Similar to a lot of the tribal dances that find their connection and power within dance circles, street and club dance also thrive in cipher circles. Whether the spirit and energy of the dance is an aggressive battle or a sharing and exchange of expression, the dancer in the circle connects to those surrounding them and there is a dynamic reciprocation that truly takes the dance to a different level.

In the mid 80s and early 90s, I felt a shift in dance begin. Street styles were depicted in media and in pop culture as "old school" and "played out." Sadly, dancers and DJs shifted from being in front as headlining acts to becoming background for singing artists. The rise of New Jack Swing music became apparent and "housin'" crews started popping up in Southern California. They were called housin' crews in my community because these crews would perform or battle other crews at house parties. It was the generation of the party dances where there were many common names for each dance move such as "the Robo-Cop," "the Smurf," the Roger Rabbit," "the Kid n' Play," "the Reebok," and "the Wop." Instead of breakin', poppin', or lockin' sets and freestyles, choreographed routines with complex formation changes, ripples, and levels were imminent. Pop music had transitioned away from soul, funk, disco, and break beats to rap, pop, and R&B music.

I had witnessed my cousins perform at our family parties as well as dope crews from Cerritos composed predominantly of Filipino-Americans such as Funki Junction and Johnny's Quest perform and battle at house parties and party events. The energy of house dance battles reflected the competitiveness of crew battles from the 70s and 80s, but the spirit was definitely much more playful, fun, and fitting for a party atmosphere. Bragging rights were now earned within the parties. I also became aware of East Coast–based legendary dance crew Elite Force, who combined freestyle and choreography to really create a dance movement recognized many places as "new skool."

Aside from party battles and performances, dance crews in my area were often seen at school talent shows as well. Thus, in high school, I joined up with three other close friends and created a crew called P.D.P. We rocked polka dot rayon shirts, Z Cavaricci pants, polka dot socks, and shiny wing-tip shoes for one performance and air-brushed hooded t-shirts, Guess overalls, and sneakers for another. With our routines, we entered talents shows and performed for parties. Similar to the cultural dances that represented the provinces of our parents, as second-generation Filipinos, we used dance to express our life experiences, our camaraderie, and our local communities. It was an era of dance that was fun, hype, and prevalent in Southern California Filipino-American communities.

My interest in dance traveled with me when I moved to Irvine to attend U.C. Irvine. Kaba Modern was created in 1992 as the plans and rehearsals for U.C. Irvine's Pilipino Culture Night (PCN) were underway. As I reviewed, learned, and choreographed Filipino cultural dances, a thought crossed my mind: "If PCN is about sharing our pride as Filipino-Americans, shouldn't we have a dance suite for modern styles of urban dance?" I approached the president of the Filipino club, Kababayan, and soon thereafter, flyers were posted, auditions were held, and Kaba Modern was born. The very first Kaba Modern performance was in spring 1993 for U.C. Irvine Kababayan's PCN. My intent of creating Kaba Modern was not only to showcase innovative artistry, but to also share the

SOUL IN THE WHOLE | 25

familial bond created within our group. I believe that this is the reason that Kaba Modern was received so well—it reflected the fearlessness of trying something new as well as pride in dancing together as a close circle of friends.

In 1992, there were no other formalized college Asian-American crews we were aware of, so Kaba Modern was known as something innovative. Other Southern California college dance companies such as PAC Modern (stemming from Cal State Long Beach's Pilipino American club), Team Millennia, and CADC (Chinese-American Dance Company) popped up years later. There were also several other notable Asian-American crews I respected and admired such as Jedi Clan/Mind Tricks, Dangerous Image, and Chain Reaction up in Northern California. Thus, the Asian American dance scene in terms of crews who did choreography really started blowing up in the 1990s. Almost every big college in Southern California had a Hip Hop dance group as part of their PCN or cultural night. While many of the emerging dance groups were different, it appeared that the spirit that fueled these groups was the same—the intent to entertain audiences with their art, the fulfillment of being embraced as a part of a group, and the sharing of a memorable experience you can collectively be proud of.

Asian-Americans had such a strong presence in underground street dance with so many poppin' and breakin' crews composed of many Filipinos and other Asian ethnicities since back in the 70s and 80s, but in mainstream pop culture, our visibility was few and far between. In fact, when I founded Kaba Modern, there were few Asian-Americans in pop culture mainstream. I think the only remotely visible role models I can remember seeing on TV were Nia Peeples from *FAME*, CarrieAnn Inaba as one of the Fly Girls on *In Living Color*, and a few back-up dancers for pop artists such as Janet Jackson and Britney Spears. This greatly contrasted what I had witnessed my whole life—the diversity of Hip Hop dance culture inclusive of so many Filipino-Americans.

In 1995, as car shows became increasingly popular in Southern California, dance crews were beginning to be approached to perform and compete at these car shows. One of Kaba Modern's first dance competitions was the Del Mar Car Show where we competed against another dance crew called Culture (later renamed Team Millennia), which was founded by Danny Batimana at Cal State Fullerton. Car show promoters recognized the popularity of dance and incorporated dance competitions into their event schedule to create an increased draw to their events.

The Asian-American dance culture (especially in Southern California) has thrived for the past decade and a half with several annual dance competitions, battles, dance showcases, and countless groups of dancers. Some of the first collegiate, urban dance choreography competitions for the Southern California dance circuit emerged in the mid-90s such as BUSTA-GROOVE presented by JALAN & Culture Shock San Diego (which later evolved to being BODY ROCK presented by Anna Sarao and Artheta Watten), VIBE presented by Lambda Theta Delta, Irvine (founded by my old roommate and Kaba Modern alumni, Joseph Lising), FUSION presented by members of 220 in San Diego, and PRELUDE presented by members of Team Millennia. These shows would sell out thousands of seats as dance groups from various areas would compete for bragging rights and a trophy. As events became produced for dancers throughout the west coast, more dance crews and dance communities were being created and our dance community flourished and expanded.

Social media also evolved to connect dancers globally. Boogiezone.com was launched by Elm Pizarro in 2003 to provide online forums for dancers to not only find out about local dance events, but also to connect with each other and exchange ideas and commentaries. With the advent of YouTube in 2005, visibility and networking between Asian-American dancers exploded not only nationally, but internationally as well. I was accustomed to watching VHS tapes and DVDs shared between friends, but social media such as YouTube, MySpace, and Facebook now made viewing international dance a finger click away.

In 2003, I was offered the Executive Directorship of Culture Shock Los Angeles and this truly evolved my views on the cultural significance of Hip Hop culture. Culture Shock, as an international non-profit organization, is focused not only on professional entertainment, but also on dance education and community outreach, so I not only grew as a dancer, but I evolved as community leader since joining the company. If we were to call ourselves "Hip Hop dancers," I realized how important it is to talk to dance pioneers and progressors of the past, so I could truly understand the rich history, the vocabulary, the essence and spirit, and the cultural significance of Hip Hop dance as an art form. I realized how important it is to know my roots before striving to create branches in the community. I now know that to be a true conscious artist, educator, and leader, I have to embrace the fact that I will be a life-long learner—pursuing the history of urban and Hip Hop dance from others and with others, so I can be better able to be a part of preserving and progressing our dance community.

My past of growing up through the era that marked the birth of Hip Hop culture combined with my pursuit of knowledge and consciousness today help me realize that urban dance has gone through its cycles from underground to mainstream pop culture. Current shows such as *America's Best Dance Crew*, *So You Think You Can Dance*, and even *Dancing With The Stars* all had many inspiring, talented dancers and choreographers, which I believe has really diversified the face of Hip Hop dance past the previous perceptions that it was an art dominated by just one race. I felt that our presence on these shows have made our place in dance culture much more visible and respected. As these shows have been more inclusive of Asian-Americans, I am overjoyed by the fact that the face of urban street dance has diversified and opened up for all people not only in the underground culture, but in the pop mainstream culture as well. *America's Best Dance Crew* has taken crews such as Kaba Modern, Jabbawockeez, Quest Crew, and Poreotics and propelled many Filipino-Americans into the mainstream culture where we now have an international presence and a visibility to the youth around the globe. This has been such an amazing honor and blessing, but it is also a responsibility as we represent the legacy of our dance community. We have the opportunity to encourage others to be positive, innovative, and well-informed artists.

I think these shows have done four major things that are positive for dance culture:

1. It has helped to more visibly place Hip Hop dance as an art form with history and technique that should be respected in the same respect as some of the other classical dance art forms.
2. It has helped to promote the positivity of urban dance and broken down past stereotypes of negativity that Hip Hop dance artists have dealt with in the past.
3. It has helped to bring parents and youth together in dialogue and in joint respect of urban street dance as premiere entertainment.
4. Increased visibility of Asian-American dancers, choreographers, and community leaders who have diversified and expanded the perception of a career in the performing arts.

However, this is not enough. We must also make sure the stories of dancers beyond these shows are told, so as a dance community, we are inspired, understood, encouraged, and validated.

There are also inherent limitations on these shows. There is not enough history and correct vocabulary shared on these shows to truly share the depth and richness of Hip Hop and urban dance culture, so it becomes the artists' responsibility to share their knowledge and further educate themselves on the dance lineage they represent. Because these shows are obviously driven by ratings, there is also pressure on the artists to be wary of the stereotypes that can be portrayed. One of my Kaba Modern dancers on Season 1 of *America's Best Dance Crew*, Yuri Tag, had shared her challenges of not being understood by her parents when it came to her passion for dance. While this is true of many families out there, Yuri and the rest of us shared a concern that this televised story may negatively portray a lack of support from Asian-American families for the arts when this is obviously not true of many families who actually encourage the arts. Luckily, the show ultimately portrayed a positive resolution of understanding, but that is the danger of these shows—anything said can be cut, edited, and produced to negatively reflect upon a community. Being backstage and on set of various reality dance shows, I have seen that there is always a pressure by producers to tell a controversial story. Thus, aside from showcasing their talent, it is important for artists in the public eye to also be conscious that their voice can positively or negatively impact the world's understanding of Asian-American culture.

I have witnessed some of the other challenges Asian-Americans face on these dance shows. With the noticeable success of many Asian-American dancers from the West Coast on many of these dance shows, I have heard of casting directors turning away dance crews composed of Asian-Americans in efforts to diversify the faces of their show and optimize ratings. Shouldn't these shows be based on talent, passion, and attitude? Have we seen this happen when shows feature too many Caucasian cast members? "Yes" to the first question and unfortunately the answer to the second question is "no." I have witnessed casting directors request a change in the composition of dance crews or even cut dance crews based on efforts to limit the number of Asian-American dancers or to cover other areas of the country on a particular season. Because of this reality, it is important that when given visibility on these shows, we seize the moment to use our voice wisely and powerfully to represent the beauty of our culture and identity. It also points to the importance that we, as community leaders, produce our own projects, events, and publicity that also bring our important stories to the public.

After over two decades of both Kaba Modern and Culture Shock International, I am grateful to have been a part of the evolution of our dance community. The future of Asian-American dancers can be bright because not only in California, but nationally and internationally, there are countless phenomenal dance crews, dance companies, choreographers, dancers, directors, and community leaders who continue to make a huge artistic impact on their communities.

The key to keeping it strong is for all of us as artists and leaders is to stick together in our mission to keep the dance culture positive and artistically innovative. We need to understand the history and culture of Hip Hop dance and understand how this history has paved the way for urban dance today. We need to not repeat mistakes of the past where ignorance, money, and fame have divided talented artists. I also hope that Filipino-Americans can see how urban dance parallels the generations of cultural folk dances of our Filipino ancestors in the sense that dance is an expression of our experiences of joy, cultural pride, struggle, strength, and growth. Just as our Filipino cultural dances represent a province, community, and culture, each urban dance crew represents the social movement or their community. Thus, in this way, dance can be a vehicle for creating and bridging communities and generations of thoughts, experiences, and life lessons. We need to connect not only through social media and televised media, but more importantly through dialogue, in-person connection, print, and community events. Lastly, it is important for us to push creative boundaries to pave professional paths for artists beyond what has already been done.

I hope one day to open or support the opening of a community center that utilizes innovative arts and wellness programs to promote creative expression, improved health, and community outreach for people of all ages. While the stereotypical career for a Filipino-American was once to be doctor, engineer, or lawyer, I now know that it is more important to choose a career that brings authentic and meaningful fulfillment. Thus, I have chosen to be a doctor of occupational therapy *and* an artist—it doesn't have to be an either/or situation. Whether it is a lawyer and marathon runner, a marketing executive and a parent, a graphic design artist and community activist, a photographer and writer, etc. everyone should find that purposeful, healthy life balance that makes most sense for them. Together as a community (local and global), it is up to us to be courageous, informed, innovative, collaborative, authentic, purpose-driven, and positive-minded artists to not only keep urban dance alive, but growing, thriving, and visible for generations to come.

THE STRUGGLE & SURVIVAL OF EMPRESS MILAN

EXCERPTS FROM AN INTERVIEW WITH MILAN ZANOTTI

By DJ Kuttin Kandi

"I'm Milan Zanotti"

A lot of people know me as Empress Milan, the artist formerly known as Nano Reyes. I am a modern-day female. A lot of people might not know what that means but in layman terms, I am a transsexual woman. But I don't label myself a transsexual woman. I am a woman, period. That's who I am and that's how I feel inside. So, I choose to live my life as a woman every day. I take the necessary hormones to minimize and totally deactivate any type of testosterone in my body. As of late, I've got some new triple D titties, so my tits are huge. But that was a big accomplishment for me. Because coming from where I come from, I never knew that I could do this to myself. I am so much happier in my life.

"I was brought up around the party lifestyle, the gang lifestyle"

As a kid, going back to as a kid, my mom had me at a very young age. My mom—she's filipino, she's Spanish-Filipino, and my father is also Filipino mixed but he was born in Manila and he was raised Fil-Am when he moved to America. My parents had me at a young age; they were 17 years old. They were young teenagers that liked to have fun and party. So, I was brought up around the party lifestyle, the gang lifestyle. My father got incarcerated when I was 2 years old. The relationship that him and my mom had from what I remember was very abusive and not healthy. And that stuck in the back of my mind as I was growing up. Part of my life growing up, I seen everyone in my school at Father's Day, their father would come. Their dads come pick them up and I felt a little awkward and I felt a little weird.

"I used to pray to God at a young age, 'What do I do?'"

There was something [about] me, besides not having a father—I always knew there was something different about me. I felt like I never really considered myself gay. Unfortunately, society has made the label "gay" so wrong, so in my head I tried to deprive that feeling. And I've always had fantasies of sexual desires, you know, for a man. I love my gays. I love them but to be intimate with one, I never really was turned on by it. And I always wanted, like, a straight man. In my mind as a kid, I always said I was a girl. I didn't know how to go about that as a kid. Where I am from in California, there's not a lot of people that are G.I.D., which is gender-identity disorder. I didn't know what that was, so growing up, I thought I was crazy. And that turned into a lot of anxiety, a lot of stress inside myself. I started to lock myself in the room at a very young age, confused. I used to pray to God at a young age, "What do I do? I don't know what to do." I didn't know what was going on.

"I use music as an outlet to let go of frustrations and emotions that I have within myself."

My mom, she partied a lot. I love my mom. My mom has the most amazing heart, but the downfall of it, she was a young girl looking for love. And that's how I put it, even now. My mom is a woman of love and that's what she's looking for. I know she loves her children, but the most important thing [is] for her, was for her, to be loved. Growing up, when I was a baby, my mom partied. So, that took a toll on me as well, being locked in my room. I would pray to God, "This is not what I want, this is not who I want to be. I don't know what's wrong with me." I [was] crazy, I felt I was an alien. There were times I felt like I was possessed by a demon. "This is not who I am. God, if this is the life that you don't want me to live, I know you don't want me to be gay or [have] whatever feelings I have—change me." So, I started going to church and I became real active in church. At those times, when I locked myself in my room, I started to write. I started to write a lot of poetry, I started to write a lot of my feelings down in journals.

"I was getting bullied back before it was such an anti-bully thing."

Growing up as an adolescent, I got picked on a lot at school. People would call me faggot, queer. I would get pushed on, people would write things about me, post pictures about me. I dropped out of school in 8th grade, in Peters, California. This guy got one of my pictures and made 100 copies on white pieces of paper, blew it up and [wrote] "I like dick." And this was before "bullies" was in the media. I'm 29 years old now; I was getting bullied back before it was such an anti-bully thing. I wish we had these campaigns growing up, because otherwise I would have finished school with high grades. Being bullied as a young kid and my mom not being there, I became suicidal. I didn't know what to do. I was so confused, I hated myself, and everytime I talk about it, I get emotional because it really took a toll on my life growing up. I hated my life, I hated waking up in the morning. I just hated it; I hated everyone around me. And that made me become rebellious. At 16, I met my first boyfriend, and me and him were together for 2½ years. He got involved with heavy drugs. I never really got involved in the same drugs he did, but I started to get involved in the same activities he did. We would rob people, we were stealing cars. We were hurting people to get money. I was with a group of people in San Jose, and we ended up being in the news and getting arrested November 16, 2001. I ended up doing some time. Nothing hard—we got arrested for robbery, for car theft and a whole bunch of stupid things that I did as a teenager, that I did because I was angry inside, and I hated myself. So I didn't care what happened, so I was doing a lot of crazy things.

"I love the Lord, and I'm not going to deny that, but I was still suppressing who I was."

I ended up leaving my boyfriend. I turned to this place called Victory Outreach and it's an international ministry. And they also have some in metro Manila, Philippines. I was in San Jose, so I gave my life back to God because I was confused. Because this is not who I am, not who I want to be. Through my artistic ways, I started to write music and I made Christian raps. I used to go by the name by Lil' ANT and it was an acronym: Life is Living Anointed and True. So that was my name, for a long time, I was going out. I would reach out. We would do like an events, we would go out every Tuesday and every Thursday, and we would go to the dirtiest hoods of every city and we would reach out to the drug dealers, the gang members, the prostitutes. At that time, nobody was really out gay, like being gay was not popular. And people knew I was gay. I would admit it. That was my testimony. That God saved me from a life of being gay, from a life of robbing people. At a young age, at 14–15 years old, I was pimping women. I was pimping these girls to get money. And God pulled me from that crazy lifestyle and being suicidal. I had a lot of hurt and a lot of anger in me. Like I said, I became a testimony for a lot of young people out there. I would share my testimony how God took me from the streets, and God took me from all this hurt and all this pain and now I'm living this great life. I love the Lord and I'm not going to deny that but I was still suppressing who I was. I was truly happy with the Lord but as soon as I began to travel more and see things, I still was unhappy with who I was. My pastor ended up sending me to this bible school, called the UTC. It's located in Los Angeles, California. There's one in Africa, in the Philippines, one in Mexico, and one in Connecticut. I went to school in LA, I was there for 9 months, and I was doing really good. But I was still struggling with who I was, like my sexuality. After I graduated he sent me to London; I came back home a few months later to America and I told my pastor, "You know what I can't do this anymore. This is not who I am. I am not happy, I love the Lord and I love you guys. You guys are amazing." This is an amazing establishment and they truly have a heart for the lost generation and that I can give to them. They were there for me and the Lord was an amazing God to me. But I couldn't lie anymore inside, I couldn't suppress who I truly was. So I left.

"Nano Reyes is someone I will always love and respect because he held it down without giving up."

I got involved with a radio station in Salinas, Santa Cruz. There was this radio station 102.5 KDON. I was interning there for a while and I became this personality named Nano Reyes. I met a really good friend of mine—her name was Mari-Jane and the day I met her she told me she had cancer, and I knew that one day I was going to lose her as a friend. But Mari-Jane was vital to my growth in the radio industry. I started hanging out with her. I was interning, she got me a spot on weekends, and I got a spot with her as a co-host for a love show called Night Moves, so I started to give love advice on the radio. So I was doing that for a year, [and] I started getting bookings to speak at different high schools locally to be there for young people. Any time anybody needed someone to talk, they would call me to let [young people] know about bullying, about staying in school, staying focused, [about] staying off the drugs. I was doing that for awhile.

I had just got signed to Downlow, Deadlee and all that gay, out hip hop stuff. I [had] got signed to Clyde N' Clyde records with Downlow from Arizona, Deadlee from Los Angeles. But I parted ways with them and started to go independent. And Nano Reyes started to make a lot of his own music.

At that time, I was claiming to be gay. But I didn't feel gay. I was dating other gay boys and I wasn't happy. I was not happy with that lifestyle. And shout-outs to my gays 'cause I do love them, I love them, no doubt. But like I said, where I am from, there [are] not a lot of transsexuals. Maybe now, but there [weren't] a lot of transsexuals [then]. So, I didn't know.

Nano Reyes is someone I will always love and respect because he held it down without giving up. I will always remember him—I just don't want other people to remember him like that, because they will use that against Milan negatively. As a person, I will always remember who I once was, and I will always love and respect that person because that person [was] strong. Even at times when [I] felt weak, Nano was always there. As Milan, I will always be there to protect Nano. But as far as videos go and stuff like that, I don't want them out there publicly.

"Every single day I am thinking about ways I can kill myself."

I was doing my hair and I was so frustrated. And you know how sometimes, when you're doing your hair, the rubber band snaps, like it broke? And once that rubber band snapped, I snapped. There was an antique mirror. I punched it straight through and it broke. I started throwing everything. "I've had it, I'm fucking done. Fuck this life, I can't do this no more." I'm telling you this story but throughout this whole time I'm fighting suicidal tendencies. Every single day I am thinking about ways I can kill myself.

"Now I'm Milan, I'm more happy inside."

My mom calls my best friend who I call my sister, Kyra. She calls Kyra and she's in New York. Kyra gets with me on the phone, "I'm here for you, I'm going to buy you a ticket." Two days later, I ended up in New York. She bought my ticket to New York. I started to see a lot of transgender people in New York. I told her, "I think that's what I am." And she told me, "Don't just do it for the glamour." And I told her, "I'm not, you know." So, I started doing some research, and I thought to myself, "This is who I am." I started hormone therapy and I continued with music. And through that time, I became Milan. And I was gonna do a reality show called, "Becoming Milan." But then I thought about it; I don't want people to look back on it and YouTube [and see] all my crazy-looking days, my awkward stage. I have grown—I'm not where I wanna be, but I'm not where I used to be. And right now, I haven't been working on my music, but I've been writing. But I haven't been in the studio as much because I've actually been living my life. And I have material to fall back on, so when I do go in the studio and what I write and what I spit, people will be able to feel it because I've lived it. Now I'm Milan; I'm more happy inside. I don't think about being suicidal no more. I still write music. I'm actually doing my own documentary on my own life. I've been recording little bits and pieces as I travel the world. Trying to keep myself happy. Right now, I'm working on a mixtape. Actually, I'm working on an album with Last Defense. He's an amazing mentor in this whole scene. I'm working on myself and I'm upgrading me as much as possible. The best for Milan is yet to come.

"No one can ridicule me"

As a Transgender Fil Am artist I feel like, I will say, there is discrimination, not just in America, but probably in the Philippines. I am able to be vocal because I'm just living the life. I feel like I've lived a crazy life. No one can ever say anything to make me feel any type of way to make me feel less than I am. You get what I'm saying? No one can ridicule me. I am the kind of person now that I have no filter. I lived a hard life that I can just go out there and people can say things and I won't get offended. I deal with discrimination every single day. I deal with it and it's horrible. I hate it. But it is what it is.

"To not just live and die, but to live and tell my story"

Well, based off of this world, it's very visual, so image is everything. As a boy, I was very awkward-looking, but as a girl, it's weird. I have this sex appeal that I've been told [about]. I only say what people tell me. I know that I haven't uploaded any new videos, but it's been a year that I have triple D titties. I've just been working on my beauty and trying to stay focused. And just keeping my eyes on the prize. I think this generation, it's still like the south… there's still discrimination but it's getting better, as we grow progressive, as more and more transsexuals are coming out. And they just legalized gay marriage, so we are making some type of progress. In the industry, it's like a taboo. I think they are going to have a transgender famous rapper. And I know I'm definitely going to be in the Hip Hop scene. I'm definitely going to be one that's known. I've lived a crazy enough life. To not just live and die, but to live and tell my story and let it be effective and let it touch others who lived similar lives or if not, worse. So, I can be there as an outlet, to let them know not to give up. Cause there's been time I wanted to give up. There's so much hate around this world. And there's so many times I wanted to give up. But if I give up, the world wins. I wanna win. Before I die, I wanna experience life. I wanna know what it's like. That's the only reason why I'm not giving up, because there are young people out there that were once like me that need to hear a story of success and survival. And I wanna be that voice, I wanna give back to the community. I wanna travel the world and reach out to young people that are struggling, that have no one to talk to. I wanna be there for them. My story is going to be told and it's going to be told in the utmost truth. So, I just can't wait.

"There are a lot of people that are not accepting about me"

Fortunately, our culture being that we're Filipino, from the Philippines—a lot of people from our culture, I've noticed growing up, are very welcoming and very warm-hearted. One thing about Filipinos is that they're very loyal. A lot of people are not like that in this world. There's a lot of shady and evil people. There are a lot of people that are not accepting about me, but if they're not accepting of me, I don't need them around me. I don't need anyone's attention that doesn't wanna give it to me. I'm not gonna beg for someone to accept me for who I am because I accept myself. And there are others who don't know who they are, but I will accept them too. This world is getting better, but there are a lot of ignorant, naive people out there. And they take it out on us for not knowing what it is—they take it out on us.

"I came out to them and they met Milan."

(In my experience), the Filipino community is more accepting [of people who are] transgender. I've never been to the Philippines but I really wanna go. I don't go to a lot of Filipino functions because my family from the Philippines is in California and now I'm in New York. When I was growing up, they were really accepting of me. They still love me the same. They made me feel part of the family. At first, growing up, my stepgrandmother—she's real Filipino—she was all like, "I don't want you to be gay growing up." But that was as a kid. They didn't know. But as I grew up, I started to live my own life. I came out to them and they met Milan. And they treated me so lovely, they showed me so much love. And I am just so grateful that I was able to move to New York and become Milan. 'Cause if not, I would have died. I really would have killed myself. I think about it everyday. I still cry myself to sleep.

"My music is my love"

Sometimes, I feel like I will never find true love because it's so hard to meet someone that is actually genuine and loyal; that's why my music is my love. And right now I've been living my life. I'm living my life to make me happy and it's time for me to let all my stories and my life unfold before the eyes of the world. Because I know if I don't belong to anybody, but I belong to the world.

On other works

I'm working on a book. I'm trying to put this book together as soon as I can but it's very emotional. It's an autobiography about my life. I know I haven't accomplished great things but I am starting it now. I'm writing my destiny and fulfilling the legacy that I'm supposed to leave behind.

"This is like a new form of bullying"

It's an easier way through YouTube to be known. This generation that we live in, you can be famous and your name can be known overnight. They were sharing my video on the transgender network. And a lot of transgenders were hitting me up: "You're so inspiring." I am not perfect because a lot of crazy things been taken place lately. But I'm just grateful because God is good and He's had my back the whole time. YouTube for this generation is good, for whoever has the voice to be heard. It's kind of like, wow. This is like a new form of bullying. But I already know how to deal with it. It's people behind the screen and you can just actually erase it. It just goes to show you that no matter how good you try to do, there's always gonna be someone right behind you doing bad. And all you gotta do is live life and be successful because that's the best type of revenge. They're at a place in their life where they are unhappy. And I don't wanna be there. I wanna be happy and I wanna live happy. I just wanna love and spread love. I'm speaking and I'm speaking to myself because there's sometimes... I'm pushing an older age and I be fighting and I need to stop fighting. But we're human.

On how to support people who identify as Transgender

Questions—ask questions. No question is a stupid question unless you're being stupid intentionally, but if it's an educational question and if you're really concerned ... I think just being there for somebody. We're human. That's what I tell guys who wanna date me. I let guys get to know me first and then before it's anything sexual, I tell them, "Hey, look, this who I am. But I am a human first. I am a Transgender woman." They look at you as though you're some type of alien. And I don't understand that 'cause I'm not like that.

On describing Hip Hop sound—"It's just bonafide"

It could be gritty. I could be mainstream, but for the most part it's pretty much just real. They tell me to put a label on it, but I don't like to label things. It's just bonafide. It's the honest truth, real, the realest. I'm kind of, like, gritty, I guess. A lot of people be like, "You sound gangsta." It's not about being gangsta, it's just that passion I have within me. I could do mainstream, but it depends. That all depends. My style has changed. She's more calmed down, Miss Milan. I am more at peace with myself. I'm not where I want to be, like I said, but a lot has changed as far as me being happy with who I am. So, a lot has kinda calmed down. Because back then it was more about the struggle. My raps were more like struggling and hustling. I still struggle and hustle but now I make more money than I did before. I'm not rich but I'm not broke like I used to be. My mom is not selling drugs like she used to be.

My mom is not in prison no more. It's a different part of my life. I haven't performed any and I haven't released [any]. But there's a song coming out called "Alone," and that really says it all. It really explains who I truly am. A lot of my songs have been emotional lately, but they're good because people can understand it and feel it.

"You will make a difference"

I do want to go to the Philippines and see what I can do. Maybe do some type of reality show there, if there are more people out there that are willing to give more of themselves to help better the world. The world can be a better place. You can't save the entire world but those that you can save, you will make a difference. I feel like being that person that has the ability to travel and love genuinely—people can feel that. And they say hugs do heal. And true love from your heart, people can feel that. I would love to give a positive force for a lot of hurting people. I can't wait to start moving in my talent and traveling and spreading the word.

Milan's last words

Just spread love and be happy. No matter what struggles you go through, know that someone else out there does have it worse than you. As far as my music, be on the lookout 'cause I'm taking over.

GETTING SCHOOLED

LESSONS FROM RESEARCHING FILIPINO AMERICAN MOBILE DJ CREWS

By Oliver Wang

With any luck, this essay should appear sometime in the general orbit of the release of my book, *Legions of Boom*, a social history of the Filipino American mobile DJ scene in the Bay Area.[1] Though *Legions* isn't about hip-hop specifically—an assumption, interestingly enough, that many erroneously make, to understand the rise of Filipino American hip-hop DJs in the 1990s requires, in my opinion, an understanding of the mobile crews that preceded them. This essay is not meant to be a summation of that research, though I will be drawing from it. Instead, "Getting Schooled" is a reflection on the research process itself, ideally as a way to open a dialogue into how we approach pop culture topics in Filipino/Asian/ethnic studies, especially for those of us engaged in ethnographic/oral history projects. By no means am I suggesting that "my process" is the only "correct one." Rather, I try to explain my own evolving ideas around methodology beginning with two (deceptively) simple questions: "why?" and "how?"

"Why Filipinos and DJing?" This became a recurrent question people would throw my way whenever I mentioned my research for *Legions*. When I explained how Filipino Americans were well-represented amongst the ranks of the best DJs in the world, those from outside either community (DJs or Filipino Americans) would often ask whether or not there was a particular "Filipino style" to DJing or, conversely, if there was any innate cultural tradition or impulse that guided so many young Filipino Americans to become DJs.

I always took these questions to be well meaning and stemming from a curiosity of a community who have historically sat on the liminal edge of America's racial awareness. Many of my respondents have suffered through

---

1 Wang, 2014. Mobile DJ crews are groups/outfits organized around providing audio and lighting services for private events and parties: weddings, birthdays, school dances, etc. As *Legions of Boom* discusses, the Filipino American mobile DJ scene roughly spanned the late 1970s through mid-1990s, including dozens if not hundreds of different crews, and was an integral part of Filipino American youth culture during the 1980s. Though not ostensibly a "hip-hop scene" when it formed (indeed, the earliest crews precede the national interest/awareness of hip-hop), hip-hop became an important musical and cultural influence on crews by the late 1980s and many prominent Filipino American scratch DJs came directly out of the mobile scene, including Qbert, Shortkut, Mixmaster Mike, Apollo, D-Styles, and many others.

the all-too-common indignity of being asked some variation of "so ... what are you?" or "what is a Filipino?"[2] Therefore, for a cadre of Filipino Americans youth to become such important members in a cultural scene as visible as hip-hop DJing, can understandably engender a desire to understand "why Filipinos and DJing?"

That "why?" question often haunts scholarship that deals with race/ethnicity and cultural movements. As noted, I believe "why?" comes from a well-meaning place of inquiry but I always feel slightly unsettled by it. For me, the "why?" often flirts—however unintentionally—with one of two potential assumptions. The first is that cultural and social behavior stem from an embedded, essentialist set of community norms that are so fixed as to be readily legible to everyone else. In other words, it presumes that the phrase "Filipino culture" has a universal meaning that can be understood, and therefore, expressed. However, given what Sarita See describes as the "wild heterogeneity" of the Filipino community, it's unlikely that anyone could identify any cultural practices that would define a core, unified sense of "Filipino-ness."[3]

On the other hand, the "why?" could also represent a desire to grant social conditions causal power over cultural activities, what Robin Kelley warns as a reductive way of pathologizing culture as "compensatory behavior, or creative 'coping mechanisms.'"[4] Culture surely responds and reacts to social conditions but it'd be myopic to presume that people engage in culture only as a survival mechanism in the absence of other compelling forces (Kelley offers up "aesthetics, style and pleasure," for example).[5]

As I was mulling over how to deal with the "why?" question, a friend reminded me of Howard Becker's take on this issue. Becker, already a formative sociological influence on my work, astutely observes, "somehow 'Why?' seems more profound, more intellectual, as though you were asking the deeper meaning of things."[6] I get that; "why?" is seductive because to answer "why?" is like solving a mystery or unraveling a puzzle. "Why?" is like a secret waiting to be revealed.

The problem though is that "why?" is not a mystery just to the person asking ... it's often a mystery to the person being asked. I discovered this very early into my interviews, where I would ask my respondents questions about why they thought DJing took off so intensely within the Filipino American community. I was met with many literal shrugs and figurative head-scratches; "I don't know, I never thought about that before" was a common reply.[7] After all, in this case, asking "why?" presumes that people have sufficient awareness about the motivations and desires of not just themselves but of their peers too. That is no small thing to ask people to opine on. In a few cases, they would turn the tables around and ask, "you're the scholar studying this, why do *you* think?"

Becker's advice is to put aside the "why?" and instead ask "how?" *"How did you become interested in becoming a DJ?"* or *"How did you and your friends form a DJ crew?"* is also a seemingly basic question, much like "why?", but instead of asking for an explanation of motives, "how?" asks people, instead, to lay out a narrative of who/what/where that isn't just easier for most people to recollect, but also allows the respondent to tell the story the way they see fit. That's a deceptively simple but profound research tool as it creates

---

2   See Pisares, 2011: 426–7.

3   See, 2009: 141.

4   Kelley, 1997: 17.

5   Ibid.

6   Becker, 1998: 58. The problem with "why?" in Becker's estimation is that it tends to prompt an unintended defensiveness among respondents, as if they "understood [the] question as a request for a justification, for a good and sufficient reason for the action I was inquiring about."

7   The other common response was, "I don't know, it was just the thing to do." That was telling in itself since it suggests how DJing and the mobile party scene became so commonplace as to be common sense. In other words, if you were a Filipino teen in the 1980s, you were down with the party scene; the identity followed the activity rather than the other way around. However, this still doesn't necessarily answer the "why?" question.

the possibility for respondents to volunteer "[things] they thought was important to the story, whether I had thought of it or not," as Becker notes.[8]

The latter is especially important to research that's more inductive by design since it can potentially reap observations beyond the researcher's realm of knowledge or ability to hypothesize. As a DJ myself, I understood how (and why) any *individual* might want to become a DJ. But not having grown up in the mobile scene (let alone in any of the Filipino American communities that produced the scene) meant I lacked any personal insight to how the scene itself began and grew. By trying to answer "how?", my respondents shared myriad stories about their influences and mentors, about the importance of family and friends to finding gigs, about all these "small details" that, in aggregate helped not just answer "how?" but also, in its own way, "why?" as well. To put it another way, it's nearly impossible to answer "why did mobile DJ crews take off within the Filipino American community?" without first asking, "how did the mobile crews take off?" The narrative of that process is what gives us any kind of insight into possibly addressing the question of "why?" That is the power of "how?"[9]

Having reflected on this part of my methodological process, I want to use the second half of this essay to suggest a few useful areas for cultural scholars to consider when putting "how?" to use. These are suggestions based on my research experience/process and therefore, aren't meant to predict useful strategies for any potential study of any possible cultural phenomenon. But to the extent that cultural movements are, by definition, collective activities, I want to lay out three broad areas to consider when probing how cultural collectives—be they DJ crews, MC cliques, dance troupes, etc.—form and more importantly, persist and grow.

1) SETTING IT OFF: PEER-TO-PEER INSPIRATION

How do individuals become interested in participating in a particular cultural activity to begin with? In my research, overwhelmingly, the interest in DJing came from seeing someone else DJ, especially if that person was a friend/peer. For example, Anthony Carrion was the founder of one of the first mobile crews out of Daly City: Unlimited Sounds. His interest in DJing, as a craft, came from watching Cameron Paul, a popular San Francisco DJ, spin at a club called Studio West. However, the idea for *forming a crew* came from watching other crews from San Francisco—namely Electric Sounds and Non-Stop Boogie—perform. It was that moment, watching peers from similar backgrounds, that compelled Carrion to think: "we could do that too, what they're doing. You know, even better. So we said, 'okay, let's put something together.' Got some money from my parents, got some equipment and went from there."

Inspiration, of course, can derive from many sources: a family member, something seen via mass media, a random observation made out in the public sphere. However, there is a particular power in being inspired by a *peer*, someone who you identify with, someone you feel like you share a common background with.[10]

---

8 Becker, 1998: 59.

9 I can't emphasize enough how important this is for scholars of cultural practices/performances to consider. As I suggested earlier, "why?" is seductive in a way that "how?" may seem almost rote but "how?" inevitably yields better insights and understandings in my opinion. Cultural histories, when smoothed over for easy digestion, favor linear tales that reinforce canonistic narratives; a "top-down" explanation, in other words. However, cultural activity almost never springs forth into the world, fully formed. It builds in fits and starts; there are all kinds of actors and events that are barely (if ever) chronicled. By focusing on the social processes that influenced the shape and direction of a cultural activity, we often get the "bottom-up" stories that may yield more nuanced, more insightful appreciations as to how and why cultural practices come into formation. Besides, it makes for better storytelling and in our struggle to make our research more legible to colleagues, students and others, this is an added benefit.

10   It's the difference between watching Lebron James, a once-in-a-generation talent, accomplish something you deem remarkable vs. watching your next door neighbor accomplish something remarkable … unless of course you're living next door to Lebron James.

The recognition of, as Carrion put it, "we could do that too" is what I colloquially describe as a "lightbulb moment," that point at which someone's sense of possibilities takes a leap forward into the heretofore unimagined.[11]

Unpacking the lightbulb moment doesn't simply reveal personal stories; it also allows us to understand how cultural movements build via the interactions of people within both social networks and spaces of contact (whether physical or virtual). In other words, to be in a position to identify someone as a peer presumes a set of social relations that allow for that recognition to occur: attending the same school, living in the same neighborhood, coming into contact at a community center or a cousin's house. Collective forms of cultural activity don't manifest overnight and they don't sprout at random; they build node by node, and the relationships that tie those actors together should be a vital part of our scholarly inquiry.

For example, the two crews—Electric Sounds and Non-Stop Boogie—that Carrion named as being part of the inspiration for Unlimited Sounds were both from San Francisco's Balboa High School. Balboa is where the earliest known Filipino American mobile DJ crew formed: Sound Explosion in 1978. Members of both Electric Sounds and Non-Stop Boogie credit Sound Explosion as being part of the inspiration behind their own crew formation. To understand "why Balboa?" it helps to know how these crew members ended up at Balboa—the school is located in a heavily Filipino American neighborhood, Excelsior—and how these students met one another—they were all part of the school's ROTC-run drill team.

Cultural movements begin with small interpersonal relationships. Exploring where and how and when those relationships form is part of the richness of the overall story, let alone our ability to try to understand it. However, for a movement to grow and find new participants goes beyond just inspiration; you also need support systems.

2) WHO'S GOT YOUR BACK?: INFRASTRUCTURES

To become a DJ requires, at the very least, turntables, a mixer, ideally an amplifier and speakers, and most certainly, a constantly growing record collection. All these things require capital and though some DJ crews received their seed funding via a gift or loan from someone's family members, for any crew to survive, they need to generate income via gigs.

When I began my research, it didn't occur to me that learning about how crews would acquire gigs was that interesting a question, yet it turned out to be one of the most important things I learned.[12] The mobile crews in my study, as it turned out, made use of many different networks to solicit work or get their name out there. That could include, but not be limited to: neighbors, classmates, church mates, extended friends of their immediate family, extended families of their immediate friends, community centers, Filipino social associations based around provincial origin, et al. Especially as a community made up of largely "recent" (post-1965) immigrants, the Filipino community maintained strong social ties via these kinds of family and social networks, an existing web of relations that immensely benefited young mobile crews looking for gigs.

I describe this kind of informal support system as part of the "infrastructure" of the mobile scene: less-visible organizations, institutions, and networks that contribute to the long-term growth and success of any cultural

---

11   Describing this as a "lightbulb moment" has its rhetorical appeal but in reality, it's not usually the case that new awarenesses manifest all at once. To borrow from the phrase I used earlier, these realizations often build through "fits and starts," gradually edging into your consciousness as if it happened in a "flash" when it's actually the culmination of changes in thinking that happen over time (though perhaps outside of our immediate self-awareness).

12   This also raises another obvious suggestion when embarking on new research: beware of a confirmation bias that may curtail you from exploring other facets of a story that may turn out to be more important than you ever may have imagined.

movement.[13] Without this infrastructure, something like the mobile scene would have been vastly more limited in scope given that most crews wouldn't have been able to solicit enough gigs to support themselves and therefore, grow the scene as a whole.

This applies in other forms of Asian American hip-hop expression. For example, the incredible rise of Asian American hip-hop dance crews—manifested on MTV's now-defunct *America's Best Dance Crews* reality competition—seems difficult to imagine without the many collegiate dance troupes that develop nascent interest into professional-level talent, benefiting from rehearsal spaces, performance opportunities, travel support, etc. In Southern California alone, every large public university has at least one such dance group on campus, whether UC Irvine's Kaba Modern, UCLA's Samahang Pilipino Modern, Cal State Long Beach's PAC Modern, etc. Individual dance crews could certainly have formed in the complete absence of these supporting organizations, but it's difficult to imagine how a community of Asian American hip-hop dancers could have coalesced without these collegiate groups playing a role. These kinds of "soft" infrastructures may not seem overtly obvious to explore or focus upon but they turn out to be key to understanding the contours and directions that cultural movements take.

As it relates back to my research on the mobile crews, understanding this infrastructure gave me insight into the elusive "why?" question. Part of what "makes DJing Filipino" is the fact that so many Filipino families and community organizations helped support the DJ scene. Even if you, personally, were not part of a DJ crew, if you played a role in helping a crew survive by referring gigs to them, you played a role in helping that crew—and by extension, the scene as a whole—survive and thrive. That collective investment by various nodes in the Filipino community helps us understand the mobile scene as a "Filipino thing" in a tangible way compared to the fuzzier search for innate cultural characteristics.

3) "WHY?" REDEEMED: THEORIES OF DECLINE

The one area where I've found the most utility in asking "why?" is not around the beginnings of movements but rather, their endings. Participants in collective cultural activities aren't always aware of own motivations for getting involved but they rarely seem to lack opinions about why other people (themselves included) lose interest. Ask any hip-hop fan about why the so-called golden era of rap music—the late '80s through mid-'90s essentially—didn't last longer and they'll all have at least one pet theory, if not three.

The historical accuracy of these explanations is important, of course. It can be revelatory to try to pinpoint how key events or trends can trace the slow (or fast) decay of a cultural movement. However, it can also be illuminating to collect the subjective opinions of people and trace commonalities within them, even if their explanations don't necessarily line up with historical fact. In other words, the perception of how a trend comes to an end is at least as interesting as any "actual" explanation of that end, especially if the two don't always coincide.

For example, many people outside the scene assumed the rise of scratch DJing diminished interest in the mobile scene. There's an accessible, tempting logic in tying those two movements together, especially since most scratch DJs in the 1990s got their start with a mobile crew. However, in speaking to scene participants, what emerges is a far more complicated explanation of how and why the scene declined (and as I noted, this was one question where people almost never answered with a shrug and "I don't know" to share).

Though respondents felt that the scratch DJs drew interest away from the mobiles, they identified that as only one of several forces at play. Ironically, the mobile scene's success helped sow some of the seeds of its own fall,

---

13   I was drawn to the term "infrastructure" because it inherently communicates the idea of support systems but in concept, it's essentially a variation on what Howard Becker describes as "art worlds" in his book by the same name (1982).

especially as nightclubs and radio stations began raiding mobile crews for talent. Since clubs and radio stations already had equipment on site, this severed the basic purpose that mobile crews served. Moreover, a string of fights and other violent episodes made larger hall parties prohibitively expensive, which also fed into the shift towards clubs that could afford private security. Many respondents also identified the rise of interest in import car racing and customization as competing for the attention (and financial investment) of younger Filipino Americans.[14] By the mid-1990s, the mobile scene was 15 years old—practically venerable in pop culture time—and it's not surprising that newer cultural trends such as scratch DJing or car customizing would peel away the interest of the next generation.

My point is that cultural movements are built in discrete stages, through a variety of intersecting forces, and that their dissolution happens via a similarly complex process. However, the only way to properly uncover those stages and steps is via a research model that directly engages primary sources (if possible) and relies as much on an open-ended, inductive process as it does any preliminary theoretical frameworks. All researchers come into their work with a series of presumptions; after all, those constitute part of our intellectual curiosities that lead us to explore these topics to begin with. However, as I've certainly learned, the long-term success of a research project has to allow for those presumptions to be challenged and transformed. In this context, "getting schooled" isn't something to be embarrassed about. Indeed, it may be one of the best parts of the process itself.

SOURCES

Becker, Howard. 1982. *Art Worlds*. Berkeley: University of California Press.

_____. 1998. *Tricks of the Trade: How to Think About Research While You're Doing It*. Chicago: University of Chicago Press.

Kelley, Robin D.G. 1997. *Yo' Mama's Disfunktional!* Boston: Beacon Press.

Kwon, Soo Ah. 2004. "Autoexoticizing: Asian American Youth and the Import Car Scene." *Journal of Asian American Studies*. 7(1). pp. 1–26.

Namkung, Victoria. 2004. "Reinventing the Wheel: Import Car Racing in Southern California." In J. Lee, M. Zhou (Eds.) *Asian American Youth: Culture, Identity and Ethnicity.* New York: Routledge. pp. 159–176.

Pisares, Elizabeth. 2011. "The Social Invisibility Narrative in Filipino-American Feature Films." *Positions: East Asia Culture Critiques*. 19(2). pp. 421–437.

See, Sarita. 2009. *The Decolonized Eye: Filipino American Art and Performance*. Minneapolis: University of Minnesota Press.

Wang, Oliver. 2014. *Legions of Boom: Filipino American Mobile Disc Jockey Crews in the San Francisco Bay Area.* Durham, NC: Duke University Press. (forthcoming)

---

14   For more on the Asian American import car racing scene, see Kwon (2004) and Namkung (2004).

THE GOLDEN AGE OF THE FILIPINO-AMERICAN PARTY SCENE IN NEW YORK CITY

By Cindy L. Custodio

When I first stepped in the Filipino-American party scene, it was 1992 and I had just turned fifteen. Growing up in the intersections of Jewish, Black, and Latino communities in Flushing, Queens, my older sister Candice and I were rarely exposed to other Filipinos. The only time we ever saw Filipinos our age was at family parties and church-related events. We attended public school and our peers were mostly Black, Latino, a few white people, and a small minority of Asians. I was the only Filipino in my grade from kindergarten up until high school. We grew up in a time when being Filipino was "foreign" to people in New York City. We were often classified as Chinese with Spanish surnames by our classmates, misunderstood and mis-categorized because society didn't like anomalies. Being classified and marginalized was the standard. Oftentimes in my youth, I felt I didn't feel like I fit in, forever trying to assimilate as our Filipino parents drummed into our heads to do.

One thing that bridged the gap in our time was music. Hip Hop was a young adult a few years older than me. But she was still new to the scene, wide-eyed and bushy-tailed, waiting to spread her wings and expand her horizons. I attended my first school dance in 1992 and as I walked into that gymnasium, the track that was pumping through the speakers was Biz Markie's song, "Just A Friend." Everyone was singing that song in unison, just as they still do today. Hip Hop had just one simple edict, to love the music and to be a fan. To bridge the gap more, I was introduced to a group of Filipino peers later that year at a teen club at the church in our neighborhood. It was the first time I encountered so many Filipino youth with whom I could relate. Much can be said about the statement, "Strength can be found in numbers." Not only was I growing up parallel to Hip Hop, but my fervor was emancipating me and what arose was solidarity with my Asian brothers and sisters. Fundamentally this was key because I found others to relate to, those who grew up in quasi-households like mine, spoke the same languages, with like ideals and expectations. I finally started to feel like I belonged to a community.

The heart of my community arose from the local party scene. It started in basement house jams that were always spread by word of mouth. Local Filipino DJ groups were hired for $100 a pop to DJ a house party and that is how the community came alive. Tracks like "Insane in the Brain" by Cypress Hill rocked hookie jams and house parties on weekdays while our parents were away and on weekends when we told our parents only a few friends were coming. My first Filipino basement house party was refreshing. I met more people and forged friendships that have stood the test of time. We built the community we have today based on the music we bopped our heads to back in the days.

The first DJ group that I met was Kuya Tribe. DJ Kuya Derick was behind the tables and playing the latest track Wreckx-N-Effect's song, "Rumpshaker." I watched in amazement. A Filipino DJing—wow. What pride. But I was young to the scene. There were many before his time, doing it up and playing for other communities, close by, in the same fashion, playing the music and uniting a people. Little did they know the scene was blowing up. Homegrown Filipino DJs were sprouting all throughout the community, people I call my close personal friends. The first time I saw young Sonny D'Lite spinning was at a house party in Jamaica, Queens. The tune blasting from the speakers was Chaka Demus and Pliers' reggae track "Murder She Wrote." And *what a bam bam* it was. Picture young Filipinos cramped up in a living room, dancing close, sweating and gyrating to this Jamaican tune. Filipinos were continuing to vibe and soak in the cultural sponge of music that was growing fiercely around them.

Just a year later, I started becoming more exposed to the party scene. My boyfriend at the time hung out with DJ Sonny D' Lite's 3DS Crew who introduced me to a whole new community of Filipinos. Through hanging out with them I was slowly introduced to more people and other party-goers who introduced me to other DJs and crews. What started off as small pockets and clusters of hanging-out sessions turned into full-blown parties. More Filipino promoters had emerged and started making their way into nightclubs in the city. One of the promotions during the early 90s was for a series of Filipino parties that took place at the infamous Village Gate. Even when these series of parties are mentioned in Filipino circles today on the East Coast, they are highly revered because they had gained legendary status. These parties were a sight to behold. I remember walking into one of those parties on a summer night at the tender age of 16, full of wonder and amazement. I was immediately immersed into a sea of other Filipinos my age, a cloud of smoke lifted, and that's when I first heard DJ Roli Rho on the turntables spinning 45 Kings 900 #. It truly was epic, not only because of the size of the venue, but the gravity of what this meant for Filipinos. A gathering of this magnitude was virtually unheard of in the Filipino community. Social gatherings this large were more family-centered or church-related, very rarely for entertainment. This was concert-level and of epic proportion because of what it did to unite a huge number of people.

I had never in all my life been in a room filled with hundreds of Filipinos. It was both overwhelming and exciting. I had somehow begun to feel empowered. I had finally found people that I had a common denominator with; they were a part of my foundation, they were strangers but kindred to my heart, because they shared my roots, but most importantly, they were growing up with me in what I would like to call the "Golden Age." Hip Hop had been born only two decades ago at this time and those in the culture were also still shaping the music as it continued developing. The parties within our Filipino-American community was not necessarily new since it has been told there were parties happening in New York City since the 1970s. However, the scene was at an "enlightening" period where things were shaping into the community we all had been looking for in what seemed like a lifetime.

Reminiscing on how our community arose takes you back to the parallel teenage years of Hip Hop. From the parks to house jams to lounges to clubs, the music emerged and so did a community. No longer were we just "those Asian kids" they labeled, we were something, we belonged, we had identity.

Invites to parties during this time were spread by word of mouth and fliers passed around by promotional street teams. Teams of teenagers were creating guest lists of people they met at the mall, in the parks, at other parties. And then it happened like a bolt of lightning, AOL chat rooms became the center of promotion. Online chat rooms became the virtual meeting places for Filipinos in the Tri-State area to connect. Teenage Filipinos and other young adults in Queens were meeting up in virtual rooms like "Jersey Pinays," "PinoyPinay 21 and Up," "Flips," etc., and this is also where East and West first started to meet as well. Instead of beeper numbers being exchanged, AOL screen names were being created and exchanged. Fliers were being emailed and parties were being promoted in chat rooms. New friendships and relationships alike were being forged by the information superhighway. Big club venues like Webster Hall, The Tunnel, Limelight, and Speed continued to be booked and the Filipino parties of the 90s were the social sensation of our community. DJs from crews like IntroBass Production rented spaces at the Philippine Independence Day Parade/Festival and started DJing at their booths. This drew in more young Filipino Americans into our party-scene movement. Soon after, other DJs started doing the same, renting booths and selling their mixtapes or simply promoting their business and the after parties. Filipino clothing companies that were NYC-based were also sprouting up, which gave us pride as we wore their Pinoywear or Saluge shirts. As is any Golden period, there is great joy, entertainment, and knowledge being shared. If there was ever a time for this type of growth, it was during this party scene, never to be recreated, just only to be imitated. Eighteen-and-over parties were not only popular, but they were the key to $20 covers, $15 for guest-list names. Entrance into this scene was golden.

I was more than just the "DJ's girlfriend," as those of us who are partnered with a DJ often got labeled. I became the observer, the participating party-goer, contributor, and supporter of family members who were DJs. I was growing up with DJs all around me from my sister Candice turning into DJ Kuttin Kandi with her past boyfriend DJ Roli Rho of 8 years who was much like my brother, and to my own boyfriend, now-husband DJ LoLyfe. Having all of them in my life placed me right inside the party scene where I was fully immersed in the DJ life. I was surrounded by DJs and learned so much about what it takes to be a DJ. I even learned DJ terminology and how to set up sound equipment, and if I wanted to, I could probably learn how to mix in no time. But I was never the kind to be creative in that way. I was just happy to be sitting back, observing the scene, and embracing the beauty of being around my people. Also, being behind the scenes gave me access to see what it was like to make a party happen while I was still able to party all night. At times, the DJs or the promoters put me to work as either working the guest list at the door or occasionally security or collecting the cash. It was an exciting experience that had me proud to be both a contributor and supportive friend to making this Golden period happen.

Unfortunately, the party scene was short lived. Although there were several Filipino promoters, the rules of engagement of clubbing were starting to change. In the late 90s Mayor Rudy Giuliani started invoking "quality of life" initiatives. In 2002, Mayor Giuliani's successor Michael Bloomberg created a quality-of-life initiative coined Operation Silent Night, which combated target areas around bars and clubs that had a large number of noise complaints. Furthermore, with the dissolution of 18 and up to party and leaving only 21 to drink and party, clubs made it harder and harder to gather. The age restrictions created a void for youngsters citywide. The club scene for twenty-somethings moved from the traditional club atmosphere to a low-key lounge scene. Just when Filipino parties were starting to make noise, starting to make a name for themselves, they were done as quick as they had emerged. Gone were the days for huge Filipino parties at major clubs and smaller venues, more intimate settings were the norm. In the late 90s to early 2000s, promoters were starting to purchase their own lounges and making small niches in the party scene in their own way. Upscale, quiet, intimate gatherings took over and the Filipino club scene began to mature. The emergence of social media transformed the usage of word of mouth, guest lists, and street team promoters into online "page events." Email addresses and screen names replaced the one-on-one contact. Actual flyering became a thing of the past. Gone were the more intimate connections at our local churches and teen clubs.

As these party scenes slowly started to quiet down, the Filipino DJs who made most noise in the party scenes were also crossing over into the broader turntablist and Hip Hop community. This also gave opportunities for the younger generation of DJs to step up into the existing party scene and make names for themselves. Other DJs just moved on, some still spinning at local bars, others settled down into marriages and families who reminisce fondly about their party days.

As the Filipino youth of my day grew older, other types of social gatherings kept us linked. The same people who used to club, drink, and get lifted together are now in their mid- to late thirties and older, experiencing other walks of life. Other social events dictate modes of intermingling from weddings to housewarmings to baby showers to children's birthdays and baptisms. Every now and then, I find myself looking fondly at my friends at all of these more family-oriented types of functions. I look at my children and I look at my friends' children. As we often do, we take pictures at our little gatherings and I can't help but smile when I flicker through those pictures on Facebook or through my phone. I smile because I know that our friendships are to be valued for the lineage of our friendship comes from a period that should also be valued. Most of us, if not all of us, have met through our party scenes or at least have all been associated to the parties in some shape or form. Had it not been for the movement of our Golden Age, we might not have met. We might not have had the chance to grow old together. My friends have seen me grow up, seen me through tough times, marriage, and the birth of my children. Our friendships have a foundation because we found each other when we didn't realize we were searching for one another. Together, we were enlightened by a scene we forever will recognize as a movement that created a community. We had our days of *party and bullshit*, but most of all we've had a lifetime of meaningful and beautiful friendships.

KNOWLEDGE OF SELF

FROM ISLAM THROUGH HIP-HOP TO FREEDOM

By Freedom Allah Siyam

Philosophers have only managed to interpret the world in various ways; the point is to change it.

—Karl Marx

Hay, we can make life better, together, not divided, universal, original, creamay. The man ain't shit: whats happenin'!

—Digable Planets

Fuck the false prophecy, promising we'll all be free as long as we fall in line with the flawed philosophy of mystery gods and eternal afterlife's in heaven, while living in hell, where the militant dwell.

—Blue Scholars

I was raised by brown-skinned matriarchs from the Philippines on Beacon Hill and in the Rainier Valley of Seattle. My moral compass came from the humility of my mother's peasant-class origins and the honesty of my father's proletarian roots as a child of European immigrants. The needle on that compass was tempered through the hottest of fires and passed on to me through the wisdom of my Lola. This is a narrative of my trajectory from ignorance to knowledge, from one of the masses to an activist engaged in laying ground work for a mass movement. I would struggle with graduating high school, but would temper my ways and actions enough to obtain a Masters in Teaching degree, and much later an administrative credential to be a school principal. At the heart of all of these accomplishments would be a desire to serve the people, and build community power by creating mass organizations to facilitate consciousness-raising or politicization and discipline to carry out positive change in the world by employing a threefold formula to restore agency in our community: education, organization, and mobilization. Before we learn to walk, however, we must crawl, like an animal on all fours.

Prior to my engagement with Islam through the tradition of the Five Percent, also known as the Nation of Gods and Earths, I lived as a savage beast in pursuit of happiness, deaf, dumb, and blind to a righteous path, unaware in many ways of who God is and who I was, am, and could become; much like the allegorical 85 percent of the population I would learn about, who were "poison animal eaters, slaves of a mental death and power," and "worshiped what they knew not." I would constantly spiral and test knowledge through practice, and even slip into backwards tendencies, requiring a second rectification campaign of my own, for the process of knowledge is not mechanical or static but dialogical and fluid.

In Born-Culture (1994) I watched a friend in self-defense unload his Grendel .380 on another Pinoy brother from a rival set. This event facilitated a series of life-altering events: the car chase and the police roadblock; the guns drawn, the interrogation; and the snitches writing affidavits. All of this made me reflect upon my life choices and the impact such decisions had on my family and larger community. It was also during this time that I would seriously reflect upon my identity as a Filipino American youth questioning: why children of immigrants would bust on another who spoke his native tongue; why Moms left the island archipelago under the Pacific sun; why Pops left his home without an education or a job; how we survived through Pop's strike as a janitor or Mom's double shifts and sending money to the Philippines. I began to reflect on my practice; I began to evaluate my smoking, drinking, packing, debauchery, and began to problematize our conditions in the 98118, south side Seattle, and started looking for new companions. Companions or comrades who were not just as curious as I was at finding answers to my questions but also interested in changing the world we live in.

I would learn a lot through personal and collective study over the years, finding mentors within many, and in some ways becoming the mentor I was searching for. The Filipino Diaspora spans over 200 countries throughout the 196,940,000 square miles of the planet earth, and is a result of dictates of the International Monetary Fund and World Bank. Droves of Filipino migrants would be made warm-body exports through the Philippine government's Labor Export Program, continuing a legacy of exploited labor throughout the Diaspora. Unlike the so-called first wave of immigrant farm-working Pinoys to America, post-1965 Pinoy immigration was brokered by the U.S. and Philippine nation states and the tools of international finance capital.

For me, the timing of Digable Planets' 1994 release of the *Blowout Comb* album was impeccable. There is no other album that was comparable to the impact of *Blowout Comb* on my decolonization process. These thirteen tracks would be the soundscape that would accentuate my own journey from an *eighty-fiver* to one with knowledge of self through the lessons of the Five Percent and later anchoring my worldview in dialectical and historical materialism, the philosophical cornerstone of Marxism.

An intelligent trio, Digable had a spectrum of knowledge and a vernacular that was smooth like butter. Encrypting their language over jazzy beats, *Blowout* facilitated wonder and study. They were an inspiration to deepen my knowledge or foundation by interweaving references to the culture of Five Percent, Black Nationalism, and Third World Marxists such as the Mao Zedong, Che Guevara, George Jackson, Erica Huggins, and Geronimo Pratt. This album assisted me in developing a language that would allow me to sharpen my understanding of our conditions as *original people* or oppressed people. It was the first time I heard words like *proletariat, fascist, vanguard, systematic, oppression,* and *COINTELPRO*. From here, I decided I would pack a dictionary in my backpack and listen to music that I would have to use that dictionary for.

Back then, in the early nineties, there were not too many consciousness-raising study groups in Seattle, at least not amongst *Original People*. Through my ace boom Boricua brother from the block, I hooked up with a motley crew called the "360 Nation." I loved these folks from the jump, for they were humble and thoughtful people, dedicated to improving their spiritual lives through the study of original cultures and pre-colonial spiritual traditions. Through brother G-Hod Amen in the Central District, I learned a lot about Kemet, what black Africa's Egypt once was called, and was introduced to a number of influential writers of black history and or spiritual traditions of black people: Ra Un Nefer Amen, Muata Ashby, Cheikh Anta Diop, Chancellor Williams, Francis Cress Welsing, Manning Marable, J.A. Rogers, G.A. James, Carter G. Woodson. We also studied Santeria, Voudoun and their African roots in Ifa. In the Southend at Orun's spot, after paying homage to the *Orishas*, and as Orun practiced *bata*, his moms built with us on the AIDS epidemic in black and brown communities. She also told us about Cuba, the Bolivarian revolution, and the Young Lords. It was on her bookshelves that I saw for the first time volumes of Lenin and Leninist books.

In 360 we studied and shared what we learned through thoughtful observation and diligent study. We built, we meditated, we improved our ways and actions. We studied pre-colonial Africa, pre-colonial North and South America, and I tried to get my hands on anything about pre-Spanish Philippines, making my way to the University of Washington library just to peruse through a very limited Philippine and Filipino American section of books. I did not find anything on pre-colonial spiritual traditions of the so-called Philippines. What I did find however, were gems on Andres Bonifacio and the Katipunan revolution. I also found first-edition copies of Amado Guerrero's quintessential revolutionary classic *Philippine Society and Revolution,* one of the only books banned in the Philippines other than Jose Rizal's *Noli Me Tangere.* Through this constant search for knowledge, "from the cradle to the grave" as warranted by the Prophet Muhammad, I also discovered nationalist historian Renato Constantino and Teodoro Agoncillio. This thirst for knowledge even facilitated a well-coordinated jack move at an undisclosed library, stuffing my backpack full of books. My come up: *The Autobiography of Malcolm X, America Is in the Heart* and a secondary reference book of no real value to me other than a window to other works—*The Philippines' Fight For Freedom.*

In the builds or study sessions of 360, we practiced switching up our diction and vernacular, stretching our vocabulary bank and syntax to make sense of complex ideas and to be able to articulate these ideas. Outside of our builds we bumped an eclectic range of music in the ride. Of course, we were still products of that particular time and space and thus we slapped anything and everything from E-40, the Click and Sicwidit, and of course we rocked the gems that came out of Rapalot, Blackmarket, and Death Row Records. But we also sprinkled our late-night rides through the city with Lazaro Ros, Celia Cruz, Gil Scott Heron, and the Last Poets. We were renaissance men, searching through liner notes, looking for the credits for the samples of our favorite contemporary tracks and discovered the past by way of Coltrane, Roy Ayers, Thelonius Monk, and the like.

On weekends, after classes at Seattle Central Community College or before my work shift, I frequented used bookstores and built with folks from 360. Through 360 I met a lot of different heads from different walks of lives. The circle in many ways was an intersection that exposed me to a spectrum of ideologies—how people made sense of the world; their answers to their hows and whys. I met Greg Lewis, a quirky light-skinned Huey P.—looking brother who ran the Black Anarchist Newspaper. A booklist Greg scribbled down for me to read would be an important reference list that would develop my own perspective and ultimately lead me to a Marxist analysis.

At this time, 1995, a senior at Franklin High School, my studies on spirituality were still eclectic, with no focus or discipline. Hip-Hop tracks provided me references to further research. KRS-One's "The Truth" blew my mind: "Reading up the bible is irrelevant, you gotta look within yourself not a scripture, KRS-One comes to rearrange the God picture." Inspired by KRS-One and others, I discovered the historical process of the manufacturing the 39 books of the Old Testament, 27 books of the New Testament, the fabrication of the so-called holy trinity, and the reification of the cross as a symbol of Christ under the directives of the pagan Constantinople. The historical inaccuracies and blatant contradictions within the Bible fortified the fact I did not know what I was going to believe in, but I knew it was not going to be Christianity. Jesus is indeed our brother who endured trials worthy of recognition, but as our brother he did not teach Christianity, he taught freedom, justice, and equality. This forced me to continue to conduct my own research, in search of this Knowledge of Self the Hip-Hop gods spoke of. As Malcolm stated: "Of all our studies, history is the best qualified to reward our research."

The references Rass Kass made in *Nature of the Threat* and the Poor Righteous Teacher's *New World Order* CD slip provided an extensive reading list for me. Among the bookstores on Capitol Hill I frequented were Black Bird Books (the only black bookstore at that time in Seattle), Twice Sold Tales, and Quest Bookstore. I also hit Edge of Circle Books, a spiritual bookstore specializing in books, literature, and items of alternative spiritual practices, where I found a lot of material on Freemasonry, something that piqued my interest because of the conspiracy theories of William Cooper author of *Behold a Pale Horse*, and black conspiracy lecturer Steve Coakley. Eventually, I found conspiracy theories offered a reason that things were the way they are, but insufficient, as they did not identify how we could actually change our conditions. A principle I held firmly was if I cannot change the world and make it a better place for the human families of the planet earth, then I might as well leave the planet. Although the illuminati may fascinate the profane and inept, it is not, however, enough for the all wise and the adept. I therefore continued this search for meaning and method.

There was a study group that was supposed to happen at Black Bird Bookstore between folks from 360 and the brothers from the Five Percent. The study group was canceled, but I was intrigued by this crew who called themselves Five Percenters, Seattle Morocco, and Harlem Mecca. Divine Ruler Equality, a Ph.D. Student in Chemistry out of North Carolina posted information on the internet about the Five Percenters and I ate it up and began using D.R.E.'s website as a bastion of information for my growing wellspring of understanding.

The term Five Percenters came from the lessons of the Nation of Islam, in which it states that there are 85 percent of the population who are deaf, dumb, and blind, because 10 percent of the population kept them in that triple stage of darkness so that the 10 percent could rob the 85 percent and live in luxury. The Five Percent, however, were the poor righteous teachers and knew who the true and living god was and were a cultural vanguard to reach and teach the 85 percent "knowledge, wisdom, understanding" and "the science of everything in life" in the interest of obtaining freedom.

"The Father" also known as Father Allah or Clarence 13X, brought the teachings of the Nation of Islam out of the mosque and into the streets to teach black lumpen-proletariat youth the truth about their true selves, the legacy of their ancestors, the history of their oppression, and a guide, to the seat of authority and greatness, their original role in the universe: fathers and mothers of civilization. There were 120 questions and answers in these lessons the Father brought out of the nation into the streets. However, the esoteric values in 120 were too difficult to grasp by the demographic the Father set out to reach. In the interest of scaffolding the level of understanding of the pimps, prostitutes, and thugs the Father was teaching, he developed with his associates what is now known as the Supreme Mathematics and Supreme Alphabets to function as a prerequisite or preface to 120 (Figure 1.1 and Figure 1.2).

My last quarter at SCCC, Logic Seven-Allah Amen spoke to professor Charles Jeffries' Psychology of African Americans class about the displacement of Natives, the enslavement of Africans and the colonization of Filipinos. After class, I approached Logic in Jeffries' office and told him I was interested in being put on the Supreme Mathematics. Logic became my *Enlightener* as they are called endearingly in the Nation. He would be the conduit through

1. Knowledge
2. Wisdom
3. Understanding
4. Culture or Freedom
5. Power or Refinement
6. Equality
7. God
8. Build or Destroy
9. Born
0. Cipher

Figure 1.1

Supreme Mathematics

which I would learn 120, and between me and him, I would replicate the question-and-answer catechism that occurred when Fard Muhammad taught his student Elijah Muhammad for three and a half years between 1930 and 1934; a tradition that Malcolm X and Clarence 13X, among hundreds of thousands, would be initiated through.

At ripe age of Knowledge Born—19—in Born-God (1997), I was given the Supreme Mathematics, the first set of eight lessons to be memorized and recited, and an understanding to be drawn from. It took me my first year at Washington State University to progress through the Supreme Mathematics and the Supreme Alphabets, while snail mailing back and forth with Logic back home in Morocco as well as sending mail to the Allah School in Mecca, a youth center that was established by The Father and with support from the city of New York in the 1960s. The Gods at the Allah School connected me with another Pinoy God by the name of Freedom God Allah out of Massachusetts, whom I built with for some time through letters. Pre-email days, these letters were significant and reminded me of the letters between Elijah Muhammad and Malcolm during the latter's incarceration.

The first set of *degrees*, the Supreme Mathematics and the Supreme Alphabets are a total number of 36 principles associated with each numeral in the Arabic number system (one through nine, plus the zero) and each letter of the English alphabet. Thus, the number one is synonymous with the principal "Knowledge," the number two, "Wisdom," and the number three "Understanding." Similarly, the Supreme Alphabets had principles associated with each letter from the English alphabet, thus A was Allah, B was "Be or Born," and C was "See or Cee." The Father *scienced up* these values in a dialectical fashion summarizing exoteric and esoteric understanding, or what I now would interpret as materialist and idealist ideologies.

A	Allah
B	Be or Born
C	Cee or See
D	Divine
E	Equality
F	Father
G	God
H	He or Her
I	Islam
J	Justice
K	King
L	Love, Hell or Right
M	Master
N	Now or End
O	Cipher
P	Power
Q	Queen
R	Rule or Ruler
S	Self or Savior
T	Truth or Square
U	Universal or You
V	Victory
W	Wisdom
X	Unknown
Y	Why
Z	Zig Zag Zig

Figure 1.2

Supreme Alphabets

After completing Supreme Alphabets I had the opportunity as many Gods before me to reconstitute myself, define or redefine my identity as one who had grown from the savage *eighty-fiver* I was into the righteous God I was becoming or striving to be. I was taught through this tradition that our birth names were honorable, for the poverty our families endured did not permit them from giving us anything other than that—a name. I *scienced up* my name in "Born Build" (1998) after I completed my Supreme Alphabets. I was given the name Arthur Gatcho Cupp at my physical birth. I took the name Freedom Self-Born Allah Siyam to represent my liberation or at the very least a lengthy process of unchaining the brain.

Freedom because I had learned that no one is free while others are oppressed, and through my discipline as an educator I intended on mastering the science of pedagogy to free the dumb, deaf, and blind. *Self-Born Allah* to indicate what year I got Knowledge of Self and the year I discovered that Allah was closer to me than my jugular vein, as stated in the Quran's Surah 50:16, and Psalms 82:6, and John 10:34. And *Siyam*, for Siyam is a Tagalog and Ilocano word for the number nine, and traces its origins to the Arabic word referring the third pillar of Islam, the practice of abstaining from iniquities, particularly during the ninth month of the lunar calendar, the holy month of Ramadan.

My partner at the time was with me every step of the way in this transformative process, and encouraged me to assert my independence as an *Original Man*, and assisted me in building my new identity. For me, Freedom Self-Born Allah Siyam stated a strong sense of internationalism, relating to all the human families of the planet earth, while at the same time expressing a degree of nationalism, the most immediate or localized way to affirm self-determination. Dialectically it expressed collective struggle and individual initiative, among other things.

1.	Supreme Mathematics
2.	Supreme Alphabets
3.	Student Enrollment
4.	English "C" Lessons
5.	Lost-Found Muslim Lessons No.1
6.	Lost-Found Muslim Lessons No.2
7.	Actual Facts
8.	Solar Facts

Figure 1.3

The Eight Lessons of the Five Percent

There are eight sets of lessons one must go through to complete the rites of passage within the Five Percent: 1. Supreme Mathematics, 2. Supreme Alphabets, 3. Student Enrollment also known as "one through tens," 4. English "C" Lesson also known as "one through thirty-six," 5. Lost-Found Muslim Lesson No. 1 also known as "one through fourteen," 6. Lost-Found Muslim Lesson No. 2 also known as "one through forty," 7. Actual Facts, and 8. Solar Facts (Figure 1.3). After making *knowledge born* and building on my name, I progressed through the lessons.

I matriculated slowly in many ways and I would not finish 120 until the fall of 2001. My big brother Truth got 120 in six months—a degree a day. He was in the military and confined to barracks out in Virginia, where he built with his enlightener, Peace Justice Allah, in the flight tower; Peace spitting 120 from the top of the dome, Truth writing the *degrees* down in his own *book of life* or journal kept by Gods to document degrees they receive. Many Gods obtain *knowledge of self* (synonymous with obtaining 120 in the Nation) in prison in the same amount of time or less. There are two conditions that determine the length of one's completion of 120, just as there are two conditions for any one person's development: readiness and willingness. I did not obtain 120 until after four years, through my undergrad, graduate program, student organizing, serving as primary guardian for my younger sister while reading Frantz Fanon, Paulo Freire, Michael Parenti, bell hooks, George Jackson, and Epifanio San Juan, Jr.

The year I completed 120, I also graduated with my masters in teaching, began teaching full-time, and was hardcore organizing in light of the 9/11 attacks and subsequent attacks on Muslims, immigrants, and anyone who was different in this country (mind you, I changed my name legally in 1998, and "Allah" would spark the interest of local offices of the FBI in 2006). After finishing my Masters in Teaching Program and subsequent return to Seattle, I did not put much effort in nation-building with the Gods for a number of reasons, including the difficulties of a first-year teacher, the organizing, and the battle with brain cancer I shouldered my wife through. From the onslaught of my return, I was part of the logistical secretariat supporting my wife and her organization's efforts to host the North American Consultation for Women of Philippine Ancestry, one of the biggest, if not the biggest congregation of militant Filipino women from the Philippines, Canada, the United States, and Europe. What time I did have, efforts were concentrated on establishing a comprehensive Filipino youth and student mass organization that tied our location in the Filipino diaspora back to the economic contradictions of neocolonial Philippines. Anakbayan Seattle would be the first overseas chapter of Anakbayan Philippines, an organization whose orientation is National Democratic with a Socialistic perspective. That is, an organization with a focus on genuine sovereignty as the current objective and building socialism as a subsequent next step.

Doing the groundwork and laying the foundation for mass organizations to be the basis of creating a mass movement was my way of utilizing the tools and jewels of the nation. The God Truth once told me: "Latinos or Filipinos studying 120 are not taught to be Black, they are taught to be original; to be themselves," because through colonization and slavery black and brown people had been taught to be other than themselves. The materialist articulations of spirituality ("consciousness" à la Lenin), through the lessons of the Five Percent in many ways paved a way for me to study the history of radical movements for self-determination in the Philippines.

To this day, I hold very close to my heart the degrees and traditions of the Five Percent. I remember the sacrifice many have made to keep teaching, and recognize the influence that these poor righteous teachers have had on the entire planet. Before I was given the Supreme Mathematics, it was communicated that Gods had died for these lessons; the Father himself was shot seven times and killed in his apartment elevator. Within many prison systems in these United States, Gods are not allowed their First Amendment rights to have these lessons on their person. My word is my bond, and I have a duty to give what I am given: the lessons of Fard Muhammad as they were taught to Elijah Muhammad. These lessons would be given to the Father and the Father would give these lessons to the world, through his Five Percent in this *wilderness of North America*, and then broadcast through your radio channels, by the countless Gods and Earths of Hip-Hop.

Since I have been an organizer for social justice, against imperialism, and for a genuinely free Philippines, I keep the lessons close and carry out the teachings of the Five Percent in my personal private practice—we are not missionaries, nor do I proselytize. I strive to allow the *knowledge of self* I obtained through 120 to transpire in my words, ways, and actions. Because I do have a duty to *deal in equality*, when I am asked for lessons, I have that aforementioned obligation to give what I was given. Therefore if someone asks to be put on, I have a commitment to teach and add on. The caveat nowadays for me is that I do not adhere to the patriarchal and homophobic perspectives that often permeate the Five Percent. I will not impose my understanding of these matters on anyone; however, anyone who comes under my study must know I will not perpetuate those tendencies, and they will get an orientation on patriarchy and heterosexism as systems of oppression. The issue at hand is nation building or building community power, not preaching doctrine—even 120.

How I see it today, the greatest contribution I could make to the world-wide struggle for a just and lasting peace on the planet earth is by being part of the liberation of the Philippines. The victorious struggle for sovereignty in the Philippines would be a flaming torch and inspiration for other nations to obtain freedom through their national liberation struggles or begin to wage those struggles for national liberation and or struggles for genuine democracy. My political work today is still consistent with 120 and the teachings of the Five Percent and I still go back to 120 for my more personal intimate discourses with self, to facilitate my own reflection, humility, and compassion—my theology, if you will.

I value my process through and relationship with Islam and the Five Percent; the Supreme Mathematics and Supreme Alphabets and 120 are my foundation. These lessons have been with me through my development as an organizer and a person, while I constantly tested the truth, and took *the best part* or understanding. Mao Zedong states in his "Where do correct ideas come from":

> Man's knowledge makes another leap through the test of practice. This leap is more important than the previous one. For it is this leap alone that can prove the correctness or incorrectness of the first leap in cognition, i.e., of the ideas, theories, policies, plans or measures formulated in the course of reflecting the objective external world. There is no other way of testing truth.

Ultimately, I respect any one's own spiritual process, whether it is through Sunni or Shiite Islam or Sufism. I also admire your process if you are a Christian or practitioner of Santeria. I personally love the teachings of Tich Nhat Hanh and other Zen Buddhists. I also respect folks finding their way through Hip-Hop especially through the Zulu Nation. After Digable Planets, a number of Hip-Hop artists would sustain my morale through the study of 120, many of which are *God-body*: Dead Prez, RZA, Nas, AZ, Common, Guru, Rakim, Brand Nubian. Pinoy emcees like my brothers Prometheus Brown, Bambu, Kiwi, Power Struggle, and the Shining Suns provide the bed of music for my activities as a lover and fighter for freedom. What is important I discovered is twofold: these spiritual traditions make you a thoughtful, more compassionate and kind person. And two, these traditions are used to empower self and others for systemic change and forward a movement towards a more free, just, and egalitarian world.

HUMMING.BIRD. IN.PARADISE. LIVINGARTFULLY

By Malaya LP

O ne of my earliest memories with music was back in the Philippines with my father who used to tape me singing on his mini recorder. The first song he taught me was a Tagalog song entitled "*Dito*" (a Tagalog word for "Here") by Pops Fernandez. Early on, my parents encouraged me to sing all the time; in the car, around the house, at family parties, and pretty much anywhere, and I believe it is what fueled my passion to pursue music from such a young age. When I was little, dinner tables served as a stage, and at parties, family friends would cheer and throw money at my feet. As I grew older, my parents continued to play a supportive role in nurturing me as an artist even though at times they could foresee its rocky path.

I was born and raised in Manila, Philippines until age 8, when my family migrated to the South Bay in Los Angeles County to a city called Lawndale. This decision was driven by the aftermath of major turning point in the Philippines towards the end of Ferdinand Marcos' dictatorship, the assassination of Benigno "Ninoy" Aquino in August 1983. The event was a catalyst for what Pilipino history refers to as the *People Power Movement* and before leaving the country, my 12-year-old sister and I took the car and participated in our first political demonstration. It was a time of great political upheaval and economic turmoil so significant that it affected my father's job and eventually the safety of my family. With the uprooting, we learned to adjust to a new environment, oftentimes feeling displaced, but memories of 1984 were also filled with echoes of Michael Jackson, Prince, Madonna, Spandau Ballet, Chaka Khan, David Bowie, Billy Idol, The Cure, Twisted Sister, and the last piece of musical memory from home that I could hold in material form—Lea Salonga's Minus-One Sing-Along tapes.

My 4 siblings and I all went to private Catholic schools from preschool until high school. Our family attended mass on most Sundays, even though some unnamed persons would either doze off or hang out in the back of the church while smoking a cigarette; nevertheless, they volunteered to collect tithes and help out at Friday Night Bingo, so it all balanced out. Inside our home, in one area of the living room, Santo Niño, Mother Mary, and a cheerful, well-rounded Buddha faced one another, suggesting that although we were practicing Catholics, we also carried out traditions that were influenced by our Chinese heritage, which some visitors found very amusing.

At around age 9, I began singing in a choir that traveled to various churches and cathedrals along the California coast. As I grew older, I grew increasingly shy about singing, but continued to explore music through piano lessons and learning to play the flute. I played harmonies using my flute for the school church band at age 11, while my friend sang lead vocals. By the time I reached sophomore year in high school, music became sort of my little secret; all the while, I had this burning desire to attend a performing arts high school similar to the one in the television show *Fame*, but moving to New York with my uncle and aunt was out of the question. I grew more introverted, but found ways to harness my inner fire through running long distance with my high school team. One summer, I experienced training in the mountains of Big Bear for the first time, challenging me both physically and mentally. Running helped me to strengthen my mind-body connection, playing an instrumental role in nurturing the urge to expand my understanding of spirituality while developing a healthy inner dialogue and getting fit. During my senior year, my class was introduced to meditation by a religion teacher, while another teacher encouraged us to keep a dream journal. This encouragement was so timely because my dreams had become increasingly active and was curious to examine their meanings. Having already established an active journaling practice since age 10, I valued moments spent with each blank page, like talking to my best friend. With an expanding sense of awareness, I gravitated to books, artwork, music, people, and conversations that stimulated and drove that search for something bigger than my limited view.

By age 22, two years after reading *The Alchemist* by Paulo Coelho, a book that served as somewhat of a portal to a shift in perception, I was well on my way to developing an inner voice through journaling and sharpening my skills in both performance and visual art while attending conservatory on the Upper West Side in New York. I wrote several times a day in that city, in between dance, music, and acting classes, hanging out with friends and a steady weightlifting routine of 5 days a week. After one year, I made my way back to California where I did an intensive yoga teacher–training course in Hermosa Beach. I spent one year there and started a small jewelry design business. I got my first account at a posh children's boutique in Manhattan Beach, which helped me save enough money to return to Honolulu, the one place where I felt the most important aspects of a healthy lifestyle could be nurtured. I spent the next few years working on my ballet and modern dance technique at the University of Hawai'i at Mānoa where I also earned a minor in Dance upon graduating. It wasn't until I overcame some growing pains a few years later, at age 30, that the words in my journals would begin to crystallize through sound, beginning with my first recording, the most unexpected and organic process.

I was at a friend's office studio in Chinatown, attempting to study for my Anthropology exam. I had already lost interest in the class but felt obligated to hold on, but I decided to leave my books on the desk and join my friend who walked me across the hall to a studio where two guys were working on a song. I was invited to join in so I pulled up my laptop and sang a melody to a poem from a creative writing class I wrote a few years prior. I recorded the words over a dirty downtempo beat produced by Eugene "Slo" Carroll; it was a piece entitled *My Fruit, Your Green Tree*, depicting a close friend who was an exotic dancer and it illustrated the power female *mana* holds. That November night in 2005, the poem transformed into what we called *La Femme Nu*, it was a two-take experiment inside Fort Union Studios. That night, I decided to drop out of school and did not return to complete my degree for over five years. A few days later, Slo called and asked me if I was interested in making an album project and becoming lead vocalist for the group *Tempo Valley*. The musical chemistry between my producer guitarist Kona Askari and I was fluid, allowing us to create song after song with little effort.

It was Christmas night in 2005 when I had the pleasure of recording my first track with Seph One. The track is entitled *Dream Away*, a one-take recording for both of us; and after hearing the beat, I looked at another poem I had written and let the music write itself. For Seph One, it was an amazing freestyle session to witness, and because he had improvised, he has done something different to that song every time we've performed it. It was also through that song that I first experienced the melodic rhythms of Ted de Oliveira and fell into musical crush with his sounds. Ted is still my favorite producer and his musical intuition is certainly well developed; he also produced the song entitled *Fluffer* on the album as well as some works in progress that may be heard on the next project. Although a previous all-male group called *Tempo Valley* existed prior, their songs were not able to reach a live stage or release a recording—Slo, Kona, Seph, Ted, and I made up the core group that the Hawai'i underground music scene knew as *Tempo Valley*, a name that was a simile for the distinct downtempo/hip hop sounds, interlaced with suggestive Tahitian French undertones and native chants, a play on words to the breathtaking Temple Valley on the Windward side of O'ahu. Two years later, I invited a cellist Diane Rubio to play with the band and her velvety notes covered many of the songs on the album.

As an independent artist, I have the liberty to allow my music to mature and I am aware that the stories that are told through these songs are from truly living moment to moment. Surfing is a perfect metaphor for music and it because of this idea that I don't feel I have to surf every wave that comes my way, unless of course my life depended on it, so I continue to nurture my craft while consciously making an effort to improve aspects of my life while waiting for my waves. Although we had over a dozen songs in a year's time, *Memoirs of the Tempo* was released two years later, after we had pirated our own music—labeled with a Sharpie—which is how we gained most of our listeners, by giving our music away like business cards.

Lyrics and melodies flow like water when the practice of inner connectedness is cultivated and the same is true when working with others; our connections create a bond through it and the music can write itself. There are two types of energy, negative and positive, and to add the element of sound is a very powerful thing, because it affirms what type of energy is being intended, so I always check myself before I say a thing, because it can become a mantra. As a vessel, I know that the songs that I sing and the words I speak have the ability to affect the way I feel, so it must be true for those who listen to my music as well, so I make a conscious effort not to pour anger, hatred, and negative talk into music, unless it is what I intend for that particular song. Through whatever I do, I hope to share from an honest place, while also not taking myself too seriously. Over the years, I have learned how to listen more and say less, which is why I don't feel the need to release music all the time. In between writing and finding new inspiration, I often channel creative energy into creating visual, wearable, and edible art, as well as deepening my understanding through my roots, tuning in for the right moments, waiting for the next wave to ride with music.

Months after the passing of my father, I began a practice of chanting the Lotus Sutra mantra, which is the chant that you hear in the beginning of the *Memoirs of the Tempo* album. I chant in the morning and at night, which I find to be much like a spiritual workout, and make modifications to the sounds to suit my personal needs as well as chanting various mantras, such as the 100-syllable Vajrasattva purification mantra and the purest, simplest chant Aum. Chanting aligns all the energy centers or chakras in the body, and similarly, music has the ability to not only heal us, but it also tunes us with ancient universal sounds and ultimately our inner voice; all we have to do is stay connected.

It is the simplicity of working with individuals who just wanted to get together to play and have fun that makes a musical project such a delightful process. During the early days of working with the group, it was simple because there were no expectations, but as we grew as a band, so did our individual selves, stretching us in different directions after 5 years. Most of the tracks on the album were raw, with lots of vocal imperfections, and that was the way it was released.

I continue to journey through music with an attitude of teacher and student, and always with an open heart for the right time to share musical space with those who speak the same language. My approach towards music is often stoked by being around like individuals who challenge me both musically and personally. I am drawn to individuals who are committed to maintaining integrity in not only a musical or artistic sense, but to those who mirror the kind of person I strive to be; and I choose not to compromise these important things for the sake of expectations or projections—because like Seph One, Shing02 & CAVE said in their track *Man-O-War*, "The waves keep comin'."

JAH LIGHT AND LOVE

By Seph One

Words never used, abused, view construed … for in the midst of a feud / the truth runs through in the nude / barenaked, am I? / reflecting the damned disguised / I stand direct upon this ground as I land upon a lie / command as I apply demand and multiply / I band and boldly defy the gravity / I too can fly

words don't die / rely upon life for reply / implying that I'm flying upon the most natural high / loving life for what is true / loving life like loving view / anniversary unique antique / a universal who? / say you or me the epitome / that's word to my life

words like herbs / make sanity of the strife / Seph's search for meaning / reason and rhyme in the season / giving living loving breathing and believing / or at least what you believe's in and out of your lungs / the winds of change arrange themselves on the tip of my tongues / time sprung

words with best herbs / dreads locked with less verbs / chestbox full treasures / puttin' pressure to pervs / singular molecular manifest subliminal original intellectual / study of the spiritual individual / unscene unheard untouchable ancient ritual / that of an herbal medicinal meaning habitual / universal on dispersal I'm a human in hindsighting the mind / first but always last in line / verse two applied with ultraviolet from sun's ray / this one amazed by the net working in waves / validating the vague within a vertical masquerade / microscopic syllables through time and space

I represent enceph inside / synonymous to the left side of my brain / with steady breaths that maintain the repetition / missions by the millions relevant to the intuition / contained within a mentality that might be insane / in training, heaven is here / the seven is how I found what I thought I lost in the past within the now / present within the breath is the essence of Seph / shining with the effervescence from the rise to the sunset / treble clef with the bass all in your face / chasing the horizon / real eyes realize where this ties in / where the tides end / the beginning of brethren / breadwinning depending on your devotion to women / your mother, your lover / your sister, even the undercover up / you know wussup and what I'm talking about / the one that smothers the others without gauge / in a fit of rage, making you shout / I'm out

Rastafari in the HI…
I continue to study Ethics and Rastafari in the HI, through my collective experiences with Jah Love on O'ahu. The Children of the Most High (Haile Selassie I) in the HI refer to themselves as Na Keiki o Ke Akua Kahi Kolu o Mana. I wear an heirloom ring with the seal of the Kingdom of Hawai'i (pre-fakestatehood), which contains a coin with a shield of the Hawaiian Nation on one side and Kamehameha on the other. Inscribed are words in 'Olelo Hawai'i (the Oral Tradition of this archipelago) "Ua Mau Ke 'Ea O Ka 'Aina I Ka Pono"—usually translated as "the liberty of this land is perpetuated in righteousness." It is my belief that these days are upon us now.

I am reminded of a song brought forth by Berhane Selassie (better known as Robert Nesta Marley) in his composition entitled "Everywhere Is War." In the lyrics are the words of His Imperial Majesty during his last speech to the United Nations in 1963. The composition uses a portion of Selassie's speech that calls for equality among all without regard to race, class, or nationality in his cry for peace. It also asserts, quoting Selassie directly, that until the day of an equal society, there will be war. As I look at the world unfolding in this now, I can clearly see how knowing history can help to make sense of what's relevant today. I feel that it is my responsibility as a conscious being, having knowledge and experience in the matters of the heart, to bring forth a light unto this subject so that we may have better *overstanding* of each other, and begin to communicate a higher conscience.

I believe my connection to Rastafari and Ithiopia is a deep and mystical one. It would take hundreds of songs to illustrate the connections of this culture to my life in the HI, as the journey has been filled with song, dance, reasoning conversations, vibrational frequency manifestations, and the occasional sacramental herb to inspire the *heartical* vocalizations. I was once gifted with a book of Bob Marley lyrics, "56 quotes from Hope Road," which is where Bob used to live in Jamaica. As I would flip through its pages, I was astonished to find that the words would resonate as a tune in my heart, and his songs soon found their way to the tip of my tongue. I could mention a handful of Marley tunes that have brought forth the depth of this word, sound, and power. I could quote multiple lyrics, too. But the most remarkable gift of all entered my being through within the words, and this was the gift of song. I had learned to sing just by listening. For once in my life, I had made a connection with my own singing voice. And I had found it just by harmonizing with *Berhane* and the I-threes.

I recall the first time I listened to his music, while lightly influenced by a healing meditation. Amazingly, I had not stopped to listen to a single song composed by Bob Marley until the age of 21—and I had not been introduced to the sacrament until that time, either. From the very first time I set my heart on his music, the light came shining through. A certain truth resonated through his words, thus began my journey to study the teachings of Rastafari—though I did not know of his name.

In the process of discovering who Ras Tafari is, I have also discovered the "self" in Seph One. Aside from sharing similar initials with Jah Rastafari, Selassie I (Santiago Ilano—my middle names, Joseph Rosales—first and last names), I also share a passion for humanity. I have studied some of his works and the art of those he has inspired to create music and harmony, and I have found that these roots run deeper than I could have ever imagined.

"Today man sees all his hopes and aspirations crumble before him. He is perplexed and knows not whither he is drifting. But he must realise that the solution of his present difficulties and guidance for his future action is the Bible. Unless he accepts with clear conscience the Bible and its great message, he cannot hope for salvation. For myself, I glory in the Bible."

—Selassie I

The Direct Descendant, I am / lyrically sent to manifest on these islands / spiritually I write of righteousness / and I man, Rastafari from creation / the healing of nations / the herbal verbal ancient asian / righting right in front of your face and simply smiling with patience / ain't it amazing / the phrase that you're facing / soon to be the tongue that you're tasting / time is what you gotta stop wasting

Respect my vibe / mic check! / my childhood survived a barrio full of bad boys and bottles / batu ice up in their shabu pipes / who's got gall to make calls that mess with Mabuhay? / i told the dirty, Aloha! / this bird is up too early / you catch a contact with Seph One on track / now that's worldly / Selassie I soljah worthy / the conquering tribe / we on a journey

Until the day we rise again / this your early warning / soldiers in jah army round the grounds are forming / kalo keiki farming / solomon resounding inna your heart / it's pounding King Selassie I / until we reach the sky / Mt. Zion I / Jah Rastafari sightUP / bless it up, we rise up / wi-fi your skies up until we realize / up is the only way to recognize righteousness in fullness / yes all of we, a harmony is prophecy / an international kali green thumb / harvestin' all in season / them bastards, don't believe 'em when they're blastin' off without a reason / every single ounce in my being / for freedom

"UPSET THE SET-UP"

A PATH TOWARDS SELF-DETERMINATION ROOTED IN CONSCIOUS HIP-HOP, PIN@Y, AND PANETHNIC COMMUNITIES

By Benji Chang

CERRITOS, CONSCIOUSNESS, AND NAVIGATING PAN-ETHNICITY

My mom is from the city of Qīngdǎo (Tsingtao) in the northern Chinese province of Shandong. After experiencing Japanese imperialist bombings and the start of the Chinese civil war, she moved to Taiwan as an adolescent. Mom visited the U.S. in the mid-1960s on her own, and eventually stayed after marrying my father. My dad's father was Fujianese, while his mother was Cantonese but grew up in Vietnam. Dad was from Xiàmén city (Amoy) in the southern Chinese province of Fujian. Because of the civil war, his family moved to Hong Kong where they lived under British occupation. Later they moved to Dī'àn (Chợ Lớn) in Ho Chi Minh City (Saigon) in Vietnam, where they experienced French and American hegemony. After living in Vietnam, Dad finished high school in Taiwan. After high school, he immigrated to Northern California before the 1965 Immigration Act was initiated. I share this family history to illustrate that I'm sort of a second-generation Chinese mixed breed who doesn't fit into neatly packaged ethnic categories ordained by nation-state agendas. As a second-generation Chinese, my upbringing was perhaps not as homogeneous as many Chinese peers who claimed stricter identities like being Hong Kongnese or Taiwanese. Dad learned to speak some six languages during his lifetime but conversed with Mom in his third-best language of Mandarin, which Mom adapted to speak without her Shandongnese dialect so that Dad could understand her better. Growing up in the suburb of Cerritos in LA County, my parents did not explicitly teach me to speak Chinese as they were advised that this would help me do better in school. Due to the ethnolinguistic diversity of my parents, a de-emphasis on learning Chinese, and the fact that we had no family living around us, I didn't grow up participating in so many Chinese cultural practices. This was reinforced by a lack of Chinese neighbors for half of my childhood, with most of my neighbors being middle- and working-class white, Black, or Latin@ folks, with one family of Punjabi Sikh friends. At different stages of my schooling I hung around different Asian American groups, as Cerritos was at the time the most diverse city in the U.S. in terms of Asian Americans (Nakanishi and Nishida, 1995).

Midway into ninth grade, my critical consciousness began to have a more functional articulation, having read the *Autobiography of Malcolm X*, which complemented the conscious era of hip-hop music that I was listening to. Nation of Islam (NOI)-influenced artists like Paris provided early access to a discourse of resistance, in this case militant Black nationalism, which helped me articulate the frustration and outrage I was experiencing growing up in the context of Reagonomics, the crack epidemic, gang violence, police brutality, and the 1992 Uprisings. Helping to further refine my voice were the more dialectical philosophies of artists from the Nation of Gods and Earths, sometimes called the Five Percenters, such as Poor Righteous Teachers (Daulatzai, 2012). In terms of my identity, I knew that I wasn't Black and didn't try to emulate the aesthetic like other hip-hop heads around me. Instead, I grappled with what popular mottos notions like "knowledge of self," "no sellout," "history vs. HIS story," and "each one, teach one" meant for someone of my background. Heavily influenced by the NOI, Malcolm, and his Organization of Afro American Unity, I sought out ideas and practices based on non-European religions that took me to study Islam, Buddhism, Shintoism, and Daoism. I also sought out physical spaces for me to realize my developing consciousness. In my majority Asian high school, which had few Black or White students, the dominant Korean and Taiwanese American groups tended to be more privileged and performed whiteness (Lew, 2006). Although I could "pass" as a member of these groups, given my parents' less-than-Model-Minority status coming to this country and my burgeoning critical consciousness, I leaned towards peers who had a stronger affinity towards hip-hop, the majority of whom were Pilipin@ American. In ninth grade I shifted from an aspiring b-boy in the "houser" dance style, to a DJ who practiced mixing and scratching at my friend's house every weekend. Because it allowed me to directly interface with peer groups and be a producer of culture, DJing was my first concrete way to voice myself artistically, culturally, and politically. When I spun, I not only tried to demonstrate my individual dexterity on the turntables, but also my overstanding of hip-hop's culture of youth resistance as I moved crowds with music that was a mix of the popular and the political. Via The Teacha, aka KRS-1, I came to see hip-hop DJing as a form of "Edutainment," where I could both entertain and educate towards a higher purpose of social change. Through national coalition efforts like X-Clan's Blackwatch Movement, and local Pilipin@ American circles that we sometimes referred to as "the underground scene," I saw hip-hop as a social movement for change.

To be honest, most prominent Pilipin@ American DJs at the time didn't publicly espouse a social-change agenda. But by my senior year, it wasn't uncommon for hip-hop heads to engage in dialog around socioeconomic issues and hip-hop as a movement. Conscious hip-hop was also present when DJ Curse played at a dance, or Icy Ice made a four-track mixtape. In addition, DJs like Rhettmatic adhered to a kung fu-like code of hip-hop practitioners (Prashad, 2001), which emphasized knowing where the elements came from, and the legacies of originators and mentors in our culture. I'll never forget the time Rhettmatic invited me over to his family's home to watch a dubbed Japanese VHS copy of the quintessential hip-hop film, *Wild Style*. At the time, he was the only person in our community who had it and he made sure to "do the knowledge" on the film, and quiz me about what he taught me through the film and about hip-hop in general. Thus in addition to providing a social context of crews, party goers, dancers, graf writers, and MCs, the Pilipin@ American scene also provided me with mentorship and discipline as I developed my voice and consciousness around art and social change (DeLeon, 2004). This process continued as I became part of a DJ crew conglomerate that was active around LA County, particularly in Glendale/Eagle Rock, West Covina/Walnut, and Cerritos/Long Beach where we threw "flyer parties" at houses and an occasional "underground" where we we'd rent a hall (i.e., industrial garage, armory), print up nice flyers, hire security, and charge at the door. And yes, hiring security was even necessary for high school house parties. It was common back then for Asian gangs to pack guns, such as the time we DJed a Wah Ching (WC) party in Hacienda Heights that got rushed by Pinoy Royale (PR) and ended up in several deaths.

Stepping back from parties and hip-hop spaces in high school, there were other reasons I felt comfortable in Pilipin@ American communities. In primary school, Japanese Americans (JAs) were the predominant Asian group I was around. While I enjoyed basketball league games, Buddhist church festivals, and the apparent sense of comfort found in a multi-generational and highly "Americanized" identity, my JA friends' lack of connection to their mother tongue and family in the homeland was strange for me. Later in grade school, Korean Americans were also a dominant ethnic group in school that I hung with. While they had a definite connection to their mother tongue, immigrant families, and homeland, it was also made clear to me that although I could "pass" when I attended my friend's Sunday School, I knew I was not fully welcome when they found out I wasn't Korean. Pilipin@ Americans were the last large Asian ethnic group that I was also around. Aside from facing similar issues like learning the mother tongue, diaspora, and martial law in the homeland, my Pilipin@ friends also tended to act less entitled than peers from the other groups I mentioned. In addition, there was the infamous hospitality of Pilipin@ moms and all the social gatherings that my friends' families would have. Because of my first name, Pilipin@ parents would often assume I was Pin@y. When they found out that I was Chinese, they still welcomed me and would often make sure that I knew they were also part Chinese. At the time I wasn't as aware of the seemingly ubiquitous presence of the Chinese as settlers in Southeast Asia and the Pacific, but I was aware of skin-color politics and certain legacies of colonialism when I engaged in conversations about being Chinese, or Ilocano, or skincare products like Eskinol. Over all, through this engagement with Pilipin@ American families and friends, I felt welcomed and could identify a great deal with them. This also seemed to be true for the non-Pilipin@ members of our crew, who were of mixed Indian, Thai, Chinese, Cantonese, Mexican, Vietnamese, White, and Taiwanese backgrounds. An outcome of this for me was being able to comfortably navigate diverse Pilipin@ and Asian American spaces by the time I graduated.

THE INDUSTRY AND THE CAMPUS, FROM SAN DIEGO TO LA

When I moved to UC San Diego at age 17, the Asian American hip-hop scene, led by Pilipin@ Americans, was gaining momentum. We were beginning to get into the 1000-person capacity nightclubs in LA (i.e., Glam Slam owned by Prince). DJs from our scene were winning the most prestigious national and international battles, while also getting spotlight and regular income as mix DJs for "urban" format radio stations like Power 106. MCs were also getting some play, such as Key Kool & Rhettmatic who would eventually join others to form the multiracial MC crew, Visionaries. Pilipin@ recording artists connected to our scene, like Jocelyn Enriquez, were also blowing up on the radio. There was a growing number of entrepreneurs involved in industries such as clothing, magazines, and import car shows by promoters like Mainstream, who brought our "racer" car culture together with hip-hop DJ and dance crew battles (Namkung, 2004). My crew, Icon Events, focused on throwing events with college students, as our members were spread out around Southern California universities like UC Riverside, Cal Poly Pomona, UCLA, and Loyola Marymount. As I still held strongly to my vision of hip-hop and social change, we promoted our events as part of the true school hip-hop scene with skilled DJs who could move the crowd. Although we lacked a feminist analysis, we still felt it wrong when promoters increasingly resorted to stunts like female booty-shaking contests to try to attract bigger crowds. Conversely Icon, like a few other promoters, worked with college groups to promote events and help them raise funds. Fundraising was a way I thought we could contribute to our greater community, in addition to bringing different groups to work together and supporting their events with audio and visual tech. One example was a fundraiser for UC Irvine Kababayan at the Old World Festival Hall, which had held many of the previous generation's megadances organized by the United Kingdom crew (UK). We brought back UK DJs who were becoming even more popular as the Beat Junkies, along with performances by Key Kool & Rhettmatic and the recently established Kaba Modern dance crew that would go on to fame with MTV's *America's Best Dance Crew*. In San Diego, Icon was tied to the pioneering college hip-hop radio and TV shows I helped run, as well as guest DJ spots on Jammin Z-90 FM, an internship with Atlantic Records, and writing hip-hop articles for *The Guardian* newspaper. All of these strengthened Icon Events in the industry, and we were able to leverage famous DJs like Babu for even just our mobile DJ gigs, and hip-hop acts like Jurassic 5 for our club events.

None of this would have been possible without mentors and teachers from the Pilipin@ American hip-hop scene (although it should be noted that several of them were not Pilipin@). There were mentors like DJs Melo-D (Modern Musique/Beat Junkies), Pat-Man (Empire DJs) and Havik (Prestige/Beat Junkies, who taught me the flare scratch), who helped me develop as an artist and furthered Rhettmatic's lessons about "respecting the architects" and knowing where your arts and culture come from. Others like Icy Ice (Legend/Beat Junkies), D-Vine (Fascination/Legend/21XL the eventsco.), and Xcel (Mainstream/Import Showoff) went from being prominent DJs to leaders within their organizations and our scene, and innovators of where we could go with our people, music, and culture (Alsaybar, 2002). From them I learned to be a more inspiring communicator, entrepreneur, and leader, along with realizations about how to always watch my back in the cutthroat "hustle" that our scene was becoming as it grew increasingly commodified and aligned with the entertainment industry. Aside from D-Vine, two other mentors were more on the creative and business side. Tien Tran (Transit Studios) and Joey "Junk 1" Quarles (Inkworks Press/Mixwell Clothing) took the time out to explain to me the broader visions they had for our work and scene. Tien's visions related more to fashion, the entertainment industry, and the Asian American community. Joey, the "Original ½ Black and Filipino" as he often called himself, was a master at "flipping the script." He was known for coming up with concepts and designs for events and clothing that spoke to the existing Pilipin@ and Black hip-hop scenes, but pushed them to another level. Along with D-Vine, these two helped me understand the different roles I could play in bringing our communities together, and the level of vision, design, communications, and people power it would take to make it come together. Although it wasn't obvious to me then, these were also valuable lessons for my future social justice work as an educator and organizer. Looking back I realize that my first lessons in ideology, hegemony, panethnicity, and social movements did not come from an ethnic studies course, but in grounded practice within our scene as I sought to fulfill the dreams of hip-hop and social change that I'd been building on since the 9th grade.

After a few years in the hustle, I pulled out of a career in the industry for two reasons. One was that I felt the industry was too shady for me to be effective in my life's goals of social change. It was fun being interviewed in *The Source* magazine, rubbing elbows with celebrities in VIP rooms of Hollywood clubs, and getting shoutouts on radio stations and rap albums. There were also folks who I respected still holding it down like DJs Dwenz and Abel of the Foundation Funkcollective (DeLeon, Mabalon, and Ramos, 2002). But I became very disillusioned when so many I looked up to got wrapped up in the hype, materialism, and co-optation of our culture. Another reason I stepped back from the industry was that things had become too hectic with my family, and I decided to move out on my own and cut ties with them. Without their financial support, I had to drop out of college and work five jobs to pay rent in San Diego. At 19, this was the hardest thing I'd ever done but I was able to transcend it partly due to the support of mentors who offered me work and friends I'd made through the TV and radio shows at UCSD. With backing from mentors in the scene and UCSD student leaders of color I'd worked with through Icon, I was able to return to school with financial aid after an exhaustive application to prove my financial independence. This difficult process made my life's goals very clear-cut for me, and I vowed to make the most of the chance I had been re-given.

As the Pilipin@ American hip-hop scene continued to grow with developments in film, internet, and the cottage industry of turntablism, I focused on a career where I could make a living but also apply what I learned in the industry and pursue my longstanding goals of social change work through arts, culture, and bringing people together. This steered me towards K–12 teaching, which put me in classes alongside student activists of color with similar goals. Partly due to taking courses with critical professors like Ricardo Stanton-Salazar, and the support of student leaders during my process of independence, I became involved with student of color activism at UCSD. Operating out of the Cross-Cultural Center, OASIS Student Services, and the Student Affirmative Action Committee office suite, I threw my energy into building with Asian American student groups and coalition work with Black, Chican@, and Latin@ student groups. While much of our efforts revolved around identity politics and on-campus representation, more critical work was also being done partly due to the political landscape of that time (i.e., Propositions 209 and 227, University of California Standing Policy 1 and 2). This work solidified for me when I was approached by UCSD APSA president Jonathan Burgos, to run for the presidency of the 300-member organization. A popular student leader on campus, Jonathan explained that although I was a lesser-known member, he felt I had the skills and panethnic leadership experience given my work with in the scene. In addition, Jonathan advised me to take the time out to listen to and address the everyday needs of members and potential recruits (i.e., family, financial issues), as that was the best way to retain folks and sustain the organization. He and other APSA board members had put these ideas into practice given that in the early 1990s, APSA's membership was mostly dissolved as Asian student communities continued to create their own ethnic organizations and weren't as invested in the panethnic project of APSA. Jonathan shared that in order to rebuild the organization, its leadership had to connect the everyday issues people faced, to the skills and experiences they had, and the broader work of the organization. Other APSA leadership like Jane Yamashiro also schooled me on issues of exclusivity between those with male privilege, decision-making power, and other forms of privilege and capital (Yamashiro and Quero, 2012). Although we didn't know it at the time, our mentors' leadership advice paralleled the humanizing approaches of certain strands of culturally relevant and critical pedagogy (Duncan-Andrade and Morrell, 2008; Tintiangco-Cubales, Daus-Magbual, and Daus-Magbual, 2010). When I applied these approaches with the skills I learned as a DJ and entrepreneur in the scene, I was better equipped to support the work of an amazing cast of board and general members. Subsequently our organization grew to 400 people and we were able to further expand APSA's work with underrepresented university and high school students.

Although I'd walked away from the music industry and the Pilipin@ American hip-hop scene as my primary vehicle for social change, I did continue to promote events and DJ. In my remaining undergraduate years, D-Vine offered me the helm of Legend Entertainment's presence in San Diego, which evolved into 21XL the eventsco. With this group I incorporated the praxes of vision, design, communications, and people power I had learned in the industry and then student leadership, to a more impactful promotions group that saw itself as a supportive family that pushed the scene to be community-minded. I also encouraged the more privileged UCSD Pilipin@ and Asian American students, to work together on community-based events with eventsco. members who tended to be more working-class, Southeast Asian, and tied to the military. While we can critique the events as being too rooted in market ideologies, or college groups for not having an anti-imperialist analysis, there is something to be said about having a nuanced understanding about where the masses of our communities are, in order to better educate and organize them towards social justice movements. I remember once working with a union organizer from a similar background as me, who scoffed when I mentioned that I DJed at a prominent Asian American hip-hop/reggae club because, "that's where the people are at." He thought I meant that I worked in those spaces to get at the sistas, when I was actually referencing being tuned into popular spaces of our communities and their intersections with arts and culture. Several years later at a UCLA release for the book *The Movement and the Moment* (Louie and Omatsu, 2001), I heard similar suggestions from an activist and promoter from the International Groove company (R.I.P. DJ Hideo). He suggested that the small audience of activists look beyond universities and the non-profit industrial complex, and recruit from the night and car scenes that thousands from our communities regularly attend, including those from the working class. Well-known historical examples of critically and strategically drawing from these spaces include Malcolm's work, and the emphasis of the Black Panthers on recruiting and training cadre from the lumpen proletariat (Pulido, 2006). Similarly, this essay's title, "Upset the Setup" borrows from a song by revolutionary Pilipin@ MC Bambu, who has long emphasized building our movements by drawing from working-class youth in gangs and crews (Viesca, 2012). The significance of building relationships, educating, and organizing outside of universities and non-profits is even more pronounced when we note the creaming and elitism of UC students after SP-1 and SP-2 in the late 1990s, and how we cannot simply draw from today's campuses with similar strategies to those used with far less privileged Asian American students during the 1968 Ethnic Studies Strike and subsequent campaigns. Instead of privileging formal education and subsequent political lines of thought in organizing, my experiences with the industry and student groups tied to the Pilipin@ American scene taught me to listen more to how people talk about and navigate their everyday challenges and successes. In my years of working with youth, parents, and other members of working-class communities of color, I continue to return to the process of listening and building relationships with constituents that I was first trained in with Icon, the eventsco., and the San Diego groups. The more sustainable and transformative nature of these approaches has been reinforced and nuanced during my later graduate training in critical and sociocultural theory (Buenavista, 2010; Campano, 2007).

TEACHING, ORGANIZING AND SUSTAINING OUR WORK

In my years since leaving San Diego, much has happened within the Pilipin@ American hip-hop scene that nurtured my identity, politics, and pedagogy. Artists who came out of our scene have enjoyed worldwide respect and success, like the Jabbawockeez dance crew and the World of Dance (WOD) promotions run by the eventsco. Even more famous, but also problematic, are members of the Black Eyed Peas, LMFAO, and others who once touted our underground Pilipin@ and hip-hop scenes (Wang, 2006). When I moved back to LA for my teaching credential, I continued with the eventsco. and the recently assembled Cerritos All-Stars, a coalition of the city's most prominent DJ crews in the mid- and late 1990s. But as my life's work shifted to decolonizing teaching and grassroots community organizing, I increasingly volunteered my cultural work as a DJ for progressive Pilipin@ community groups like the Pilipin@ Workers Center, Habi Arts, and the Balagtasan Collective, as well as Tuesday Nights at the Café and Projekt Newspeak. As a classroom teacher, DJing was no longer a way to pay the bills, and I increasingly saw spinning as a skill I could contribute to social justice movements. By the time I went back to UCLA for my Ph.D., we had already begun mETHODOLOGY, a monthly nightclub event in Chinatown that was completely volunteer-driven, with all proceeds going to progressive non-profit groups. Now I've had the chance to spin in front of 2,000-person audiences and share the stage with Outkast, Ice Cube, and Far East Movement. Yet my most meaningful single accomplishment as a hip-hop artist was organizing mETHODOLOGY on a six-year run, where we raised some $40,000 and showcased Pilipin@ artists like Bambu, Kiwi, J-Natural, and Power Struggle, mentors of mine like DJ Icy Ice, and other talented artists like Skim and Dumbfoundead. After focusing my work on organizing and teaching, mETHODOLOGY was a bit of a homecoming, as it allowed me to reconnect with some of the unique skills and networks I had developed growing up with the Pilipin@ American scene.

Nowadays when I get asked about how hip-hop has influenced my social justice work, my immediate answers revolve around the politicizing music of the conscious hip-hop era, and how DJing honed much of my pedagogical sense of timing, emotion, and ability to navigate and blend across genres with audiences. I am grateful to this book's editors for their request of me to dig deeper into hip-hop's influence on me, and consider the largely Pilipin@ American context in which I came to learn about and live hip-hop. Aside from what I've already mentioned about my critical consciousness, social justice work, and educational approaches, one other anecdote speaks to the scene's influence on me. Several years ago I was organizing in Chinatown with a Bay Area comrade. An accomplished organizer, she had experienced significant hardships in continuing to do grassroots feminist and anti-imperialist work after college. She asked me how I was able to maintain positivity and resilience against the relentless dehumanization that we face with communities as we challenge the system. While there were influences I could point to from family and friends, I spoke generally about the positive and nurturing experiences I had in past leadership and organizing spaces. My comrade then talked about how she felt that much of her foundational organizing experiences were tied to anger about injustices, and a moral imperative to do what was just. This prompted me to share about the types of mentorship and teamwork I'd experienced in the scene and in San Diego. Although we made many mistakes, we still had lot of fun laughing and crying while being critical of and caring towards each other. As I continue to reflect upon those times, I've come to understand that while I hadn't been initially involved in the most critical organizing and formal education spaces, my long engagement with inquiry, leadership, and the Pilipin@ American hip-hop scene gave me a sturdy foundation from which to conceive and practice more transformative efforts at social change. Whether as a questioning adolescent, DJ artist, industry entrepreneur, or student leader, the scene has provided me with a discourse, and more importantly material spaces and people, to challenge and sustain me in what the Blue Scholars have called "the struggle protracted" (Viola, 2006), or the long march for revolutionary change.

This essay is dedicated to the mentors named above, as well as my sisters and brothers from Icon Events, Legend and 21XL the eventsco. San Diego, and the mETHODOLOGY crew. The love and growth we collectively shared over the years continue to guide me on the daily.

REFERENCES

Alsaybar, B. D. (2002). "Filipino American Youth Gangs, 'Party Culture,' and Ethnic Identity in Los Angeles." In P. G. Min (Ed.), *The Second Generation: Ethnic Identity Among Asian Americans* (pp. 129–152). Walnut Creek, CA: Alta Mira.

Brown, E. (1992). *A Taste of Power: A Black Woman's Story*. New York: Anchor.

Buenavista, T. L. (2010). "Issues Affecting U.S. Filipino Student Access to Postsecondary Education: A Critical Race Theory Perspective." *Journal of Education for Students Placed at Risk (JESPAR), 15*(1–2), 114–126. 7

Campano, G. (2007). *Immigrant Students and Literacy: Reading, Writing, and Remembering*. New York: Teachers College.

Daulatzai, S. (2012). *Black star, Crescent Moon: The Muslim International and Black Freedom Beyond America*. Minneapolis: University of Minnesota.

DeLeon, L. (2004). "Filipinotown and the DJ Scene: Cultural Expression and Identity Affirmation of Filipino American Youth in Los Angeles." In J. Lee and M. Zhou (Eds.), *Asian American Youth: Culture, Identity and Ethnicity* (pp. 191–206). New York: Routledge.

DeLeon, L., Mabalon, D., and Ramos, J. (Writer). (2002). *Beats, Rhymes and Resistance: Pilipinos and Hip-Hop in Los Angeles* [film]. In L. Productions (Producer). U.S.A.

Duncan-Andrade, J. M. R. and Morrell, E. (2008). *The Art of Critical Pedagogy: Possibilities for Moving from Theory to Practice in Urban Schools*. New York: Peter Lang.

Lew, J. (2006). *Asian Americans in Class: Charting the Achievement Gap Among Korean American Youth*. New York: Teachers College.

Louie, S. and Omatsu, G. (Eds.). (2001). *Asian Americans: The Movement and the Moment*. Los Angeles: UCLA Asian American Studies Center.

Nakanishi, D. T. and Nishida, T. (Eds.). (1995). *The Asian American Educational Experience: A Source Book for Teachers and Students*. New York: Routledge.

Namkung, V. (2004). "Reinventing the Wheel: Import Car Racing in Southern California." In J. Lee and M. Zhou (Eds.), *Asian American Youth: Culture, Identity and Ethnicity* (pp. 159–175). New York: Routledge.

Prashad, V. (2001). "Kung Fusion: Organize the Hood Under I-Ching Banners." In V. Prashad (Ed.), *Everybody Was Kung Fu Fighting: Afro-Asian Connections and the Myth of Cultural Purity* (pp. 126–149). Boston: Beacon.

Pulido, L. (2006). *Black, Brown, Yellow and Left: Radical Activism in Los Angeles*. Berkeley: University of California.

Tintiangco-Cubales, A., Daus-Magbual, R., and Daus-Magbual, A. (2010). "Pin@y Educational Partnerships: A Counter-Pipeline to Create Critical Educators." *AAPI Nexus: Asian Americans & Pacific Islanders Policy, Practice and Community, 8*(1), 75–102.

Viesca, V. H. (2012). "Native Guns and Stray Bullets: Cultural Activism and Filipino American Rap Music in Post-Riot Los Angeles. *Amerasia Journal, 38*(1), 113–142.

Viola, M. (2006). "Hip-hop and Critical Revolutionary Pedagogy: Blue Scholarship to Challenge 'The Miseducation of the Filipino.'" *Journal for Critical Education Policy Studies, 4*(2).

Wang, O. (2006). "These Are the Breaks: Hip-Hop and AfroAsian Cultural (Dis)connections." In H. Raphael-Hernandez and S. Steen (Eds.), *AfroAsian Encounters: Culture, History, Politics* (pp. 146–164). New York: New York University.

Yamashiro, J. H. and Quero, H. C. (2012). "Unequal Transpacific Capital Transfers: Japanese Brazilians and Japanese Americans in Japan." In C. Fojas and R. P. Guevarra (Eds.), *Transnational Crossroads: Reimagining Asian America, Latin@ America, and the American Pacific*. Lincoln, NE: University of Nebraska.

ALL THE WORLD'S A STAGE ... AND ALL OF US MERELY SOLDIERS

By Brian Buño

"**G**uerrilla::words—A Writers' Showcase of All Realms" was the name seen endlessly on marquees, posters, flyers, and web blasts. That in-your-face title and moniker flashed outside club chalkboards, cardboard cutouts, business cards, and off the tongues of dedicated street teamers. What started as a monthly happening quickly became a tradition, and eventually, a lifestyle that many of us still carry in our daily politics. Was it an obsession? Yes, quite possibly. A movement? I must admit, we still think it will be. Can we call it a way of life? Well, that answer is deeply embedded in the individuals whom guerrilla words has touched. Each syllable teaches us, and continues to guide us, every day.

It was the turn of the century, and spoken word and hip hop met at an intersection. The search was on for a breath of fresh air exhaling the turmoil of the world. Beyond the written word, vocalization held the power for radicalization. It was a historical pinnacle as the world was at the offensive, and we were now a war nation. We were citizens of obligation, because in one day it was the maturation of economic bliss, and then as quickly as the sun fell, night grew into social dismay. It was at these crossroads where we found the verbal equality and the likeness of expression. They were at these very crossroads where we discovered the founders of such a spark; where a pair of comrades plunged, and eventually completed their trifecta with a neighboring ally. DJ Kuttin Kandi and I created her, and J. Encite gave her life. On Tuesday, April 2, 2002, guerrilla words was born.

But before we can diverge into the creation of New York City's longest-running free open mic, I step back and reflect on the fond memories the world allowed me to experience. It was during my travels through Asia in 2001 that I was able to step back from urban wear and fully grasp the globe's grassroots. I found them to be the similar roots of life, love, politics, and economics. These were the fundamentals of basic living. Just like me, these people living across the world were moved by the same emotions, angered by the same injustices, and motivated by the same pursuits of happiness—and they all had similar tans, just like me. These same brown-shelled beings lived for today, and hoped for an elevated tomorrow. They just happened to be thousands, tens of thousands, of miles away from the asphalt I have been accustomed to all my life. For nearly one year, my soles kicked the dirt of Southeast Asia, while my soul symbiotically touched the spirits of nearly everyone I encountered. There was, however, a recurring difference that kept prickling down my spine. I instantaneously realized that everything I lived and worked for up until that point was a profligate want, and the people around me were striving for desperate needs. I suddenly felt alienated, observant, and then obligated.

What was so special about that blue passport I held? It stood out so much that I was searched by Burmese secret police, and between the borders of Communist China. It made me pay double entrance for the rows and rivers of Angkor Wat, but allowed accessibility through Saigon. I was able to stow it within the sands of Malaysian beaches, to find opiates in the mountains of Sapa, and float aimlessly along the Mekong. Even touching base in my homeland of the Philippines, from Luzon, the Visyas and Mindanao, I felt there was an internal piece that could not connect with the outside puzzle. It wasn't until I finally took off my shades and spat out the betel nut that I realized the answer was being vividly painted in front of me the whole time; it was in all the smiling faces and welcoming arms that took me in. I survived through pantomime dialogue that fed me, and the enduring need for communication. I spoke American English and was fluent in Tagalog, yet verbal speech became secondary. This discovery was a whirlwind of emotions, and I had no better answer but to write. I let poetry be my guide, and took direction from the verses and stanzas that paved the roads. Every place I stepped, I had my notebooks and ink with me, jotting everything down. It was evident that no matter what translation, no revolution could take off without conversation and communication. This dialogue had to have participants, and it had to be heard.

I landed back home to the monster concrete of New York ways, and my backpack was filled with memories, ideas, and hopes. I presented all my discoveries to my confidante, Kandi, to see how we could organize. Again, this was the time when a closing decade was emerging into a new millennium. We were saying goodbye to the 1990s and were being introduced to a transforming world, a changing society. We were now a warring nation and the tension was mounting even into our lingual world. Hip hop and the spoken word community could no longer be oblivious to this distress. In the decade prior, there was the emergence of the Slam scene transcending from Saul Williams' performance in the film of the same name. Rocky LaMontagne and Flaco gave us "All That!" every Wednesday at the Nuyorican Poets Cafe. Every Monday was "Louder Arts" at Bar13, Asian American Writers' Workshop held intellectual meetings, and the blueprints to the Bowery Poetry Club construction were being finalized. The poet was jumping out of the page. Much like the emcee battles continuing from the streets to the stage, the End of the Week-ers were also building their home (big up, BTHS!). The potholes in the New York City concrete streets kept cracking and we were left with gaps. The poets looked for their voices, the writers needed to move beyond their ink. Musicians, comedians, emcees, deejays, photographers, journalists, graff writers, b-girls, and b-boys searched attentively to fit into the scriber's circle. The disposition of the Filipino, the American, and the artist needed to eliminate color lines, deplete classes, and erase borders. It was essential for the typeface to be vocal. Fed up with the separatists, we took it upon ourselves to mend these fractures, and form a congregating oasis.

But before we could attack, our ambition needed a home. All this energy and eagerness kept growing, but we didn't want to sacrifice it to circulating locations. Yes, we wanted it to be active to our surroundings and reactive to our space, but we needed a venue to ground ourselves. We turned to our friend Teresa Lai, owner of Nightingale Lounge, and the connection bonded. It became the perfect place for our event, as the East Village already left footprints from the beatniks and "yippies" who pounded their rebellious drums years prior. From that moment on, we hoisted our flag, and every flyer read "at 213 Second Avenue, corner of 13th street; drink specials all night long." It was sealed. Nightingale's generosity allowed us to host a monthly free event, and artisans and activists from all walks of the literary, musical, and performance worlds started to flood in. It became the most talked-about open space, a true open forum, and the only open mic of its kind. The buzz was high, and word ignited. History was made as the new-century hip hop was reborn on a small corner of downtown Manhattan.

Our first show on that cold spring night in 2002 proved to be epic. The marketing was unforgettable as the flyer designed by DJ LoLyfe boasted Shaniqwa Jarvis' black and white photo of a rustic teenage Thai boy in full b-boy stance. That image will forever be ingrained in our minds as the pretense for guerrilla words that night, and for every show that followed. It was always a heightened moment for every performer who stepped on the homemade, forklift platform stage. The audience was equally responsive as they became part of the experience. Philanthropists and contributors joined the movement, and the alms race was on to this irrefutable cause. In true Marxist form, all donations to every free show were put to production and marketing costs, and given directly to the expenses of the deejays and performers. It was an economic cycle that proved successful every lunar turn. All profits and losses balanced each other out in accordance to the call and response that bounced back and forth. It was an endless cipher from the music to the speaker, and the microphone to the applause. Each learning instance and each building growth allowed the iris of the spotlight to widen out with our advancing doctrines. It was just as effective for us as it was for anyone who shared the stage, automatically becoming part of the guerrilla words family for the presentations they shared.

We may have founded the concept, but every contributor did help its cultivation. J. Encite and I motivated the crowd and Kuttin Kandi made them shake their fists. From the inaugural show and on, the 5th Platoon deejays made it bounce, and we were electrified by the acts of Immortal Technique, Wordsworth, Percee P, and Pumpkinhead. There was a showcase for every month that included Deep Foundation, Kontrast, the Anomolies, and Q-York's Knowa Lazarus. Artists like Native Guns' Kiwi and Bambu, and Invincible, flew in to enlighten our Big Apple spotlight. Stronghold and C Rayz Walz attacked the scene, and we will never forget when Poison Pen stomped a hole through our surrogate stage. Heavyweight residents like !llmind, DJ Neil Armstrong, DJ Boo, Fat Fingaz, Get Live, I-Emergee, DJ Roli Rho, DJ Daddy Dog, DJ LoLyfe, Unkle Chippy, Cru Jones, DJ Asa, Djayjung, and KJ Butta were essential to guerrilla words' fluidity; engaging every emcee who complemented them. We will never forget our fallen soldiers, Optimus Rhyme and Leftist of Mindspray, who remind us why we started the movement in the first place, and how we evolve this spirit every day. We were fortunate to watch October, Organic Thoughts, Skyzoo, NaturL, 8th Wonder, Taiyo Na, Substantial, Fresh Daily, Homeboy Sandman, Aftahlife, Kevin So, Miles Solay of Outernational, Nomi, Why-G, Concept, Broken English, and numerous, endless acts that unfortunately cannot all be named, through the many appreciative years that helped us stand. There were slams, battles, contests, giveaways, photo shoots, video shoots, art exhibits, and any possible display that entertained and educated. But most importantly, it was the tireless work of the army formed by Jose Torres, Alex Reyes, Koba, Maria Mayoralgo, Maria Oh, Lawrence Atoigue, and Freddy "EQ" Quijano that made each milestone manageable. It definitely takes an army, and guerrilla words battled through and conquered.

The most amazing aftermath is the lasting affect this journey had on every artist, contributor, and audience member who was fortunate enough to witness any part of the evolution. At any moment, there was something to take back, craft your work, and push forward to create a better community. Guerrilla words was an open space that took no grievance, accepted no guilt, and simply allowed you to speak your mind. Whether you agreed, were entertained or even disgusted, there was always a place every first Tuesday of the month for dialogue. There were no barriers or limited horizons, and at the end, only a night to enjoy. I'm still inspired that three Filipino American artists of different performance backgrounds were able to shake off superficial insecurities, took the risk, and created one of the most beautiful movements in our lives.

THE INTRODUCTION

By Deep Foundation

[Mugshot]

Mean muggin, jeans sagged, means he walkin with a swagger
Speakin street slang, in streets where talking didn't matter
Came home looking hooded out, listening to rappers
So my parents thought moving to New York was a disaster
But, I'm just the product of a normal upbringing
No need to bring it up, the middle pup was unwilling
To ignore being poor, family still involved
In unresolved beef behind closed doors under one ceiling
Holding on to feelings, that no one at all witnessed
A potential that was limitless squandered along with innocence
Evidence of struggle, was time's lingering fingerprints
A clock's hands imprisoned by twelve five minute increments
But ever since my rap discovery, something inside me
Fell in love with these, rhymes as they would come to me
I took this gift as a sign from up above of me
Knowing one day I would become someone I truly want to be

[CeeJay]

Born in New Jersey, two parents, no siblings
Early on, raised in New York, destined for big things
Asked God what's my purpose, but he wasn't hinting
"It's like I'll never know the answer" is what I was thinking
Around me, kids were rockin power moves and poppin
Others spun the records, to keep the beats knockin
Felt like I could top them, so I had to hop in
Had to participate, couldn't keep on watchin
Wanted to be Q-Bert or one of the X-Men
Then formed a DJ crew with two of my best friends
Consumed our afternoons outside of basketball and skating
Cutting, scratching, mixing records in the basement
Til Intel intro'd freestylin with peers
And this is what I did for the next five years
Then finally decided to pick up a pen
And join a rap crew with a couple of friends

[ILL Poe]

New York City, in the borough of Queens,
Where the past and the present of this story will meet
Listened to Wu in 9-3 and they talkin about C.R.E.A.M.
A young immigrant was thinkin "yo they talkin to me
Coz we all want the glory and even loftier dreams
But the poor needs a mention and we all gotta eat"
He thought. One day I'll perform and MC
Form these thoughts to release over the bombest of beats
With a charm and a swag that's New Yorker in steez
Weavin stories altogether so informatively
Reach, all of the peeps in every corner and streets
After shows they come up like "it's an honor to meet"
But the honor's been me, or rather its mine
Coz it's you I have in mind when I'm rappin my rhymes
Have been inspired all my life so I had to provide
A first draft, first chapter let's just have a good time

III.

THE STREETS IS EVERYWHERE: GEOGRAPHY
AND HIP HOP IN FILIPINA/O AMERICA

IN A STRANGE LAND

By Mark R. Villegas

You and I both children of Filipino immigrants
From the same island.
Our ancestors smilin' cuz
We found one another in a strange land
Strugglin'

—"Life & Debt,"
Geologic of the Blue Scholars

Most Filipina/o Americans don't believe I grew up in Florida. More recently, I have resided in Southern California where most find it hard to picture our ethnic kin dwelling in the Sunshine State, though in fact, we roll deep. I spent my adolescent years in Jacksonville, a very Southern, very navy town. Thanks in large part to our close ties to the navy, Filipina/o American youth were so numerous in some high schools that we would take over student governments and turn regular clubs into Filipina/o American turf. In some areas, church pews would be packed with Filipina/o worshippers. On and near the navy base, it would be hard *not* to run into a Filipina/o sailor or Filipina/o military spouse. Their children—many, if not most, were mixed-race in certain areas—were our peers, our homeys, our enemies. Although a lot of us were born and raised in Jacksonville, many of us migrated from different parts of the world where U.S. Navy ships docked, such as Japan, California, Puerto Rico, Washington State, or Virginia. And when a new kid arrived, we would be curious about his or her regional style or lingo. I moved from navy housing in Long Beach, California, where, in the late 1980s and early 1990s, I witnessed the burgeoning Southern California Filipina/o American Hip Hop dance scene by observing the antics of my older brother and his crew.

Aside from its military reputation, during the 1990s and 2000s, Jacksonville began experiencing a growth of Filipina/os who were arriving because of the family reunification provision in immigration laws and the fulfillment of the city's infrastructural needs, especially in health care. Needless to say, the city's large and geographically diverse Filipina/o population made for an interesting Hip Hop scene. Along with a historically strong African American cultural community, Filipina/o American youth were runnin' things. Without a clear agenda in mind, we became dancers, graffiti and graphic artists, DJs, and emcees. We did it for fun and because other Filipina/os were doing it. We cleaned Morale Welfare and Recreation (MWR) basketball courts, Officers' Club dance floors, and middle school hallways with our spinning backs and the tops of our heads. Because of the foundation built by older generations of Filipina/o American youth who did it for fun, popularity, and love of the craft, a more solid and at times financially lucrative Hip Hop scene now flourishes in Jacksonville.

Beginning in the 1980s, Hip Hop connected geographically disparate Filipina/o American youth. Whether at college conferences, b-boy battles, choreographed dance competitions, or large-scale partying, Hip Hop became a space of recognition. In Jacksonville, before there was YouTube, we learned the latest dance styles from worn-out and overdubbed videotapes that circulated from Seattle, California, and beyond. In college, the Filipino Student Association hosted an annual mega party that brought in young Pinays and Pinoys from all over Florida, Georgia, and elsewhere to battle it out, grind, and see the latest up-and-coming Filipina/o American acts.

It may be hard to believe, but the Filipina/o American Hip Hop scene is not just concentrated in the cultural meccas of the San Francisco Bay Area or Southern California. As Kandi and other contributors in this book show, New York has been a key, though somewhat autonomous, and self-sustaining region in the cultivation of Hip Hop among Filipina/o Americans. Even though Filipina/o American Hip Hop scenes around the country (and around the world) often overlap and cross-pollinate (as do all cultures), many of our peers have yet to imagine self-thriving Filipina/o American Hip Hop scenes in the most unexpected places.

Just as Filipina/o American Hip Hop scenes are everywhere, the streets is everywhere. As a global phenomenon, Hip Hop has brought the streets—with its reminders of institutionalized benign neglect, police abuse, chronic violence, and racial segregation—to the world. Hip Hop's real and metaphorical streets are crucial to its lore and political stakes. The streets have become central to the Filipina/o diaspora's material world and cultural imaginary. The streets have connected a loose network of Filipina/os in the diaspora, providing its members with a cultural—and often political—compass. And, as if through cosmic reciprocity, the "streets" have brought Filipina/os notoriety around the world as highly sought-after dancers, DJs, emcees, and other Hip Hop performers.

In the bluest of blue states and the reddest of red, in small navy towns and cosmopolitan centers, Filipina/o Americans—the second-largest Asian American group and the second-largest immigrant nationality in the United States—are geographically dispersed. In the first half of the twentieth century, the earliest large-scale Filipina/o migrants settled in and around plantations and farmlands in Hawai'i and the continental American West. Before the passing of the Tydings-McDuffie Act of 1934, which effectively barred Filipina/os from migrating to the United States, Filipina/o agricultural workers flowed to Hawai'i and the U.S. continent fairly unobstructed, compared to their other Asian counterparts, because, as colonial subjects of America, their migration was legally protected. With the arrival of a more diverse group of Filipina/os after immigration laws were liberalized in 1965, and with intense Cold War U.S. military recruitment in the Philippines, Filipina/os began to settle in urban areas all over the country (and in U.S. Navy bases around the world). Many members of the farmworker communities began leaving their rural towns for opportunities in larger cities.

As navy brat Geologic aka Prometheus Brown says in the Blue Scholars "Life & Debt" from the epigraph above, we found one another in a strange land. For many of us, we found each other through Hip Hop. Hip Hop has been an integral part of Filipina/o American culture—that is Filipina/o American culture *everywhere*. The geography of Filipina/o American Hip Hop scenes reflects the expanse of Filipina/o American communities in general. In "So Many," Bambu reps for the mass of Filipina/os in California, throughout the U.S. continent, and in the Philippines:

> *Yo, California Filipinos, yo we down as fuck*
> *My whole West Coast Filipino fam (brrraat)*
> *And out in the South and out in the East*
> *Midwest and B.C.*
> *All over the Philippines*
> *Tsinelas and white tees*

Bambu reps the grandness of our migration. Hip Hop can teach us a lesson about the nature of the Filipina/o diaspora. It can also help us raise questions about why we migrate to this strange land in the first place and lead us to appreciate the wide variety of Filipina/o American communities, so that we won't be surprised to see that there are so many of us everywhere.

		Jacksonville, FL		Virginia Beach, VA		San Diego County, CA		Bremerton, WA	
Total Population		821,784		436,979		3,095,313		37,933	
White	White %	488,473	59.4%	301,492	69.0%	1,981,442	64.0%	28,615	75.4%
African American	African American %	252,421	30.7%	84,807	19.4%	158,213	5.1%	2,388	6.3%
Asian (total)	Asian (total) %	35,222	4.3%	26,720	6.1%	336,091	10.9%	1,656	4.4%
Filipino	Filipino %	14,458	1.8%	17,003	3.9%	146,618	4.7%	1,053	2.8%
Filipino % of Asian		*41.0%*		*63.6%*		*43.6%*		*63.6%*	
Chinese	Chinese %	2,500	0.3%	2,138	0.5%	49,395	1.6%	50	0.1%
Chinese % of Asian		*7.1%*		*8.0%*		*14.7%*		*3.0%*	

Racial and Ethnic demographics of select cities/counties with a large U.S. Navy base, 2010 (U.S. Census Bureau)

TRAVELLING MAN …

By Mario "Nomi" De Mira

The first time I grabbed a microphone was at local MC battle in Minneapolis back in 1996. Out of the ten MCs, I was probably one of the worst. My ego was crushed, and it felt like every dis that was thrown at me was true … I was wack. However, out of those same ten aspiring rappers, I was one of the few who would actually get an opportunity to take my rhymes beyond the block, the lunchroom table, the house-party freestyle, or even the local venues. I was a young Filipino kid who grew up in one of the most non-Filipino cities in the country … St. Paul, Minnesota.

I grew up in midsized Midwestern city that was more known for churning out soul legends like Prince rather than hardcore rappers. On a national scale when you say the word "Minnesota," the first thing that comes to people's minds is white; white snow and white people. And although the majority of the city was (and still is) made up of multiple generations of European immigrants, communities of color have planted their roots to create neighborhoods like Frogtown, Selby, South and North Side, Westside, and so forth. The neighborhoods that I lived in were an amalgam of colorful people and their stories. Black families had moved north escaping the behemoth ghettos of Chicago. Southeast Asian families from Vietnam, Cambodia, and Laos were packed into public housing projects forced to flee US imperialist wars that had ravaged their homelands. Native youth and their families were stockpiled in urban reservations that we properly referred to as the ghetto-rez. And of course there were the poor whites who feared the changing tide as the city began to tilt to a darker hue. The kids of these families would form the hip hop scene that raised me, and between the years 1993–2001, I think I was the only Filipino rapper in the entire scene.

For me hip hop was all about the rush. As a young graffiti writer, my crew took major physical risks by infiltrating train yards or crossing train bridges that stood hundreds of feet above the Mississippi River. Writing graffiti is a weird addiction. It's one of the few things in life where you have to put in crazy amounts of time, energy, and resources, with the least amount of recognition. As a matter of fact most people actually despise your existence and would prefer you dead. Most writers have their reasons for writing graffiti. Some do it for the rush, others see their work as fine art, some are trying to make a political statement, but most are just out there to break the rules, drink beer, and fuck shit up. My love for graffiti was an equal balance of all the things mentioned. But like all high-risk activities, my career as a graffiti writer came to an abrupt end. At some point the police chased me through a swamp; I managed to escape, but my partner didn't. He snitched on me, I got arrested the next day, and the rest is history.

But before I close this section, it's really important that I recognize Mike "Dream," the legendary Filipino graffiti writer from Oakland, CA, who was one of the most respected kings in the international graffiti game during the late 90s. I used to collect underground graffiti magazines as a way to understand the culture, while also trying to figure out why I was so enamored by it. One of the magazines had a centerfold of a bunch of Dream's pieces. The one that had the greatest effect on me was the "Tax Dollars Kill" piece. This simple statement would never lose significance, and would become somewhat of a mantra as I got older and started to develop my ideology towards life and the world. It wasn't until I moved to the Bay Area that I learned that Dream was Filipino. As a teenager I idolized him because he was a graffiti writer who had so much style and skill, yet always seemed to be dropping some sort of social commentary in his work. Once a year folks in the Bay Area put together a commemoration event to celebrate his life. I heard that before he was murdered, his political consciousness was becoming even sharper. Like all inner-city folks who lose their lives way too soon, I often wonder how his art would respond to the social ills of today. You know that question that people ask about which famous person (dead or alive) you'd like to have a conversation with? Dream would be one of my top five. I often wonder what he would think about my music and political work.

To be perfectly honest I can't tell you why I started rapping. At that age I don't think I made too many conscious decisions. One of my first rap partners was this kid named Michael Larson, who would be later known as Eyedea. A sick-ass fourteen- or fifteen-year-old battle MC who ended up destroying rappers from well-respected scenes in both New York and LA. This dude was doing nationally televised battles before things like Grind Time or Fliptop ever came into play. Many years later Eyedea would pass away from what some said was a drug overdose. I'm not sure why I feel compelled to mention Eyedea in this piece; perhaps because he represents the list of friends who lost their lives all too soon. A lot of kids in the hip hop scene have died similarly, or at least because their bodies couldn't take the excess they had to endure. The hip hop kids I knew loved to party hard, like they were always chasing the rush while running to or from something else.

In 1997 I managed to squeeze out of high school with a diploma. I wasn't college bound so I ended up working a long and uninspiring list of grunt jobs. Everything you can think of in the service industry or manual labor, I did. I worked with a lot of older people who had kids my age or younger. As a matter of fact, I worked with a lot of the parents from my neighborhood and high school, doing shit like pushing mops and saying scripted lines like "thank you come again." It was an unglamorous existence. Yet my experiences with working-class folk became the backbone of my social and political outlook. I would need volumes of pages to be able to give a justified or concise breakdown of my social, political, and class analysis of our society, so for now I'll just say that the proletarian themes that come out in our music are pulled from the decade and a half I spent as a basic laborer.

Fast forward to 2001 and my rap group Oddjobs decided that we wanted to be famous. And like so many artists from unrecognized cities and towns throughout the US, we believed that the only way to make it big was to move to New York City. We became part of the tradition of artist/transients who unintentionally contribute to the gentrification of a neighbor-"hood." We moved right in the middle of Fortgreen, Brooklyn, a black neighborhood through and through. I was happy to move to NY, I felt like I had roots there since it was the entry point for my family when we immigrated to the US in the early 80s. New York City had become a different place from what I remembered from my childhood. New York City in the early 80s is what Detroit is now, an economically depressed city falling apart at the seams. When I returned to it in 2001, it was now the Rudy Giuliani Disneyland, a gentrified police state where all the inhabitants of Manhattan looked and acted like extras from the TV show *Friends*.

Like so many others, I can share a thousand NY stories of adventure, peril, and ecstasy. But for now, I'll keep it basic. My group moved there just a few days before 9/11, and to be there to witness the tragedy, the remorse, and the recovery was something that will forever be etched in my memory. The nation went bloodthirsty on its witch-hunt of Arabs and other communities of color, while gearing up for war in Iraq, Afghanistan, and the Philippines. There was so much happening as communities were being targeted by the state, immigrants were being attacked by patriotic white mobs, and selfishly all I could focus on was trying to get this rap career off the ground. I had made friends with people from various social justice organizations but wasn't really ready to participate in their work. I'd perform at the occasional open mic or fundraiser, but I was doing it to promote my music instead of being invested in the issues that they were trying to address.

There is nothing untrue about the statement that New Yorkers are constantly hustling. This competitive culture either pushes you to achieve your goals or breaks you in the process. There are those rappers who try to get the attention of major labels, and there are those who try to make their own lane. Oddjobs was trying to play both angles. Through some inside connections we were able to meet with the full spectrum of record producers who were out there. There was your standard A&R who looked at Oddjobs as a multicultural hip hop boy band with immense crossover appeal, and there were the fresh-out-of-college kids with start-up record labels that would never actually make any money but would throw some amazing parties. We ended up signing with the latter.

Between 2001 and 2004 Oddjobs was on the full-time music grind. We were able to sign with Third Earth Music who had acts like Jean Grae, The Master Minds, and Pumpkinhead. We signed on with a booking agent from a pretty reputable company that opened the door for us to do national tours. We hit the road playing the backpack hip hop circuit from Boston to San Diego, Vancouver to Miami, and all points in between. Touring the country as a hip hop act is probably one of the best ways to learn what this nation is all about. The quintessential stories about the traveling musician are all true. The debauchery and recklessness that happen on the road are addictive, and as a young man in my early twenties, I loved and loathed every single mile of it. There were so many cities and towns that we played where there was no one who resembled me. Sometimes I felt the crowds didn't know what to think of me when I stepped on stage. Yet, it didn't bother me very much. I grew up in Minnesota where I didn't even know what it meant to be Filipino, so how was I supposed to expect a bunch of white folks to understand? Playing gigs on the road wasn't that much different than playing in my own hometown.

I fell in love in California, literally. In 2004 the Oddjobs decided to move to the San Francisco Bay Area. California was always one of the best places for us to perform. The shows were always packed, the crowds were always lively, and there were always hella Filipinos in attendance. It was also a personal decision because my girlfriend at the time had moved there for grad school, and trying to maintain a long-distance relationship was agonizing. The excitement of living in New York had plateaued. It didn't feel like I was growing as a person, and what was once excitement had turned into anxiety. However, shortly after moving to Berkeley, everything began to fall apart. Within a few months the Oddjobs broke up and most of the members moved back to the Midwest. Once my girlfriend and I were reunited, we had suddenly fallen out of love. The money from the tours and record sales was drying up and I was back to working some shitty service job. It was kind of a dark period. I had no family in the Bay Area, and the only member of Oddjobs who decided to stay was DJ Deetalx. [If you ever get a chance to listen to our (Power Struggle's) first album, *Arson at the Petting Factory*, you'll see what I'm talking about.]

Despite all of this, for some reason I felt compelled to stay in the Bay. I wasn't ready to head back to Minnesota. Moving back felt like defeat. The road was for me to conquer, and to turn back would mean it had conquered me. In retrospect, the real reason I stayed in California was that it felt like home. And even though strangers surrounded me, everywhere I turned I ran into Filipinos. What was even more amazing for me was going to different parts of the city and seeing enclaves of Filipino communities, both multigenerational and recent immigrants. I was nearing my mid-twenties, yet so many questions about being Filipino began to form. All of a sudden I was no longer this strange racial anomaly who walked my high school hallways. I was part of a larger community that had strong roots, a community that was proud to celebrate its languages and cultures.

As time went on, I began to meet Filipinos who looked beyond the simplicity of Pinoy pride nationalism. They were pushing new ideas and concepts related to the emancipation of women, youth, gays, workers, and all other marginalized sectors of society. These folks who I would later call my kasamas, or comrades and friends, would bring me back to the Philippines and expose me to the National Democratic (ND) movement. A movement that through study, analysis, and practice, has identified US imperialism, feudalism, and bureaucratic capitalism as the main factors that keep the Filipino people oppressed. The analysis of the ND movement helped me understand so much about my own life and how my family's migratory experience was similar to millions of other Filipino families who had to leave the homeland.

An internal revolution had begun, and my aspirations to become a successful rap artist lost its sense of urgency. I wanted to write songs that would inspire people to join the ND movement, songs that made poor people and workers proud of where they came from. I wanted to write about the class love and the collective well-being of a people versus the longing for the love and admiration of some sexy dream woman whom your typical hetero-male fantasizes about.

In 2007 I had hit a fork in the road and had to make a decision. A few years prior, after the Oddjobs broke up, four of the five members (including myself) created a new group called Kill The Vultures (or KTV). KTV has a sound that is often not as accepted in the US. The sound was super low-fi, and the content sank deeper in the doldrums of life. And that's why we ended up being such a big hit in Europe, so big that in 2006 we did a national tour in Italy. Then the following year KTV was asked to do an even larger tour throughout Europe. At the same time, I was also becoming more involved in social justice work, and an opportunity came for me to go on an exposure trip to the Philippines through Bagong Alyansang Makabayan or Bayan Philippines (an alliance of workers and peasants in the Philippines). The exposure trip would give me the opportunity to experience the lives of various sectors of Philippine society like peasant farmers, students, and workers. I was at a crossroads because I had to decide whether I would go on tour in Europe or go back to my homeland.

This was one of those moments in life that really determine one's future. I had two options: I could go to Europe and live the life that I had dreamed of since the first time I grabbed a microphone, or I could go to my homeland and learn about a nation that so many of us Filipino Americans so proudly claim, but know so little about. Since my first exposure trip to the Philippines in 2007, I've gone back almost every year since.

I'm in my early thirties and life is starting to feel a little more balanced. Music is still a huge part of my life, and I consider it an effective tool for me to project and propagate political issues that are important to our community. For the past 4 years I was blessed with the opportunity to work as a community advocate and organizer with the Filipino Community Center (FCC) in San Francisco. So much of Power Struggle's content, especially from our last album *Remittances*, was derived from what I've learned and experienced from the people I work with and for. These days I think more about organizing strategies than how to promote a new release.

With that said, I'm grateful for all the rich experiences that hip hop culture has given me. Without hip hop I don't think I would have ever had a reason to leave St. Paul. I would have never moved to New York and California, where I was exposed to radical ideas and progressive Filipino culture. I chose organizing over the arts because I felt the urgency to be on the ground, as part of a movement to build people power. And I also think I chose organizing over the arts because I came to the realization that mainstream America is too racist, and not ready to accept a Filipino/Asian Pacific Islander rapper. I had spent my adolescence, teen years, and early twenties trying to live up to the expectations of bourgeoisie white people; now it's time for me to live up to the expectations of my own people ... it's time to serve the people.

Y'ALL WANT THIS PARTY STARTED RIGHT?

FIL-AMS GETTING DOWN IN JACKSONVILLE, FLORIDA

By Leo Esclamado

D *J Neptune was spinning on the 1s and 2s. The party was on at St. Catherine's Social Hall, newly renovated with nice shiny floors. Lights dimmed down on decorations. It was Trina's debut and the fog machine had pushed out the steam of Filipino fried lechon. Aunties and Uncles just finished serenading the floor with line dancing. Pinays with elegant Cotillion dresses slowly transformed into baggy jeans, baseball tees, and hoop earrings. Guys took off their button downs to rock Polo shirts, khaki, or Jynco jeans and shell-toed Adidas. I rocked my white fat laces and Pumas with the green suede. I was ready to battle, and Emerson from the Southside was in the Westside—our side of town—and I couldn't wait to hear the right song to throw down.*

The BOOM-BOOM—CLAP-CLAP of Debbie Deb's "Lookout Weekend" opened up the dance floor. Anthony threw his first round of Flashy uprocks. Flares. Footwork. Freeze. He got up with a smirk. Emerson stepped in, rocked his tops and went straight to his iconic power combo: hops on to a 90 to flare to crabs, pumped never-ending jack-hammers—aka one handed crickets. Folks looked at each other like, "Who's next!?"

In middle school in the mid-90s, we would always hear from classmates with older siblings what went down at these parties at the church halls, naval bases, or club associations. Filipino American (Fil-Am) party scenes, particularly debuts, birthdays, and church functions were centerpieces for 2nd-generation Fil-Ams' introduction and expression into hiphop. It was a scene completely led by Fil-Am youth growing up in the "New South" city of Jacksonville in Duval County, Florida.[1] It was organic, and not necessarily the kind of Hiphop[2] from a purist New York City perspective.

---

1   Jacksonville, also referred to as Jax, J-ville, "The Ville," DUVAL, or the 904.
2   "Hiphop" refers to the traditional cultural forms of Hiphop that include DJing, Breaking, Graffiti Art, and MCing. Lowercase "hiphop" refers to more of the local flavor that sometimes isn't recognized or as uplifted compared to NYC's version.

We would get the updates who battled who every weekend. This after-school grapevine was like our sports news or Twitter feed. My mom would call it chismis. When we got older, we used chismis to find the closest debut or birthday party. My parents weren't so connected with the Fil-Am community, but I did have older cousins. Since a lot of the partyers were in high school, I didn't have friends from the Westside of town to learn how to break. My friends just recommend I watch the old breakin' films *Beat Street* and *Breakin'* to learn the basics.

One day, a friend from my Legion of Mary youth prayer group threw a despedida in her garage with her friends from nearby Forrest High School. The bass-thumping opening sounds of Afrika Bambaataa "Planet Rock" came on. When I saw older kids who looked like me (but dressed differently) create patterns with their feet on the floor or fly off the ground, this 12-year-old Filipino Catholic boy was hooked! I made it a point to learn how to break on my own. When I first popped in *Beat Street* and a bootlegged copy of *B-Boy Summit '96* on VHS, I couldn't stop pressing pause and play. I would memorize Ken Swift's footwork, Remind's burns, and Crazy Legs' freezes.[3]

Schools from the Westside of St. John's River to those in the Southside of Jacksonville had all kinds of hiphop dance crews throughout the 1990s. I used to hear stories of dance circles, or cyphers, and battles breaking out before the first homeroom bell. High school events such as Stanton's Spring Fest, Sandalwood's Talent Show, and Forrest's Rebel Yell were all places to see b-boys and b-girls throw down. To get a feel of Jacksonville's Southern vibe, we had high schools named after a rolling list of white Southern heritage leaders: Nathan B. Forrest, Ed White, Robert E. Lee, Edwin Stanton, Andrew Jackson, to millionaires Terry Parker and Louise Wolfson. Filipinos dabbling in hiphop were representing from an earlier generation dating back to the 1980s. We had City Street Breakers (CSB) in the Westside, Flips in Effect (FIE), Evolution of Boogie, The Chosen Onez, Violent Funkadelic Movements, Southside Asians, East Coast Rockers, Dimensions of Style, all in the Southside/Jacksonville Beaches; and those of the younger generation like myself—First Class, SADIDA in Orange Park, Nex Level, Isotonic Mango Flavorz, Phatfoot Breakers, Bodies In Motion (BIM), Junkniqs, and the new generation of CSB, and Wrektekz, which eventually formed the world-renowned b-boy super crew the Main Ingredients.

Chris Salvador, aka DJ Slue, was affiliated with one of the first hiphop crews in Jacksonville: City Street Breakers (CSB). He shares, "The music of then was essentially our 'mainstream' music. So just with any cultural phenomenon, I think it was just something that the majority of Filipino kids identified with, as it primarily flourished from within minority communities." I was actually introduced to Hiphop, rap artists, both music and culture while hanging out with Chris' younger brother, Kenny Salvador aka Kenski, who would later elevate Jacksonville's Hiphop scene throughout Florida and eventually throughout the world.

As Emerson got up in a b-boy stance and dusted off his shirt, people started chanting their local allegiances: "Southside!" The opening keys of Freestyle's "Don't Stop the Rock" crept in. I took a deep breath and circled the dance floor to hit my uprock: right when the beat dropped, I swept to my footwork so fast it felt like my Pumas were burning. I took one look at Emerson and rocked a bridge freeze to his face. The crowd went "ooh" and started chanting, "Westside is the best side!"

Jacksonville's Fil-Am community is a relatively newer community with navy families who arrived throughout the 1970s and 1980s (compared to earlier influxes of Filipino bachelor communities settling on the West Coast beginning in the 1920s). Throughout this time, newer Fil-Am communities with similar Fil-Am hiphop scenes

---

3   Now keep in mind, this was pre-YouTube, so VHS tapes were our connection outside of Florida. We used to trade tapes from with students from each high school, watching b-boy battles in Seattle, seeing California's Fil-Am parties, B-boy Summits, Rocksteady Anniversary's New York, and even footage of Battle of the Year happening in Germany.

started springing up with the influx of Filipinos associated with the U.S. Navy, such as notable scenes in San Diego, California and Virginia Beach, Virginia.

In the 1990s, Jacksonville was home to at least three naval bases—Naval Air Station Cecil Field and Naval Air Station (NAS) Jacksonville in the Westside and Mayport Naval Station in the Southside, which boasts one of the largest fleets in the nation. During the Viet Nam war, my uncle served in the U.S. Navy at Clark Air Base in the Philippines and eventually relocated to NAS Jacksonville. He petitioned my Lola and Lolo and set the family chain migration process for all of his siblings, including my mother. This process took over 20 years to complete. The navy is still one of the major employers in the city, with 16 out of every 100 Jacksonville residents being connected to the U.S. Navy.[4]

"Crazy to think a place like a navy base would be the setting of parties and gatherings, but it was just from where everyone was fostered and grew up since a lot of families in Jacksonville were military based," Chris shares. Chris's family also has roots in the navy. His parents were involved in Filipino fraternal organizations like the Knights of Rizal. The local chapter of the Knights of Rizal had a mission to continue teaching Filipino traditional values and the stories of Philippine national heroes like Jose Rizal. With the youth chapter, Knights of Rizal Youth, they produced plays and musicals relating to the Fil-Am experience. Families connected to organizations like the Knights of Rizal had close-knit networks that fostered a second-generation Filipino community who would find expression with hiphop.

Angela Magpusao reflects, "Hiphop as a whole was introduced to me by my older brother. I remember he had a lot of hiphop CDs like N.W.A. They were making a lot of noise in the media at that time and I thought it was so cool that my brother had their CD. My brother attended Ed White High School and of course I heard about FIE (Flips in Effect). That was the first Filipino dance group I heard about. Turns out the kids in that group had parents that were friends with my parents so of course I would see them at the different Fil-Am parties. ... Knights of Rizal Youth played a big part with getting me in contact with other kids that loved hiphop."

While making connections in schools and organizations, it was our parties that connected all the different Fil-Am communities in Jacksonville. There would be no party without a good DJ. Jeff Enriquez, aka DJ Neptune, remembers, "I was in middle school and a lot of high school guys started DJing and b-boying. There was a crew called the Chosen Ones. DJ Sector Six, Loran David, was in that crew. He started DJing small house parties that I would go to and I wanted to be like him." Jeff grew up in Jacksonville's Southside and was one of the popular mobile DJs for Fil-Am youth parties during the mid-1990s. Local DJs like Neptune took their influences from local radio DJs from 92.7 The Beat and Invizbl Skratch Piklz from the Bay Area and X-ecutioners in NYC.

Why did young Fil-Ams flock to the parties? Jeff shares,

"I think during the time, everyone was trying to identify themselves with something. Hiphop gave people something to be a part of. Once we realized we could be like all of the hiphop greats, we started wanting to be a part of it more and more. The cool thing with hiphop opposed to other things was that hiphop was a culture. You could be a part of it in so many ways, as a DJ, b-boy, emcee, a graf artist, or just the way you dressed, or the people you hung out with."

The crowd cheers became louder: "Southside!" and "Westside!" Tension was rising and out of nowhere came out a surprising all-female crew repped by Angela. She Rock Crew was in the house, and they were rockin fresh. They rocked 90s hiphop party moves, uprocks, clean footwork,

---

4   (2012) Benner, C., Pastor, M. *Just Growth: Inclusion and Prosperity in America's Metropolitan Regions.* "Getting It Right" Chapter 3. This is a case study of Jacksonville's successful economic growth as it addressed harsh racial and class conflicts in the 1960s.

and poses. It shut everyone up and the whole circle cheered, "DUUUUVAL, DUUUUVAL," the most neutral chant to represent all of Jacksonville.[5]

In a split second, DJ Neptune threw on trumpets from "Esa Morena!" by DJ Laz. The rest of the girls would come on the floor with a mix of merengue and booty shaking and the circle closed up. The floor got flooded to the sounds of Miami Bass. People were scrambling to find a partner to dance to Freak Nasty's "Da Dip." I caught my breath and gave Emerson a dap for respect.

"I started my own girl crew just cause there was no girl crew in Jax. She Rock Crew! (HA!) People still talk about us," Angela reflects on a memorable party. The Fil-Am party scene, while the breakers tended to be guys, also fostered a sense of inclusion. DJ Neptune reflects, "Girls didn't really dance much to hiphop back then because everyone would be in a circle watching the b-boys battle. So I started spinning a lot of reggae, freestyle and booty (Miami Bass) to get them to dance."

As second-generation Pinays and Pinoys partied, oftentimes it was alongside first-generation titas and titos. They represented shared social connections through church or community groups, but also that shared spirit of dance. In any given party there would be at least a handful of aunties starting an impromptu salsa line dance. Any song like Daniela Romo's "Todo Todo" would either signal to the young ones "it's time to take a break" and to make room for the flash mob of 40 or so aunties about to take over the floor!

"Fil-Am parties were sweet 16 parties. Meaning, there was a bunch of silly traditional stuff going on and great food to eat before anyone could get some breakdancing in. The scene was full of aunties and line dancing. I guess this made kids even hungrier to show off their skills when a decent, danceable song comes on," shares Fred Fajardo, aka Fredneck, an early funk-styles enthusiast who started as a popper in the Westside with the Isotonic Mango Flavorz.

Around the scene were a lot of our parents' connections to churches. With Filipinos being majority Catholic, in addition to an active Christian reformist group such as Iglesia ni Cristo, Jacksonville had a long history of regional charismatic movements, these places all had components where Fil-Am youth and families got together.

I met my future crew, the Mangos, while practicing Tinikling, a Filipino traditional dance preparing for a local Catholic fiesta in Argyle. In between practice we would break, this is also how I met Kevin Cajusay, who would be later known as the internationally renowned B-boy Kevo. Sometimes, I just joined some youth groups to be connected with other dancers.

> *"Church was a good place to see all the Filipinos that had kids and*
> *have potential parties.*
> *Getting invited to a garage or a church hall was vital to a young*
> *b-boy's dance life."*
>
> —Fred Fajardo

Youth for Christ (YFC) was the youth chapter of the Fil-Am charismatic group Couples For Christ (CFC). YFC had its main chapter in the Southside of town. They threw one of the bigger parties, but I remember hearing a tito say you couldn't play the "rap with the bad words." Youth groups at these faith institutions would be common ground for connecting with other dancers, across town and even across country. When Jacksonville hosted the 1999 YFC National Summit, fellow attendees Kid Reinen of the future Jabbawockeez, breakers from New Jersey and Chicago hiphop heads who would beat-box, and MC found time to join the cypher. The respective Iglesia Ni Cristo (INC)

---

5   Jacksonville city consolidated all of its townships into one county known as Duval, and it makes it the largest city by area in the continental U.S.

locales also hosted regional gatherings and house meetings that served both as general member recruitment and a place to dance.

"Between school and YFC, I met a lot of people in Jax … being a part of YFC let me share my love for hiphop with new people. We would b-boy at YFC meetings all the time. I would DJ parties. The group was a lot of fun to be a part of."

—Jeff Enriquez, DJ Neptune

During DJ Neptune's Miami Bass set, the party was in full swing. Luke's "Scarred" and "I Wanna Rock" followed Splack Pack's "Scrub the Ground." Bodies bounced and knees dropped on the floor in however fast beats per minute. The sounds slowed down and turn a bit more North towards New York: Mary J. Blige's "Real Love," Biggie's "Mo' Money and Mo' Problems," De La Soul's "Saturdays." The crowd's heads were bopping, everyone had their favorite hiphop move from the cabbage patch to the Kid-N-Play, until the boom-bap swag stopped and the Quad City DJs' remix of "Tootsie Roll" ushers in chants of "WHOOP!" Everyone dancing in the WHOOP! circle hit moves of popping & hydraulics stops, swings, and b-boy suicide drops.[6]

There's a saying around Florida, "the more north you go in the state, the more Southern you get." The Fil-Am party scene was a mecca of different regional influences. While Jacksonville was in North Florida, Fil-Ams were right in the center of the Miami Bass/Reggae scene from Orlando and Miami with its Caribbean influences. There were military families who migrated to Jacksonville from the West Coast who were "housin'" & breakin' in California and brought a local Cali-inspired street racing culture that represented some of the AZN pride movement (aka "Got Rice?"). All of this was alongside a vibrant local Black community nationally known in rap culture for fostering the 69 Boys, 95 South, and the Quad City DJs. Within this spotlight, there was also a budding underground hiphop scene led by Filipino American youth that took its cultural cues from New York City—notably represented by people such as DJ Basic, or Buddy DeCastro, CSB, the MCs and DJs who would make up Asamov (now the ABs), and the record digging crew, the Little Green Apples.

Paten Locke, aka DJ Therapy, who is African American, was exposed to hiphop from Chicago and Boston by hanging out with famous producers like No I.D. He moved to Jacksonville in 1995. DJ Therapy reminisces, "I met Base (DJ Basic) while working at the Avenues Mall, being new and being in the South, I was looking for that true school Hiphop. I noticed Base's fly sneakers. His whole style was NYC. When I asked where he got those sneakers, he gave me a smirk and said 'New York'… Later we found out we both loved collecting dope records. He told me he would search for records that hiphop songs would sample, and would follow that history. That changed the trajectory of our lives. That was the start of Little Green Apples."

Between sharing a love of Hiphop records, the Little Green Apples, made up of DJ Basic, DJ Therapy, and DJ Slue, the group of friends would help foster a northern influence of Hiphop and build the local b-boy scene heading into the late 1990s. They started bringing together the hiphop community with spots in downtown Jacksonville such as The Cave. At The Cave, DJ Therapy would help bring in underground MCs such as Molecule, Willie Evans, Jr, J-Wonder, and local DJs Sureshot, Thoro, Ruff Rob, Wish, and Zane, with b-boys from DJ Basic's CSB crew. Angela

---

6   Jacksonville is known for a regional African American Vernacular dance called "The Whoop", that also is similar to the "Peanut Butter & Jelly" Dance from Miami, but The Whoop is iconically danced to Strafe's "Set it Off"

points out, "the real hiphop I saw was at The Cave. I got introduced to the world of The Cave thanks to Kenny Salvador's older bro Chris. We would go there just to watch CSB dance all night."

The first time I saw b-boys Kes-Rock, Stix, and Strike-3 from CSB, I knew I had to change my game and learn more breaking fundamentals because I wanted to flow and freeze just like them. Everyone I knew throughout the Fil-Am parties said the CSB crew had the original style and you weren't really b-boying if you couldn't hang with CSB. They were essentially our city's "Rocksteady Crew." CSB was also known to travel all the way down to Miami for Speedy Legs's Pro-Am competition.

> *"(CSB) would rent out our old birthday party venues like the Lions Club. Basic and Slue were my two favorite DJs at the time and of course Kenski. They would play that real hiphop. None of that commercial stuff you heard on the radio: no MC Hammer at those parties."*
>
> —Angela Magpusao, B-Girl and Graffiti Artist

The connection between DJ Therapy, an African American DJ from the northeast, and DJ Basic, a second-generation Filipino American from a navy family, is a critical bridge of the Fil-Am party scene and local underground hiphop movement. "We came from two different walks of life and were straight-up hiphop heads, sharing commonality as people of color. When I look at Base, I see myself, I see my brother," shares Therapy.

With Filipino Americans in the mix of race relations in Jacksonville, Therapy critiques there is a certain privilege Filipino Americans have in choosing to assimilate to White U.S. norms and "adapting to existing rules" and not "changing the rules." Therapy shares his critique of Filipinos, who can behave like other immigrant communities: "With a tight-knit community that has a lot of strong parenting, I could often see a Filipino kid saying, 'I'm done with this [hiphop].' There's often a throw-away aspect of [hiphop] culture for folks who aren't Black. I credit Base for showing people you can do both."

By the early 2000s, the 90s Fil-Am generation who threw the hiphop parties were moving on and I vaguely remember the scene going in different directions: the older generation raising families, the next generation choosing to attend electronic dance raves, and the die-hard Hiphop enthusiasts with a younger b-boy and b-girl generation becoming part of the mainstream Hiphop and b-boying competitions.

DJ Slue's younger brother, Kenski and the Wrektekz b-boys would host one of Jacksonville's first b-boy style competitions: Got Skillz & Civil Warz. This was the first time I remember seeing b-boys and b-girls from the rest of Florida: Ill Immigrants & Mind 180 from Orlando, Skill Methodz from Orlando and Tampa, and Ground Zero from Miami would come up. Kenski with DJ Basic, and apprentice DJ B-Ryan, ensured each jam came with the hard-to-find and classic breaks b-boys and b-girls loved.

These jams brought together the best of the best of Jacksonville's b-boys and b-girls and the next generation of CSB, Wrektekz, would eventually form a supergroup, Main Ingredients. Main Ingredients would represent the 904 throughout Florida, on TV, and around the world with b-boys like Kevo, B-Ryan, Julez, Gee, Gritz, Stripez, and Obtek. DJ Basic is now known nationally as one of the premier b-boy break DJs.[7] Kenski has launched a successful hiphop apparel company, Nufsed, and still designs and supports b-boy competitions from Florida to Germany.

---

7   DJing on the break is where the DJ isolates the open drum break or "bridge" in a song, usually from funk, soul, or rock song of the 1970s. This is done with taking two records and extending the "break" to a danceable rhythm; e.g., Incredible Bongo Band's "Apache" or James Brown "Sex Machine" are b-boy staples.

In looking back, while most of us growing up in Duval swore we had "nothing to do" in our Southern town, we did invest in a lot of time making our own fun in our own ways. We found hiphop to be our cultural expression. In our search to be down with our own Filipino culture, and our own adjustment being a growing minority group in the South, we adapted a Fil-Am culture that was definitely different from our parents, but similar in our connections. We helped resurrect a love for old school hiphop in our parties. Some of us have moved on and look back with nostalgia for the high school drama, thrill, and fun of those days. Some of us point to those local parties as the identities and passions we found each time we rep our scene, our dance, our musical taste, our dress, and our art everywhere we go. Some have continued their passion and love for hiphop and have moved to New York, California, Atlanta; a lot have started their own families; some have continued the tradition through their own promotional companies. The question from some of us may be: will there be another generation?

The echoing, shimmering drums and steady whistles of Strafe's "Set It Off" crept in the last high hats of 69 Boy's "The Train." People shimmied a "WHOOP" but began to clear the dance floor. The chorus kicked in: "Y'all want dis PARTY started RIGHT?" A fellow dancer lifted another and swung him around to create a small space for someone to step into the circle. A friend said, "I'll go if you go," but nothing broke the ice. A sister urged her little brother to dance. Someone pushed the kid against his will. All eyes were on him. He did a little uprock. And that's the last time we saw him on his feet: he jumped to do flares for days, into 90s, and a little footwork hops. He rocked buddhas in perfect form for the next minute.

He caught enough air to do a move that no one ever saw, leaping all of his body 180 degrees in the air—an airflare. His name was Kevin. His family just moved to Jax from a navy base in Japan. The circle became empty. Everyone looked around and wondered, "Who will ever top that?"

--

Special thanks to: Angela Magpusao, Jeff Enriquez, Chris Salvador, Fred Fajardo, and Paten Locke for the interviews. Shouts to all the 1990s hiphop crews, DJs, dancers, and artists who have repped and continue to rep the 904! And a very late apology for all the birthdays and debuts I crashed.

A CERTAIN STYLE

A CONVERSATION ON VIRGINIA BEACH

With DJ Kuya D, DJ Delinger, Martin Briones, and DJ Kuttin Kandi

DJ Delinger:
My name is Jeremy, aka DJ Delinger. My crew is the Kuya Tribe. I started in New York. I've been DJing for nineteen years. I started because I was watching my brother.

DJ Kuya D:
Hey, what's up, this is Derrick, aka DJ Kuya D. I'm reppin' the Kuya Tribe. Been DJing for 25 years. Started out in NYC, Queens with DJ Roli and the IBP [IntroBass Productions] and a whole bunch of other fine DJs.

Martin Briones:
What's up, this is Martin Briones—that's my producer and artist name also. I've been writing and producing for probably fifteen, sixteen years. My crew is SkyHigh music. I'm from Virginia Beach, Virginia originally. I got a team in New Jersey and New York also.

Kuttin Kandi:
Do you think there's been some kind of influence of a New York-style coming into Virginia?

DKD:
What I brought to Virginia was the influence of party-rocking. When I used to go out and see DJ Enuff [in New York]. Just the real party-rockers, that's my opening in DJing. I was never really much of a turntablist, though I have much respect for it. But that was my thing [party-rocking], I have love for it. We brought that to Virginia Beach and most of Hampton Roads and pretty much took it over by storm. It was something that the Filipinos or mostly urban people haven't seen before. For me that was one of the biggest accomplishments for me here in VA. I mean

you had all the minority clubs here and they were always gettin' it and rockin' it, but when I came here and we started doing our thing, it changed the whole scene as far as the party scene. Not just for Filipinos of course, but more the urban scene.

DD:
I just grew up with that [New York] style and when I brought it out here, a lot of DJs—they mixed but there was a certain New York style that you bring that they didn't have here, just the way we threw the music in, things like that. And I think that influenced a lot of other DJs out here. What they would say to us is that we brought a certain style down here. That's when they knew me and my brother were going to be, like, trouble out here as far as DJing.

MB:
I can speak from the standpoint of being from Virginia and seeing the influence from New York before South music was even big. Before that era, it was all about New York. All rap music was mostly about New York, and then Cali. So definitely there was an influence from New York that came out to Virginia.

KK:
So what was the scene like in Virginia before you all came there?

DKD:
From what I remember, we came out here like '93, '94. West Coast influence was real popular at the time [from] what I could see. A lot of them were playing—people at the parties were playing freestyle still, and a lot of West Coast music. NWA and all that. Just not really New York. What I did play at parties, I would throw on the usual—the stuff I'd play in New York. Reggae—there was no dancehall [scene in Virginia]. We really boosted the reggae scene out here [in Virginia]. But folks out here—I can't really explain it—there were no real parties or clubs. Just get-togethers and a lot of gang fights. It was really—as far as West Coast influence—like that when I got here.

KK:
What do you think brought that strong West Coast influence?

DKD:
From what I saw and heard is the navy or the military. It's a broad mix of where people come from here. You know navy babies who travel a lot from the West Coast, back and forth, here and there. Honestly, I always thought, like what people said, all around the United States, they try to copy the West Coast. You don't see anybody trying to copy New York—you can't copy that style. At that time I thought that was true. New York was the shit. It still is. But I'm talking about the music scene and just everything. Hip hop to me, it was loud and big.

DD:
When I moved here, to be honest, I didn't know about West Coast music. I grew up to a lot of reggae and R&B. When I came here I was influenced towards what was being played on the radio because at the time radio music to me was real good. Like Gina Thompson—I dunno, just the whole hip hop, R&B-style, and then reggae. That was my influence that started back in New York. And then when we came here, whatever we were playing then, we brought it out here. A lot of people wanted to hear us because of our style—you know that New York, hip hop,

R&B, reggae style. We were packing up clubs on Monday nights. You know what I mean? We definitely brought it. People liked what we did. So, we were definitely doing something good.

MB:

Just to build on what they said, Virginia is a military town. So growing up here, there was always people coming and going. We always had people from New York coming down, moving here, going to school with me. But then we also had people from California or from the South that would also come here. So it was a wide variety of influences.

KK:

I'm trying to get a feel of what Virginia is like, especially as a Fil Am, especially in hip hop, especially as a producer.

MB:

As a producer I know that because I'm Filipino people will support me, but I try to look beyond just being Filipino or touching, like, an Asian market. I shoot for the same goals as black artists or any artist of color would aim for.

DKD:

I always found that—I wouldn't want to say "handicap"—but something that was always against me—I would face a lot of that, especially in the urban and ethnic clubs. As an artist, you're usually behind the scenes, and as a DJ, you're in the light, especially at a club. We would be setting up at a club—and you know I tell this story time and time again because it's one of those times I'll always remember in my career because you'd set up in the clubs here, and they'd be looking at us like, "Oh what is this guy going to do? I paid $20 to get in here, how am I supposed to have a good time?" By 1:00 the same guy that was talking all that trash, his boys is popping bottles and lifting his champagne bottles to me. You know what I mean? We always get that handicap in the beginning. And I always want to overcome that. That's just a feeling to me, that accomplishment. Not only rocking the crowd, which is what I DJ for—I live for that, I DJ for that—but to feel that sense of, yeah, it's all the same love, it's music, it's not what I look like, it's all in my hands and my mind. We didn't feel appreciated or respected, but I got used to it. We earned our respect here in all the clubs in Hampton Roads. People heard of us, it took a while, but it's something that, yes, we dealt with.

DD:

As a Filipino DJ—I think we have a really strong name as far as DJs and skill out here. Kuya Tribe is one of the big names out here as far as DJ crews. We definitely earned our respect from the day we moved here. We had to because at the time, we were doing clubs for radio stations. At the time, it was predominantly—they would throw parties for predominantly African American clubs, and whites. And we would get there—like my brother was saying, they were questioning just by our looks, but then at the end of the night, they were praising. But now, to this day, 2013, it's totally different now. They know who we are. Now, I'm not saying we're the best at it, but we're definitely on top. We shouldn't be considered Filipino DJs, we would should be considered one of the better DJs. It's not about race now as far as the Filipinos. Filipinos got skills out here.

DKD:

I'm proud to be Filipino. I'm Fil Am to the heart, til I die. I love my culture, I love my heritage. I try to spread my love, my talent to all. But for me it was hard to shine, to get on the radio, have our own show. I just felt I was discriminated against—this is just my personal opinion. We were overlooked. You can't really see a Fil Am shine out here. Chad [Hugo] of course did his thing. Big up to Chad Hugo, Pharrell, and all them. Chad has been doing his thing for a long, long time. When I moved here in '94, he was already doing his thing. Glad he got his break, you know. And Pharrell.

KK:

Do you think Chad Hugo really broke down doors for Fil Ams in Virginia?

MB:

As far as Virginia alone, it's hard to tell—what Chad and Pharell have done as producers goes far beyond just Virginia.

DKD:

I'm not hating on Chad. Did he open doors for us? We were kind of tight with Chad, and I don't know how this is going to be put out there. We didn't even get no vinyl from Chad. Pharrell showed us more love. We knew Chad on a personal level—he's doing his thing. But, if you're asking me if he opened doors for us? As far as putting Filipinos and a Fil Am face out there? Yes. If that's what you're asking. VA has so much talent, there's so much Fil Am talent in VA right now, and it's ridiculous. I'm not saying we need to lean on him for a break. But you know, if we all work together to get Fil Am artists more respect, that would be kind of nice for me. No hard feelings, Chad. I'm gonna tell it like it is. You might have been too busy to help us out, but you gotta understand—not to help the hungry but help the talented. Put the talent out there. It's very important to me. I saw the talent, but we didn't receive the help. That's fine, you know. I'm gonna play what I need to play. Even if we didn't get no love for him or not. Chad, he put the Filipino American face out there, if that's what you're asking.

I don't wanna put nobody on blast. But, I'm just telling you what it is. This is my experience with him [Chad]. As Kuya Tribe, we never really saw him at any of our venues. We saw him once in my whole career. Pharrell, you would always see. He would call my brother up and talk. But I understand he's a busy guy. I'm not hurt. I'm not hatin.' I'm just saying that as far as helping the Filipino get out there—he knew how big we were. Hopefully. Maybe he doesn't. That's just my personal experience. I'm sorry if I offended anyone, that's just my personal experience. I'm just telling the truth.

[Simultaneous chatter]

MB:

We're not saying that to be controversial.

DKD:

We're not hatin.' He did bring the Filipino American out. Boom. Yes he did.

MB:

He was a face.

DKD:

He blew it up. He put us on the map, you know what I mean? Like what Manny Pacquiao did too, you know?

DD:

I guess from a business perspective, putting an Asian face on a magazine, sure. I guess, personally, I've hung out with the dude plenty of times at his studio. Regular guy. Cool guy [everyone laughs]. I can't tell what goes on in the studio [laughs]. As far as business-wise, as far as Fil Am, there's not much more that he could say putting anyone out there, as far as another Asian artist really.

DKD:

Pharrell put out the Clipse. He opened up the doors for his people, and everything.

KK:

I think you guys are opening up doors too. Not in a Chad Hugo way. You're opening up doors by bringing the element of party-rocking to Virginia and all that. Your style, your influence.

DD:

Back in the day, we would walk into a club and they're second-guessing us because we're Asian or Filipino American. But now I have DJs from different races asking me to teach them. Asking to pay me just to give them lessons. So it's definitely changed in a good way for our culture.

KK:

Is there anyone else in Virginia who is killing it right now?

DD:

As far as Filipino Americans—well there's two Kuya Tribe members, there's Disko Dave, he's with Better Beat Bureau and Kuya Tribe. He's a producer as well. He's on YouTube getting over six-figure hits, so he's killin' it right now. And we got another Kuya Tribe member, Mike Rizzy. He's one of the main advertisements on Mixcloud. He's killin' the online scene. He got a Greek radio show. So he's doing his thing online.

DKD:

That's our national rep right there.

TUNNEL TO JERSEY

GUERRILLA WORDS AND THE HIP-HOP CROSSOVER IN THE NORTHEAST

By Jason "Encite" Hortillas

BEGINNINGS

April 2002. I was a student at Montclair State University working on my degree in English. In my wide-eyed ambitious nature, I felt like I wanted to find my own niche covering things in the Filipino community that did not get much publicity. Procuring a contributor position for the online version of a publication called *Brownscene*, a Filipino entertainment mini-mag, my initial idea was to be the New York beat writer, finding what was hot in the music scene provided by Filipinos.

You have to keep in mind that unless there was a college-based Filipino cultural association attached to an event, happenings such as Guerrilla Words fell on deaf ears. I found the announcement of an open mic showcase in the East Village featuring poet Brian Buño and turntablist Kuttin Kandi of the legendary 5th Platoon crew. At the turn of the decade stemming from the late 1990s going into the early 2000s, New York Metropolitan Filipinos put a lot of pride in their turntablists. They were our main representatives in Hip-Hop and the battle DJ game was at its pinnacle in that era. I loosely knew Kandi after having seen her perform at a college showcase in 1999 with my first crew Constant Elevation of the All I Ceeing camp. I was 18 at the time and I'd admit I totally bombed my performance as a young buck, this being one of the first instances of my own battles with social anxiety. Later on in my career, however, I'd be the primary host of what would become Guerrilla Words.

I decided to attend the first Guerrilla Words. I e-mailed Brian Buño about my arrival and my intention to cover the event for *Brownscene*. I jumped on a DeCamp bus from Upper Montclair, NJ headed toward New York Penn Station. I did not frequent New York on my own that much at the time, and feeling somewhat prideful as well as apprehensive, I didn't take the easier decision to ride the subway. Instead I took a walk.

As I arrived at the bar, I fumbled through my wallet to find my driver's license and parted the navy blue curtain to a dimly lit bar packed with people. In the back of the venue stood a turntable set up with a piss-poor PA system to a minuscule riser that would insult any concert venue builder. Yet in all its shortcomings, my eyes opened up to see a crowd of such diversity, varying in age and ideology, all in the same area held together by two Filipinos.

I shouldered toward the crowd trying to get the attention of Brian Buño and Kuttin Kandi. Between sets I introduced myself and my intentions for my attendance. The rest of the night was a blur until headliner Knowa Lazarus, a Filipino rapper from Queens, did his set. I later linked up with him to work on promotions; during this time I was also working with another Filipino group from Chicago, The Pacifics.

"Guerra" is translated from Spanish to mean "war" and, in turn, "guerrilla" means "warrior" or "solider." The showcase called Guerrilla Words was indicative of the Filipino warriors fighting their own battles of acceptance and recognition in a land not native to their own. Compared to many other immigrants coming to the United States, Filipino people as a whole, for one reason or another, feel the need to assimilate their children into society by first choosing not to pass on one of the most important parts of our culture—language. Put a group of twenty Filipino teenagers together and ask them to raise their hand if they speak Tagalog or another Filipino language. Unless they are direct immigrants themselves, my estimated guess is one or two people—if you're lucky. I didn't put out an official survey in regards to this, but the point being you can see why a showcase such as Guerrilla Words was formed. It was created to express an overall injustice as well as the complex disconnection among Filipinos in America. Embracing Hip-Hop provided a better understanding with African-American culture and a disassociation of Caucasian-influenced American history.

The explanation of Guerrilla Words' initial foundation must be said because those political aspects were in many cases diluted when I eventually took over the reins of the organization. I wouldn't categorize myself as an activist. Not that I disagreed with what that title would entail, but I felt like in order to put Filipino people on an even playing field, I didn't have to wear it on my sleeve. My optimism for Guerrilla Words was that this would be a go-to Hip-Hop event, hands down. And looking back in its five-year history as a monthly showcase and the people who set foot in that tiny venue in the East Village, mere steps from Stuyvesant Town, the impact on artists today is prevalent. We did make a difference and if many people still don't know, these words will serve as evidence.

Unaware of it at the time, Brian Buño and Kuttin Kandi were my mentors. They took a chance on a hungry young kid from Jersey. We depended on each other to achieve the ultimate goal of making GW a success. Brian's personality was both enigmatic and candid. His poetry was distinct and self-assured. Brian shot words like a cannon and when he was finished, his demeanor came off like he never fired a round. With that free-flowing structure, Brian's ability to be the figurehead of GW was omnipresent even when he passed on the reins to me. The transition was rather fast as I took the helm. Brian and Kandi were pursuing their own careers, leaving the window for me to take over primary duties of planning Guerrilla Words.

Brian and Kandi authenticated our existence by bringing in their friends like fellow 5th Platoon members Neil Armstrong and Daddy Dog and Krazie Charlez. They would casually invite emcees to provide impromptu performances like Punchline and Wordsworth or Immortal Technique. The early days brought in flagship artists that would dominate the stage like the Mindspray Crew, headed by Koncept and Leftist. Other regulars included Soce The Elemental Wizard, the first openly Gay emcee I ever saw, who wore it like a badge of honor even in the midst of a conflicted crowd of Hip-Hop bravado and civil rights fighting activists. Composed of Koba, Sketch, and DJ Boo (of The Jugganots), Kontrast were a staple act, providing both the activist perspective while relating the Filipino experience by releasing the album *Pencils* in 2006.

I think I was more floored by Brian's and Kandi's simple phone calls to friends to just support this small production. With that attitude, I felt like I needed to step up my game. Instead of just reaching out to similar acts, what I brought to the table was my own experience. We all shared Filipino roots but what separated me from the founders was my innate responsibility to rep where I am from: New Jersey.

BRIDGE AND TUNNEL THE GAP

The creative connection between New York and New Jersey is understated. These states are close in proximity yet are considered light years away. "New York, New York" is sung by Frank Sinatra, who hails from Hoboken. John Coltrane drove over the George Washington Bridge to Englewood Cliffs to record "A Love Supreme" at the famed Van Gelder Studio. Jack Kerouac scribed the exploits of the protagonist Sal Paradise in *On the Road*, escaping his New York City beatnik circles to reflect at his aunt's home in Paterson, NJ—the hometown of his comrade Allen Ginsburg. "Rapper's Delight" by The Sugar Hill Gang and "The Message" by Grandmaster Flash and The Furious Five were recorded at Sugar Hill Studios in Englewood. Today, you can watch any Hip-Hop-centric reality television show and notice that even though they claim New York, they lay their heads down in the Garden State. New York Hip-Hop was not only a product of its own terrain. Even if Guerrilla Words was ultimately a New York institution by our creation, with my own inclusion, it developed into a representation of Jersey.

One of the first acts I booked under my term as general manager was Organic Thoughts. The New Jersey–based group was a combination of Filipino, Korean, and Dominican emcees and DJs. Diwrect, El Gambina, and Tonio provided vocals, while DJ OnPoynt and DJ Reason held down the turntables. The group's de facto leader Jon "Jonyfraze" Bonilla served as an emcee and producer, and brought in his battle-tested skills as a turntablist in to the music. The group dropped their first album in 2004, *The Purest Form*, which resulted in a Top 10 ranking in College Music Journal (CMJ). Organic Thoughts brought in guest features like Large Professor and Organized Konfusion's Prince Po. The accomplishment emboldened my hope for this trend to continue.

> *"What I loved most about Guerrilla Words was the diversity of those who participated. People of all walks of life and every facet of hip-hop were represented as a community. Seeing other Asian Americans perform was truly inspirational and made me feel less of a minority within hip-hop."*
>
> —Jon "Jonyfraze" Bonilla

The album also featured a collaboration track with The Mountain Brothers, a Philadelphia-based group of Chinese emcees. This fueled the fire that the East Coast was stamping their own ticket for Asian folks earning recognition in the game. Jonyfraze brought in a couple of emcees from Rochester, New York named Raks One and Hassan Mackey. Fraze produced for the two artists who later would make their own names, as Mackey was selected in Rawkus Records' "Rawkus 50" campaign, while Raks One, later known by his given name Emilio Rojas, staked his claim through his work with DJ Green Lantern. Another emcee named Snacky Chan I met through El Gambina. One of the godfathers of Korean-American rappers, his records with Breeze Evaflowin and C-Rayz Walz were unheard of being aligned with underground heavyweights. His own solo career continues to shine in his native country. For a brief time I served as his hypeman.

New Jersey is known for great producers like Just Blaze. But out of the Organic Thoughts camp, an up-and-coming producer from Newark would later rise among the top beat makers of today: Ramon Ibanga Jr. aka !llmind. He provided most of the production on *The Purest Form* and later bringing in OTS in for "The Groove" on his own album, 2005's *The Art of One Mind* with fellow rising producer Symbolyc One.

These accomplishments were admired by the Guerrilla Words family as another notch into our involvement in getting these artists recognized. There was a necessity for GW to provide a venue for this work to be seen and not only heard. Brooklyn emcee Skyzoo came through to one of the later GW showcases from his work with !Ilmind. We later became the planning team behind the release of his *Corner Store Classic* mixtape. Months later Skyzoo was signed to Duck Down records. We won't take credit for that accomplishment, and if you know the work ethic of Skyzoo, getting on a label was an inevitability. After working on numerous projects, Skyzoo and !Ilmind decided to put out a record together called *Live from the Tape Deck*. Unbeknown to the duo, it stands as a testament to the Guerrilla Words credo of connecting New York to New Jersey, discarding background and coalescing creativity based on talent and drive.

What we could also take some credit for is the connection between !Ilmind and El The Sensei. As of half of the legendary group, The Artifacts, we had him as a guest at our Guerrilla Words Radio show in 2005 held at WMSC, Montclair State University. As I kept the GW name uniform to our events to bolster patrons for our events, we invited Sensei with help from a friend Steve Halo, co-host of our sister station WRSU from Rutgers University. Their show Radio Ruckus, a longtime indie Hip-Hop haven for the university brought in acts I only dreamed of seeing. Through our camaraderie they invited Sensei and DJ Kaos to the station. I invited !Ilmind with the intention of the introduction. Not aware of !Ilmind's work previously, Sensei later told me he did not expect anything from the meeting until I moved the pair to Studio B and popped in a beat CD !Ilmind recently produced. The "Wrong Side of the Tracks" emcee was impressed. That chance meeting led to the lead single of Sensei's Fat Beats solo effort "Crowd Pleasa" a year later. I was interviewed by Asian men's lifestyle site *Gumship* in 2013 about the encounter and I recounted the experience stating "having a hand, even so minuscule, was a sign that this was something I had a passion for, not just to make money from."

Before seeing !Ilmind, whom we affectionately called just "Junior," rise to the ranks of Hip-Hop's elite, scoring collaborations with Kanye West and 50 Cent, we already knew how good he was. Now everyone else does. The fact that he is of Filipino descent is just an added benefit.

> "Guerrilla Words was a movement that I'm honored to say I was a part of. During its run, it was a meeting of incredible minds and passionate Filipino people. Lots of memories and incredible connections happened because of Guerrilla Words. I think it sparked a feeling in us all to know how powerful it could be for Filipinos to unite and become one."
>
> —Ramon "!Ilmind" Ibanga, Jr.

HOMEGROWN CONNECTIONS

From the encounter with !Ilmind and El The Sensei, my partners on the wheels were DJs Unkle Chip and Jay Jung. Growing up with Chip in the early '90s, he took me under his wing, immersing me with the graffiti culture in the suburbs of Piscataway, NJ. Founding partner Mike "Mpos" Balint was my first DJ as I tried my hand as a performing emcee. A college town, the area was progressive and largely multiracial, where Indian, Filipino, Colombian, and African residents all called this town their own. In retrospect, it was unique in comparison when hearing Filipinos speak of their American upbringing outside of New York and California. The connection of music took shape as it led us to work together on Guerrilla Words–related business.

> *"Guerrilla Words was a positive and creative outlet for many artists,*
> *including myself and my crew. It was inspiring for us as GW paved*
> *the way for so many by simply allowing them the chance to go on."*
> —Anthony "Unkle Chip" Fernandez

The entire crew was composed primarily of Filipino DJs including Chip and Jung as well as Mpos, Frankie Five, Jayvee, Mike Intellect, DJ Naz, DJ Sickroc, and now Kevlove. We ran a two-tiered operation. Half of the crew would dominate Jersey venues in New Brunswick and between the lanes of the New York metro area automobile haven Raceway Park in Englishtown, NJ. Frankie Five would later utilize his talents to form Eat Sleep Race with his brother Brian Mabutas, who helped revolutionize the merchandise apparel game in the import racing community. The other half would commute over to the city to rock the party circuit, first in Filipino-centric nightlife events and later moving on to Hip-Hop crowds like Guerrilla Words showcase. Today the crew holds residencies in key venues like Le Poisson Rouge. Jay Jung now holds the title of instructor at Scratch DJ Academy, the same DJ school founded by the legendary Jam Master Jay of Run DMC.

Mike Intellect also had a connection to Guerrilla Words although he already made California his home. He was the DJ for a Filipino Hip-Hop group called Deep Foundation. The crew was a combined effort of Queens and New Jersey emcees. Even unintentional, the cross-state connection once again proves the recurring connection of Northeast Hip-Hop. Held together by Mark "Illpoetik" Malacapay, the group made one of their first New York appearances at Guerrilla Words:

> *"Guerrilla Words played an instrumental part in my development*
> *as an emcee. It gave me a forum to not only explore myself as an*
> *artist, but be inspired by such talented individuals who dropped by*
> *on a monthly basis. As for its place in the history of Filipino Hip-Hop*
> *in New York, I believe it really brought us together. It brought all*
> *these Hip-Hop heads from the Tri-state area and created a true com-*
> *munity. New York can be a ruthless and ultra-competitive scene, but*
> *GW reminded us the value of community and strength in numbers."*
> —Mark "Ill Poetik" Malacapay

As the group went through lineup changes and hiatuses while finishing up their university degrees, they finally released their first full-length album in 2008, *The First Draft*. Held together by the remaining group members including Mugshot, Ceejay, Proseed (who would leave the group after the album), Illpoetik, and later addition Hydroponikz, their lead single "Children of the Sun" became their biggest hit among Filipino Hip-Hop fans. The 2012 Boxing Writers Association of America Boxer of The Year Nonito "Filipino Flash" Donaire took notice of the song. A version was made for his entrance theme bout against Fernando Montiel. The remix, which I am personally a part of as well as fellow Guerrilla Words alum Koba, is possibly the only song that represents the legacy of Guerrilla Words.

SEEING THE BIGGER PICTURE

One of the biggest contributors to Guerrilla Words was in fact not Filipino at all. Stan "Substantial" Robinson was an emcee out of Maryland who came up to New York for his music and made significant connections with the community, aligning himself with the founder of Hip-Hop Kool Herc. He became one of the members of the popular indie collective QN5. While his counterparts graced the stage including Pack FM and Tonedeff, Stan would become one of GW's greatest allies. Initially, he performed while promoting his product. His appearances would become more frequent as Guerrilla Words gained momentum. With a resume including performing alongside The Roots, scoring hits in Japan with production legend Nujabes and later having his videos air on MTV, Stan became a flagship GW artist. One of the best stage performers in GW history, he became a mainstay that showed we were not just a Filipino open mic.

> "When I think of the New York underground, for me, Guerrilla Words definitely comes to mind. It was as awesome place to share and develop your talent while witnessing the growth and rubbing elbows with the likes of Kuttin Kandi, Fresh Daily, & of course !Ilmind to name a few."
>
> —Stan "Substantial" Robinson

Substantial's QN5 connections gave the impression he was from New York. I would later find out he was a DMV representative when he formed his own crew of emcees and brought them to GW. Our largest event was at Nightingale Lounge. The "Make The Face" showcase included members of Stan's label Unlimited Vinyl Ink. Artists out of the group included Insanate, Gods' Illa, and newcomers Fresh Daily and Naturel.

Unlike the rest of the group, Fresh Daily, known then as Ill Tarzan, was a local Brooklynite. With vivid hand-drawn mixtape covers at his side, Tarz would complement Substantial, reminding you of Mos Def and Talib Kweli in their early Black Star days. Tarzan would become Fresh Daily due to a cease-and-desist letter from Disney, which I found out during a Guerrilla Words event where he proudly explained to the crowd the name change was a testament that someone was listening. After numerous albums, collaborations, magazine ads, and corporate sponsorships, the man now known to the world as Fresh Daily graciously considered Guerrilla Words as one of his early locations to hone his craft:

> "Guerrilla Words was a place where I saw polished performers and producers right next to up-and-coming artists. It was a space to foster creativity in a communal sense while unknowingly procuring tomorrow's cream of the crop in Indie music."
>
> —Michael "Fresh Daily" Richardson

Another artist Substantial brought to the fold was Naturel. His connections to our extended family included being classmates with GW graphic designers Gregory Flores and Romeo Tanghal, who also were good friends with Elite Camp's Unkle Chip. Call it fate, coincidence, or just the result of the small world of New York's Hip-Hop scene, it eventually led to our own work with Naturel. His rhyme style was superior to any Pacific Islander we ever saw, and ultimately his talent superseded the necessity of a Filipino emcee representative. Both Fresh Daily and Naturel were introduced to Emilio Rojas when he decided to move to the city. Through Jonyfraze and me, tying into the network with !llmind solidified the GW connection. Naturel's "The Bullets" produced by !llmind remains one of the most slept-on indie singles out and one of my personal favorites.

> *"Guerrilla Words was my proving grounds, much like the Shelter was to Detroit rappers, or like CBGB's was to the NYC Punk scene. So many other talented folks came through week after week, I had to consistently elevate my craft just to keep up with them. Before GW, I was just a rapper—But after, I was a recording artist."*
> —Lawrence "Naturel" Atoigue

Maria Mayoralgo posted a memorable picture on MySpace. Maria, a long-time supporter, was a rising writer whose career led to positions at *The Fader* and *Buzz Media* and later assisted me with work on event planning with !llmind's *Blaps, Rhymes & Life* series. The picture featured Skyzoo, Fresh Daily, !llmind, Emilio Rojas, and Naturel. Ironically, I loved this picture because I wasn't there. Months earlier I put these guys together in addition to Substantial on a showcase at the original Knitting Factory in Manhattan before it moved to Brooklyn. Musical history was being made after I decided to group these individuals based on a feeling that I knew they all would do major things. These were cases where I felt like a proud papa before I actually became one.

I remember the eccentricities of Homeboy Sandman who let out a prideful laughter when he signed with the legendary Stones Throw Records. I remember cats like 8thw1 also taking his trek from Jersey to the East Village and working his way forward just like I did. I remember Daniel Joseph with his crew Bullymouth rocking for Smacks Records representing Mr. Len (Company Flow) and the future of Newark Hip-Hop. I was proud to see family from Philly like Illvibe Collective and Fatnice and the homies from Fortilive who moved all the way from Hawaii to grind out East. I know there are tons of artists and poets, comedians, and freedom fighters who all took something from what Guerrilla Words tried to accomplish.

Some walked away having learned something either on stage or off. I ultimately got over my own social anxiety by seeing smiles on people's faces. Being a host and performer made it worth the dreaded nerves. But as I present you with my written history of what I thought Guerrilla Words was, is, and what it can still be, we did make an impact not only in the history of Filipino Hip-Hop but Hip-Hop as a whole. Because yes, I did name drop and I did brag because if I didn't, who would? Filipino humility, although admirable, gets discarded here. Guerrilla Words speaks and speaks loudly.

SOMETHING OUT OF NOTHING

By Michael "Suitkace" Capito

I didn't even want to be a b-boy. My relationship with hip hop wasn't quite the conventional one you'd hear from other people. I never really immersed myself with or followed hip hop, until I eventually realized several years into my b-boy career that I had been essentially living the hip hop culture all along. I heard a fellow b-boy from Queens by the name of Rocism once describe hip hop as "making something out of nothing." I feel like that's exactly what happened to me. As a kid I was timid and sheltered. Hip hop helped me break out of that shell and gain confidence in myself.

My story begins in freshman year of high school. I had thick glasses, a mushroom haircut, and was decked out in the least stylish gear. I was really into Star Wars and paleontology and wanted to be a Broadway actor. I memorized a whole bunch of musicals and would recite them when I got home. I went straight home after school and wasn't really allowed to go out. I was definitely far from the coolest kid on the block.

My friends and I went to different high schools. We all pretty much stayed within the Jamaica, Queens Filipino scene. We didn't get along too well with the kids a year ahead of us. They called themselves the Junior Freakz. Some of those guys were getting into b-boying and I decided I wanted to try to be better than them for once. So I found a mutual friend, a younger kid by the name of Andrew (now DJ RawBeatz). He taught me all the basics—toprock, six-step, and the baby freeze. My friends and I often hung out with another group of Filipino kids who were getting into b-boying too from the local Catholic high school. Freshmen like us, they were called "the Frosh."

The summer after freshman year, the Junior Freakz called out the Frosh as well as me and my friends to a battle at an upcoming birthday party. That battle was the catalyst for my life as a b-boy. For me it felt like the scene from the movie *Beat Street* with the battle at the Roxy. The battle was in the basement of a Chinese restaurant. It was hot and the floor was slippery from the humidity in the room. The tension was high between both squads and no one held back that night. There was no declared winner but if you asked my friends, they'd tell you we won and if you asked the Junior Freakz they'd tell you the opposite. For me it didn't matter too much. I was far from the best that night, but I remember feeling alive on that floor.

After the battle, I found myself practicing every day. I wanted to be the best. So, I would wake up at 5AM on a school day and took every opportunity I could just to practice. I found other b-boys at my high school and we formed an official b-boy club. My friends would come over and we'd rearrange the furniture in the living room or lay out the cardboard on the driveway. We called ourselves the 2 Intense Crew. We often teamed up alongside the Frosh, especially whenever we ran into the Junior Freakz at parties.

One of the best b-boys on the Junior Freakz was a kid named Wayne. Although he was on the opposing crew (and talked the most smack), I respected him a lot because he took b-boying as seriously as I did. I always looked forward to going up against him. He always brought his A-game, which forced me to be on point whenever we battled.

The November after the battle in the Chinese restaurant, a Filipino organization called F.A.H.S.I. (Filipino-American Human Services, Inc.) hosted a one-on-one b-boy battle. Needless to say we all entered. It was my first tournament and with all the practice I put in, it was my opportunity to shine. I found myself in the semifinals against Wayne—a battle I looked forward to. I knew he threw his best moves at me and I answered back with my best. We went to a tiebreaker and the judges brought it to a crowd decision. Somehow, the crowd chose me (probably because there were a lot of Jersey heads in the crowd and Wayne had taken out one of their own). In the finals were me, Charn who was another one of the Junior Freakz, and Brian Hernandez. Hernandez was older than the rest of us and was one of the first and best b-boys out of the Filipino scene in Queens, so we all looked up to him. The judges decided on another tiebreaker. This time, I was placed against Hernandez. At that point, it didn't matter about winning. I was just surprised I had made it that far and could battle on the same level as Hernandez. After making it through the brackets and tiebreakers, I ended up winning the entire competition. Sure, it was a small-scale competition, but it was enough to drive me to get better and better.

From that point on, I was practicing a lot. As the fad of breaking wore off, I noticed several of the guys in our little Filipino b-boy scene fall off one by one. The rest of the guys in 2 Intense Crew found other niches in life. It seemed the only b-boys left were me and Wayne. Having respect for one another, Wayne and I began practicing together. He introduced me to another Filipino b-boy from around the way named Seano, who would later be known as Evil Skwerl. The three of us formed our own squad. It wasn't necessarily for battling but just a small clique that was just really passionate about perfecting our art. We found ourselves performing occasionally at local events like the Barrio Fiesta at St John's University with a few friends under the name of the Flying Jalapeño Popper Stick Avengers. That was my first taste of being on stage and performing in front of a large crowd. Little did I know that it would be a precursor to things that would come to into my life as a dancer several years down the line.

In the early 2000s, we collected b-boy videos. Between the three of us, we had a lot of b-boy tapes. And, yes, by tapes I mean VHS tapes that you watched on a VCR and had to wait three weeks to a month after ordering it to arrive via snail mail. This was the era of the 56K modem. A time when you listened to a giant track listing of break beat mp3's that took you twenty minutes each to download. Most importantly, this was the time before YouTube. Videos for a lot of b-boys were the only connection to the outside world. Watching *Freestyle Session* and *BBoy Summit* videos you were able to see the legends of our time go at it, and what they were doing to "innovate" within the scene. Most of the videos were from the West Coast. They had their own style that was clearly different than the more foundational New York style. They used a lot of abstract moves that somehow worked. I found out I was pretty damn flexible (at least for that time period) and incorporated it heavily into my style.

It was during the fall of 2000, that Seano convinced me to enter a b-boy battle hosted by the Rocksteady Crew in the Bronx. The jam was called Break Beats, and after shopping for b-boy videos at Fat Beats, I was familiar with the event but only in VHS form. I was nervous but I was hyped. Bottom line though, I just wanted to dance.

I remember that day pretty well. I had told my mom I was just hanging out with Seano around the way. She knew I was dancing but she didn't know how serious it was. On top of that, I was still pretty sheltered, so if she found out I was going to the Bronx she would've killed me! So we made the journey up to the legendary venue, The Point. As an amateur b-boy with little knowledge of the b-boy scene outside of our little crew, it was like going to the mecca of b-boying. I finally saw other b-boys apart from ourselves. I saw cats from the videos, which got me even more hyped. It was my first true taste of the scene.

We were the last crew to get called up to battle. Crazy Legs was hosting, and I remember him calling out our names. "Suitkace and Evil Skwerl. ... Nice names guys," he said reluctantly. I think it was one of the funniest moments of my b-boy life. We got matched up against two out-of-towners, Itchy and Husein Money. The battle was two rounds a person and I had little to no foundation compared to the other New York dancers. What I did have was my superior flexibility and the crowd went nuts for it. We lost, but I knew from then on, that flexibility was going to be the key to making a name for myself.

From that time, we started going to practice centers around the city and put ourselves out there. In no time, I ended up meeting all the big names in the New York City scene. Everyone thought I was from California. One—because of my clearly evident West Coast–influenced style. Two—because I was Filipino. There weren't really many Filipino b-boys in the New York City scene at the time, or at least not in the competition circuit. As I got better, I took pride in knowing that although I grew up knowing mostly Filipino b-boys, I was the one representing us in the overall hip hop scene.

One practice, I finally ran into B-boy Chino. He was a Puerto Rican b-boy out of the Bronx and was one of the key members of one of the best crews in the city, the BREAKS Kru. Chino's major focus was on power moves. It was one thing to see any other b-boy do power moves but watching Chino do power moves was incredible. His speed was unlike anything I had ever really seen before. All the guys with BREAKS Kru that day ended up having a cypher battle with all the other dancers at the center that day. I remember jumping out and busting out my weird flexible moves. That got Chino's attention and I remember him coming at me after my throwdown. I introduced myself to him and we actually became pretty cool.

Seano and I ended up practicing with BREAKS Kru quite often and decided to attempt to get down with them. They were very reluctant and initially declined. One day, I went to practice by myself. When I got there, practice turned out to be closed but a bunch of BREAKS Kru cats were hanging out at the basketball court nearby. They were having a meeting about what was going on with the crew and initiated two b-boys who had been down with them for a while. After their initiation, Chino, out of nowhere, pointed at me and said, "This guy still gotta get down." I didn't know Chino had his eye on me to join the crew, and honestly I was in disbelief. I didn't know what to do. I came that day just to practice and already accepted the fact that I wasn't going to get down with BREAKS Kru. Then I just let all my inhibitions go and found myself going one on one with WaAaK, the president of BREAKS Kru. We went a few rounds on the concrete and on that hot summer night in the Lower East Side, I found myself inducted into BREAKS Kru. I couldn't believe it. I was actually pretty honored.

The years I had with my little crew in Jamaica, Queens was merely the precursor for what I was about to find myself getting into. Joining BREAKS Kru opened up many doors for me. I went on to compete with them all across the map and making a name for myself as Suitkace around the country. When I was still immersed in the Filipino scene, I remember restricting myself to just the Filipinos. I remember all the sessions I had were predominantly Filipino b-boys but not necessarily guys who ventured out into the rest of the b-boy scene. Looking back on it, I realized that for a lot of them it was more about getting props from each other, instead of going beyond our little scene and experiencing the true essence of it. Initially, it was about the fun from the innocence of just dancing with my friends and getting known amongst my Filipino peers for being the "b-boy guy." When I found myself with BREAKS Kru however, I learned that I might have been hot stuff with the Filipinos but I was merely a drop in the ocean within the larger hip hop community. My outlook on things had changed from that point on. I wanted to make a name for myself in the b-boy community. Part of the culture is competition and that is what drove me to continue to be better than who I was the day before. That timid nerdy kid was no more. I was confident and assertive. I did what I could to be the best. I went from being nothing to something. Something substantial. Eventually, I went from wanting to make a name for myself to spreading knowledge so that others might have the experience of enlightenment through hip hop that I had.

BUILDING HIP HOP FROM THE BAY TO THE WORLD

By Rob Nasty

My name is Robert Creer, better known as Bboy Rob Nasty. Both me and my twin brother Profo Won—together known as The Dirty Pair—have been considered pillars for the San Francisco hip hop community for the last twenty years. We have also made our mark on the international bboy scene as teachers of hip hop culture across the globe. Representing Floor Gangz Worldwide, our reputations have allowed us to travel to places like Taiwan, Russia, Philippines, Denmark, and Korea. As a member of Forever We Rock, I have had the honor of introducing dancers around the world to "rocking," which is a little-known style that preceded hip hop styles. But before me and my brother became influential dancers, we were just two kids who were trying to find our place in the world going through the challenges of growing up as two young Filipino Americans.

I was born in San Francisco in the mid-70s, along with my twin brother, Ron, to a newly divorced mother who recently migrated from the Philippines. We were a lower-middle-class income family. My mother was employed by the San Francisco Police Department, working administration for adult probation. My father was a seaman for the U.S. Navy, but unfortunately, he was never able to adapt to the social standards of American life and never finished his naval tour. After a couple years of divorce and bad life decisions, he returned to my grandparents in the Philippines.

Both me and my brother were latchkey kids while my mother was gone working for most of the day. This situation gave us ample time to get into different kinds of trouble. We weren't bad kids but without any parental supervision or guidance, we were certainly a handful for my mother. Traditionally, the father is the head of the household, primary provider, and disciplinarian. Without my father present in our lives, my mother was blazing trails for a divorced immigrant mother of the 70s. She showed great independence and tried her best to fulfill both parental roles. She was able to enroll us in an expensive Catholic school and did her best to make sure we were raised comfortably.

My mother's native tongue was Visayan and she was also fluent in Tagalog, but she made the decision to have her children speak strictly English. She had a new family in a new country with new opportunities. It only made sense to sever the ties that made us "foreign" and adapt to our new surroundings. Like most Filipino transplants, speaking the English language was a butchering process, at best. In retrospect, this was a very bold choice. Learning the native language could have infused stronger connections to our island culture and better communication with my mother. Not learning Visayan or Tagalog, however, caused rifts between an immigrant mother and her two American-born teenage boys.

My earliest experience with hip hop music was through the radio. The radio stations at the time were predominantly rock and soul music, but every now and then there were inklings of something rare. It was 1981 and the first rap song I heard on the radio was, "The Rapture" by Blondie. I was six years old and what I heard was impressionable to me. At the time, my musical ear wasn't developed enough to make any distinction between "Rapper's Delight" and "Good Times." I think it was probably hearing a white woman talking in rhyme over music that intrigued me.

Not even a year later, me and my brother were first exposed to breakdancing. My first glimpse of breakdancing was on a television show called *That's Incredible*. We did not know it yet but this experience was to change me and my twin brother's lives forever.

A memory that I will always cherish is when I saw breaking in real life.

Usually, my mom would take us downtown to shop on the weekends. What we saw this one particular weekend amazed us. Cardboard was laid out in front of the train station at the cable car turnaround. Dancers in tracksuits acted like robots and spun on their backs, hands, and heads. Music blasting from a boom-box stereo flooded the ears of pedestrians. I remember watching breakdancing on TV but to see it in real life and in person was like seeing Michael Jackson in the flesh!

My cousin was part of a breakdancing group called Zero Gravity. His crew had recently won a trophy for a breakdancing competition in San Jose. My auntie invited us over for the weekend so our cousin could teach us his prize-winning moves. My mom didn't really approve of this "street dance" because she had better aims for us in the future. For her, it was just another weekend with her sister and her family. For us, it was the foundations that would take us beyond our own imaginations.

I didn't realize at the time but as the breakdancing craze carried on, I noticed more and more Filipinos heavily engaged in the dance. This was my first time seeing Filipinos and non-Filipinos taking part in something cross-cultural. I was used to seeing Filipino relatives at family parties and gatherings, but to see Latino, Black, and Asian dancers together in a social setting was something entirely new to me.

I was a teenager in the 1990s when hip hop started to take real meaning in my life. At the same time, hip hop music had reached its Golden Era. The breakdancing fad had phased out in 1986, but rap music was climbing the Top 40 charts and gaining commercial success. After the media over-saturation of breakdancing, it was easy to disconnect and move on to the next fad. As I started getting older I began to have a rebellious attitude towards commercial music. West Coast rap was breaking off into two directions: Glamour Rap and Gangster Rap. East Coast rap was producing very Afrocentric music. I felt like I could not relate to these any of these genres.

Before I got into hip hop I turned to the sounds of heavy metal to quench my thirst for defiance of the status quo, the status quo being the mindless following of mainstream media. I had angst and contempt. These feelings derived from being alienated from my classmates and a noticeable difference of being raised with an absent parent. I was never athletic growing up and was grouped in with the dorks and nerds. If I were to be an outcast, it would be on the terms that I chose. I quickly turned to the sounds of heavy metal while all the "cool kids" listened to rap.

It wasn't until the summer of 1991 when hip hop took a full effect in my life. My mom relocated us to El Sobrante, a suburb 17 miles away from San Francisco. She felt that city-living was beginning to have a bad influence for me and my brother. We started high school at De Anza High. At the time me and my twin were still avid followers of heavy metal music and still considered outcasts. Then something truly significant left an impression for us.

Our freshman year of high school was over, it was summertime, and we were watching a local television show called *Home Turf*, which usually aired on Saturday mornings. *Home Turf* would feature local and national talent connected with urban culture. The show had been running for a couple years, and even though we were metal enthusiasts, we always tuned in and always had interest in the subject matter they televised.

There was an episode when they featured DJ Qbert and the Shadow Posse along with rap duo FM20 and their dancers the Knuckle Neck Tribe. I was instantly captivated. It was my first experience seeing an all–hip hop ensemble. These were not the usual African-American faces associated with rap music, but people who looked more like us: Filipino American. This was the defining moment that would build a greater understanding of hip hop culture and connection to our own Filipino heritage.

The segment focused primarily on DJ Qbert, Apollo, and Mix Master Mike. This was right before the Shadow Posse became world champion DJs and held international titles throughout the 90s into the early 2000s. The Shadow Posse offered something different aesthetically. This was something I've never seen or heard before. It was typical to hear "scratching" in rap songs, but this was the first time I'd seen a turntable band!

They were animated and stylistic, each DJ bobbing and weaving, catching sounds with their hands. It was like hearing lasers, bells, and whistles in symphony. Patterns of sampled recordings in an arranged-broken uniform. They felt a little like punk music and freestyle jazz. I related to the alternative, unpolished, and underground style.

All the members of Knuckle Neck Tribe were Filipino Americans. We experienced the breakdancing movement 10 years ago, but what we were watching now was a fusion of dance styles that were unrecognizable yet very familiar to us. Their style was a unique twist of soul and tribalistic rhythm-riding while combining moves from breakdancing. This was the pinnacle of a major shift in our perception of how we looked at ourselves as young Filipino Americans and how we fit into American Culture.

During the following fall semester of our sophomore year, me and my brother broke out of our social shells and started scouting for dancers at our high school. We immediately found other Filipino kids who knew about DJ Qbert and Knuckle Neck Tribe. Upon deciding to be dancers, our social status in high school skyrocketed. All of a sudden we were making a lot more friends and meeting a lot of girls. We went from being outcast heavy metal rockers into quickly becoming the popular "twin brother hip hop dancing duo."

We were no longer 80s breakdancers, we were now called "houzers," the label for a freestyle dancer at the time. This is not associated with Chicago's house music movement of the 90s, but it was a style of dance that Filipino and Black kids were doing exclusively in the Bay Area. After establishing our first dance crew, Animal Kwackaz, we found out we had many rivalries when it came to dance battles. We would dance anywhere and everywhere! We would crash parties looking for a place to get down and dance. Whether it was garage parties, family parties, cotillions, or high school dances, as long as they had a DJ who was playing some hip hop, we were there ready to dance. We would travel up and down Northern California—from San Jose to Sacramento—looking for parties to crash and for more members to be recruited in our "tribe."

With Filipino artists like DJ Qbert and graffiti legend Mike Dream getting international praise, this created an atmosphere for a grass roots hip hop movement for Filipino Americans in the San Francisco Bay Area. This attracted many hip hop pioneers from the East Coast to visit and mix in with the San Francisco hip hop scene.

In the mid-90s bboying was being further defined by breaking legends like Crazy Legs, Ken Swift, and Mr. Wiggles. At the same time 80s Bay Area breaking crews were reviving their lineage to this culture and establishing themselves with the growing online international breaking community. Bay Area Crews like Renegade Rockers and Rock Force were making comebacks by adding new generations of bboys. Both myself and Profo Won were involved with this revival and were later inducted into the bboy crew Rock Force, which had begun in the early 1980s. I can write more about this occurrence but our history in Rock Force should be a separate article by itself that I hope to write in the future.

Since the 90s, my brother and I have remained constant figures in the Bay Area and global hip hop community and still battle as The Dirty Pair. We continue to spread hip hop cultural awareness across the globe by teaching workshops, judging battles, and building a community with a network of dancers—who we consider family—in every time zone. Be on the lookout, because we may be teaching lessons in your neighborhood next.

CRITICAL NOSTALGIA AND THE TRANSNATIONALISM OF APL.DE.AP

By Ethel Regis-Lu

"No matter how successful he gets, Black Eyed Peas' Apl never forgets his roots in a Filipino barrio, and his all-Tagalog hip-hop hit proves it."

—San Francisco Chronicle

Apl.de.Ap or "Allan Pineda Lindo of Angeles, Pampanga" is a Filipino American rapper, songwriter, producer, and member of the popular, multi-ethnic hip-hop group The Black Eyed Peas (BEP). In an August 2005 piece, *San Francisco Chronicle* writer Benjamin Pimentel features the Filipino American rapper's personal story and his "all-Tagalog hip-hop hit" song "Bebot," which was included in the BEP's then-recently released album *Monkey Business*. Apl's personal history, as an adopted child from the Philippines who immigrated to the U.S. in his teens, influenced his music as songs such as "The Apl Song" and "Mama Filipina" highlight the lives and experiences of Filipino Americans, although in the instance of "Bebot," cultural references and representations proved to be problematic and controversial due to the problematic sexual representation of Pinays in the video.[1] Apl's story and success resonate among those who draw inspiration from their ethnic heritage and mark traces of the Philippines in new cultural practices and productions that traverse national boundaries. Apl has become an example of a member of the Filipino diaspora who has effectively negotiated and reconciled his ties to the Philippines and the United States, even as he can be appropriated as an objectified Filipino American celebrity used as a means to sell a product and a culture.

Since breaking ground in the U.S. with "The Apl Song" and "Bebot," Apl has focused much of his professional energies in transnational work, including a collaboration in 2009 with the Philippine Department of Tourism to

---

1   The song "Bebot," which means "hot chick" in English, received scrutiny from some in the Filipino American community for its stereotypical portrayal of Filipinas, particularly as hypersexual, objectified subjects for male consumption in the music video.

produce the "Take U to the Philippines" video.[2] Philippine media facilitates appeals for the millions of Filipinos outside the Philippines to intervene in "home" country conditions through Filipino American celebrities such as Apl.[3] Even as Apl successfully traversed barriers and gaps—first as a Filipino American rapper and group member of BEP in the U.S., second as a Filipino American returning to the Philippines to establish solo, his involvement in state-led efforts in the realm of tourism demonstrate how his transnational Filipino American identity informs institutional projects used to reach the Filipino diaspora and reinforce the notion of *global Filipino*.

As an honorary ambassador for the Philippine Department of Tourism (DOT), Apl.de.Ap wrote and performed in the DOT's video "Take U to the Philippines." In it, he is depicted as a contemporary *global Filipino* who has returned to reconnect with his roots and even as he serves as a personal tour guide. Aimed at young, overseas Filipinos, the video was distributed and aired on MTV networks across Asia, shown on The Filipino Channel (TFC) around the world through various satellite and cable providers, as well as made available via YouTube, and promoted the Philippines as an exotic destination and a familiar homeland open to new generations of Filipino and non-Filipino visitors. Through the campaign, Apl assumes the role of *global Filipino* who embodies the desired multicultural tourist and consumer particularly selected for his diverse, international reach. In the Philippines, visitors can expect to be exposed to an array of local cultures, landmarks, and destinations in an infrastructure that is efficiently linked through tourism.[4] In the video, Apl is tactically positioned to be both a tourist and tourist guide for a country in a quest to be a "tourist destination" and an "investment haven."[5] Rendering his identity as a Filipino American consumer and promoter of displayed Filipino culture, he was tasked with supporting an industry that, according to a 2011 report by the Philippine Department of Tourism, supplies 6% of the country's gross domestic product (GDP) and 10% of the jobs in the country.

"Take U to the Philippines" paints an intimate picture of a tropical paradise full of excitement and adventure: "Jump on a plane, pro'ly jump on a train/Just you and me yeah just you and me/I can take you where I come from right/Where the water's so warm with the sunlight/Shine all day, Really shine all night/Ma I like you, Yeah I like you/She shine all day, all night too/I could be your boyfriend, I could wife you/Let me take you to the place where I come from/Take you to my hometown cause I wantcha." With Apl positioned as a guide and seductive lover for the listener (gendered female), the song calls on its audience to be ready and open to go anywhere, from the "rugged hut" of rural, provincial towns to modern, "splendid villas in the city." Apl, as depicted on the video, raps the names of one local destination after another, each location captured and identified, as names of different towns and cities flash on the screen. This declaration promotes the diversity of a variety of local cultures and destinations, despite the fact that in an interview, Apl admits that his travels have only been to Pampanga (the town he grew

---

2   In "The Apl Song," he draws on elements of Filipino culture that have been brought over by previous generations of Filipinos in the United States. The racialized and gendered depictions of Filipinas in "Bebot" brought about contentious elements of Filipino American representations in popular culture in a struggle to find a place in mainstream U.S. music industry.

3   The Filipino diaspora is largely composed of over 8 million of Filipino migrants who have departed the Philippines for the Middle East, Europe, and North America in pursuit of a "better" life for themselves and their families. Reports often declare that one out of every ten Filipinos lives outside the Philippines. Women comprise most of the overseas workers, particularly in Asia, North America, and Europe, while men are generally recruited and placed for work in the Middle East. Of the 8 million Filipinos abroad, permanent migrants comprise approximately 3 million, many in North America and Australia where paths to citizenship are available. Temporary overseas contract workers (OCWs) make up approximately 3.5 million who work abroad for extended periods of time, while 1.2 million are considered "irregular" migrants, including migrants who stay abroad with undocumented status.

4   In *Destination Culture*, Barbara Kirshenblatt-Gimblett argues that "heritage is created as a process of exhibition...adding value to pastness, exhibition, difference, and, where possible, indigeneity"—and it is increasingly so because of the way that tourism packages travel. (149–150) Tourism that, as Kirshenblatt-Gimblett suggests, compresses and displaces the world as it is typically experienced, is in effect in Tourism Enterprise Zones (TEZs) established by the Philippine Tourism Act of 2009.

5   These phrases stem from President Gloria Macapagal-Arroyo's speech at the opening ceremony of the first Philippine Tourism Congress meeting, November 25, 2009. The Philippine Tourism Congress was established after the passage of the Tourism Act 2009.

up in), Boracay, and Cebu (where the DOT had toured him in preparation for the campaign).[6] As he takes his guest and the audience on a virtual, whirlwind tour, images of him dancing, traveling on a tricycle (a local form of transportation that is a motorcycle with a covered sidecar) or riding a *jeepney*[7] overlap vibrantly colored names of towns and islands for potential travelers to remember and eventually visit.

The visual effects are colorful and festive, though the images are not photographs of places but rather computer-generated graphics of moonlit hills, coconut trees, waterfalls, and cityscapes that are juxtaposed with text that spell out names of famous tourist destinations in the backdrop. As such, the video categorizes these places under the umbrella of an exotic, tropical paradise, even as the names distinguish the different destinations from each other. The computer-generated effects provide a futuristic, dream-like mood while the catchy upbeat sound orients the listener to the future and positions the listener-audience as one who has only dreamt about the Philippines. The intended audience of mainly members of the Filipino diaspora may identify with the symbols as images or objects they have encountered only in travel brochures, advertisements, or souvenirs, unlike life-like, realistic depictions such as photographs or video footage where audiences directly or narrowly identify with a place or object as some place they have been to or as something they have experienced in the past. Moreover, the futuristic feel of icon-like images from the Philippines created from computer animation conveys a kind of modernity—one that is hinged on symbols of heritage and markers of authenticity. The video poses Apl as one who is able to show the audience around the country (in this case, virtually), particularly because of his identification as a Filipino American, positioned as someone who can bridge the native elements of the Philippines with international tourists. This position of tour guide that Apl inhabits glosses over any possible contradictions or reservations and instead assumes a natural relationship to the Philippines.

Apl alludes to the political and economic hardships of life in the Philippines in his songs, and in "Take U to the Philippines," he does so by acknowledging that even in such a beautiful, exciting place "Everybody's workin'/They survivin'/They want peace/No more fightin'/Wanna see the world?/Don't be surprised when/I take you to the Philippines." This stanza, perhaps, is a remnant of Apl's song titled "The Island Song," which has a reggae-like sound, a nostalgic yet critical sentiment, with more explicit mention of the political and economic ills that plague the country. Instead, the catchier, livelier "Take U to the Philippines" was favored by the DOT to use in the promotional campaign. Even as Filipino Americans like Apl.de.Ap may search for inspiration from ethnic heritage because of their disidentification with U.S. mainstream culture, transnational Philippine media also rely on such nostalgic sentiments to conjure "Filipino-ness" and include Filipinos in the diaspora in representations of *global Filipino* to promote Philippine tourism.[8] Transnational projects instituted by state apparatuses like the DOT capitalize on the desire and increased ability of Filipinos outside the Philippines to maintain homeland connections.[9] And, similar to the Philippine Overseas Employment Agency's (POEA's) strategy towards overseas Filipino workers and migrants—an approach that employs a neoliberal strategy in social and economic discipline guised as empowerment[10]—the DOT's approach evinces efforts to capture the Filipino diaspora by reclaiming and reconfiguring a once-lost son in support of larger neoliberal nationalist projects.

---

6   From "Story Behind 'Take U to the Philippines'" with Apl.de.Ap and former Tourism Undersecretary Ace Durano on YouTube at http://www.youtube.com/watch?v=HtKbhBoblgQ.

7   The *jeepney* is a form of mass transit used primarily by the working class and urban poor. These colorful, ostentatiously decorated vehicles originated from surplus American Jeeps left after WWII that were converted to accommodate more people.

8   Based on my interviews with DOT officials, I learned that cultural awareness is a key strategy for marketing the Philippines to members of the Filipino diaspora as a place to discover and expand knowledge of ethnic and family heritage.

9   These connections can be tangible (e.g., money remittances, care packages, returning to visit) or intangible (e.g., regular conversations with family members because of ease of communication, memories, or plans of visits to the Philippines).

10   Guevarra, Anna. *Marketing Dreams, Manufacturing Heroes*. 2010

Transnational productions play on feelings of nostalgia as they extend state-initiated projects. Maintaining the "ethos of labor migration"[11] institutionalized by government agencies such as the POEA, media representations of Apl tout inclusion and acceptance, with undercurrents that prop up the myth of meritocracy and the American Dream. Media efforts to reach the diaspora through celebrities like Apl.de.Ap revamps the country's image beyond that of a country that exports domestic helpers, nurses, seafarers, and construction workers. Rather, Apl stands in for a different kind of Filipino—one who has successfully entered and impacted the American music industry at the same time that he signifies a degree of multicultural acceptance—wherein differences have been resolved but not further interrogated. Breaking barriers and dissolving difference, Apl's "value" is partly derived from his racialization as a dark-skinned Filipino and his personal story of transnational adoption[12] such that media representations featuring Apl.de.Ap as a global Filipino conveys the notion that Filipino-ness absorbs anyone who is of Philippine ancestry (regardless of class, skin color, regional, or other differences). In the case of the DOT, this is in order to market the Philippines as a diverse, tropical playground with lots to offer young, new, and returning Filipinos and foreign visitors. Second- and third-generation Filipino Americans who are seen as having comparable spending capabilities are called to take part in experiencing the newly developed Philippine tourist industry. By raising cultural awareness, the DOT and TFC tap into their racialized identities to call them back to reconnect with their Philippine heritage. These institutional efforts assume a narrative of "rescuing" Filipino Americans from cultural amnesia even as they position them to economically "rescue" the Philippines.

From the standpoint of the Philippine government, the idea of a *global Filipino* is a strategically useful concept in line with its efforts to generate interest and investment from overseas Filipino migrants, and by extension, Filipinos who span generations. Famous Filipino Americans such as Apl.de.Ap are instrumental in state efforts to reach a broad demographic of Filipinos and non-Filipinos alike—especially through nostalgia and affective ties that especially draw younger generation outside the Philippines to reconnect with what their parents or previous generations have left behind. Varied pasts all linked by "the ghosts of a traumatic imperial history" and the experience of migration can differently shape these knowledge, feelings, and practices with which Filipino Americans must come to grips.[13] Confronting these ghostly matters, these hauntings, is necessary to bring to the fore histories that have been rendered invisible and to understand how the subaltern Other is constituted.[14] As a way to confront these conditions and gaps, Filipinos of the diaspora in search of wholeness can look to the past for affirmation of identity and draw on material traditions for notions of authenticity to find meaningful connections between two or more homes. In the process they may reconfigure their inquiry into expressions of critical nostalgia.[15] And, the politics of belonging may also come into play as cultural boundaries and political commitments are defined, challenged, and assessed.[16]

How might Apl inspire a global awareness centered on critical nostalgia? How can his story of being in the margins and emerging in the mainstreams encourage meaningful and effective strategies for providing direct resources and support to those who need it? Apl's popular global appeal can link the chasms across communities

---

11   Guevarra, Anna. *Marketing Dreams, Manufacturing Heroes.* 2010

12   Parallel to what Guevarra has argued as the racialized and gendered ideologies about Filipina women's labor that characterizes them as having "added export value" because they are thought to be more qualified and naturally primed for care work.

13   Capino, Jose. *Dream Factories of a Former Colony: American Fantasies, Philippine Cinema.* 2010.

14   Avery Gordon, *Ghostly Matters: Haunting and the Sociological Imagination.* 1997.

15   Critical nostalgia critiques the present by drawing on the past, albeit at times a romanticized past (Clifford, James, *Writing Culture: The Poetics and Politics of Ethnography*, 1986). As James Clifford puts it, critical nostalgia is "a way to break with the hegemonic, corrupt present by asserting the reality of a radical alternative" (Clifford, 1986, p. 114). First used by Raymond Williams, critical nostalgia is a useful term to describe how diasporans construct a sense of belonging and forge community in imagined ways.

16   Maira, Sunaina. *Desis in the House*, 2003

of fans by making his personal story and efforts palpable to the greater public. Through his transnational humanitarian efforts, he calls attention to social concerns to incite positive change and symbolically flexes his hybrid and multiple identities to channel resources into non-profit advocacies that support Amerasian children and public education in the Philippines. Beyond his work with the Department of Tourism and his solo music endeavor, Apl has maintained transnational ties through philanthropic efforts that involve his Apl Foundation alongside education initiatives by other non-profit groups. Apl can represent how Filipino Americans engage and reimagine immigrant cultural practices by acknowledging and connecting his transnational family and global community ties. For example, the "We Can Be Anything" campaign, launched in 2011, is a partnership between the Apl Foundation and the Ninoy and Cory Aquino Foundation. It was largely promoted in the Philippines and targeted overseas Filipinos through the "We Can Be Anything" music video shown on TFC. He actively took part in the 25th anniversary celebration of the first People Power movement[17] and flew to the Philippines in Feb 2011 to accept a position as education ambassador for the Ninoy and Cory Aquino Foundation (NCAF) EDSA People Power Movement, in conjunction with his Apl Foundation efforts. Out of the partnership between the Apl Foundation and the NCAF, the "We Can Be Anything" video was produced to promote and secure donations for the foundation's education advocacy projects. As a transnational adoptee, music artist-philanthropist, and entrepreneur, he reestablished ties with his country of birth in an effort to embrace his two homes, which today continues to deepen and resonate in his growing transnational commitments.

---

17   In 1986, the People Power Movement, emboldened by the martyrdom of opposition leader Benigno "Ninoy" Aquino, stood ground in the streets of EDSA (Efinanio de los Santos Avenue) and ousted the longstanding military dictator Ferdinand Marcos. This led to the re-establishment of democratic government in the Philippines with the election of Aquino's widow, Corazon "Cory" Aquino.

FROM QUEENS TO THE PHILIPPINES

By Knowa Lazarus

Growing up in Queens, New York, I thought of the Philippines as just a place my family was from. It was as far away as another planet where my mother and father once lived hard lives. My mother spent time having to scavenge and steal food in an orphanage in Manila. My father, who was at one point valedictorian of his class, had to drop out of school in Davao to work to survive. My Lola Naty immigrated to the United States and was working as a teacher for years in New York. She saved up money and through the open visa process in the 1970s flew my mother and her three brothers to the "land of opportunity." My father, who moved to Manila to work as a waiter, luckily saw an ad in a newspaper seeking restaurant workers in New York. He replied and interviewed for the company, then next thing he knew he was on his way to America.

I remember my parents being really in love up until I was about two years old, then I just remember this huge fight and my father left, and I didn't see him for two years. They got divorced, and I only saw my father on weekends. It wasn't pretty and even until now, I rarely see my father and mother in the same room at once. I would also get severely ill as a child, as I was born with asthma and eczema. The doctor told me as a child I would never be able to play sports. As a teenager, I would run and ride my bike everyday coughing up phlegm and using my inhaler whenever I was short of breath. My eczema was so bad I had to wear turtlenecks in the summertime to cover the open sores. Kids were pretty mean, so most of the time I was the outcast. On top of all of this, I was one of only three Filipinos in my elementary school. I remember being made fun of, being called ching-chong, egg roll, wanton soup, all of that. When I would say "I'm Filipino," they'd say "same shit!"

As you could imagine, I kept to myself a lot but I found salvation in art. I needed ways to express myself, so I would draw, write poems and stories, and even sing and act in school plays. I remember my mother working, going to school, and trying to raise me all on her own. She couldn't do it alone, so I had a Dominican babysitter during the week and even sometimes weekends. I spent a lot of my younger years in the house and actually learned how to speak Spanish, dance merengue, and all that. No matter what I did, however, kids would still give it to me and call me "chino." I remember wishing I wasn't Filipino and I tried my hardest to stay away from my identity, even denying it at times, saying I'm half this or that. It was in this house that I was first introduced to Hip Hop. My friends and I used to play basketball in the backyard while playing cassette tapes in a portable stereo.

When I reached junior high, I decided to try to live with my father for a bit since my mother and I weren't getting along. He had remarried, but my stepmother and I didn't really get along at this point, and it was still a better option than the constant fighting with my mom at home. My father lived in Forest Hills, which on the surface was a nicer neighborhood than where my mom stayed, but looks can be deceiving. The first day in orientation of my new school, there was this kid throwing quarters on the floor, saying "I'm rich, I have so much money, I can just throw whatever I have away!" I saw this and started picking up the quarters thinking to myself, "Shoot, that's candy and lunch money!" He then walked up to me and said, "Why you picking up my money, chink? Are you poor? You need my money?" I just shrugged my shoulders and said "Yeah, you're throwing it away, so why not?" He then spit on me, told me to go back to my country and said, "Outside after school 3:00, you and me!" Great, it was my first day of school in my new neighborhood and I had to fight already. I always hated fighting, but I remember my Uncle Willie (who was like my second father) telling me, "Don't start fights with anyone, but if someone pushes you, stand your ground." So I mustered all my courage and met him outside after school where a crowd was already waiting. He pushed me and took the first swing. I dodged it, and then he tried to grab my jacket and pull it over my head. I don't know how I did it, but somehow I flipped him over and threw him on the floor, and was sitting on top of him and punching him. His lip was bleeding then he finally cried out, "That's enough!" We actually became really good friends and people didn't really mess with me after that.

I began flirting with music as I became a lead tenor saxophone player in the school band. My Uncle Willie would take me skiing, and I ended up breaking my collarbone and wrist in three places. No more saxophone playing for me! I remember listening even to more Hip Hop at this point, from Cypress Hill to Das Efx. I even wore my pants backwards to school like Kriss Kross. I also began playing basketball religiously and vowed that by the time I got to high school I would play for the school team. Things didn't last long at my dad's house, so I ended up moving back home with my mother.

The high school that I was zoned for in my mother's neighborhood wasn't the best. You basically had to stay with your homeroom class throughout the day, and you were only exposed to the students from other homerooms during gym, lunch, and recess. Although I was one of only two Filipinos in the entire school, my skills in basketball and sports allowed me to earn the respect from other kids. I vividly remember this one instance of a Chinese student being pissed on from the top of the staircase by some of the gangsters. I didn't do anything at the time, but deep inside I started feeling a responsibility to help out people of "my kind." I didn't know how to start.

Most of my close friends from my neighborhood were pretty much becoming gangsters at this point. They were selling drugs, carrying weapons, and starting fights. Although my mother and I weren't exactly getting along, she always told me I could be anything I want. I knew I didn't want to be like them. I applied and got accepted to the SMART (Science, Math, and Arts) program at Bayside High School, which is as far as you can get from my neighborhood without leaving Queens. It took me an hour and a half to get to school everyday on the bus, but to me it was something I had to do.

During this time, all my friends were African American and Latino. I tried out for the basketball team and made starting point guard for the junior varsity team. During away games we'd take the bus together and me and my boy Dacian would rap. He would always tell me I had skills but I'd always take it as a joke. My stint as starting point guard for the team didn't last long, as I started seeing how athletic and natural the game came to some of the other players. I would have to work so hard to keep up with some players who didn't even practice. It was a reality check, but I kept playing. During lunchtime at school I would always spit rhymes while Dacian would bang beats on the lunch table. Crowds would form and it would be a good time.

I remember meeting a son of my mom's family friend. Jastynne was one of my first close Filipino friends. We were both into music, dancing, partying, and having a good time. He asked me to come with him to a party in the Manhattan. I wasn't old enough yet, so I saved up money from my part-time jobs and got a fake ID card. It was the first "Filipino underground Hip Hop party" I went to, and it was kind of crazy. I told Jastynne and the people that were with us that I knew how to rap. I spit some freestyle verses and they thought it was cool.

Next thing you know we were inside club "Ukrainian." It was a completely new experience for me. There was a Black rap group on stage. The crowd really didn't respond to them and the group ended up cursing out the crowd. They said, "Fuck you Filipinos! Ya'll don't know nothing about this Hip Hop!" The crowd reacted by booing them. I told my friends, "I can do better than that." Then someone gave me the mic and I went on stage and freestyled. At the end I recited the lines of a popular Filipino house song "Aye Naku, Putang Inay Mo!" (which doesn't mean anything good). The crowd joined me and started pumping their fists in excitement. The feeling I felt on stage was undeniable, and I knew that once I got off of the stage that this is why I was born and that music was what I wanted to do for the rest of my life.

One day I was freestyling on the back of the bus and some dude came up to me with a business card saying I should enter a talent show. I called up my friends and we made a group and entered the contest in the South Bronx. We were outsiders and the only "Asians" but somehow we ended up winning the contest. We supposedly won a record deal, but in the end it wasn't real. However, I was able to hone my skills as I took trips every week to Bushwick and Flatbush, Brooklyn to improve my rhyme and songwriting skills.

I was taking the train back one day when I heard someone talking about this Filipino DJ, DJ Roli Rho, and how he won the Zulu DJ Battle. I was in awe hearing about a Filipino making noise in Hip Hop. So back in Bayside High School I ended up meeting these two Filipino kids, JC and Noel. They mentioned they knew Roli and I told them that they had to introduce me to him. They passed some of my tapes to him and he agreed to meet me. This is the time I met IBP (Intro-Bass Productions), DJ Kuttin Kandi, DJ Junior, DJ Lo Lyfe, and DJ Jay. They gave me so much love. I remember they would invite me to their parties and I would just hang out. They'd let me get on the mic and mc and all that. They also taught me what they knew, and a lot of the foundations of what I do now, I learned from them.

By the time I graduated high school, tensions were also growing at my home, so my mother ended up moving out and I was living on my own. I ended up doing a lot of things I shouldn't have, but that's a whole different story. Let's just say I partied a lot and was pretty reckless. I was actually on probation at my college because I just wouldn't go to class. This was something completely new as I maintained pretty good grades up to this point.

I had a multi-racial rap-group at this time called Da Paradoxx. It was me aka Knowa Da Unknown, Agony Within a Trinidadian MC from Brooklyn, and DJ Fat Fingaz, a Latino from Jamaica, Queens. One day DJ Fat Fingaz (who is a really dope DJ and is now a Heavy Hitter) told us he couldn't do the next upcoming show as he was training for the International Turntable Federation competition. Agony's girlfriend had a cousin, DJ Flava Matikz, who she mentioned could spin for us. We ended up linking up and it clicked, he spun at our shows and that was that.

Back at home, things were getting worse. My mother told me I needed to focus on school or she would kick me out. Music wasn't paying the bills as I was working two jobs still, so I decided I needed to take a break and focus on my education. We were in the process of recording our demo and there were also tensions in our group. So when I said I needed to focus on school, the group dissolved. Once the group dissolved, people who we worked with before started to come out of the woodwork saying they wanted to help me, but they couldn't before because there were negative vibes in our group. Chuxter, who was an engineer at the Hit Factory, would sneak us in after artists such as Mariah Carey, Jay-Z, Eminem, and Nas used the studio. He would tell us all the secrets; it was amazing how much he would share, and I soaked it up like a sponge.

Chuxter hit me up and said he wanted to record an EP for me. He was my coach. We recorded eight songs and I presented it to my boys. They all told me they liked it, but that something was missing. I needed some beats that were more "street." One day when I was driving on the Williamsburg Bridge, I get a phone call from DJ Flava Matikz who told me, "I'm making beats now! Come through and check it out." I ended up stopping by his place in Woodside and we clicked full force from that day. Under the guidance of Chuxter, we built a home studio in Flava's place and started recording and playing basketball pretty much everyday.

As me and Flava Matikz grew closer, we started to realize a lot of our upbringing was the same. We were both from single-parent households, and both grew up mostly away from our Filipino culture. We began recording and released an independent album, *Let the Truth Be Told,* along with beatmaker/producer T.H.E Menace. The album built a buzz and we did shows up and down the East Coast. We decided we should call ourselves something, so Flav came up with Q-York, which is short for Queens, New York because that is where we were from. We all thought it was genius and ran with it. We put our music online and started getting a lot of feedback from people in California. So we decided to visit. We stayed there for six weeks and did shows and met with people.

The thing that stood out to us most was seeing how many Filipinos were living in California. It was something we never experienced before. We went back to NY, inspired, but went back to our same life. I was in my fourth year in college when the head of the music department pulled me aside. He told me, "What do you want to do, Cedric? You have talent, but your talent won't succeed in this classroom. You have to be out in the world and meet people, and let them see you shine. This institution will always be here, you can always go back to school, but if you want to be a musician you have to go out in the world and get it!" That was that; I decided it was time to take a chance on myself.

I asked Flav if he was down to move to LA. He just shrugged and said "yeah." I worked for a year straight and saved money to move. We only knew a few people in LA but we knew somehow, someway we'd make it. The night before it was time for me to leave, I came home to my mother lying in bed. She said, "I am going to sleep forever." I walked into the bathroom and saw pills scattered, and I called the police. We went to the emergency room, everything was going to be ok, but the drama was tough. I just told her I loved her, and I had to find my own way.

On a cold, snowy day in February we packed up our U-Haul truck and drove across the country to a studio apartment we only saw online on Craigslist. We lived for a year in that studio apartment and I don't' know how, but by the graces of God we made it. I remember almost having a nervous breakdown not being able to pay the bills when Lakers player Ron Artest, who we knew back in Queens, hit us up to help him make 10,000 CDs. That saved our lives. From there we realized we should make CDs for other people, so we bought a CD printer and CD tower. More help followed as some of our friends from NY decided to move out to the West Coast, too, so we could join forces together for the movement. Together we ended up having some success. We made local TV, we were making CDs for the top DJs and independent artists in LA, and our graphic artist Def Case did 50 Cent's and Funkmaster Flex's websites. We even released a mixtape, "Step Ya Game Up Rapper, Vol. 2," which was mixed by Power 106s DJ Turbulence and featured tracks with Far East Movement, Ron Artest, and many other celebrities.

In 2004 I remember doing a show and cursing on stage at the Lotus Festival and seeing parents pull their kids away. I made a vow from then on to not use profanity on records and also to be conscious of my lyrical content. I really started getting into what it meant to be a Filipino. I started reading and researching about Jose Rizal, Bonifacio, the Katipunan and Philippine history. In 2005, we ended up doing an album entitled *Jose Rizal*, which contained songs inspired by Rizal's life and message. I also started getting involved with the community and began speaking at high schools in San Diego thanks to a good friend Joann Fields. I would basically talk to the kids about Hip Hop and how they didn't have to be a "gangster" to "be Hip Hop."

Eventually the larger group we had of Q-York dissolved, and it was back to just me and Flava Matikz. My mother ended up moving to California and buying a house. Me and Flava moved in there and built a studio in the basement. Things were ok for a bit, then tensions began to rise again between me and my mother. We were like fire and ice, and we just couldn't coexist in the same place. I didn't know what to do, but I started to accept that if I just made records from my basement and let people talk about it on the internet, I'd be fine with that. Flav and I would joke around about maybe going to the Philippines and that would be our last shot, because if we couldn't be successful in our motherland, than maybe this wasn't for us. The problem was we didn't know anyone, and our families didn't make it easier as they would say we'd get kidnapped or robbed or killed.

Our good friend Joann had a trick up her sleeve. She wanted to introduce us to the Philippine Allstars, the award-winning dance crew who were in town from the Philippines for a competition. I saw them dance and they were really good. I thought to myself, these guys don't want to meet us. Joann took Flava and me to their hotel room and there were fifteen of them in one room, five on each bed, people on the floor, under the table etc. It was crazy. Joann told them to give me a word and I would freestyle about it. I just went for it and ended up vibing with a few musicians in the group. We ended up recording "Caught Up" with Kenjhons of the Philippine Allstars for our album *L.I.F.E.—Lyrics Inspired From Experience* produced by Elevated Soul. The group stayed a little longer after the competition, so some of them crashed at our place. We gave them jobs in our CD business to help them out. They went back to the Philippines and our song "Caught Up" reached top eight on the radio charts in the Philippines.

Flav and I decided to visit the Philippines. We fell in love with the country once we got off the plane and stayed for ten weeks. We realized at that point where all our creative energy came from when we saw the lavishly decorated jeepneys and heard music playing everywhere. We toured and did some shows with the Allstars. Time flew by and we had to head back to Los Angeles. Upon our arrival in the states we decided Q-York was going to move to the Philippines and that it was all or nothing. We had to take a chance. We saved money for a year and worked on our business. Through God's graces we did well and were able to move. We packed up all our equipment in ten balikbayan boxes and padded it with our clothes. Flav sold his whole record collection, which I know was really hard for him.

So once again, we were in a new place trying to make something happen for this undying passion we possessed in our hearts. But now we had a true purpose, to help be a voice in and for the Philippines. Sort of like the book *The Alchemist*, where everything you're looking for has been at home the whole time, but this time it was a home we never saw or knew.

Continuing our collaboration with the Allstars, we decided to finish the song we started in LA "Mainit" and shot a video in a style that had never been seen here in the Philippines. It contained dance, R&B, Hip Hop, basically all of the elements that we had going for us all together in one. The song exploded into the Philippine music scene and became a dance craze throughout the country. It was surreal. But as always with success comes struggles, and the collaborative effort began to deteriorate as people wanted to go in their own direction and try to will everyone else to move their way. We had record labels interested but were never able to finish our collaborative album.

Things became real once again as I fell in love with my wife and had a daughter. It forced me to grow up in a lot of ways, as I didn't party as much anymore and I really wanted to be there for my family and knew what it was like to be raised in a broken home. Once again, we were at a crossroads and I didn't know what to do, so we turned to music again. We decided again we had to create a completely new album in the shortest time possible. So in two to three months we finished *Q-York City*. We didn't know what was going to happen, but we just knew we had to do it.

JayR (the "King of R&B" in the Philippines) heard our music and decided to help us out. He distributed and helped us promote our album and we won some awards for it in the Philippines and we were back in the game. That same year, we also ended up getting accepted to the 7101 Music Nation Songwriting Camp and we were mentored by legendary musicians of the Philippines such as Ryan Cyabyab, Gary Valenciano, Joey Ayala, Noel Cabangon, and many others. It was surreal once again, and it opened my eyes and heart to a scope much larger than what we've been doing. I actually ended up starting to write songs for other artists, not just Hip Hop, but pop, R&B, and everything, and Q-York started becoming more of music producers, which was something I never thought would or could happen. We even ended up having our song "Fallen" featuring me singing and Flava Matikz rapping, which charted for three months straight here in the Philippines. A new world was opening to us.

The next year, my girlfriend (who is now my wife) got approved for her Visa. So she went back to the US. I went with them, but she knew what was in my heart, so she told me to go back to Manila. Back in Manila on my own this time, it was like starting all over again, and I had spent all my savings on my family. I was still earning, but the buzz had started to die down from our last album. I only had $200 dollars in my pocket, but I was blessed with a place to stay, and I was back on it. It was actually really tough because I had no idea how I would be able to see my family again. Then we ended up winning the KBP pop song contest with a Hip Hop/fusion song entitled "Lead The Way feat. Kat Lopez." With the prize money I was able to buy a plane ticket back to LA and, through a movie soundtrack deal, had enough money to get married.

After a year my family came back to the Philippines. And now here we are. I am currently working on our latest album *Q-LaboNation* and have been blessed being able to collaborate with world-class artists from the Philippines. We hope to help inspire others to live their dreams and bring our Filipino people together. Filipinos are all over the world, we are strong, and we are smart and big-hearted. However we are still divided and separated by distance, walls, financial inequality, language, and generations. I pray one day we can solve this and stand up unified to show the world we are destined for greatness. Pinas Pa Taas!

"A MELTING POT FULL OF DIVERSE STYLES"

By Creed Chameleon and Roderick N. Labrador

RL: Tell me about yourself and your family?

CC: I was born in Guam and mostly raised in the island of O'ahu. My parents were both from the Philippines, Cavite to be exact. My grandparents were also raised in the Philippines. Our family settled in HI around 1985 or so.

RL: How did you get interested in Hip Hop?

CC: I first started to fall in love with Hip Hop was when my cousin introduced me to RUN DMC. I was only in the 2nd grade at the time but was deeply connected to the beats and rhymes. I started to emcee or write rhymes when I was ten due to my love for poetry in school at the time. I delved into some graffiti and b-boying but emceeing was definitely my craft.

RL: Why did you choose Hip Hop?

CC: I felt Hip Hop did not have any restraints or boundaries as far as what was said or how it was created. Hip Hop now is so diverse with different sounds that we have to make different categories for them, such as underground, west coast, boom bap, trill, etc. I chose Hip Hop because it allowed me to be who I am.

RL: Are there any particular childhood experiences in Hawai'i that speak to your experiences as being Filipino?

CC: One experience that stands out was when I was living in Kalihi [a neighborhood in urban Honolulu with a high concentration of Filipinos] during elementary school and there was a very significant separation between Ilocanos and Tagalogs. At the time, Ilocanos were the most dominant language group as far as Filipinos go. I remember Ilocano kids not thinking fondly of me because I could not understand certain words they would be saying when they addressed me or get me to dialogue.

RL: How do you think growing up in Hawai'i has shaped your understanding of and use of Hip Hop?

CC: I felt Hip Hop has helped me convey my thoughts and emotions more especially coming from the islands. Growing up, Hip Hop has helped me channel some of my negative emotions into rhymes and essentially grow stronger as an artist and an individual. Hawai'i Hip Hop to me is a melting pot full of diverse styles that all represent Hip Hop forms. Similar to other regions in the U.S., Hawai'i has a different struggle as far as high cost of living, tourism, ice epidemic, etc., which makes Hawai'i Hip Hop display a different side to the spectrum.

RL: In your opinion, what makes Hawai'i different than other places?

CC: Hawai'i is different than other places because I feel that it's the most predominant place where all cultures in the world cross and meet; therefore diversity in the cultures itself creates a whole new breed of music and is why Hawai'i Hip Hop is the way it is now.

RL: What are you trying to express about yourself and about Hawai'i in your music?

CC: I feel that my music has influenced the younger cats to express a lot more deeply and not "dumb it down" for the masses to hear. In my music, I try to express that Hawai'i is so different compared to other parts of the U.S. and world but it still has the same quality Hip Hop music just like the others, and even better.

RL: How would you describe yourself? How would you describe your style?

CC: I would describe myself as someone from the working class trying to express himself through emotional verses laid out on instrumentals. I would describe my style as more towards significant concepts pertaining to realistic events that may sometimes be understood as story-telling or just plainly speaking the truth through the music.

RL: Where do you see your place in the history and culture of Hawai'i Hip Hop?

CC: I see myself as one of the first underground Hawai'i emcees that was able to drop multiple albums available in stores and online and was able to perform in big shows and tours along the way. I first recorded back in 1999 with Mana, which was my first album attempt called *Sentimental Value*. Mana or Mana Buck was an old producer based out of Moanalua that has created numerous beats with Nomasterbacks back in 1999–2000. *Sentimental Value* was pretty much a test-run album. There was no concept on where the album was going but it was a stepping stone to more things to come.

RL: What about your other albums?

CC: *Love Potion Cyanide* was an album I definitely put a lot of soul and heart into. At that time, I was going through a lot of drama … between child custody, relationship issues, and even drug abuse. I am surprised by how much people love that album and how much attention it has gotten. Definitely an album that helped strengthen my passion towards music making … *SIQ of Lazy* was an album more towards proving a point that a Hawai'i-based emcee can spit just the same as any mainland artist and maintain that substance that a lot of Hip Hop emcees back at the time were losing. It definitely was one of my hardest-working albums I put out and had a lot of help from friends to help build the album to what it is … *The Ultimatum* was just a bridging point when I merged with Flip The Bird Entertainment. Tassho Pearce and I united in late 2009 in order to help push the envelope in Hawai'i Hip Hop. Although this project was an EP, the release was treated as if it was a full-fledged album. I also teamed up with Osna on production, though at the time a lot of well-known artists were very skeptical about working with the dude due to his brash style of Hip Hop. I always thought Osna was dope … being versatile with his stuff, which made him a musical genius. I'm thankful for that … *The Vanishing Act* was pretty much a concluding mixtape project, saying farewell to the islands due to my quick move to Arizona in 2011. I just gathered all the beats and collabs I had done and had DJ Jimmy Taco mix it up. The mixtape has a variety of sentimental songs and head-nodding tracks. I had fun making that one.

RL: What rap groups were you part of?

CC: I was with a group called Direct Descendants. We had some really good times performing and recording together. Due to creative differences, we split and I delved into my solo work. I felt being in the Direct Descendants hindered me from branching out or shining more than the rest of the older emcees of the group. I then signed with SIQ records where I succeeded in my solo Hip Hop career. Right after, I joined FTB on wanting to build with other artists in order to push the Hawai'i Hip Hop movement hard.

RL: If you could pick three songs you've done that best represents Creed Chameleon, what would they be and why?

CC: I would say "Flesh and Blood" because it represented how much I sacrificed … how I would put in so much work just to make the music felt for the masses. "White Flag" represented my admission to letting go at times in my life, that sometimes it was just hard to let go. Whether it be relationships, work, or life struggles, giving up doesn't necessarily mean that you lost in life. It just means that it just wasn't meant to be, so move on. "Morning Blessing" because it represented my love for this music scene and how much it is a blessing to live day by day in Hawai'i. It also represented the drive and passion that cannot be stopped unless it's my own intentions to do so.

RL: That's one of your more popular songs. How did the song come about?

CC: "Morning Blessing" was actually inspired by the beat alone. It was the first time I started working with Osna and he gave me the "Morning Blessing" beat. I automatically thought about how blessed and cursed it is to be living in Hawai'i and came up with my rhymes along the way. The video was created by Ryan Miyamoto, and he came up with the visuals as far as showing the beauty and traditional side of Hawai'i. The people in the video were mostly from the FTB camp, alongside with DJ Packo, the Angry Locals' Big Mox and Mic 3, and other close homies. As far as the meaning of the video, I'm just trying to push the envelope in the Hawai'i scene and say that obstacles in life should not hinder you from grasping that "Morning Blessing" or new day.

MASCULINITIES, POWER, AND HIP HOP PINAYISM

HIP HOP PINAYISM FRONT AND CENTER

CLAIMING SPACE, EXISTENCE, AND THE SOUNDTRACKS OF OUR LIVES

By DJ Kuttin Kandi

"As all advocates of feminist politics know most people do not understand sexism or if they do they think it is not a problem. Masses of people think that feminism is always and only about women seeking to be equal to men. And a huge majority of these folks think feminism is anti-male. Their misunderstanding of feminist politics reflects the reality that most folks learn about feminism from patriarchal mass media."

—bell hooks, *"Feminism Is for Everybody"*

I was always used to being that "only female in my crew" that Lil Kim kicked in her verse with her all-male crew P-Diddy and Biggie. It was cool to be the sole female of the clique. The rarity of being an "only female" gave status and spotlight. It was all a game and to maintain in the game, you had to compete. After all, "It's all about the Benjamins baby."

This is what the *industry*, not what the culture, taught you.

Lucky for me, I never considered myself "industry."

"It is time to return to the malls in our lives, to resist the question 'To dog or not to dog?' and to begin to engage in a discussion that should be a repetitive process of reevaluation, reconstruction, retransformation, retransgression, and, especially, relove for one another."

—Allyson Tintiangco-Cubales, *"Pinayism"*

I remember the day it was no longer just about me anymore. I said to my friend Helixx, "Hey, you're an MC and I'm a DJ. We just need to start our own group..." A few days later the all-female Hip Hop crew of over 20 womyn called the Anomolies was born.

I didn't realize it then and I most certainly never claimed it till years later, but Anomolies was my form of feminism.

In an industry that was primarily male-dominated toppled with misogyny, sexism, and a whole lot of patriarchy, there was a need for womyn to come together. Initially, we didn't necessarily have a statement; we just knew we were womyn and that we had talent. But the more we got together, the more we talked. The more we talked, the more we realized just how important it was for us to exist. We later realized that being Anomolies was a statement within itself.

Eighteen years later and the Anomolies are still together. Throughout the years each of us have received accolades, been featured in Hip Hop timelines and have been highly talked about in books, museums, and magazines for simply starting our all-female Hip Hop crew. But Anomolies wasn't the first to do this nor would we be the last.

Many would say we were a rarity. I beg to differ because us womyn in Hip Hop were definitely out there; we just didn't always get the respect we deserved. True, back in 1995, I could count how many of us were present at all the Hip Hop events in New York City. But that didn't mean we didn't exist or that we didn't aspire to *become*. But in those days, we didn't have the internet to tell us there were more of us out there and so we leaned on our camaraderie to get us through the difficulties of an industry that so often tried to leave us out.

But I'm proud to come from New York City and to have contributed during the last leg of the 90s that has been coined as "The Rebirth" post "The Golden Era of Hip Hop." I am honored that I was given the chance to shine, to rock, and to learn from some of the best. I have been blessed to have been able to contribute during a time where the sound was authentic, gritty, and real. I've got a whole lot of pride because the struggle was real but it was also hype.

The womyn in Hip Hop I knew were raw. We rocked hard and we also brought flava. These were the days when Jean Grae was What What (I can't help but still call her What to this day) of Natural Resources, Apani B Fly was releasing her herstoric compilation song "Estrogen" featuring all-female MCs, Lyric (now known as Sara Kana) was rippin' the mic and Pri the Honeydark was winning most of the MC battles nationwide. There was also Toni Blackman, Yejide the Night Queen, BGirl Rockafella, DJ Rekha, D'Jeannie of the Lamp, Infinitee, DJ Mocha the Sunflower, Queen Godis, Honey Rockwell, La Bruja, Sofia Quntero, DJ Reborn, Lazy K, Cocoa Chanelle, Jazzy Joyce, Beverly Bond, TooFly, Spinderella, PebbleePoo, Sha Rock, Roxanne Shante, Rosa Clemente, Cristina Veran, Jlove, Allison Joy, April R. Silver, Christie Z. Pabon, and so on and so on and so on.

As I began to tour I quickly learned of other womyn in other cities doing it Hip Hop. They were womyn, womyn of color, white womyn, adoptees, (im)migrants, lesbian, gay, bisexual, transgender, queer womyn of color from all different classes, backgrounds, ethnicities, abilities, spiritualities, political ideologies, indigeneity, ages, and sizes. I met them in my travels to Austin, Champaign-Urbana, Atlanta, Seattle, Detroit, Wisconsin, and from countless other small towns to big cities around the world. Although we were different, we shared a common love of Hip Hop and each of us had a story to tell. And so we spoke stories through six steppin', sprayin' cans, rockin' mics, and spinnin' vinyl. We went beyond the limits through fashion, business, promotions, event organizer, chantin', rhymes, ink, film, song, poetry, and the written word. Sometimes the stories were of funk and it "locked" out the truth. Sometimes they were stories that beat-juggled the anger out of us or sometimes it just made us laugh till we couldn't scratch no more. And oftentimes the music was so inspiring that we cried it out in 16 bars.

There were days it went real smooth like the wax off a power-belted drive. And there were days it was as rough as spinning on your back on concrete. Yet, no matter what, we told our truths. Whether it be Helixx spittin', *"I don't wanna be an MC,"* or Mystic singing her famous, *"the life, the life, the life …,"* they were stories of survival and it spoke of beats stolen from a song and instead given to a "celebrity male emcee." They were about sound technicians giving us the hard eye because they didn't think we knew how to set up our equipment or it was about the disrespectful gropin' done to us backstage. We told stories about that typical Hip Hop Macktavist who rapped political conscious music but was a homophobic womanizer behind our backs. Then we can never leave out how there were too many men headlining with only one spot in the line-up for that 1 sole female from an all-male crew. But then there were also triumphs and celebrations, where we didn't always speak of our struggles. There were party anthems that had us breakin' to Missy Elliot's "Work It" or simply just chillin' at the bar on an open mic night where we were fallin' in love and head-noddin' to Bahamadia's "I Confess."

This is how we rolled. And these were all the womyn I rolled with. I had the honor of meeting and working with some of them over the years, and some whom I have yet to meet whom I just honored in return by spinning them on my two turntables.

Finding Hip Hop or rather Hip Hop finding me was like waking up in the morning to "Here Comes the Sun" by Nina Simone. And when I found other womyn like me, especially other Pilipinas who loved Hip Hop just as much as I did, I often had to pull a reverse on that old 45 because it held that much soul. I always carefully place those kind of rare jewels in special record crates, never letting them turn to dust, making sure they are cared for in every sleeve because I know how golden each of them are. I stack them high and not by BPMs but by the height of how high I get off of each memory. They are memories of ABGirl taking on 1 on 1 battles, a rare performance by the Rhapsodistas, Ruby Ibarra politically spittin' pure fire on her "Lost In Translations" mixtape and YouTube videos of Empress Milan speaking truth to power. I know exactly where they are on my record shelves and all I have to do is pull them out of their sleeves right onto the silver platters whenever I need to remember who I am. I can pick each one of them out without looking—Rocky Rivera, Hope Spitshard, Jocie De Leon, Faith Santilla, Alison De La Cruz, Joy De La Cruz, JNatural, Bgirl Magno, Allison Joy , BGirl AntEye, BGirl Baby Angles, DJ Malia, DJ Raichous, La Femme Deadly Venoms, and more. Each one's artistry comforts me and sets me at ease; taking me to places I never think I could possibly reach. This is what it means to be a feminist; this is what it means to be a Hip Hop Pilipina head.

I just had no idea it would help me find my Pinayism.

To claim my Pinayism means to claim my space, my very existence, my love for self.

> *"Pinayism should belong to Pinays and Pinoys who are willing to engage in the complexity of the intersections where race/ethnicity, class, gender, sexuality, spirituality/religion, educational status, age, place of birth, diasporic migration, citizenship, and love cross."*
>
> —Allyson Tintiangco-Cubales, "Pinayism"

To claim Hip Hop means to claim my truth.

It was revolutionary Assata Shakur who once said, *"I believe in the fire of love and the sweat of truth."* Well, I believe that when Hip Hop and Pinayism meet it is my fiery love and the sweat of my truth converging into endless possibilities, hopes, struggles, passion, and dreams.

And it takes me on quite a ride; a ride that politicizes me and teaches me a lot more about feminism than any academic book ever could. It also gets me closer to understanding that the world we live in is filled with systems of oppression that colonize, imperialize, globalize, capitalize, and commodify us. To do this, they must occupy land. They seek colonial conquest. So, as they obtain all of our resources, they occupy womyn in order to occupy land. They occupy us womyn through physical conquest of our bodies, spiritual dynasty, and psychological warfare. This occupancy exists not only on our homeland(s) but is also rooted in the streets of our very Pilipina/o American experience. It lies amongst our media, seeping through our neighborhood blocks, homes, schools, families, and on a good number of those repetitious songs we blast on our radios because of an illegal practice called *payola*. This form of colonization is lethal because as they intend to colonize our mind and our bodies, they also colonize our existence. It seeks to erase everything we know about our own rights to self-determination and any herstory that speaks resistance.

In a time where sex-trafficking and mail-order brides have long been on the rise, where suicide amongst our Pinay sisters is at its highest, and where a Rick Ross song promotes date rape, more than ever we need to (re)claim with a response that is up for the challenge against white supremacist patriarchy. We need a rally, a dialogue, and a song for the people; one that puts us womyn at the center of every movement.

My friend and famed author Joan Morgan who coined the term "Hip Hop Feminism" writes in her book *When Chickenheads Come Home to Roost: A Hip-Hop Feminist Breaks It Down*,

"More than any other generation before us, we need a feminism committed to 'keeping it real.' We need a voice like our music—one that samples and layers many voices, injects its sensibilities into the old and flips into something new, provocative, and powerful. And one whose occasional hypocrisy, contradictions, and trifeness guarantee us at least a few trips to the ter-rordome, forcing us to finally confront what we'd all rather hide from."

My response has always been with Hip Hop but through a Pinayist consciousness.

As a Pinay, it has always been about "keepin' it real" but more so gettin' real with myself. It is about that, *"checkin' ourselves before checking others"* that Allyson Tintiangco-Cubales spoke about in her 1995 article "Pinayism." Hip Hop Pinayism allows me to do this through the ways that I turn down gigs and flossy offers that contradict with my Pinayist consciousness. It teaches me about sisterhood rather than the competition to be that "only female" in the spotlight. It inspires me to be out and proud; to claim my queer identity while learning to check my straight-marriage privilege. It teaches me that while we as womyn of color and queer womyn of color should be the center of the dialogue, we also shouldn't be tokenized or compartmentalized into just one chapter, for our stories inked in depth carry purpose and truth. They're narratives that are far too important and they deserve to be the center of every page and weaved into every chapter, along with still having our very own chapter with each of our names being the very title of a book. Because we know very well that we're worth more than just myself name droppin' every womyn I know on this section intro. We know that we're worth more than a bunch of shout-outs on some album cover.

Through Hip Hop Pinayism I was able to see the ways in which I perpetuated patriarchy in not just Hip Hop but in my whole being. It got me in touch with the uncomfortable and painful process of checking privileges but understanding that transformation is possible, forgiving, compassionate, and healing. My Hip Hop Pinayism travels on my journey, guiding me through near-severed relationships; it teaches me trust, connectedness, and real community-building that need to be maintained rather than cut. While I am still in the process of doing this work, Hip Hop Pinayism has got me that much closer to truly understanding the meaning of solidarity and ally-ship. Hip Hop Pinayism is where the Pilipina/o critically confronts, deconstructs, decolonizes, and dismantles sexism, misogyny, and patriarchy. And as it became my everyday consciousness, it became everything I embodied and inspired to become. I learn to live with this new embodiment knowing that even though I carry much of my own contradictions, "it is still going to be okay." I learn that perfectionism is a product of assimilation, colonization, and imperialism that I am socialized as a Pilipina American to believe and this too, needs to be dismantled.

Through Hip Hop Pinayism I found the soundtracks of my life. And I made so many mixtapes out of them.

For it gave me hope during my own hardest times of depression as I struggled out of suicidal ideation. It found me the love I've been looking for my whole life; a sense of enlightenment where the intimacy and the ability to be vulnerable got me in touch with the real me.

This is what saves me, every single time.

I'd like to hope that Hip Hop, Pinayism, Hip Hop Pinayism, Feminism, Womanism, whichever terms one prefers (or perhaps no labels at all) does the same for others as it has done for me.

Either way, I'm simply just thankful to be alive, to claim my existence, and to be able to share another herstory with you.

RESISTANCE AND STRUGGLE ARE SISTERS

By Allyson Tintiangco-Cubales and Dawn B. Mabalon

Bulosan said: If you want to know what we are, we are revolution

Ninotchka Rosca said: Do things on your own, in your own way

If you want to know who the Pinay is, she is resistance
        If you want to know who the Pinay is, she is struggle

Walking forward into a storm
Born in displacement meant
To exist we had to resist

Born into a life of hardship
        Each day a war
        Our bodies are the battlefields
        Our souls the soldiers
        Our lives are lives of struggle

Racist
Sexist
Classist
Ageist
It is rape culture and we must resist

Colonialism
Takes our land
But not our souls
And we must struggle

Sister
Daughter
Babae
Babaylan
Mom
Inay
She is Pinay
She is resistance

Ninang
Tita
Manang
Auntie
She is Pinay
She is Struggle

Resistance
Through Wars we have led the struggle
On many levels
Guns across our souls
Shields protecting our minds
Fighting to maintain our culture in an insane rape of our motherland

Struggle
They came slinging Colt 45s and different flags
To kill and burn
Kill and burn
To turn our homeland into a firestorm
In its eye, we hold our family close
With strong brown arms
We have known starvation and disease
Sexual enslavement and devastation of death
And still we survive

Resistance
Contracted by Amerikkka to move from nation to nation
Being stationed in sweatshops
To sex brothels

Seen only as a maid
Bodies laid
Dignity Stolen
Hearts and Dreams broken
Many words unspoken
But yet we seemed to survive

    Struggle
    Is a love so deep
    That leaves the comfort of a motherland she birthed
    To pick cotton
    To can peaches
    To cut asparagus
    To clean the homes of the oppressors
    To care for white babies
    While her own cry thousands of miles away
    Her hands bleed as she feeds a Pilipino nation

Resistance
Through Pinoy colonization
Looking for someone who's down
'Cause we're not willing to take
The Pinoy's excuses
About why he erases
The Pinay's struggle from his own
And we demand that every Pinoy man
Take a stand
Because this hand is the hand
That gave birth to your existence

    Struggle
    Against colonized brown minds
    Which negate our lives, our spirits, our self-determination
    Told we cannot be who or what we want to be
    By our own
    Uncles fathers brothers pares lolos boyfriends
    And even by ourselves
    Our aspirations left in the sink
    Or in the laundry
    Silenced into a culture of complacency
    Ask us what we hold inside
    And our dreams are a deafening roar

Resistance
Through the neglect of my mom and your mom too
Heroines with stories unwritten
About many people
Spitting on their souls
Even their own
Disrespected and rejected by history
Not even seen as political
But step back and check out her ways of being
'Cause you'll be seeing and feeling
How being Filipino has really stayed alive

Struggle
To be recognized
Because without us,
There would be no Pilipino heroes
So check that
With your HIStory books
Original warriors, priestesses and matriarchs
Lola and mom are queens
Her everyday struggle makes her a heroine
Like our Mare Emily says, "Stronger than Eve she is"
Pinay
Who marches and toils
Feeds and clothes
Pinay in the trenches of wars
Past
Present
And future

So if you want to know who the Pinay is, she is resistance.
So if you want to know who the Pinay is, she is struggle.

—*Allyson Tintiangco-Cubales and Dawn B. Mabalon, 1995*

RESISTANCE AND STRUGGLE, THE HIP HOP REMIX: MEMORIES OF SPOKEN WORD, SISTAHOOD, SCHOLARSHIP, AND SERVICE

Allyson Tintiangco-Cubales (Resistance) and Dawn Bohulano Mabalon (Struggle)

"To speak a true word is to transform the world." (Paulo Freire)

For us, doing spoken word truly transformed our worlds. Our sista/friendship, which is entering its third decade, began at a poetry reading. We met in October, 1994, at a Pilipino American History Month (PAHM) spoken word event at UCLA's Kerckhoff Gallery. It became clear early on that day, we were birthed from the same story and together, we would write more stories. Dawn had just graduated from UCLA and was working as director of the Samahang Pilipino Education and Retention Project; Allyson was a first-year PhD student in education at UCLA. In 1995, Dawn entered the MA program in Asian American Studies at UCLA. We had so much in common: we were both UCLA graduate students in a mostly male, white world. We were granddaughters of Manongs, and came from working class families who emigrated from the Philippines to Northern California in search of salvation in a place that promised much more than it was able to provide. We had schooling experiences that deemed us unworthy of higher education and both of us had initially ended up at community colleges. Schooled and guided by ethnic studies professor-activists, we were able to defy the odds and transferred to two of the top universities in the nation—UCLA and UC Berkeley. And with mentorship and support, we both ended up in graduate school together at UCLA and became roomies in 1995.

Although it wasn't clear the role Pinays could play in the very masculine world of Hip Hop, we found that the burgeoning West Coast Filipina/o American intellectual and art world and renaissance of the mid- to late 90s—with its poets, writers, musicians, Hip Hop artists, scholars, and spoken word performers—gave us a space to forge a lasting sistahood that sustained us in a lifelong journey, toward a life of scholarship and service. Now we are in our early 40s, tenured profs with books, poems, and articles under our belts. We sat down one summer day in 2013 to reflect on and dialogue about the last two decades and what Hip Hop and spoken word meant to our lives. In 1995, we wrote a spoken word piece called "Resistance and Struggle Are Sisters" that we performed all over nation and was included in the 1997 limited edition indie vinyl record *Elements of Hip Hop*, an early release by Jaime Munson (the producer Poet Name Life) on his label Listen Deep Records. On that cut, Allyson was "Resistance" and Dawn was "Struggle"; we decided to dialogue using these pen names.

SPOKEN WORD AND SISTAHOOD

Resistance: My introduction to spoken word came from ethnic studies. With professors like Barbara Christian and June Jordan at UC Berkeley, poetry was always in the context of political struggle and resistance. In my first Asian American Studies course taught by Ron Takaki, I distinctly remember watching *The Fall of the I-Hotel* documentary by Curtis Choy and hearing the voice of Al Robles reciting a poem about the "manongs." I learned early on that spoken word had a role in political activism. In my classes, I was also introduced to Filipina/o poets such as Jessica Hagedorn, Emily Cachapero, Shirley Ancheta, Jeff Tagami, Luis Syquia, Oscar Penaranda, and Jaime Jacinto. In many ways they were our foremothers and forefathers. Filipina/o American spoken word started with them. To apply what I was learning in my classes, I found my voice in *maganda* magazine, a Filipina/o student literary publication where I served as managing editor and as a copy editor. It was there that I met Pinay poets like Barbara Reyes and Vanessa Deza who inspired me to write. *maganda* was my entry point into the Filipina/o American Literary World.

Struggle: I often think of the time we met—the early to mid-90s—as this golden time to be young Pinays in college on the West Coast. At the time you were doing *maganda*, I remember being at UCLA and reading your pieces. In 1994, I was fully immersed in this new and breathtaking world: taking Asian American and Filipina/o American Studies classes from folks like Uncle Roy Morales, Prof. Steffi San Buenaventura, and Prof. Pauline Agbayani-Siewert, and getting involved in the Filipina/o student and larger community, getting more political and radicalized. I was already politically left and feminist, but I think being at UCLA at that time, with all the mentorship and influences and community, made me a *Pinay*, a Pinay feminist, a *Pinayist*, though that term was yet to be articulated by you for a few years. My senior year at UCLA, I took a writing workshop with a then-up-and-coming writer, Han Ong, along with my friends Francis Tanglao Aguas and Robert Karimi (both of whom have since made amazing careers in art, theater, and performance). I started writing poetry then, but I wasn't thinking of it as "spoken word." I devoured my aunt's tattered first-edition copy of *Liwanag*. I loved Jeff Tagami's reading of "Now, It Is Broccoli" in the documentary *United States of Poetry* on PBS, and the poetry of Shirley Ancheta, Virginia Cerenio, and Al Robles, and the way they talked about the themes closest to my heart—the experience of growing up in rural California as the child and grandchild of *Manongs* and *Manangs*, gender, memory, culture, and home. My father was still working the asparagus at the time. I was also deeply influenced by the spoken word movement happening on the East Coast. While at FANHS in NY in 1996, I went to Nuyorican Poets Cafe and felt like I had been transformed. Around that time, I remember seeing the poet Emily Porcincula Lawsin perform in LA. Emily was a few years ahead of me in the UCLA MA program and her poetry and performance was always so mind-blowing and it still is. Really, Emily Lawsin just blew open this world for me. She was really our ringleader and mentor. Her piece "Dear Kuya Oscar," written for Al Robles' 1996 LA book launch for his *Rappin' with Ten Thousand Carabaos in the Dark*, is this really special piece that just really encapsulates those golden times of rich Pin@y artistic and cultural production and poetry up and down the West Coast.

Resistance: I remember the first time I heard Emily spit fire on the mic. She blew me away with her non-apologetic neck-rolling self. She was always unafraid to take risks, call people out, and resist the racism and sexism that we faced as Pinays—in academia, in spaces that were dominated by white people, and even in our own communities. Like you, her presence gave me courage to speak a "true word." I remember following Emily at the Kerckhoff PAHM event in 1994 with a poem that I read called "Finding Words." At the end of the evening you introduced yourself to me and friend, Rico Reyes. Then our journey began. We began to hang out together reading, writing, and studying at Lulu's cafe in Santa Monica and 6th Gallery in West Hollywood, and started frequenting poetry readings and open mics throughout LA. It was when we started collaborating that I felt our words became more powerful because we were better able to articulate our stories together.

Struggle: When we began writing, we were battling sexism on so many levels—and within our own community. We were struggling to articulate so much of what we felt as brown women, as Pinays, as writers, as artists, as feminist scholars, and here was poetry, and this new space—*spoken word* and Hip Hop—suddenly giving us this place to articulate what we felt, what we experienced in our lives, what we were reading and discussing in our classes, all this theory and praxis and pain and growth. Now we had each other and we had this community that was growing. By 1995, spoken word and underground Hip Hop and this whole world of radical art being made by

Filipinas/os were all around us. In 1995, one of our UCLA classmates, Wendell Pascual, who was the founder of the Downright Pinoy clothing line, created an LA Filipina/o American spoken word series called *Our Path to Follow*. At these events, we met more writers and DJs and MCs, like Faith Santilla, Kiwi, Irene Suico Soriano, Napoleon Lustre, Joel Tan, Allan Aquino, and Myra Dumapias, too many to name. Wendell Pascual and our friend Jose Buktaw went on to create the underground Hip Hop collective Foundation Funkollective in 1996, and they used to have these open mic nights where we'd have MCs, DJs, poets, and all these other artists at venues like Marvin Gaye's old house in LA. That was where we met this dance group called Atban Klan, who became Black Eyed Peas. And the soundtrack to all of this was underground as well as mainstream Hip Hop, everything from Biggie Smalls to Common to Tribe Called Quest to Bahamadia to Guru to Kiwi to the Fugees, and of course mixtapes, and the Beat Junkies and local artists and DJs.

Resistance: I also remember Tupac and Invisibl Skratch Piklz on those mixtapes. Simultaneous to the Filipina/o Hip Hop scene forming in LA, the Bay Area was also growing a Filipina/o American arts movement. Events like Lapu Lapu Day, organized by Klay Ordona, aka Bruddah K or Kayumanggi, featured generations of poets and performers. Our friend Aleks Figueroa organized Filipina/o Spoken Word events called *Represent*—held at both the Upper Room and 330 Ritch—where poets from both the Bay and LA performed. Along with the LA folks that you mentioned performing at *Our Path to Follow*, they would come up to the Bay and also perform at *Represent* with featured poets like Barbara Reyes, Celine Parreñas, Olivia Malabuyo, and Christine Balance. There was this organic synergy between the two communities. Our spoken word pieces often spoke to each other. In both LA and the Bay, one of our biggest honors was to share the stage with bigs such as Al Robles and Jessica Hagedorn. One of the high points was the *Our Path to Follow* event at the UCLA Pilipino Studies Conference event in April, 1997, when Al Robles and Jessica Hagedorn shared the stage with all of us LA poets. These events became our midterms and finals as spoken word artists. Often writing last-minute poems, collaborating before we had the internet and formats like google drive. I even remember the one time that you were driving up to the Bay to meet up with me to go to one of the *Represent* events and you were writing in the car in response to one of my poems, and by the time you got to the Bay, the poem was written. Then we performed together that night for the first time. This led to our writing of "Resistance and Struggle Are Sisters" in October, 1995.

Struggle: I remember you had written your half of the poem, the "Resistance" part, one morning. I read it and then we went to Prof. Agbayani-Siewert's graduate research methods seminar. When we got back to our West LA apartment, I banged out the "Struggle" half. It really came out of all these conversations we had had about gender and women and history, and our own painful experiences as Pinays.

Resistance: Actually, I think what had really happened was... you wrote the "Struggle" part of the poem in Prof. Agbayani-Siewert's class. Maybe that's why we *struggled* in that class. LOL. Regardless, we wrote the poem for the Pinay Event organized by Cindy Evangelista for the UCLA Pilipino American History Month Celebration. I had just finished my article on Pinayism for *maganda* magazine and much of my work was trying to understand the relationships that Pinays have and don't have with each other. Honestly, there would be no Pinayism without my friendship with you. I'm so thankful to have met you when I did. I felt I had a partner in the journey to figure out how to be a critical Pinay. Also, being involved with Gabriela Network, we were both learning about the struggles and resistance of Pinays across the diaspora. Resistance and Struggle became our herstorical documentation of our political development as Pinays.

Struggle: Ok, haha, you're right. I wrote it in class. No wonder she gave me a B-! But yes, I agree, having you as my sister in struggle at the time made me fearless. I don't know if I could have written and performed what I did at that time without you having my back and I'll always be thankful. At the time we were writing "Resistance and Struggle," I was writing my MA thesis on Pinays who had been invisible in the Filipina/o American experience—the pre–World War II Manangs in Stockton. And I had all these feelings of loss and pain, anger, and regret as I was doing these oral histories and reading feminist theory, and at the same time learning about the global sexual and labor exploitation of Filipinas. A critical mass of Pinay feminists was gathering in LA, at UCLA, and in the larger community, and we had a strong home with all of them. Spoken word gave me a place to articulate what I was thinking and feeling about being a Pinay, and our place in history and the community.

Resistance: After reading "Resistance and Struggle" for the first time, I remember feeling a sense of power and agency that I believe gave me the courage to take on my future. The second time we read the poem was at Coco Jam at UCLA, organized by the filmmaker Ernesto Foronda. Then we read the poem at many open mics and readings from LA to the Bay, and then even across the nation in places like Virginia Beach at the FANHS conference in 2000. We were honored when our friend Jaime Munson, then a young budding Hip Hop producer who now produces for Black Eyed Peas and other groups, asked us to perform it for a record he was doing called *Elements of Hip Hop*. "Resistance and Struggle" became our anthem for many years after.

Struggle: I still can't believe our piece is on vinyl! One of these days I'll play it again. And now Munson is famous. I remember seeing BEP on the Super Bowl last year and just amazed that he was the DJ. Anyway, back to the 90s. By the time both of us moved to San Francisco in 1997 (Allyson to go back home and finish her dissertation, and for me to get my PhD at Stanford in history), the Pin@y spoken word and literature scene had really grown. We started collaborating with Bay Area poets like Olivia Malabuyo and Christine Balance—one of my favorite pieces was this totally irreverent yet very political and Pinayist piece we four did together called *Reflections* for a Justice League Pin@y poets night, and again for the *maganda* magazine launch in 1999, in which we made fun of ourselves as Pinay spoken word artists. Spaces in the city like Justice League and Bindlestiff Studio also provided more venues for underground Hip Hop, spoken word, and art. In 2003, I organized the launch party for the all-Pinay anthology *Coming Home to a Landscape,* edited by Marianne Villanueva and Virginia Cerenio, at Bindlestiff.

Resistance: Along with these readings and books, we were also very fortunate to have been included in some of the first Filipina/o spoken word CDs such as *Infliptration* curated by Aleks Figueroa, *Evidence* curated by Catalina Cariaga and Theo Gonzalves, and *Re-evolve*, organized by Reno Ursal and Tony Santa Ana as a fund-raiser for Filipino Youth Coalition in San Jose. Along with these CDs, we were blessed to be published in 'zines started by such creative and productive artists like Michelle Magalong who put together *Pinaytration*, Ryan Yokota who published *This World Is Ours*, and Wendell Pascual who created *deKonstruk*. I am now honored to teach these CDs and 'zines in my classes. It actually has inspired many of my students to produce their own CDs and publications.

SCHOLARSHIP AND SERVICE

Struggle: In the spring of 1997, I took what I thought would be an easy elective at UCLA—Asian American Videography—with esteemed filmmaker Jon Esaki. My classmates Lakandiwa de Leon and Jonathan Ramos and I decided that for our class project, we would try to document the burgeoning Filpina/o American underground Hip Hop scene in Los Angeles. Justin Lin (now a famous director), who was a recent graduate of the UCLA film school, was the TA for the class and he helped us a lot. For seven weeks, we interviewed artists who were going to Foundation Funkollective, like Kiwi and Faith, Jaime Munson (Poet Name Life), Pia San Jose, Immortal Fader Fyters, Kid W.I.K., Icy Ice, DJ Symphony, Rhettmatic, DJ Babu, DJs, dancers, graf artists. We wanted to interview Apl of Black Eyed Peas by himself, but Will.i.Am wouldn't allow it, saying it had to be all of BEP or nothing. We knew them personally as friends and as a group because of Foundation Funkollective. Our friend Terry Valen interviewed them after they performed at UCLA because we had to all run to class after the show, so we tossed him the camera. We were so pissed at Will's controlling nature that we cut BEP out entirely, because we didn't think they'd make it big anyway. Ha! Remember, this was pre-Fergie! The twenty-minute doc became *Beats, Rhymes, and Resistance: Pilipinas/os and Hip Hop in LA*. It screened at Visual Communications' festival Chili Visions. I'm still so proud of it—we had no idea really what we were doing then, but we just really wanted to show how honest and raw and beautiful this scene was in 1997, with Hip Hop and politics changing our lives as young Pin@ys. You can find it on Vimeo now. We can't formally distribute it because we can't afford the music permissions.

Resistance: Regardless, *Beats* was an amazing video that I still use today in my classes, especially in my Filipina/o American literature class. Yes, Hip Hop is literature. Spoken word is text. Our experiences matter. Now that we're both professors at San Francisco State University, you in History and me in Ethnic Studies, I sometimes look back and think about how much spoken word and Hip Hop have shaped the scholars and activists that we've become. I can't imagine gaining the confidence, courage, and criticalness it gave us anywhere else. People may wonder how the two of us—former spoken word Hip Hop shorties—were able to finish our PhDs, become professors, get tenure, publish books, and start organizations like Little Manila and Pin@y Educational Partnerships when so many people didn't believe in us, in Pinays like us.

Struggle: Yes, it's amazing how we bucked the odds. We came from working-class backgrounds and graduated at the bottom of our high school classes. My book is coming out this year with Duke University Press: *Little Manila Is in the Heart: The Making of the Filipina/o American Community in Stockton*. It's the culmination of 20 years of research, back to when I was an undergrad at UCLA. And now that I'm reflecting on it, I realize how many of the themes in the book were first explored in my spoken word pieces: asparagus in Stockton, food and culture, gender and family, farm labor, even the urban redevelopment and destruction of Little Manila is in one of my early pieces. I did a spoken word piece on Filipino food in 1994 and now I have an article in the recent Asian American food anthology, *Eating Asian America*, on the history of Filipina/o American food! The spoken word scene gave me a place to think about these ideas, to articulate my feelings about myself and my hometown, to learn how to be fearless and speak my mind. And when I co-founded the Little Manila Foundation in 2000 in my hometown, my many years of performing my poetry in front of people gave me the training and much courage to speak out against the destruction of the historic Little Manila. The Pin@y Hip Hop and art and intellectual world in which I found a home in LA and the Bay, and my sisterhood with you, made all of this possible. I don't write much poetry anymore and I've left performing poetry and spoken to the next gen, who have taken it to the next level and I give them all the props they deserve. But my PhD, my job as a history professor at SF State, my activism, my writings, my books, even my dabbling in documentary filmmaking—you can draw a direct line back to LA in 1994 and meeting you at a spoken word event to find where it all began.

Resistance: I never realized while we were so immersed in the moments that being a Pinay spoken word artist would really matter in our futures. We lived for the moment. We spoke our true word. And somehow it helped us find purpose. In my second year of teaching at SF State in 2001, I started Pin@y Educational Partnerships (PEP), an ethnic studies educational pipeline that currently has nearly 60 volunteer teachers and two hundred youth at five schools. PEP gives kindergarten to doctoral students opportunities to learn about how to "lead the world to transform their worlds." Hip Hop exists in every PEP classroom, whether it be graf-writing, emceeing, dancing, and/or turntablism. Hip Hop has truly shaped my pedagogy. My lessons have soundtracks and lectures are in the form of mixed tapes. On some days, I even reminisce and teach through spoken word. It is so a part of ourstory, it is a part of our journey, it is a part of you and me. Lastly, I want to talk what it means to have a sistafriend like you. Beyond the poetic memories of performing, recording, publishing, teaching, and serving our communities, I'm blessed to have met you twenty years ago because I met my best friend, my sister, my comadre, and the ninang to my daughter. In many ways, I have to thank you for keeping me alive. And yes—you can draw a direct line back to LA in 1994 and meeting you at a spoken word event to find where it all began.

Struggle: Awww, now I'm going to cry. I love you, my comadre!

As we sat down to write this memoir in dialogue, we realized that we've moved at such at fast pace that we've never really reflected on the last twenty years. So much of what we've been through as spoken word artists, as scholars, as Pinays, is too much to tell in this short piece but what it comes down to is that without the struggles that we've survived, our collaborative resistance would not be as strong.

THE QUEEN IS DEAD …

By Bambu

"this is not a song to gas a girl's head, or get a girl to bed, a proclamation that the queen's been shot and dead … "

this is how a song i wrote in 2009 begins, prefaced with a disclaimer stating that the song is not another attempt to woo the woman listener into putting her guards down and buying into the deceptive colloquialisms of a "conscious rap song." i was super jaded when i wrote it. i just found out that the man responsible for teaching me to understand gender balance and apply my gender politics had just been caught in a long-standing affair with his co-worker. i was hurt. he called his wife his queen. he paraded his adoration for her at every turn, and he jeopardized it all. he was the framework for me, and many other young men he mentored, as the man who challenged patriarchy and misogyny and won … so we thought. admittedly, i disregarded his humanity and his allowance to make mistakes, but i was young and idealistic, so *fuck him* was the foundation at the time. i was conscious about not including details surrounding the incident into the song that might've caused harm to a family already going through it. in retrospect, i'm glad i had that much restraint.

"… grind on a woman at the club while his wife spends the night with his kids, he sees his life like a bid …"

i recognized early in life that our society is structured by class. i recognized that those classes were usually patriarchal—meaning the men dictated the division of classes—and women have been marginalized outside of those classes. not truly being included, but instead being patronized and objectified, paraded at every turn as an accessory. whether it be in the workplace or in popular culture, there is a very visible glass ceiling for our sisters. as men of color, we are plagued with the feeling of being second class in a world being molded by white supremacy, and because of this, we are conveniently ignorant to the oppression of women of color. with that said, once this

155

veil of selfishness is lifted, we try to play catch-up by trying to cut out words used to oppress women, embracing a misguided sense of monogamy and gravitating toward women who don't *seem* to conform to the societal confines of femininity. we do all these things without checking in with ourselves and properly processing our own histories. as a pilipino man, the cultural stigma surrounding gender equality is steeped in the country's marriage to dogmatic catholicism. that's to say, women came from the rib of adam and therefore are indebted to man. this marginalization of women has become the status quo of the pilipino and the greater culture—and manifests in our own personal lives.

"… i know some players out here, gon' say i'm blocking that cock, thing is i'm man enough to step up and the rest of y'all not …"

arrogant. at the time though, i felt like i had unlocked something that my conscious rap counterparts had not. i felt special that i believed i had recognized and was willing to write about something we kept under wraps: sexual opportunism, macktivism. this is a by-product of not going through the processes of checking in. a consequence of not challenging preconceived patriarchal perspectives. the learned behavior can be greatly outweighed by the generations of sexist "cultural norms" passed on by the father figures in our lives. whether biological father, step dad, older brother, teacher or too short, we find our own personal models as men and we carry on tradition. unless we are earnestly fixed on walking the walk, the surface attempts to play the part will eventually give way to *carrying on tradition.*

maybe you have no idea what i'm talking about it. maybe you truly adhere to the principles of a gender-equal philosophy, but for those of us who are welcoming of the challenge to surface chauvinist ideals embedded into your hypermasculine foundation, then i encourage you to indiana jones the *shit* out of your personal history. you'll find the bedrock. don't be afraid to be ashamed of what you've been led to believe. the process and how you deal with what might materialize during your search is to become your footing as a feminist ally.

"this is why i don't refer to women as queens, 'cause you got fingers like me could squeeze an m-16 …"

here's a great example of my own growth. there are two problems with the line above: my belittling of the word *queen* could be easily misconstrued as me telling women that the appropriation of such a word as a means of empowerment is bullshit … that's not what i'm saying at all. though the term *is* rooted in a typically oppressive societal structure, i understand the need to empower as a means of coping and strengthening the fight. the second issue with that line truly reflects what i was just talking about in regard to personal process. *the queen is dead*'s second verse exposes a few flaws in my own understanding in that i use a masculine-based aggressive, combative, and violent tool to draw the line of balance. violence, combat, and aggression make up a large part of my interpretation of what it means to be a man. now, since i was also raised with the misguided perception that my station in life was that above a woman's, in that same line, i'm kind of saying that in order for a woman to be considered my equal, she has to come up to *my* level. violent. aggressive. combative. problematic. violence and aggression should not be synonymous with manhood. a woman does not need to appropriate masculine traits in order to garner genuine respect as an equal. recognize the problem. dissect the problem. process. build. apply.

these self-imposed studies of past works are examples of me weeding through my own shit to find out where my current view of feminism lies and where i ultimately want to take my feminist understanding. the day before finding out about my mentor's indiscretion, my comprehension of gender equality and gender balance was frivolous, at best. i stopped saying "bitch," i thought "*being honest about it*" made womanizing okay, i shook my head at misogynistic hip hop lyrics and i wrote songs calling women queens and regurgitating chestnut phrases from feminist slogan boards ... it was frivolous as shit. no genuine understanding was built. i just followed along with the new circle of friends i'd made—they just happened to read cooler books. that's the point of this whole thing, right? to be genuine. to keep it real. there's nothing realer than owning a critical grasp of your imperfections and having the honesty to tackle them as a part of a collective principle.

writing, recording, and releasing songs like *the queen is dead* was therapeutic and crucial in documenting my development. along with the peer-building, the conversations with elders and my community work, studying my own sonically documented history has proven to be the greatest contributor to my maturation as a pilipino man.

WRITING WRONGS

I wasn't a writer until I realized I had a story.

Now, I can't shut up. Which is good. Well, it feels good … which is what "good" should mean.

When I first found out I was supposed to write music, I listened to Biggie, Tupac, OutKast, Nas in my room on my cheap headphones. I sat by a boombox all day recording around the DJs and radio drops, transcribing the lyrics, rewinding, risking accidentally deleting the whole joint, and wasting a whole afternoon waiting for them to play that shit again. Then, I'd practice and practice until I memorized everything, and perform in my mirror. I didn't realize it then, but I was learning about cadence and breath control and rhyme schemes from some of the greats. Still, aside from just enjoying how words bounced around in my mouth, and consonants fought over where to land, I also enjoyed the anger. These dudes were angry—they were sounding off about their environment, so determined you could hear the saliva popping off the mic. In my household, there was a lot of anger, but you wouldn't say a fucking word about it. You couldn't, or else. Here, anger could jump off the whole conversation, a conversation I wasn't allowed to have.

Well, I was 11 or 12. I was an immigrant. Lyrics about Biggie's Bed-Stuy and OutKast's East Point Atlanta felt a world away, because these were stories about the underbelly of America, the harsh reality of the American system, and I wasn't *American. I observed, I understood, but I couldn't participate. Not me—a Pinay whose family left during the fall of the Marcos Administration, so that I could have a bright future and eat steak dinners and drink whole—not powdered, not evaporated—whole milk. I'm one of the lucky ones. Look at your cousins who live in shanties without shoes or any education. And, you're uncomfortable because the police come around the block bothering the boys standing by the 7-Eleven? Your mother was a lawyer; now, she works as a cashier at the Chinese grocery. This was done for you.

No, I was meant to write.

There were so many like me … I grew up in San Francisco's Sunset District, where the population was predominantly Asian—as in *Asia* Asian. You could hear every Chinese, Vietnamese, Cambodian, Lao, Filipino dialect before hearing a butchered English word. You could smell the fish market next to the liquor store next to the fish market next to the liquor store, all run by a husband-and-wife team, with their listless teenagers as the cashiers. My friends, all children of immigrant parents, came to school with putrid, generic Tupperware lunches in plastic bags. The select few proudly waving their shiny plastic lunchboxes probably didn't know how obvious it was that their prized cases bore telltale signs that they were fakes purchased from Chinatown. No, we were blissfully unaware …

Until we went home, and no one was there, because our parents worked double shifts. My best friend, Laura, youngest of 13 to two Chinese immigrant parents, took the L train from 41st and Taraval to Westportal Station, and transferred to the T train to Hunter's Point for a dangerous, 1½-hour trip to and from third grade because she didn't have anyone to pick her up. The mischievous girl at my babysitter's house told me a secret about her uncle while she showed me my first pornographic magazine. My downstairs neighbors hosted a constantly changing community of transient immigrant relatives whose clutter piled to the ceiling in the moldy one-bedroom. We all had cockroaches. We all had sad, robotic parents. This was life in an immigrant community for an aloof child placed on a pathway to be railroaded by the American Dream.

Me, personally? I was in a loving family of sorts where my parents looooooooved me, but not one another, really—or, at least, not in the *right* way. I was so desensitized to the turmoil in my family that when my friends came over, I was completely oblivious when they'd cringe as my dad beat up my poor mom who would try desperately to keep her voice down in the next room while we watched S.N.I.C.K. This was daily. But, they worked their asses off at menial jobs when they had been upper class in the Philippines—they, the children of three lawyers and one doctor, met in law school, had maids, had drivers—just to provide for their Hope. They took their time to help me with my homework, teach me math, and have conversations with elementary-school-me about religion, politics, and the law, which is, I feel, why I skipped from kindergarten to third grade, and would eventually continue on to law school. My childhood was bad, but my parents were good.

We came to America due to a combination of the fall of the Marcos Administration as well as the turbulence of their relationship and how they feared it would affect me. But, life in America as an immigrant is rough as a single parent, so their paths kept colliding, whether out of monetary necessity or an actual love for one another. I was a good kid, precocious and well behaved, until I hit junior high, then I wasn't. I looked around and decided I was angry. By then, my parents had broken up for good, and I was living with my mom and 5-year-old sister in spare rooms provided by people from church. Then, understandably, the effect of her abuse took a toll on her mental health, and she started hitting me. I moved in with my dad, but he couldn't afford me, so I had to pay rent at 13. He was really an awesome dad, but he was a terrible husband and an alcoholic. I learned too much as a kid—and, I'm sure other children of immigrant parents will agree when I say, because they were assimilating while I hit puberty—it felt as though we were raising one another, like I was a third parent. Well, I was arrested twice in high school—once for shoplifting and once for possession with intent while under the influence, etc. I don't want to get too into it, but it's safe to say that you do these kinds of things when your family life is insane, you're poor, and you're a teenager paying rent.

I want to say that this is very hard to write, because it's intensely personal and because I don't want to seem ungrateful. But, just because it's uncomfortable to talk about, or just because I've come to completely accept and even appreciate the way I grew up as an integral part of why I am who I am—both of which are true—doesn't mean that my experience is invalid or irrelevant for the purposes of reflection or stimulating conversation. And, isn't that what hip hop is? What's more hip hop than an uncomfortable conversation about personal hardship and circumstance to which other people might relate and maybe even feel a freedom from sharing a common experience? What's more hip hop than the feelings of a disenfranchised youth cracking under the weight of the realities of the American Dream? To me, the immigrant experience is hip hop, and that's how I realized I have a story to tell through music.

I'm meant to write.

I started rapping heavily in high school. By then, we had been moving a lot, and it was my sophomore year when my dad and I wound up in Daly City, a city bordering San Francisco. At 35% Filipino, Daly City has the highest concentration of Filipino people of any other city in the U.S. Because I was surrounded by Filipinos, all the kids I rapped with were my own race, and my identity as rapper changed; I wasn't defined by my ethnicity anymore, but by my message. Suddenly, I felt for an instant how it might feel as part of the majority, which, if you can imagine, is just the opposite of how being a minority feels. Unencumbered by the ridiculous weight of racial divisions, I was able to focus on who I was as an artist.

This was also around the time that mainstream hip hop artists were evolving, as well. I had been in love with Missy Elliot in middle school—*Supa Dupa Fly* was one of my favorite CDs. When I first started tinkering with music, I thought I was a singer-rapper hybrid. No one embodied who I wanted to be more than Missy. That was until I met Erykah Badu. Then, Lauryn Hill shut it down. Having been in a political household, and encouraged by my parents at an early age to chime in on conversations about America's involvement in the Marcos Administration and immigration reform, I was highly aware of my own political and social compass. By the time *The Miseducation of Lauryn Hill* dropped, I already knew I wanted to be either a lawyer or a politician. Then, I heard Ms. Hill rapping, and I saw my two loves—politics and hip hop—reside in one woman. There was no brighter, more encouraging beacon of light than Ms. Lauryn Hill.

I met Nina, a *mestiza*, in high school and we became best friends fast. In her I found acceptance personified. If I ever felt like too much of an anomaly in a teenage world where girls cared too much about gossip and boys, Nina was readily available, in her hoodies and baggy Gortex windbreakers, to assure me that a 14-year-old adolescent girl who was equal parts obsessed with hip hop as well as political theory could coexist with the Brendas and Donnas off our hallways. Nina and I spent every afternoon trying to catch cyphers after school, or sticking around after the janitors were done sweeping when the breakdancers slid out to go crazy in the hallway. Hip hop was such a boy's sport, whenever there was just one chick rolling bolo with a group of dudes, usually it was to tag along with her boyfriend; she was not a participant, she was a fan, or a "breezy." But, with Nina and me, we were just all about music, and the boys had to respect us. We weren't trying to catch boyfriends; if anything, we were trying to check all the boys who would treat us differently by schooling them. We hung around this all-boy crew who would rap into this shitty karaoke machine all afternoon recording shitty-quality tapes that were the most awesome thing ever. Finally, the kid whose parents owned the karaoke machine said there was a space on one of the tracks for me. I was juiced, and I went home and wrote with Nina. But when I went to his house for our session, he had written my verse for me, ready for me to learn. He looked dumbfounded when Nina and I went bad on him—something about "fuck you" and "women's lib." I defiantly spat my own verse, which impressed everyone, and I felt amazing. I'm sure if the song is still in existence somewhere on tape, it is horrendous and I'd probably want to burn it before it found YouTube, but it was everything to me at the time.

Between high school and college, I discovered several locations in the city for open mic nights—The Cellspace, Rockin Java on Haight Street, etc. I was at City College of San Francisco by then, and, like most community colleges, we had a collection of students who were committed to reading Noam Chomsky, smoking weed, and complaining. I feel like the college experience is usually intensely political, especially in the Bay Area where our roots are firmly planted in grassroots mobilization propelled by counterculture movements. Compound that with the dense population of young immigrants at our 'hood community college, and you find yourself in the middle of walkouts protesting tuition hikes, and rap cyphers featuring dudes in Che Guevara shirts dropping lines about labor laws, all on a Tuesday afternoon by the humanities building. My days were filled with politics, and my nights robust with hip hop. It was nice. I joined a band where I sang and rapped, then, I learned how to play the drums. We had a monthly party at a bar I was too young to be in for 10 or so of our underage friends. I changed my major to political science. I went to protests and raves alike—protests to see Dead Prez and Dilated Peoples, and raves to see Aceyalone and KRS One. I chose a new favorite member of the Living Legends every month, and I lived to see the free Hiero shows at UC Berkeley. Underground hip hop in California was an incredible force. People worshiped these legendary rappers strictly based on the strength of their performances and word-of-mouth advertising. I didn't know I'd be rapping with some of these underground heroes somewhere down the line, and, if you'd told me then, I wouldn't have believed you.

Between high school and college, several circumstances accelerated my interest in law. Besides my personal run-ins with the law, which led to a brief probation period wherein I dealt with probably the least-interested juvenile probation officer, as well as a court-mandated counseling-based deterrence program, which only really introduced me to more kids in my school with the plug good weed, my friends and I were constantly harassed by police. We weren't the best kids, but we were corralled and treated like second-class citizens. Then, two of my friends were murdered—Fernando was beaten to death (killer not found) and Justin was shot in the chest (killer in prison)—within months of one another. Then, a month after Justin's death, a man with a knife broke into my office and tried to rape me. The police officer who responded to my 9-1-1 call accused me of covering up for a family member or a boyfriend who had gone too far one day, but now I didn't want to get him in trouble. I felt helpless and angry, but my resolve to become a lawyer to help people like me in situations was the salve that eventually allowed me to heal.

I started recording here and there, and haphazardly finished an album as a member of a group by the time my MySpace page caught 6Fingers' eye. 6 had just released a project with Vallejo rapper Topkat, and, that year, Topkat's "Here to Stay" was hot in the Bay with something around 10,000 YouTube views in one day. I met with 6Fingers in his studio, which he called "The Guts," and we eventually recorded my first album, *The Diamond Dame*, in eight months. I didn't know what I was doing recording *The Diamond Dame*; I had been rapping here and there for several years, but never thought I'd actually get to work on my own full-length with a producer of such high caliber. Recording in The Guts was not glamorous: The Guts was a home studio in a garage in inland Vallejo, which, if anyone knows Vallejo, is an icy tundra in the winter and an inferno in the summer. Plus, 6 had a thing for cats that had a thing for inflaming my sinuses, and the mic was situated somewhere by the dryer and the water heater in the laundry room where the cats run shit. I didn't drive, so I'd take an hour BART train ride to Concord, where 6 picked me up to drive the remaining 20 minutes to Vallejo. We independently pressed and distributed *The Diamond Dame* and it was one of the most glorious times in my life.

I was also in my first year of law school at Hastings. All the crime books in high school, and political theory discussions in college, and I knew that I could either spend my days complaining by the humanities buildings of life, or transform myself into an advocate for others in my community who've been bullied by a system that wasn't made for them. I grew up a poor, immigrant child, the product of a broken home, and without health insurance. My family was shuttled in and out of dilapidated apartment complexes, makeshift in-law units, and spare rooms, some not suitable for human inhabitants. God blessed me with strong resolve, and I'm proud to say that I turned out all right, but I didn't want my experience to have been in vain. There are lots of lawyers in this world, but not all of them can speak from this platform of truly having been in their client's position, living through the unique hardships one faces as a young child in a country that will not slow down for a small immigrant family to get it together.

We released *The Diamond Dame* during the summer break between 1L and 2L, and I'm still unsure how, but it sold copies without my doing any real promotion aside from a YouTube vlog and some MySpace posts. Maybe in exchange for the bad luck bestowed upon me in my youth, the gods decided to cut me some slack and smiled favorably upon my music career. This was evidenced in a number of ways, but most notably in the following: Firstly, what I can only describe as a Hail Mary move of blind bravado, 6 sent Del the Funky Homosapien of the Hieroglyphics a MySpace message with my URL. Surprisingly, Del responded favorably, recorded "Whatta Ya See" for *The Diamond Dame*, and eventually continued on to become a mentor of sorts for me as an underground Bay Area hip hop artist. Secondly, I moved into an artistic, female-led household in the Excelsior District of San Francisco with a photographer named Kirstina, who snapped *The Diamond Dame* cover and album artwork, and Krish, who would become another powerful figure in the Filipino American hip hop community, Rocky Rivera. She began seeing Bambu, then of The Native Guns, while we lived at the infamous Brazil and Madrid house, and the three of us continue to make music to this day, which is amazing. It's difficult not to feel empowered as a Filipino American in hip hop when you're living under the same roof as some of our community's pillars, all marching side by side to the beat of our own *tinikling* sticks. Thirdly, shortly after releasing *The Diamond Dame*, I was nominated by *URB* magazine in their annual Next 1000 issue highlighting who they believed to be the next 1000 up-and-coming hip hop artists in the country. I think this, along with the favorable response to my album in general, and a kooky music video for "Yummy," caught the eye of MURS, former member of the Living Legends crew and organizer for Guerilla Union's annual indie hip hop music festival, Paid Dues, which I performed in 2010.

I would graduate from Hastings in 2010, and, in 2011, I released a string of music videos and two albums, *Dulce Vita* and *Raw Gems.* My approach to music has never changed from when I was in high school, or when I was a kid, really. I approach music with reverence; I understand that I'm lucky to be a participant and that nobody—not music, not the audience, not myself—owes me anything. When I keep this focus, the music comes out purely, and not forced. I know I'm lucky to be able to continue making music. I'm not trying to actualize an illusion of grandeur here; music is already the reward.

In February 2012, I returned to the Philippines for the first time since we left, and the Philippines was not what I expected. When I was a kid and I was naughty, my mom would scold me saying, "If you act up, I'm sending you back to the Philippines," the implication being, of course, that life in the Philippines was undesirable, and you were much better off here in the U.S. than back to that place we left so long ago. Well, in 2012, the Philippines had its own growing art scene. I palled around with a painter, Dee Jae, a transplant from the Bay Area who is now living off his murals in Manila. He introduced me to rappers, photographers, videographers, producers, everybody. I did an internet radio interview, a photoshoot, a mag interview, and two shows—things I would try to do during a tour stop in any city in the U.S. was available for me in the Philippines. My big homecoming show was on my second-to-last night at B-Side in Makati, Metro Manila. Dee Jae painted a 4x8 foot mural of me holding a microphone. My mom came and stood on a chair drinking a San Miguel beer during my set. The girl in front row with her hair cut exactly like mine was in my "Yummy" music video from four years ago knew all the words. It's curious how much you can feel at home in a place you haven't been in over twenty years, but I felt home.

Now, it's 2013. I'm at Oakland International Airport writing this piece for a book about the Filipino American experience in hip hop. I'm on my way to Las Vegas to meet with some promoters. Since yesterday I received 1,000 units of my new album, *Sugar Water*, from the pressing company. They were delivered to the modest law office, my mom's, where I work as an immigration and bankruptcy legal assistant. Oh, and tomorrow, the California Bar Association releases the results for the February 2013 bar exam, which I actually took not too far from here in downtown Oakland. Full circle much?

I'm a sack of nerves. I'm drinking whiskey at four in the afternoon and I've barely slept or eaten all week. But, this moment is unlike any other moment, and I'm savoring it. This moment is the exact culmination of everything I've been through, everything that was strewn upon me, and everything that was withheld from me. I let it mold my approach to my careers—music and law. Instead of letting it destroy me, I let it create me.

This story wrote itself.

BOOTY POP MADNESS

THE NEGOTIATION OF SPACE FOR GAY PILIPINO AMERICAN MALES AND CHOREOGRAPHED HIP HOP

By Joseph Ramirez

INTRODUCTION

As hip hop has begun to be redefined and articulated as new forms of expressive art, a younger generation has come to understand hip hop as more than just songs and music and have critiqued the historical pillars of hip hop as restrictive and, at times, "old fashioned." With the growing sensation of choreographed dance performances with a younger generation and capitalized by MTV through their show *America's Best Dance Crew*, hip hop has been redefined through stylized and highly choreographed sensations. This has been called "choreographed hip hop." Choreographed hip hop has taken many forms with stylized techniques and fashioned story lines or scripts that blend music, dance, and theatrical dramatization as a form of stage performance. From high school air bands to college cultural nights, formalized dance companies to dance schools, choreographed hip hop has transformed how youth express their understanding of hip hop culture. Yet, unlike many venues of hip hop expression, choreographed hip hop has also pushed the boundaries of the stereotyped hypermasculine and homophobic hip hop scene. For many who identity as gay males, choreographed hip hop has allowed them to not only express themselves through art and dance, but also receive acceptance and respect from their fellow dancers. Choreographed hip hop has accepted queer-identified individuals far more than those who follow the traditional pillars of hip hop, and especially for gay males, has been a venue to not only express their sexuality, but also find community and camaraderie where they will not be judged because of their sexuality. This article looks at interviews that were conducted from various hip hop dancers who are self-identified as gay males, Pilipino Americans, and who belonged in the choreographed hip hop scene. Though this article seeks to raise awareness of the experiences of Pilipino American gay males in choreographed hip hop, there are some struggles I faced in trying to find qualitative data to analyze. First, all individuals whom I interviewed referred to choreographed hip hop as merely "hip hop," not differentiating the uniqueness of their expressive art form from other pillars of hip hop; second, the genre that has been expressed by dance companies, dance schools, school cultural shows, and school dance teams to categorize this type has also been referred to as plainly "hip hop"; and third, those whom I interviewed and those whom I chose to mention in this article are not the shared experience or does it seek to homogenize all the experiences of gay males in choreographed hip hop. Though my interviewees did not touch on race directly, they see hip hop as part of a growing Pilipino American culture that is unique to what their parents know as Pilipino/American culture(s). This ethnography also does not seek to state that this stylized form of contemporary hip hop expression aims to our demand to be incorporated into the hip hop genre as it also seen by many as a counter-culture to traditional notions of hip hop, a form of cultural deviance from the stereotypes that bound hip hop into hypermasculine, sexist, and queerphobic spaces. I argue, however, that through "hip hop," gay Pilipino American males are able to find acceptance of not only their gender identity and sexuality, but also find a place where they are not racialized or othered. It is through the performance of choreographed hip hop do race, gender, and sexuality blur and find acceptance, where in traditional hip hop, such intersectionality is rarely acknowledged or accepted.

REFLECTION ON INTERVIEWS

> "Hip hop has changed and unlike rap and other hip hop forms, this form of hip hop is more accepting of gays. Especially rap where it only talks about sex and is gay-bashing. The hip hop now allows gays to be accepted."
>
> —Raphael V.

My interview with Raphael was unique in that he is connected to various hip hop dance teams ranging from California, Nevada, and up to New York. In our interview, Raphael expressed how hip hop dance teams are more welcoming and accepting of gays and lesbians and are usually the center of attention during complicated routines or sets. He did express that it was a challenge at first because the hip hop dance scene had a stereotype by others in hip hop as not being considered an actual hip hop expression or genre and how it attracted gay and lesbian dancers. He views other forms of hip hop as sexist and queerphobic, but it is through choreographed hip hop that gays (and lesbians) find acceptance and community. One follow-up question that I did try to address is the location where Raphael has had a deep connection with choreographed hip hop scene. San Francisco Bay Area, Los Angeles, New York, and Las Vegas have a different social and cultural acceptance (or tolerance) of queerness and he admits that location can contribute to how gays (and lesbians) are accepted in the hip hop scene. Also, these places have a high population of Pilipino Americans in a concentrated area. Raphael has expressed that Asian Americans who are queer-identified in these regions are very visible in the dance scene. It is at times when their families do not accept their identity as being queer that their adoptive hip hop family does. This rhetoric of the "hip hop family" not only creates an imagined space and familial bonds with other dancers who identify as queer or heterosexual, but also becomes a sustainable venue to be queer without judgment.

The "family" unit is very common in the choreographed hip hop scene. Whereas it does enforce a particular non-queer-based notion of a family unit, it does, however, queer the traditional notions of what a family may be socially accepted as. Raphael navigated these terms in his interview referring to both family units as his "original family" or "family-family" and his "hip hop family." This trend of classifications became a common trend in all my interviews as each of the Pilipino American males referred to both types of family units that they are associated with. For Pilipino American males, this negotiation of familial bonds allows them to find a form of imagined acceptance from a family unit that is unique to queer youths trying to find validation for their gender and sexual identity.

> *"[Choreographed] Hip hop respects gay dancers because they can do moves that both guys and girls can do and we're respected because of our talents. The straight guys don't care about us being gay. They care if we can dance the next piece."*
>
> —Frank H.

Frank's experiences in hip hop stems from trying to find acceptance from others and not necessarily be judged by his sexuality. Though Frank is also from the San Francisco Bay Area region that has a more liberal stance on diversity, the negotiation of space with heterosexual males in the same team is a phenomenon that he was able to navigate through. Our discussion brought up issues of initial discomfort and fear of others finding out his queerness and how it might contribute to how others viewed him. Though this phenomenon with Frank can be presumed to be a unique experience, many gay males do find comfort in choreographed hip hop scenes alongside heterosexual-identified male dancers. Though usually it is heterosexual-identified female dancers who are the first to find out about queer dancers' sexual identity, the fear of coming out to heterosexual males is not as violent as to coming out to heterosexual males outside of the dance scene. Frank expressed how his queerness has actually contributed to his acceptance in the group and how, though gendered and sexualized in a unique way, allows him to be versatile in feminine and masculine types of dances and allows him to participate in dance sets that are reserved for a particular gender. In his perspective, his versatility has contributed to his success and respect from others in the dance group.

> *"I demand respect when I teach hip hop. No one messes with me or other gays in the dance team because they know that we bring in dancers to the team and we bring people to watch us. An all-straight dance team will not have a lot of followers. Us gays come to watch each other and dance competition is like gay church… all the gays come out."*
>
> —Teri J.

Teri self-identifies as a fem-dancer, a genre of dance found in choreographed hip hop that is gendered to be (hyper)feminine and dramatic. Fem-dances incorporate moves that are hypersexual and draw from dance moves from famous hip hop and pop singers. Teri explains that these types of dances are usually reserved for gay-identified males and females (regardless of sexual orientation), but is received differently by audience members if a known heterosexual-identified male performs it. For heterosexual males, this form of performance excites the audiences and, according to Teri, boosts the respect of the dancers for their versatility. Yet, it is also known by dancers that such performances are done with the approval of female dancers and queer male dancers. This power dynamic between heterosexual males and queer males is unique to the choreographed hip hop dance scene. Queer males have a sense of authority and power of the performance of femininity, which is ironically accepted by female dancers as well. Many queer male dancers in their understanding of gender roles and enforcing an environment that is accepting of differences embody this authority of feminine performativity.

As Teri also expressed, gay males in the dance company also attract other gay males to participate as audience members during competitions. Referring to dance competitions as "gay church," they raise awareness of the social and cultural investment of gay male youths to the choreographed hip hop dance scene. Though there is no actual explanation of this phenomenon, Teri expresses that there is an un-talked-about understanding of gay males' (especially gay Asian American males) direct contributions to the social climate of hip hop dance competitions. Calling the social and cultural investment also as a form of "gay pilgrimage" brings a different phenomenological socio-cultural understanding of how gay Asian American males travel to different competitions to watch their peers or favorite dance team. Within these settings, gay males are also reunited with their gay peers as they participate in the dance competition as spectators. Teri (along with Raphael) expresses how for many gay Asian American males, the distance of travel also shows the commitment they have to the team of their choice. As gay male spectators, heterosexual males also experience a phenomenological relationship with gay spectators. Teri calls it "ego boosting" when gay male spectators surround heterosexual male dancers after the performance demanding pictures and/or autographs. Here, if not acceptance, tolerance of gay male spectators by heterosexual male dancers becomes a normative experience. Teri jokingly stated that heterosexual males who are not acknowledged by gay spectators sometimes feel left out and hurt.

CONCLUSION

Choreographed hip hop blurs the lines of gender identity and sexuality through the performance of dance sets and theatricalized story lines. The interviews conducted with Raphael V., Frank P., and Teri J. are but a mere glimpse of the complicated relationship with gay-identified male dancers and a traditionally masculinized hip hop scene. Though choreographed hip hop is still being debated within many hip hop circles on its role in and contribution to the scene, participants give little concern to criticism from those who practice traditional notions of hip hop. This genre, if you would like to refer to it as one, of hip hop is both a deviant form of socio-cultural understanding of the hip hop scene as well as a form of self-expressive counter-culture and counter-narrative that demands to expand not only the understanding of contemporary hip hop but also the cultural acceptance of non-traditional bodies. For gay Pilipino American males, choreographed hip hop offers a multiplicity of counter-culture and counter-narration to hip hop and dancers' relationship with their families, which helps them understand their own cultural identity as Pilipino Americans. As a springboard to future research, the role of queering hip hop and critically looking at performative bodies must be addressed not only in academia, but also on stage and in the streets.

V.

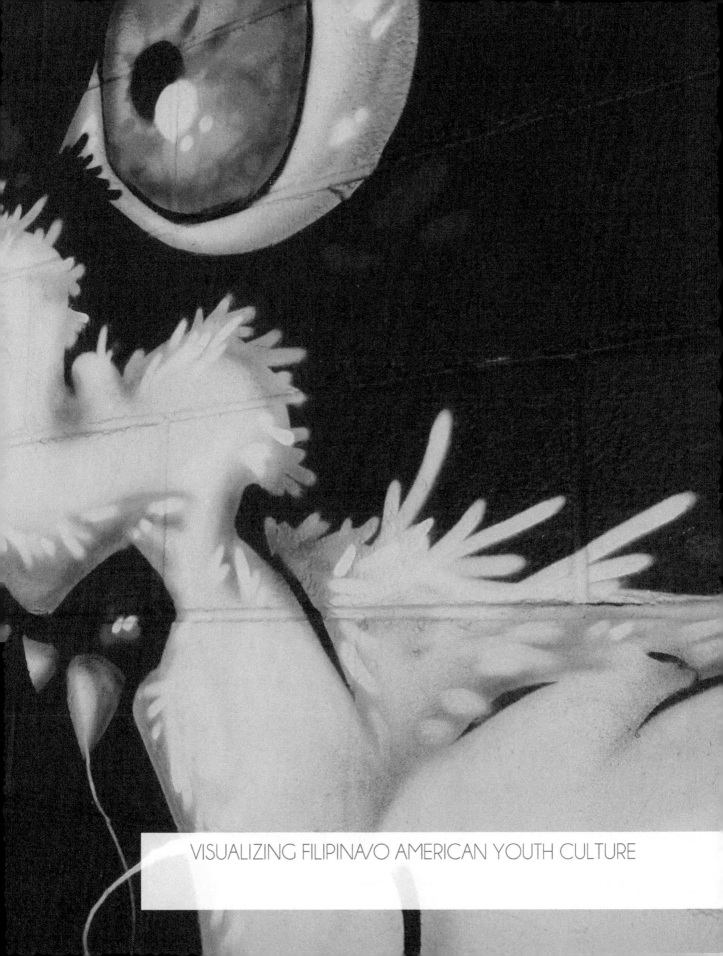

VISUALIZING FILIPINA/O AMERICAN YOUTH CULTURE

FILMING APPEAL

A CONVERSATION ON FILIPINA/O AMERICAN REPRESENTATION

With Gene Cajayon, Patricio Ginelsa, John Castro, DJ Kuttin Kandi, and Mark R. Villegas

Kuttin Kandi: Can you give us a brief introduction about yourself?

John Castro: My first short film was *Diary of a Gangsta Sucka* that I did while I was a student at Long Beach State University. It was a short film about Filipino American wannabe gangsters. And then I followed that up with writing *The Debut* with Gene (Cajayon) many moons ago … Following *The Debut* I also went to culinary school and I created a comedy, a political cooking show along with Robert Karimi, a spoken word artist. I toured that for a couple of years and I also dabbled in stand-up comedy recently.

Gene Cajayon: Been working in film for twenty years now. *The Debut* started out as my thesis project when I was in film school [at Loyal Marymount University]. For my degree I shot a trailer of the first few minutes of the early draft of the script. That's how I got my degree and how I got started working on the film. And it just kinda grew into this feature length project and when I saw *Diary of a Gangsta Sucka*, John's legendary student film, I asked him to come on board to work on the movie with me because he offered a very different perspective than what I had growing up in Orange County, and we worked on it ever since. It took us about eight years to finish the film, then another three years to get the film distributed so that people could see it. And since *The Debut* came out, I've worked in what they call in the industry "development hell." I've been working on one screenplay after another. Getting close in some situations but no cigar. And I'm still doing that. I've got several projects in development right now, writing with a number of different writers, and hoping that one of these days, if I'm lucky I may get a chance to make another movie. But if not, that first was a pretty special experience. I'm very grateful to have been a part of it.

KK: How did you get into filmmaking? What were the deciding factors that led you to filmmaking? What led you to the path of making the types of films that you've made?

JC: Initially, I was inspired by the movies by Spike Lee. He really started the whole consciousness thing and putting images of your people on film by any means necessary, as he said … . And I really took it to heart. Prior to that, Filipino Americans, Asian Americans, or Pacific Islanders, we didn't have our own Spike Lee out there, so he was the closest thing. There were some early filmmakers like Wayne Wang, but Spike Lee put politics behind it, and his politics behind it and hip hop culture. And as Filipino Americans, we embraced that scene also. It was a natural thing to gravitate towards Spike and be inspired by what he was doing. That made me do the crazy thing and jump into film as opposed to the more safer stuff that we, as a community, would like to do. Engineering, physical therapy, or something like that. But yeah, it was a really tough decision, too. I racked my brain around it. I went through a lot of ups and downs whether to do film or not because there was no real precedent for it … But I was lucky to meet a fellow Filipino American filmmaker named Rod Pulido. Rod and I had the Beginning Film class together and we latched on to each other, supported each other throughout film school, and we were like brothers from another mother. It was good to have another Pinoy in the program with me, to give each other support, because film school is like a miniature Hollywood with all the white kids thinking they're all hotshots even though we were all starting on the ground level. And Rod and I were like, "Fuck that! We're going to take over this film program or the class, at least." We were coming up with the better product and a lot of these kids had nothing to say and Rod and I had a lot to say. Because of our community, we had all these stories that needed to be told. And it showed through our work.

MV: *Diary of a Gangsta Sucka* is a satire. Can you go into the motivations behind that and what you were trying to get at with this satire of this Filipino gangster wannabe?

JC: It was '93 when I shot it, and prior to that, I was seeing the shift in hip hop and in our community. The shift from the late '80s to early 90s, from political, fun-yet-conscious hip hop to more gangster stuff, and then I saw the shift in some of the kids in the community, acting like gangsters even though a lot of them were from the suburbs, they acted like they were from the 'hood and "Here's my EBT card" and shit like that. I though it was a zeitgeist moment for me. I just wanted to capture what I was feeling at that time and it was the perfect thing to poke fun of. Actually for that film, I saw this film from France called *Man Bites Dog*, which followed this assassin. It was a fake documentary about him and following him and his various killings. I was also inspired by Monty Python and stuff like. It seemed like the perfect time and moment to spoof the scene because at Long Beach State, I saw all of these nursing students who were acting like they were hoods, and therapy students acting like they were gangsters, and it was hilarious.

GC: For me, I fell in love with movies when I was a kid, when I found out there was this thing called "Film School" where you could go to college and study how to make movies. I was fifteen years old when I found that out and from that point on all I cared about was film school and movies, and I didn't really want to do anything else, fortunately or unfortunately, depending on your perspective. When I was younger, when I was a teenager, before I got to college, I thought I was just gonna go out and make movies that were just your Hollywood popcorn, big blockbuster movies. And then I got to college and I remember seeing *Do The Right Thing* when I was a freshman. Similar to what John was talking about, Spike Lee was very influential on me, too. Watching *Do The Right Thing*, I remember it vividly when it was screened at the university theater. I was sitting in one long row of film school students. I didn't notice this at the time, but everybody was white and I was the only person of color in that line of film students. And the row directly in back of us was the Black Student Association and they covered that whole row. And I remember at the end of the film, when the pizzeria gets burned to the ground, I was feeling very emotional. I thought it was really intense and I felt so bad for the Italian family. I looked down my row of film students and they were all crying, too, and were just like, "Oh my god. That was just horrible." And then I looked one row in back of me and there is this whole row of Black students and they're cheering. I remember thinking to myself, "Holy fuck! That's just amazing how people can experience a film so differently." It was the very first time that I realized that films were a lot more than just car chases, and explosions, and action scenes, and sexy girls, and this, that, and the other. Then I started taking Asian American Studies courses and kinda came into my own political awakening. From that point on, for me, movies were about trying to say something bigger than just offering us entertainment. Not that there is anything wrong with that, you know; I've developed over the years my fair share of my version of commercial movies, but the whole idea and the reason why I still do this, twenty years on, is the hope of making movies that add to the dialogue. Hopefully to add to the conversation of American film, what it truly means to be an open and diverse society. Challenging the whole concept of a "post-racial" society that we're supposed to live in and all those big issues. If it wasn't for that, I would've quit this business a long time ago. Otherwise, it's not worth working that hard in the entertainment industry if it doesn't mean something more than just the end product. It has to be what that end product does for society and for people around the world. To this day, we still get random emails from people around the world talking about what *The Debut* did for them. I'm the first one to admit that *The Debut* is a deeply flawed film. It's got a lot of heart. It's a good film, but it's nowhere near as good as what I would have hoped it would have been because I made every rookie mistake making that movie. But it's still gratifying [to hear from] random people from all over the world—like I just got an email from a woman from Texas talking about how it saved her marriage. There were also all these crazy stories, from when we went on tour, what it did for people and how it changed their lives. It was pretty cool. And that's the reason why you keep working.

KK: Can you talk more about what you would do differently now if you were to remake that movie?

GC: It's a bit of a trick question … If I were to make that movie now in my 40s as opposed to when I first started the film when I was 20 years old, 20 years ago. And now, I'm a dad, I got two kids, I got a lot of life experiences—a lot of challenging things and a lot of amazing things have happened in the last twenty some years. If John, Pat, and I and the whole *Debut* crew were to make that movie today, it would be a very different film. Who knows what it would be about? Who knows if we would cover that same material? I would like to think that we wouldn't and that it would be a much more mature look back at a very important time in people's lives, their teenage years. But hopefully, with not quite as a simplistic view as the first film had. It's a tough question to answer. I don't know if you can answer that question or that we should because we're very different people now. I feel fortunate that Pat, John, Lily, and all the other *Debut* people are still in my life because we did really go through an amazing experience making that film.

MV: It seemed like everyone was connected from '95 to 2000. Folks were producing video, film, poetry, and hip hop. What was that moment? Why do you think from the mid '90s to the late '90s there was this Filipino American renaissance? What was it about that moment that made it so ripe?

JC: I've been trying to rack my brain with that same question. How *did* that happen? Was it a generational thing? Was it the generation before us that set the table to be able to eat off of it? I don't know how or what happened. I'm amazed by it, too. It was a magical moment where everyone was just coming out doing their own thing, doing amazing things. It seems that we've gone backwards since then. We had Classified records and we had Pinoy and Pinay groups coming out and with the whole DJ thing. I don't know how that happened…

Patricio Ginelsa: I think it's a mixture of generations, technology, the rise of hip hop music. I think pop culture got more prevalent and the rise of MTV. I think our generation was when when movies and blockbusters became very mainstream in a way. When you think of blockbusters, you think *Star Wars* and *E.T.* We grew up with those kinds of movies. I call that period the "search for identity." In the '90s, for me growing up in Daly City, we had such pioneering things happening, like Qbert, who was one of the first FilAm celebrities who came from there. Qbert allowed us to grab a piece of hip hop we weren't known for, the whole turntablism thing. Then of course, you had Classified Records who was creating Jocelyn Enriquez and the whole freestyle movement, and that created a sense of pride; that decade was the golden age of Filipino American pride. I remember Friendship Games when I was going to USC … . Everyone was there. And you compare that to Friendship Games now, it's much different. It's just a college club now. Back then, even people who didn't even go to college headed there promoting stuff. Everything was ripe. The Filipino culture was in the creative mode, finding their identity.

GC: I guess I'm a little skeptical. I used to think that, too, that we started all of this bad ass stuff and the kids coming up after us just didn't have their shit together and they dropped the ball. It's easy to say that and it makes you feel better about yourself, I guess. The whole thing of, "My generation is best and everybody else sucks." But I guess I'm skeptical of that because a lot of it makes me wonder if there is any more or less energy in the Filipino American community, at least the youth community, the Filipino American second generation that has come up since we came up. I get the sense that there is just as much energy—it's just spread out among so many other areas. With YouTube, and with the democratization of media technology, where anybody with a laptop and a prosumer camera from Best Buy can go out and make a professional-looking music video or short film or whatever it might be and you can upload onto YouTube. The unfortunate side effect of the democratization of technology and YouTube and the internet is that everybody can now have voice. So when you have that many more voices out there, you don't get as much attention on a handful of individual, big voices, like there was in the 90s. You had Classified Records, you have One Voice, Premiere, our film, *The Flip Side* from Rod, Jocelyn Enriquez. So these are a handful of voices and of course, they are going to get a lot more attention because there's not a thousand other voices competing with them on cable, the internet, YouTube, and everything else. So I question whether or not the generation coming up after the '90s in the FilAm community is any less competent or artistic or creative. I just think there are so many more channels to absorb this content that it just doesn't stand out as much as the time that we did it. Maybe if anything, we were just there in a Goldilocks age where there was just enough media and just enough interesting stuff happening where people noticed more often than they do today. But I don't know, I could be wrong about that. There's a lot of people out there, a lot of arguments out there that say, "If that really is the case, then why haven't any other Filipino American feature films broken out?" But then you just look at what Ron Morales just did with *Graceland*, you look at what Richard Wong and H. P. Mendoza did with *Colma* and their other stuff. These are all interesting films. For me, *Graceland* is the best film that's come out this year.

PG: But I would argue that *Graceland* hasn't gotten the kind of attention and hype and the community support that *The Debut* has gotten and the whole phenomenon.

GC: When Ron contacted me earlier this year before *Graceland* came out in theaters, to try and reach out to the Filipino community and try to see what he has to do to get the kind of grassroots support. I told him very honestly that because of what the movie is, you're not going to be able to outreach to the Filipino American community the way we did simply because of the subject matter. It's a kidnapping thriller set in Manila and it's in Tagalog. It's a tweener film. It's not going to appeal to the ABS-CBN, *Wowowee*, first-generation, new immigrant crowd—the ones with satellite dishes who are watching ABS-CBN or GMA all day. It's not going to appeal to the second generation, hipster, hip hop kids who are consuming KevJumba videos and Patricio's work because it feels very old-school Filipino. To look at *Graceland* and not see a world-class example of filmmaking is not to know what a good film is. You watch that movie and that's the reason why he's got representation now and he's making his rounds in Hollywood. He's doing super well because of the fact that he made a really good fucking movie. Our movie was a John Hughes movies but with a Filipino American cast. And so of course we're going to get a huge turnout from the Filipino American youth community because that's the audience it was made for. *Graceland* wasn't made for teenagers. I used to think that perhaps there was something about the fact that after *Flip Side* and *The Debut*, nobody stepped up to the plate, but if you look at the amount of feature films that have been made, it's just really tough to break your feature film out these days. The media landscape out there, it's really a thousand-to-one shot that your film will break out. If you look at Sundance, they get maybe three thousand applications every year and they take in 50-ish feature films and at most a hundred, if you look at international stuff. And out of the 100 movies or so, may 20–30 get any meaningful distribution going forward. If you compare 30 films getting meaningful distribution and you compare that to 3,000 independent feature films getting made every year, then you are talking about a 100 to 1 shot for your film to get noticed. Plenty of Filipino American feature films have been made; *Cavite* is another excellent example. But it's really, really hard to get your film breaking out. … [W]e self-distributed our movie. We drove around the country for two years going from one city at a time, hitting up every high school, college, church, restaurant, social group, you name it, to tell them about the film, pretty much one-on-one, which is why to this day, *The Debut* is the highest grossing Asian American self-distributed film of all time by a long shot. Nobody has ever tried to mount that kind of an outreach program before or since. So we were hard for that gross, that nearly 2 million dollar gross, but I don't fault the other filmmakers for not having the huge gross *The Debut* did because you have to give up two years of your life to self-distribute the film the way we did it. It's not something most people can do. So it comes back to this thing where we have a very different media market and landscape today than we did 10–15 years ago.

JC: *Graceland* and *Cavite* are really good films, but I'm thinking no one is going to watch these films if they don't put their own effort into the marketing. It's cynical but I'm watching these films thinking they're not gonna make any money or get the support we had because they're not going to spend two years marketing and getting their team together. I don't want to make a movie just so you can burn it or see a stream on the internet. I want to put people in seats. But the whole paradigm has changed since we made *The Debut* and now we could have made it on HD and spent less money.

MV: What about a sequel?

GC: We would love to make a sequel but it's not financially viable. If there is an investor out there who wants to get behind the highest grossing Filipino films of all time—the movie grossed over 5 million dollars worldwide, which is a decent amount of money, but it's not a slam dunk in terms of getting financing for the next movie.

MV: Can you talk about comparing the immigrant generation versus the Fil Am second generation? What are the necessary components to make sure that you are speaking to a second-generation audience? This goes for the music videos as well. What needs to be there to show that appeal?

PG: That feel for the Fil Am community? There's two things: it's usually an issue that's important to the community, and number two it's always like a twist—like something you see in mainstream or Hollywood but then you "Filipinize" it, if that makes sense. For example, when I tackled the "Apl Song" music video—I didn't just write that and throw in the whole WWII Filipino veterano into that story because it's such a big issue. That's not how I tackled it. I tackled it more from a story perspective first and what the music meant and basically about Apl's journey of being adopted and the rags to riches story. But then, after I thought of that story, then it was about the old guy stuck in a convalescent home, which was based on a true story.

I treated this video like, if this is the best platform to showcase our community and this is a music video that can say something positive about our community, what would it be? I didn't tackle it in a sense where this is a commercial that's promoting the Black Eyed Peas and we are helping them sell records. I didn't treat it where this is the music video that's going to introduce Apl as the Filipino in the Black Eyed Peas, and not Taboo. Because everyone thought at that point that Taboo was the Filipino guy. The whole thing with the Filipino vets was very hot then and it came natural to weave it into the story line. I kind of approached it that way. More like a responsibility versus it being a commercial piece. Come on, a music video in a convalescent home? Number one that's already a different kind of music video. But to actually talk about an issue that even if a lot of people in our community know about it, that my job was done if a young kid—Filipino or not Filipino—saw that would say, "What the hell is all that protesting going on?" And made him research it more and learned more about the issue, then I felt that I did my job.

There's no formula. I can't tell you this or that because even with "Bebot," sometimes it doesn't work. There's things we might not agree on. The last video we did was with Bambu and Prometheus Brown, "Books," and that was a different twist on the sitcom. You can't define our community by just one thing. A lot of people think that you can define our community by certain images. What makes our community so unique, I think, is the fact that we are so diverse and different in our culture and religions and even our languages, we have so many dialects. But I think one thing that unites us all is that—we saw this first hand when we did the tour for *The Debut*—all of us as Filipinos, we have that bond, that brotherhood, that sisterhood that we really know. It's the same thing when you see a Filipino [and] you do that little nod.

I want to capture all of that. There's no one visual. That's a key a lot of people try to break. I think that's why Ron Morales had such a tough time marketing *Graceland* and why you don't get that phenomenon like with the *The Debut*. There's a code that people are trying to crack.

GC: Going back to your original question, I think there are elements that unite the second generation of the Filipino American community. It does tend to revolve around what your book is about: hip hop. I think for all people of color, but for Filipinos especially, there's at least in the subconscious but sometimes a very conscious understanding that hip hop speaks to the experiences of oppressed minorities. I think that the fact that *The Debut* was chock full of hip hop, all of the top Filipino American hip hop groups were in that film—we have up to three dozen Filipino artists from all across the world in the film; a majority of them were all hip hop artists. It's what speaks to the second-generation community.

There is that really big generation gap. If a movie is perceived as one of your parent's Filipino movies from the Philippines, you can pretty much guarantee that the kids are not going to be that interested in seeing it. You guys remember when we were on tour, we heard that all the time. A lot of the kids would be like, "Oh, it's not one of those corny movies from the Philippines, is it? I don't want to go see a movie like that." There's such a huge difference in perceived quality when it comes to Filipino movies from the Philippines versus American films.

But at the same time, *The Debut* was a unique kind of history because not only did we have a significant budget to make the film, we also had so much support from the community itself, especially on the music side. If we were able to organize that much Filipino American talent at that one place at that one time for one movie, again, the same thing would happen today. It might be a little bit more internet-heavy, and there might not be as many people in the theaters if we did it today, but it'd still be a very significant cultural event for the community. I don't think that's changed.

JC: I think a lot of the choices we made for *The Debut*, including the music, I think a lot of those were marketing decisions too. We wanted a variety, and we also wanted artists from around the country. Because if we had a group from Virginia Beach or New York, those locals from those cities will hype it up. That's why we had the girls from [the R&B group] Premiere in the film, because they also had their own built-in marketing. A lot of it was very conscious, from the casting to the music to the locations. We wanted to make it as universal as possible. We didn't really name [the location where the family in *The Debut* lived] "L.A." either. People thought it was L.A., but we didn't want it to be city-specific, because we know how our community could be when it comes to claiming cities.

KK: Has there been any negative feedback or responses to your films? How did you all respond to that?

GC: I would categorize it from two camps: hate from the first-generation community because we specifically chose to show a working-class family, because that is the reality. The Filipino American community is a working-class community. And so a lot of the white-collar, richer, more upper-middle-class Filipinos were embarrassed—because white folks are going to see us on the screen for the first time, we shouldn't show those "other" Filipinos. When in reality that's how it is. The other big category of haters were second-generation Filipino American kids who were hating on their community. It happened all the time. They would see our presence in the movie theaters, they would see the posters and stuff and they would just laugh at it, saying that, "Oh that's one of those Filipino things. That's lame." The common theme that unites both categories is just your typical colonial mentality. Your classic Filipino, thinking yourself as less than, inferior to your white colonial masters.

PG: There are a lot of Filipinos who see the Bambu videos that we did, the "Crooks and Rooks" and the "Old Man Raps" videos based on Bam's life. But they say, "Why is he acting black? I'm ashamed for them being Filipino because they are acting so black." A lot of that comes from people who don't understand what it's like growing up in the U.S. and coming with a different perspective.

The big controversy was the "Open Letter" with "Bebot" that was back in 2006, right when the video ["Bebot"] was released. The challenge of producing that video was difficult because we had shot "Bebot" unlike the "Apl

Song," which was funded by the label, [and] we had to do it independently by Apl and myself because the label didn't get behind it. We did two versions of the video ["Bebot Generation 1" and "Bebot Generation 2"]. The "Open Letter" was drafted by professors and grad students. The issues were complaining about the portrayal of women. Basically the whore, the virgin, and the shrill mom were the three stereotypes that they were calling me out on. While I felt that those were issues that were important, I just didn't think [those issues] related to my video because—and I can talk forever about this topic—I felt they didn't give me enough credit for what we did. When we shot it, I didn't do a cattle call. When I shot the video, me and my crew made sure that everyone who came on our set, we told them, "Dress like you would, like you were going to a barbeque or going to a house party." We wanted people to dress individually how they would, and not tell them what to wear.

It does take a whole village to make a video. And we had a lot of community support making it. I even had support from Dawn Mabalon and Dylan in terms of helping them. Because if the "Apl Song" was trying to talk about the issue of Filipino veterans, I was trying to wrap the whole "Bebot" video around support of the Little Manila Foundation, and try to get them support and acknowledge their preservation of the two buildings that were part of Little Manila in Stockton. And I felt that the whole controversy kind of overshadowed it to the point where the Foundation tried to distance itself from the video. So all the plans that we had—we were planning a charity concert for the Black Eyed Peas in Stockton—all that just kind of hit the fan because of this controversy. And in a way it affected my relationship with the label.

And to this day, I second-guess myself what I could have done differently. But it hurt. That controversy hurt a lot. Whatever momentum I had at that point, it stalled my career, and I had to reset and figure out what I wanted to do. It took me two years to get back on the horse again after that controversy. And it's a controversy that people basically forget already [laughs]. But it definitely affected my career. To this day, what kind of pissed me off about that whole thing is that this is a topic that even if these academics felt it was an important issue, they felt they couldn't talk to me directly. They just put it out there in an uncontrolled environment online and not continue the conversation. It was almost like: throw it out there. Anyone who knows me I do a lot of talks. I go to high schools, I go to colleges, I do this thing called Pinoy Sightings all the time. And yet all the forums that everyone tried to create, whether it was in Santa Barbara or even a taping on ABS-CBN, and any of the writers [of the "Open Letter"]—because there were like six people who wrote this thing—none of them wanted to join this forum. Or even talk in a debate. It was almost like they threw it out there, and didn't continue the conversation.

For me, I felt like I was in a defensive mode immediately. I had to not only protect my reputation, but I had to show them my point of view. To this day, I still feel like I'm doing that.

GC: I think there's an interesting point to be made here. Whenever you have a scarcity of images—see Pat's made a ton of music videos, but the obviously the most high profile of his music videos were the Black Eyed Peas ones. And so whenever you have a little bite of the apple, and you have a lot more people who want a bite of the apple, there's going to be a really healthy, and at times counterproductive dialogue about those images. Whatever your feeling is about how Pat dealt with those "stereotypes" about Filipino women, at the end of the day he did not get enough credit getting the video made in the first place. Otherwise, there wouldn't be anything to talk about. So because of the fact that there is so few of those images out there, his video comes along and all of a sudden everybody gets overly critical for their own good because there's nothing else to compare it to, so you're going to focus all the energy on this one thing that doesn't deserve that much negativity. It's an unfortunate side-effect of not having enough representation in media.

JC: Imagine if the African American community protested every music video that was on B.E.T. It'd be non-stop. With the dearth of images, we have to single out the few that come out. If we had the same amount of images that the African American and Latino communities come out with, then maybe we'd have less controversy. Pat's was one of the few Filipino American videos coming out that year, he had to be singled-out. It still pisses me off today what Pat went through.

PG: I'm still waiting for the "Open Letter" for Far East Movement or Bruno Mars.

KK: As men making music videos, are you conscious of the way you portray, or what you shouldn't portray—is that something that you consciously do in that context? Like having a feminist lens in some way? And when you do have those responses—and I do feel as well, especially if you know people in the community who are criticizing your videos and to send an open letter out, there could have been a conversation there, especially if you have close connections to them prior to the letter going out. Is that something that you consciously already do, prior to making films, thinking about a Pinayism perspective as male producers, filmmakers? Is there something in practice that you try to be aware of in choosing to portray or not portray?

PG: I'm always conscientious of what I portray, not only for the women, but any group, religion, or whatever. For me, I always talk to people, when I write something. It's like getting feedback from your colleagues. I always talk to people. My wife Melanie always helps me out in telling me what's right or what's wrong. I talk to my brother a lot for what's funny or not. In a sense, I'm not going to censor it because for me, my goal as a filmmaker is to not only take the good, positive stuff of any community and put it out there. I think, for me, my goal is to portray the human qualities of everyone. And not every is going to have a positive image. In a way, what's more appealing as a storyteller are the negative aspects of a character. The character flaws.

Right now I'm re-mastering my old movie, *Lumpia*. We're celebrating ten years, even though I shot it like seventeen years ago. I do find myself filtering the language of that movie more. Even though I'm keeping a lot of "fucks," "shits," and all the bad words, for the new version that I'm releasing next month, I've actually kept all that bad language, but I can't bring myself still—I censored all the "n words," "niggas," and there's instances of them saying "faggots." It happens twice in the movie I wrote when I was seventeen. Even though this is what kids would say at that age, I even censored myself because I can't bring myself to even include it this new version now. I think it comes with age and being mature, I think. In a way there's a responsibility. I feel I'm catching myself a little bit. I don't know if it's because of the "Bebot" controversy.

GC: Every filmmaker is different in how much political consciousness they're gonna have. I think of myself as—on a scale of one to ten, ten being super-politically conscious, I would probably put myself somewhere on the seven or eight range. If you're gonna write, you have to write from the heart. You have to write what you really feel. You have to find the right balance between trying to be respectful and trying to give voice to all the different characters and different experiences out there, and then staying true to the story that you're telling. So you're not always going to completely address feminist perspectives, gay and lesbian perspectives, whatever different perspectives as much as everybody would like. You have to let your story and your characters be your compass.

And sometimes you're not going to satisfy people as much as you would like. And that's what makes this line of work more interesting. Because not everybody will be happy with what you do. Especially with the internet, where anybody can go out there and say horrible things anonymously, so that's what they do. You can't let it stop you. You gotta get up and keep going.

KK: I think that's always been discussed in not just film, but theater as well, "I'm not going to satisfy everybody." Especially when it becomes art and something being "controversial." What do you think is the fine line when it comes to things like that. The fine line of, "We're just trying to show these other perspectives... ."

GC: The line is always moving. There is no line, because the line is different in every single case. It's always going to be different depending on the circumstances. That's why for me, whenever I have political questions, I'll send the script out to a handful of people whose opinions I trust, and they all happen to be academics. They can kind of vet the screenplay ahead of time and inform me what kind of trouble I might get into, and what issues I may be stepping into that I didn't realize I was stepping into. Once I understand what I'm getting into, I'll make reasonable efforts to address issues that might be insensitive to groups. But I'm not going to completely gut a script, or completely change my vision because it might piss somebody off. There's always going to be somebody who's going to get annoyed. It's inevitable. Especially when it's a minority community where they don't have enough representation. Again, it's that whole scarcity thing.

PARTY FLYERS

By Glen Parin, Mark Pulido, and Eric Sanford

Spectrum Entertainment throws a jam in San Diego, 1988. Art by Glen Parin.

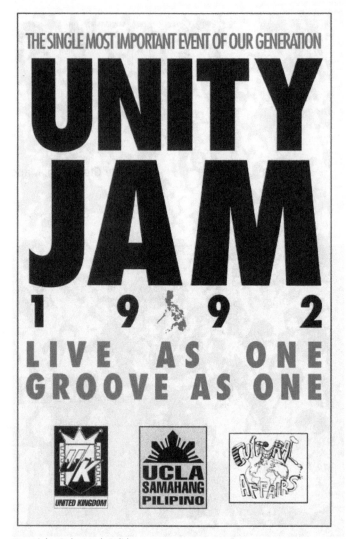

Copyright © by Mark Pulido

Unity Jam was one of my proudest organizing achievements during my college years at UCLA because it took the collective effort of so many good brothers and sisters to converge our generation from up and down the state at UCLA's Student Union in Ackerman Grand Ballroom for what we billed as "The Single Most Important Event of Our Generation." It took the shared leadership of my roommates (ICEBOX) and United Kingdom Attractions managed by visionary Tom Corpuz (pioneering mobile DJ crews from Cerritos and Los Angeles: Publique Image Musique, Majestic Productions, Ultra Dimensions, and Double Platinum), b-boy Crews, UCLA Samahang Pilipino and Southern California Pilipino American Student Alliance leaders, and UCLA Student Government leaders.

We collaborated to bring our unique scene and the elements of Hip Hop, at the height of the Stop The Violence movement, to UCLA. In our take on that sign of the times, we succeeded in inspiring and uniting (for at least one

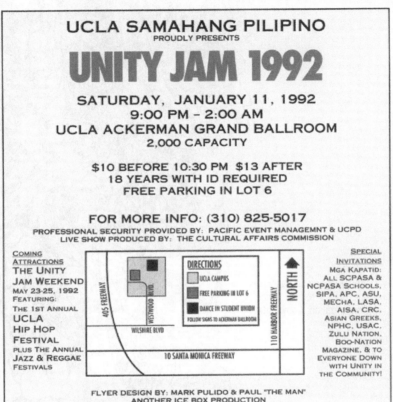

night) the once warring factions of our youth generation throughout California (gangs, car crews, dance crews, etc.) for the jam to end all jams—2,000 strong with lines out and around the building and all the way down Bruin Walk. The event featured a showcase of up-and-coming Filipino American entertainment from the Bay Area to LA to San Diego that no one had ever seen before. From that night, I knew that my life would never be the same. I learned that through organizing and sheer will, anything could be possible for our community. I knew then that I would run for UCLA Student Body President four months later, to build upon that positive vibe we created together and to build momentum for our future that would hopefully propel us from campus back to our respective communities to serve the people.

—Mark Pulido

DJ mega crew United Kingdom collaborates with the University of California, Irvine's Kababayan student organization. Copyright © by Eric Sanford.

HIP HOP, FILMS, AND BEING FILIPINA/O

EXCERPTS OF A CONVERSATION WITH FILMMAKERS AND PRODUCERS

With Rik Cordero, Eric Tandoc, Corinne Manabat, Christina Dehaven, and DJ Kuttin Kandi

On who they are and their filmmaking works:

Eric Tandoc: I was born in San Diego, but I grew up here in west side Long Beach. One of my first projects were on my skateboard crew on the west side. It was during the mid 90s when there weren't many skater kids of color. In Long Beach, it was mostly white kids. The history and growth of our multi-ethnic skateboard crew here and all the things we had to deal with from the police to gangs to the growth of the crew beyond it originally was. My most recent project, which has been in different film festivals around the US and also in the Philippines, is the *Sounds of a New Hope* in 2009. It's about a Filipino American Rapper, Kiwi, who was based here in LA and was involved in gangs, but through Hip Hop he was able to get involved in community organizing. He went on a trip to the Philippines to integrate with the urban poor, urban slum areas and doing Hip Hop workshops out there. He did the same thing out in San Francisco using Hip Hop as a way to organize and empower young Filipinos. Right now, I'm also the National Secretary General of Anakbayan USA which is a progressive youth organization that's struggling for genuine freedom in the Philippines, genuine freedom and democracy and it's all over in the Philippines and we have eight overseas chapters here in the US. For me, filmmaking is more of an extension of community organizing and a way to really spread the message and raise awareness and motivate people to action in a way that will not just let people know what's going on but be a tool of organizers to bring people to make change.

Corinne Manabat: I've done mainly documentaries, one of them on an Asian American woman who was in a gang in the 90s and her transition of getting out of a gang. And I'm currently working as a co-producer on a documentary feature called *What Happened to Danny?*, which is Private Danny Chen who committed suicide due to racial hazing in the military. I also made a documentary about three brave Asian Pacific Islander youth who have struggled in their lives due to their immigration status and that is currently online on Vimeo. And I guess I got started in filmmaking. I'm also a media educator and I teach young people to empower themselves through video making. I think for me the filmmaking that I have done especially with the background of community organizing and dealing with youth of color.

Rik Cordero: I'm from New York, born and bred. Actually, I got started as a DJ. I started in the mid 90s. I went to college, to art school at the New York Institute of Technology and graduated with a computer graphics degree. Then I got into filmmaking in 2007 after shooting a music video trailer for Jay Z off his *American Gangster* album. That's how I got my foot in the door in the music industry. Through that, I was able to shoot a bunch of music videos which led to a nomination for the BET Awards, Video Director of the year. That same year, I won a Best Film award at the HBO New York International Film Festival. After that, I was doing more music videos that led to some commercial work. In 2011, I won an American Advertising award for the US Marines Corps commercial which won a National Campaign. And recently I was nominated for Best Music Hip Hop video at the MTV VMAs [in] Japan for a Japanese artist named AK69.

Christina Dehaven: I've worked as a production manager, line producer, co-producer and producer on numerous short films, features, documentaries, commercials, and music videos, including for the Grammy Award winning group, The Black Eyed Peas, and participated in the production of *The Debut*, serving as assistant to director Gene Cajayon.

On how they bring Hip Hop culture into their films

Corinne: My love for Hip Hop—I guess that brought it in tune with my love for Hip Hop because the music I was really into was tuned in with me. I love it. I can relate to what they're saying, their lyrics. I love to dance, it's kinda the way I can express myself. I myself back in the day used to breakdance, be a b-girl. I love my 90s Hip Hop. In my filmmaking, just for some reason, it's natural for me to incorporate Hip Hop music, especially underground Hip Hop music, from the Asian American community because I would feel inspired when I would listen to the music and sometimes that would prompt me to incorporate [it] into my documentary films. Especially when it relates to struggle and the stories that I hear from young people in New York City talking about separation of family or talking about identity. It was just easy for me because I loved it, but also because the communities I was working with were young people, and they have love for Hip Hop ... it was natural to incorporate [it] in the filmmaking that I have done. Hip Hop in my own life has been influential. It just made sense that it became part of the filmmaking that I would do.

Eric: Like Rik, I myself was a DJ. Ever since the end of high school, I started getting into filmmaking. Through the documentaries I was making, I approached it as a DJ. From everything down to the editing. It's kind of like making loops, cutting to the beat. Actually, the way that I visualize the approach to creating documentaries is like a video mixtape where each topic or scene is like a song in a mixtape and a mood. And it's just a transition from different moods as the story progresses. So, the music aspect is a really huge part whenever I create any pieces. It's kind of like the heartbeat behind the content of whatever the subjects are talking about. One of the ways I more explicitly blended the two, the passions for DJing and filmmaking, is that we created in the past few years this live performance of my new film, *Sounds of A New Hope*. I used video-DJing, using the technology of Serato Video, and broke each scene into it's own video file, which can be manipulated by vinyl control records and performed by mixing and editing the film live, throwing in new scenes with each new performance. And in between scenes, I would throw in video instrumentals, kind of like music video instrumentals that depict what the rappers are talking about. And Kiwi and other Fil-Am rappers who are also part of the same progressive movement that we're part of come out and perform to add a more Hip Hop performance element to the presentation of the film. So, it's really like a culture production rather than just a film screening. That's a live remix aspect of it.

Rik: I guess [for] most of us, Hip Hop was a huge influence growing up. It was everywhere, at parties and everything. So, it was just kind of ingrained into a lot of creative stuff I was into. I guess my bread and butter was music videos for a long time, primarily Hip Hop music videos. I guess it just came natural with the DJing. Like Eric said, kinda just hitting these beats and knowing timing and all that stuff. A lot of my treatments reflected that and the way that I edited the aspect of my Hip Hop education, so to speak. And then I guess, my music videos were primarily Hip Hop. I guess a lot of my narrative content purposely tried to make it something other than Hip Hop, just to experiment and whatnot, as well as other music videos in different genres. What's weird is that when I first started, a lot of my early music videos were for indie rock bands from Brooklyn. I was trying to be really experimental, I was still learning, so I was just trying different things. Some of them weren't executed that great but I was learning how to tell a story. I felt like that community back then, 2007–2008 for indie rock bands, I felt like I never really got the same kind of love that I would get for experimenting for a Hip Hop artist. A lot of those videos I did for the rock bands never really did anything or never went anywhere. It wasn't until I started shooting for some up-and-coming Hip Hop artists from New York is when I felt like my work was actually appreciated and I was bringing something to the table. So, that was good and that was definitely gratifying. On the other end of that, after doing it for so many years, sort of like being this Hip Hop music Video Director, you sorta get pigeon-holed in doing the same things, getting pitched the same things. They kinda want you to repeat yourself; that's the drawback. I have so much love for Hip Hop and doing so many videos for low budget and for free sometimes just because you're so passionate about the culture. It's sort of like a curse sometimes because you may not get the big opportunity or something that is not Hip Hop that you're interested in because all of your work reflects something that's just urban culture. That's some of the struggle that I deal with day to day, but Hip Hop is definitely a part of me, and it comes out naturally in the work that I do.

On the challenges of navigating mainstream and independent films as Filipino American:

Christina: It can be sometimes [that] the struggle [is] between "independent" and "industry." In some ways, I kind of think of independent as industry, but it really kinda depends on the project. But I think in terms of the complete independent spirit defined as telling a story without any restraints, without anybody like a producer or money person breathing down your neck, calling the shots, without telling you what to keep in or what to keep out. I think our production of the "Bebot" video (for The Black Eyed Peas) is a great example. I've been so blessed in the few experiences that I've worked with fellow Pinoys in Hip Hop music. I think "Bebot" is a good example of that, working with the Peas is a good example of that. I've been real blessed to work with somebody like Pat Ginelsa, who has such a love, and he is an activist in the community as well. He has such a love for story-telling particularly. As a lot of people know, he focuses on Filipino- and Filipino American-centric content and subject matter for just about everything he's done for his career. He's wonderful to work with and when we approached the Peas for the concept for the "Bebot" video. It was very much a historical piece like I knew Pat to be capable of, to create a historical piece about the manongs from Stockton from back in the day. Just to create something really beautiful that was reminiscent of the spirit of Michael Jackson but also the spirit of our community and many centuries of migration especially to the West Coast. And you know, Stockton, California is such an important part of our history as Filipino Americans. And he'd been dying at that time to incorporate it into some sort of story-telling narrative. So, this was an opportunity to work with the Peas coming along to do this video. Every once in a while, I've experienced this in other areas of my professional filmmaking career where you also sometimes have to give and take. And then you make a decision of how much you're willing to do and how much you're willing to sort of negotiate particularly with the artists, in this case essentially bankrolling through a project. One of the beautiful things that we were able to do with The Black Eyed Peas I have so rarely come across since then with other clients and other production companies that I've worked with is the ability to make two versions of the video. One that really spoke to the original narrative that Pat had in mind, which was the period piece version of Bebot set in the 1920s and 30s in Stockton, California and then there was also the version that the Peas were asking for, which is a little bit more contemporary that complimented sort of what their vision of the song which was essentially was a dance song. And that story wasn't exactly what we were going for in the beginning. It was really just more of like a house party with more of just a party vibe, something light, something fun. We found a way to come up with two versions by some miracle under the same budget, which I don't even know how we managed to do. And that really fulfilled Pat's desire to represent the community in a positive way and represent the community in a historical way—but also [to] satisfy the other part, which is purely Hip Hop, which is purely dance, which really is just fun, for the sake of fun and to show both sides of our community both past and present .... .

[W]hat happens often when you have such a small minority of artists in a bigger community, particularly in the Filipino American film community, [which] is so, so small—it sometimes lends you to criticism from your own community, and that was something we had to interface with especially when we released the second version of "Bebot," which was the more contemporary sort of dance-party one. I was really calling on the opinion of fellow well-respected members of the female Filipina American community to sort of get advice about that video. You also open yourself up to with that kind of opportunity, which is great. You also expose yourself in a way to criticism from all aspects of the community. Some people will be supportive of it and some people won't. I think in this case that I was referring to was the fact that we had some women in the video that were—what's the word—I wouldn't say they were very provocatively dressed, but they were very sexy. It was not in a way that I as a Filipina American woman [can say] that I was personally offended by it, but there were some members of the community [who] were. And you can take that in one or two ways; you can say, well, this is just a reflection of one of the many by-products of what it means to create successful content in the community and in the industry, and you're gonna be subject to all kinds of feedback, be it positive or negative. That is just the one experience that I can speak to that sort of addresses the question of what are some of the challenges and some of the advantages when you have to balance that independent spirit of filmmaking that we know and love versus the industry spirit which can sometimes align with your own personal beliefs and values and your version of story-telling, but it can sometimes require you to negotiate and sort of question and sometimes either make compromises and compromise your vision like Rik sort of mentioned earlier for the sake of incorporating with your clients or whatever it takes to keep the client happy versus sticking 100% to your own vision. Sometimes you do have to let go of creative control or you will be put in a place where somebody is telling you, "Hey I'm asking you to relinquish some of your creative control because I have the authority to do so." And at that point you have to ask yourself is this really a situation that I move forward in this direction or do I split off and do something on my own. And that is sometimes the choice [for] a filmmaker and a story-teller, going the independent route versus the industry route.

Rik: That was an interesting time navigating the Hip Hop music video landscape back then, like 2007, which is kinda when YouTube just started and street videos was only primarily distributed on DVDs and things like that. The internet was still being formed. When I started doing these music videos independently, it was amazing because

I did most of them for free and most of them because I really just love the artists and I really just wanted to experiment and shape my craft. That part, that early beginning is really awesome. When you start out that way and you're young, you get a crew together; you have like-minded individuals and filmmakers who have the same vision and the same passion. It's just an amazing time and eventually it turns into a career and it turns into working with corporate executives and understanding the marketing aspect of it, that music videos are essentially commercials and you have to make them accessible sometimes. And that could compromise your vision if you are trying to do something different. That's something I've always felt like I've always experienced a lot of times. The one video that I had the most freedom with that I didn't have anyone telling me to change anything was the video with the Roots. It was the song called "Fire," featuring John Legend. That was the one with the World War II period piece. And so they said specifically that the Roots don't have to be in it which basically meant that I could write anything that I wanted to write. They totally believed in the vision, Questlove definitely championed the idea and that was like the moment where I felt supported by both the label and the artist. And that is a very rare thing. I don't think I ever really experienced the perfect alignment of the stars. Thats pretty much my experience with the independent route and dealing with the corporate stuff.

Corinne: Unfortunately, I haven't been as in the film industry in the mainstream, but having some of these films at film festivals was cool—to have it so that it went to a broader audience—but for myself, it was so important as a filmmaker to have my film be shown to different communities. Because at film festivals I feel like people would go to them because people have a love for film, but the people that mean the most to me were probably the ones right next door to me. Deep in Queens, they can't go to film festivals, so it's like, let me bring your stories in film that're not in the mainstream and bring it to them. I feel like that's my motivation of being a filmmaker.

On bringing in the Filipina American identity into their films:

Christina: I grew up in a very diverse neighborhood. We were probably the only Filipino family in that particular corner of Philly. There's a very, very small contingency here in the East Coast, let alone the South Jersey, Philadelphia area—it is very, very small. When I went to college , when I went to NYU for film school, you [could have] count[ed] less than five fingers for Filipinos who were in the undergrad film program at the time. It wasn't until I got this job in *The Debut* as Gene's Director Assistant that I was motivated to think about what it meant to be a filmmaker of color, let alone a Filipino American filmmaker because I never really put quite the two in the same context. I never really thought about that, and frankly, it never mattered to me. I always thought about being Filipino as family; that was what I defined as family and culture for myself personally, and my film-makng was something different. But working on *The Debut* had opened me up to a much larger conversation and to think about it particularly in terms of casting. Because one of the first things I encountered was when one of my jobs on *The Debut* was to help with the casting. I had just flown out of New York and started working in our office down in Venice at the time, and it was right in the middle of casting. And we had already locked Dante as the lead and we were looking for our lead, our Annabelle, the girl that Dante falls in love with. So, one of the things that Gene kept emphasizing to me was that it really had to be a darker-skinned Filipina girl. I never really thought about how important that was, and for some reason it was incredibly important to him and when he explained to me why. He just said that there was so much of an image of the Filipino look especially in the mainstream media in the Philippines that is very Mestizo-looking. And of course, I'm Mestizo 'cause I am half. And it was something I just never really thought about, how important that was that we focused on a particular look, particular skin tone for Filipino because to me we are such a tapestry, different looks and different skin tones that really run the spectrum. But that was something that was really important to that film and that was something that I really started to think about it and started to respect. And I respected what he was trying to do, and he was very particular with the casting of all those roles. But that was really important to him because the film was 150% Filipino American culturally-centric and I got it. It was really interesting for me, a game changer in my career, because I was halfway through my college career at NYU. And here I was, working on the first professional feature film I ever worked on and I was working on it with 200 cast and crew members of the Filipino American community. It was such an exciting experience. It was such an interesting and powerful introduction into the two things I love the most or eventually realized I love the most, which was being Filipino and being a filmmaker. And it was the best amalgamation of the two.

So that was really a game-changing experience to me. I would say that moving forward in my career as a woman of color and a Filipina American filmmaker, I'm still in the minority. I try not to focus on it, I guess. I don't know if there have been many experiences that I had to focus on it to be able to do my job as a producer. But it's something that I think about all the time, and quite frankly, it's something I cherish and it's something that makes the experience in film production and being a producer much more interesting to me, to add that flavor to that mix. I look back at all of my experiences, because I've been teaching for almost ten years now and I've been line producing for just as long. And I've worked on so many different projects. And it's been a really long time since I've worked on a project with my fellow colleagues like Pat and Gene and hopefully we do something again together soon. But I haven't really been able to find a project that really impacted me on those personal and cultural and professional level the way that *The Debut* and the way the Peas video did. It's been a good 15–16 years since we did that stuff. But I think about [it].... Those projects, especially *The Debut*, I feel privileged, quite frankly, for my first professional experience in the industry to work on something that was so close to the two things in life uncomposed of, the two big pieces of me which is being Filipina and being a filmmaker.

Corinne: From my experience, I guess it's a little bit different from other folks because I'm mainly a documentary filmmaker. And I think [that] for myself growing up in Staten Island, kind of similar to Christina, in which I was living in Staten Island, in my neighborhood [was made up of] a lot of white folks. We were the only Filipino family on my block. And I'm really proud of that, but growing up, I was facing a lot of racism. I wasn't so much into narrative filmmaking as I was into documentary only because I was asking "How come I am never seeing any of these stories about Filipino Americans, their stories that weren't so model minority?" We're a whole diaspora of lives and stories that haven't been told in the mainstream or even not in the mainstream.

Rik: Not a lot of my work represents my Filipino identity, but it's definitely in a lot of my work—I guess more so in the process of it, more than the actually product. It was definitely an interesting experience trying to navigate the Hip Hop world when it was changing. So, a lot of the artist that I worked with were sort of adapting to a different model of filmmaking, which was a little more guerrilla, a little more gritty. A lot of people know me as kind of soft-spoken, this really quiet and almost introverted person. I had to develop a way of communicating to get a lot of my stories out there. That's just who I am and how I was raised as a Filipino American. It made that process pretty easy; it's really about the hard work, the due diligence. And doing everything you can to achieve your vision. Me and Candice grew up around the same circles and so that sort of was my training with all the DJing and experimenting and being creative, whether it was [through] websites or trying to come up with a skit for a party. That sort of honed a lot of my skills, and so when I started to navigate the waters of the music industry, there were definitely a lot of other Filipinos that I learned from, that I got some great advice from. Back then there weren't a lot of Filipino American music video directors who I was bumping into in New York. I was trying to figure it out. And now I always reach out to a lot of Asian American filmmakers and we always share the same stories and same struggles when it comes to doing a lot of these videos for the labels. So it's an identity that I've always felt part of and proud of. I think it's just certainly a great time for our community of Asian American filmmakers, there's just so many that's going mainstream, getting a lot of accolades and breaking a lot of barriers. I'm just happy to be contributing.

On the intersections of being a Filipina, womyn-of-color, filmmaker:

Corinne: I went to school at SUNY, New Paltz. I was involved in the media department there. I was known as the Asian American girl who loved media. I was totally tokenized, but I was like, you know what, if I am the only one doing it, so be it. But I loved it so much, it didn't matter to me. But I felt like … where are my people of color to help be that supportive network, [or] women in the industry or within filmmaking who were proud to be where they were coming from and to represent women in circles that were predominantly [run by] men? I feel like there were two things happening for me growing up in doing the filmmaking I was doing. I was self-conscious that, in a room, I was the only person of color and the only woman of color. It was a double-standard for me. I feel like … Hip Hop [also is] male-dominated in many ways in the mainstream. A couple of years ago, I worked on a documentary with Roc-a-fella … called "All the Ladies Say," which talked about the trials and tribulations of a b-girl. Because you always see the b-boy but you never see the b-girl and their struggles as women. They always talk about their love for dancing but there's more to that. You love dancing, breakdancing, so much and even after you have children, you still want to dance, but no one really talks about that in these spaces. I feel like I'm always about telling the story of the underdog. I guess it's something I can relate to, and I guess it makes sense that I'm also a media educator because I educate youth to empower themselves through that, through things that they love through video-making. Growing up I didn't have a chance to express myself in that way … I felt like growing up I never had that access. In terms of filmmaking, growing up, I didn't know anyone else, even in the arts I didn't have anyone to look up to. Documentary filmmaking resonates with me more because it's the only way I know that I can help in bringing change to the community.

On community organizing and filmmaking:

Corinne: But in terms of my filmmaking, for story-telling, I'm always fascinated by the marginalized story we don't hear. For me, when I'm finding a character or my subject, I'm just building those relationships for my background as a community organizer as well. Finding those stories, such as working on a documentary about Filipino domestic workers, what's happening in New York City about unfair labor practices, and documenting their stories because its not being shown in the news … that would be the motivation for me to tell that story because I haven't seen it before—and building those relationships and making that documentary for presenting that message out for whoever watches the film to be aware of their stories and the issues that are happening around us.

Eric: I have a lot of similarities with Corinne. For me, even in approaching film in terms of the subjects that I choose is really something that's complimentary to the community organizing work. Before the skateboard film, it's not really about Filipinos, but there are Filipinos in my neighborhood. There's actually a really huge population of Filipinos but it was really more of like our lifestyle growing up here in the west. Later on as I started getting deeper in community organizing I really wanted to start integrating my passion for film so that it could be something of service, something bigger than myself. I also agree with Corinne when she was talking about when you show your film in spaces where there are diverse audiences. It's really important to do that because it's sharing the struggles and issues of our community beyond our community, and we can't just speak to ourselves. We really need to expose [our stories] as far and wide as we can. And I guess in terms of what I want to do as a Filipino, I just feel that there are a lot of stories and struggles that are going on here in the United States and back home in the Philippines that aren't widely known about that need to be known. I really think that film is a powerful way to do that. The project that I'm working on now is really about thinking ahead for the future. [I]t's about the community of political refugees from the Philippines that live in Europe, in the Netherlands, who are politically exiled, who are pioneers of the current national liberation movement in the Philippines and are living in Europe doing international work. It's too dangerous for them to live back in their home country because there's the real threat of violence and assassination. And these are folks who are getting older in age, in their 60s and 70s, who have a wealth of knowledge and experience and insight on the ongoing people's movement that's happening in the Philippines. I just felt that it's very important to chronicle and capture their stories while we still can. Especially for all the future generations that are going to come after them and the youth today who they did start the movement for and who will be the one to carry it on and see it through until victory. So, I guess now a lot of my work is towards specific local campaigns or international campaigns or the longer project of capturing the stories of the veteran pioneer organizers and revolutionaries.

On Filipino American Hip Hop influences:

Rik: I feel like I learned so much and I think it was more than DJing. We all identified as DJ crews, but I feel like it was life lessons I learned and ways to hone my skills because everyone was so talented. And that was really something special. When you're that young in high school, you don't really understand—you just want to do something cool. I look back on it now, and I realize how blessed I was that I was surrounded by so many talented individuals, whether they were writers or dancers or DJs or producers or promoters. All of those different skills I now apply to filmmaking because filmmaking is education, lighting, management, and organization, and telling a story, and editing, and being creative—and so it combines all of these things that I learned by my peers. I guess every now and then, I have to go on Facebook to see what everyone is up to. We have a great tight-knit community of different Filipino American artists that I am grateful to be around and part of.

On the challenges that lies ahead:

Christina: Leading up to this call, one of the things I was thinking about was how many filmmakers I know who are making so much great content. I really hope to be part of this too; it's not really a criticism towards the Filipino American film community but just an observation, that of all the other big Asian American communities that are putting out content internationally … I just think of all the talent that we have both here and in the Philippines, there's so much content out there that's deserving of great exposure. We had in recent years really amazing movies that came out of Manila, came out of the Philippines, independent work, nominated, screened at Tribeca, getting Oscar nominations in the past 5–10 years. I just wish we had more of that. I wish we had another *Debut*, not an identical story, but another Filipino American featured filmmaker out there, or a television producer on that note. To really put something out there, more mainstream exposure is basically what I'm craving, personally as a Filipino filmmaker. I don't know what it's going to take. I really would open this up to everyone—what would it take for us to put us on the map and really get the kind of exposure that our colleagues in the Indian American film arena have had, [or the] Chinese American, [or] Korean American? And to just continue to put out more content. And the truth is, in order for us to be able to put out more content, we really need support—not just from the Filipino

American community; that's the first community we target with our work. And maybe this is me being a little bit naive and overly optimistic, but I think we live in a different environment now than we did 15 years ago when we were trying to raise money for *The Debut*. I don't know if this is necessarily the type of society that we live in now where our first target audience and our first target demographic when we're looking for funding for our project is specifically the Filipino American community. I wish it was be that easy, but I think we have to be able to expand it in a global support to be able to tell the type of stories we want to tell. And the reason why I say that, the reason why I am pretty optimistic about that, is I see it happening with other Asian American themed projects and Asian American themed content. They're not getting all their financing just from their particular ethnic group, they're getting it from all over the world. And I think we just need to open ourselves up and find global support. And of course request and anticipate the support of our own ethnic community, but also try to look at it on a more global scale. And I think maybe starting to open our minds to those kind of possibilities would really help us to get the funding for the projects we really want to do. I don't want to say that everything comes down to money, but the truth is, at the very least it comes down to resources. And it comes down to finding the people that you need to align yourself with to get the resources, to get the access that you need, to great talent, great equipment, to great stages to be able to facilitate your creative vision. So, that is something we're always up against. Money is always going to be a bit of a challenge. But it doesn't have to be the roadblock. It's really just more about resources and what you define as resources, whether it be the support of your community that really supports and loves the type of story-telling that you're interested in and supports your talent and creative vision. And that's really just something that's an ongoing conversation. I just really hope that the outcome is that we all of us have a bigger, stronger platform to create content to get bigger exposure than we are [getting] now.

Corinne: I agree a lot with Christina is saying, especially with access and resources. I know with transmedia, digital media, and the internet, I feel like that's ever-changing, even in the independent world. How do we fit in? How do we have our film incorporated within that realm, because it's changing so fast? But at the same time, it's beneficial to independents like myself in which now we have things like Kickstarter or Indiegogo and all of that, creating that, building that audience online with what's happening right now. At the same time, I'm thinking, will it change again? So, I feel like I don't know if there's a definitive answer or solution yet. But I feel like having these options, alternative ways of thinking about and being familiar with them and always being in the know about it that I myself have been struggling with, dealing with, besides creating my own stuff.. What are the other outlets I may not be thinking of? That's a really, really, big, big question that I would love to someday talk about further, if possible. But I do believe that I want to be optimistic as well about what's going on, but it's changing so rapidly. I just hope I can keep up with what's happening.

Christina: I think that's good news that there's more transmedia. I just came back from a Producer's Guild conference in Los Angeles where this is all we talked about, the fact that there's so many ways to distributing content thanks to video-on-demand. You have Hulu and Netflicks, online streaming. You've got so many different outlets. Youtube created this monster for the entire industry, and the industry capitalizes on that and now we have at least 5–10 different additional mainstream ways for distributing content and that helps everybody, especially our community of independent filmmakers. I see it as a good thing that it's constantly changing. The content that you create doesn't have to necessarily have keep up with the distribution; it's more like, make your content and choose the best distribution outlet for your content.

Rik: I can only speak for New York. I feel like I'm going through that struggle right now, trying to find different ways for distribution, funding, finding an audience. It changes every single day. A lot of the features that I've produced, they [didn't cost] a whole of money. It took a low budget, but even that amount of money seems like a lot right now because technology is getting better, obviously, and there's so much video content that's being distributed on social networks. For me anyway, the video production has a serviceable industry and is kind of dwindling. There are a lot of lighting houses that have closed down in the city. I have a couple of good friends whose bread-and-butters were coloring and editing, and some of those major houses have been laying off people. It's changing, and we all have to adapt. Finding the audience is really what's going to be important, getting the support of the community and finding those stories and developing those stories. Just seeing what's out there. Being amongst the people and the culture. And having something that can connect with people because there are so many great original programming that's coming out on cable as well as some of the series that are coming out on Netflix. There are avenues and there are outlets that we can [use to] reach our audience. Just kinda telling the stories that we can all identify with, now is the great time to do it. I would definitely love to see something that features and focuses on Filipino Americans. I think I'm dying to see another *Debut*. I really wanna see what that's like, like a modern day version or something; it was something so pivotal for me growing up. I kinda wanna see who the next film maker who can deliver these stories is. It's an exciting time.

Eric: I think more subversive things are really challenging the system. One of the challenges that I see coming, growing now and even more in the future, is really the repression that's happening. Especially if you're trying to tell a story on human rights violations. Those are some things that I see in terms of the political climate that could be a challenge for progressive filmmakers to think about. We don't really know how much harder it's going to get in terms of that … that's one of the issues I forsee that could be a possible challenge. As far as future generations of filmmakers, I think it's just part of our role to help encourage and develop younger filmmakers to tell the stories of our community, to do that mentoring and education. I have to really give it up to the folks who came before who helped to guide me on this path, like AJ Calomay from Xylophone films. He would really take me under his wing to go to shoots and things like that. I think it's now our time to do that for the younger folks.

LEO DOCUYANAN

(Photography Series)

Portrait of Bambu.

Portrait of Kiwi.

Portrait of DJ Neil Armstrong.

JONATHAN "TOOK" EVANGELISTA

(Photography Series)

Bboy battle, APEX x Loft In Space present Trilogy II, July 2012 at Fresh Café, Honolulu.

DJ Revise performs at The Loft in Honolulu, March, 2013.

Krystilez of Angry Locals, The Bar Concert, March 2013, at Next Door, Honolulu.

Geologic, aka Prometheus Brown, The Bar concert, March 2013 at Next Door, Honolulu.

Hopie performs at Blue Ocean Thai in Honolulu, April 2011.

Ruby Ibarra performs at Respect the Mic II presented by WorkHouse, June 2012, Hawaiian Brian's, Honolulu.

RIANA "RUDIFIED" STELLBURG

(Photography Series)

Rocky Rivera performs at The Loft in Honolulu, October 2011.

DJ Tittahbyte at SoHo, Honolulu, on March 2013.

DJ SSSolution pumps up the Get Right party at The Manifest in Chinatown on December 2012.

Werdupstu of Audible Lab Rats performs on the MPC at Hawaiian Brian's for the "Mic Check" show on August 2012.

AARON "WOES" MARTIN

(Photography Series)

Panda King Resin Bust, 10-inch resin figure, Hawai'i release.

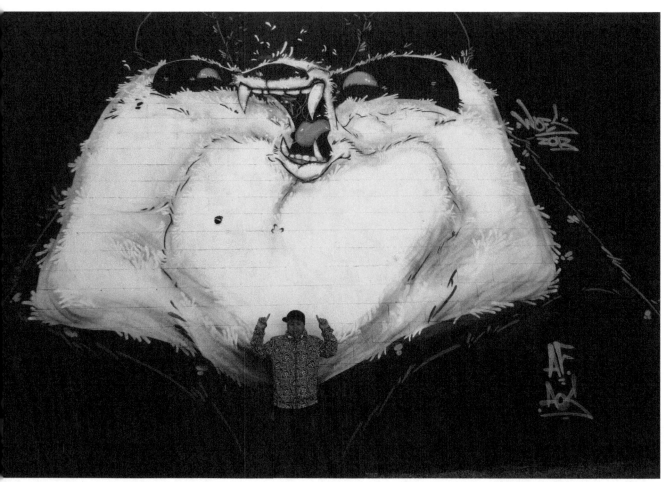

Giant Panda Mural, Arts District, Las Vegas, Nevada.

Pow Wow Hawai'i 2012, Fab 5—Peap Tarr, Woes, Will Barras, Mr. Jago, Meggs, and Aaron De La Cruz.

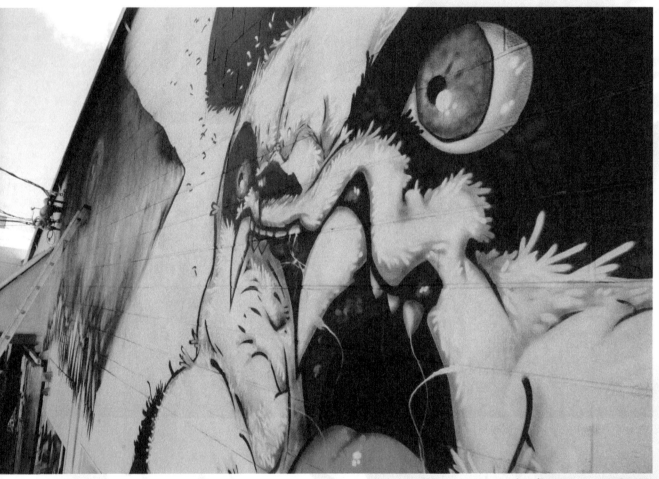

Super Angst, at Fresh Café, Pow Wow Hawai'i 2013.

THE LEGACY OF MIKE "DREAM" FRANCISCO

(Commentaries by John Francisco)

THE BEST OF BOTH WORLDS

This one-man production is what put Oakland and Dream on the map. Dream was still in high school when he painted this production. It's really significant as far as the Bay Area is concerned because circa the late 1980s, two of the most prolific graff crews were battling it out for style supremacy, The Mellow Fellows and Together With Style. TMF was more of the traditional East Coast "funk style," whereas TWS was innovating with abstract "new wave" computer rock style. Dream was down with both crews and when he

The Best of Both Worlds.

rocked "Best of Both Worlds" he shook up the Bay Area by rocking both "funk" and "new wave." He basically was saying, "Y'all could battle it out, but for me I could rock 'em both." And he did. This garnered him worldwide attention, and soon cats from New York, Philly, Japan, Europe, and Hawaii started to take notice that he was one bad cat to be reckoned with.

Plan Bee Memorial.

PLAN BEE MEMORIAL

This production is dedicated to his best friend Plan Bee who he grew up with. Plan Bee was a member of the Hobo Junction Crew along with Saafir and the Whoridas. Plan Bee's album was set to drop, but just before it did, he was shot in a case of mistaken identity. This is one of the longest-running murals in Oakland to date. It was painted in 1992 not long after Plan Bee was murdered. My brother put a lot of heart and soul into it.

Silver.

SILVER

This is the Silver piece at the Alemany Farmers Market/Projects. This is one of the last pieces Dream did before he died. He only used two colors for this burner, schooling all the heads/toys on the wall by proving it's not about how many colors you use or how vibrant your background is. It's all about style. You could burn a whole ten-man production with just one piece if you come correct with style. Style to Dream meant everything. It's what separates you from others. It's a form of identity.

ART AS POLITICAL WEAPON

By Manila Ryce, with Commentaries

PAPER CUTS

One way or another, whether children end up in college or prison, there is a concerted effort to institutionalize them. Children in communities of color are particularly expected to obey, repeat, and follow orders as part of an indoctrination process that punishes independent thought. The artwork for *Paper Cuts* utilizes the cover of a school textbook as a visual representation of the educational system through which cultural genocide and mental occupation are employed. However, the owner of this textbook has actually cut into

Album cover for Bambu's *Paper Cuts.*

John "Manila Ryce" Harrison, "Art as Political Weapon." Copyright © by John "Manila Ryce" Harrison. Reprinted with permission.

this manual of repression with a razor blade to reveal the free-thinkers and revolutionaries that the system "fails to mention." This blade, placed between Bambu's teeth, symbolizes the sharpened words of a rebel. Independent thought is not merely enough to challenge this system. Revolutionary action is needed to destroy it. Overall, there is a wide representation of people from varying cultures on the album cover to convey that the struggle of the proletariat is the same around the globe. It's important to recognize that your personal struggle is part of a larger global struggle. There is no true change without intersectionality and revolutionary internationalism.

WALK INTO A BAR

In recognition of the fact that the Hawaiian tourist industry appropriates native culture for the benefit of corporate imperialists, the artwork for the Hawaiian-themed *Walk Into A Bar* album is inspired by the ongoing movements of resistance and reclamation of dignity still present on the islands in the face of growth and development. As an homage rather than appropriation, the album art depicts the rappers Prometheus Brown and Bambu as tiki idols, with one as documentarian and the other raising his fist in solidarity. On the cover, a firedancer prepares to throw a Molotov cocktail. These figures are no longer novelties, relegated to the role of tourist attraction and consumptions, but rather proud symbols of locally aligned defiance.

Album cover for The Bar's *Prometheus Brown and Bambu Walk Into A Bar.*

...ONE RIFLE PER FAMILY.

Decorative metaphor is abandoned with the cover artwork for ...*one rifle per family.* in favor of the direct representation of armed struggle. Being the face of Bambu's "last album," this piece marks the final stage of progression from civic engagement to direct action, from advocating for what is rightfully ours to taking it by force, if necessary. With the family unit being the sole subject of this piece, the struggles for victims of US imperialism are humanized within their faces. In this Moro family portrait, traditional gender roles are challenged, as is the misconception that Filipino culture is a monolithic body. In highlighting the underrepresented Moro struggle for liberation, the definition of what it is to be Filipino is broadened beyond Manila-centered conceptions to include more than just the paternally racist perception of the "little brown brother" we too often embrace ourselves. Filipino culture is presented here as a living, breathing tapestry of resistance rather than a single characterization commodified for easy consumption.

Album cover for Bambu's *One Rifle Per Family.*

PNOY APPAREL/ KAMPEON

(Zar Javier Photography Series with Commentaries)

SAMMY THE SUNSHINE TEE 2008

Shirt The Kids (STK) is PNOY Apparel's way of giving back. With every Sammy The Sunshine shirt purchased, a Sammy The Sunshine tee, food, and/or education items are automatically purchased for an economically disadvantaged child in the Philippines.

PNOY Apparel, Sammy The Sunshine Tee 2008.

I returned to my birthplace in 1993. Humbled by my experiences, I always wanted to not only give back to my family but also to economically disadvantaged kids. In 2008, we started a one-year campaign entitled "Shirt The Kids." Experiencing the first drop-off in Pampanga was emotionally fulfilling, and we vowed to continue our responsibility. The overwhelming support resulted in 5 drop-offs and numerous charity events that spanned the globe. STK is the catalyst for all our philanthropic duties today and helped solidify our mission.

REVOLT JACKET 2009

Half zip, 100% cotton hoodie, with fully embroidered sun and stars, baybayin, and PINAS, inside lining, welted pockets, and stuffed embroidered pullers.

PNOY Apparel's REVOLT jacket is a combination of modern styling with cultural awareness. The jacket represents the foundation of four different Philippine flags through years of war and strife: (1) Emilio Aguinaldo's victories became the basis and reasoning for the design of the revolutionary government—The Sun of Liberty with a face uses the 8 rays for the 8 provinces that supported the Philippine revolution; (2) the flag by Gregorio del Pilar, the youngest Philippine general, was patterned after Cuba, which also broke away from Spanish control, and was the first to use the three colors. The flag took its last stand against the Americans; (3) the Pio del Pilar, aka "Ang Bandila ng Matagumpay" or "The Flag of the Victorious," for his many victories—it was the first to use the equilateral triangle with the Katipunan "K" in each corner and the rising sun; and (4) the evolution of the

PNOY Apparel, REVOLT Jacket 2009. Half zip, 100% cotton hoodie, with fully embroidered sun and stars, bay-bayin, and PINAS, inside lining, welted pockets, and stuff embroidered pullers.

modern-day flag was sewn by Aguinaldo's wife in Hong Kong that referenced the shades of the American flag and the three stars—we took each aspect of each flag and combined them to form the Revolt flag of PNOY Apparel.

When we started the company in 1999, cut-n-sew was the epitome of any clothing company; it gave the impression that a brand had taken the next step. At the time, the lack of knowledge, resources, and finances made cut-n-sew unattainable. So the day we had the opportunity, we took the challenge head on. After we spent countless hours working on the design, hundreds of back and forth emails with our manufacturers, and dozens of samples, the REVOLT Jacket was born. After 10 years of designing t shirts, we never thought we would still exist… let alone release our very first cut-n-sew project.

THE PI/LA SNAP BACK 2010

The Soul Assassins x Bambu x PNOY Apparel snap back with puff Philippine embroidery in an old English style font. Flip upside down to reveal an ambigram of Los Angeles. Head hunter tattoos under bill, PNOY App Sun Logo, SA Logo, and quote from Bambu himself, "Tell the story of our people that they forgot to mention."

The PI/LA snap back was a huge milestone for the company. Not only did we combine our efforts with community leader, father, and MC Bambu, we also teamed up with one of Hip Hop's own DJ Muggs of Cypress Hill and Soul Assassins. Growing up, I was a huge fan of the Cypress Hill and it was honor to design the hat inside and out, hand deliver it to Muggs, get the thumbs up, and sit in on the exclusive Souls Assassins x Bambu x PNOY App mixtape mastering. We are currently in our fourth installation of the exclusive hat with the previous three all sold out.

PNOY Apparel, The PI/LA Snap Back 2010. The Soul Assassins x Bambu x PNOY Apparel snap back with puff Philippine embroidery in an old English style font. Flip upside down to reveal an ambigram of Los Angeles. Head hunter tattoos under bill, PNOY App Sun Logo, SA Logo, and quote from Bambu himself, "Tell the story of our people that they forgot to mention."

PNOY Apparel, Kflag Tee.

KFLAG

The Republic of the Philippines flag has taken many shapes and forms through the years. The KFlag tee is a timeline of some of the well-noted flags throughout Philippine history. There is the oversized print from General Llanera's cement "K" and dark red skull, the final Katipunan flag of the sun with facial features in teal, and Bonafacio's "K"atipunan KK (Kataastaasang, Kagalanggalangang Katipunan ng mga Anak ng Bayan—The Highest and Most Honorable Society of the Children of the Nation) in lavender all on the front of the tee. Finishing it off is Magdola's "Ka" in alibata in lavender, General Pilar's sun and mountain in teal, to the modern-day flag.

The KFlag shirt was a very controversial design as it showcased a very well-known symbol, "KKK." The "Know History" ideology was about our customers using our shirts as vessels for learning about Philippine history. This came to fruition when I received an email from a customer. She said she wore the shirt to school and was told by a teacher to turn the shirt inside out. She described the meaning behind the shirt, and the teacher did not accept her explanation. She stood her ground, refused to deny her culture, and was escorted to the principal's office. When she got home, she emailed us and told her that she proudly accepted detention and a call to her parents and thanked us for designing the shirt. That email and her experience explain PNOY Apparel's KNOW HISTORY ideology.

VI.

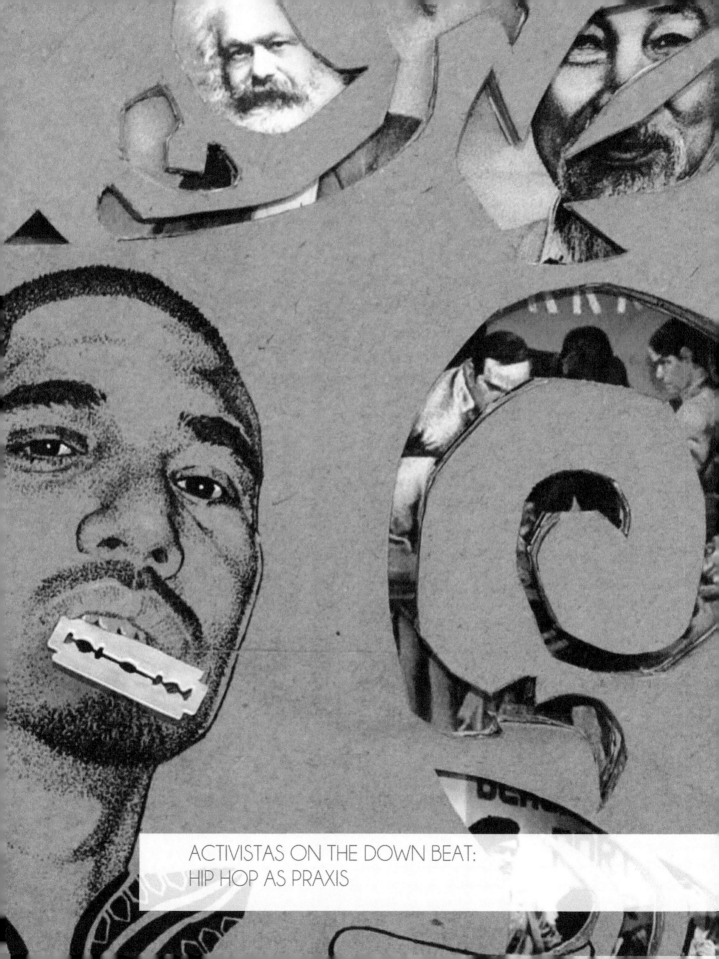

ACTIVISTAS ON THE DOWN BEAT:
HIP HOP AS PRAXIS

TOWARDS PRAXIS-ORIENTED FILIPINA/O AMERICAN HIP HOP

By Roderick N. Labrador

It's 1988. I'm in high school in southeast San Diego, in a low-income community that at the time is largely composed of African Americans and Mexican Americans. Growing up, I'm one of the few Filipina/os in the neighborhood. Emboldened by youth and thumping bass lines, my friends and I cruise down the street in my Pinto, mega-blasting the NWA and The Posse tape while dreaming along with Eric B. and Rakim of getting paid in full. The tales about poverty, drinking, gangs, aggressive masculinity, and the informal economy resonate with us. They reflect the realities around us in our neighborhood, the consequences of the post-industrial, late capitalist Reagan era.

Months later, we're testing the limits of my swap meet car speakers with *By All Means Necessary* by Boogie Down Productions, *It Takes a Nation of Millions to Hold Us Back* by Public Enemy, Eric B. and Rakim's *Follow the Leader*, and NWA's *Straight Outta Compton*. These albums give us something to dance to and something to talk about. When I'm in school, while I'm hanging out, and during the breaks at my first job flipping burgers (and sneaking chicken nuggets), I'm having conversations with classmates, friends, and co-workers about bean pies, bow ties, the Black Star Line, and the Five Percent. During these early moments of the "golden era of rap" the videos we saw on Yo! MTV Raps and the rap songs we heard on the radio were explicitly political and commercially viable. Through the songs and videos, we learned about Black Nationalism, the Black Panthers, Malcolm X, Pan-Africanism, and the politics of resistance. Chuck D. and others were our "prophets of rage" who created layered sheets of oppositional music, constructing narratives that challenged those in power, reframed knowledge and understanding about our current social, political, and economic conditions, and pointed to the possibilities of subversion (see Tricia Rose's book, *Black Noise: Rap Music and Black Culture in Contemporary America*, for a further discussion). These rappers gave voice to the marginalized and oppressed. They unveiled "hidden transcripts," loudly articulating the truths of our everyday.

It's 2006. I'd already gone to college, graduate school, and earned a PhD. My partner, Christine, buys me Nas' *Hip Hop Is Dead*. She buys me the album because she knows I'm a Nas fan, but she also does so sarcastically because for years, she's had to listen to me lament the demise of rap. *Hip Hop Is Dead* generates some public debate about the state of Hip Hop and rap, specifically. Like many others, I saw the album as a criticism of the declining artistic quality and substance of mainstream rap due in large part to the corporatization of Hip Hop, where the earlier prophets were transformed into profits (see Imani Perry's book, *Prophets of the Hood: Politics and Poetics of Hip Hop*). By the time Nas' album was released I was already deep in my grieving period, especially when one of my rap heroes, Ice Cube, had already deafeningly declared in film that rap's death wasn't in some future, we were already there (yes, that's a reference to the 2005 film, *Are We There Yet?*). Nas' album validated what I had been saying for years. I felt that my Hip Hop, the Hip Hop that I grew up with had already died or at least I had already buried it.

A couple of months later, while I'm prepping for a lecture on contemporary Filipin@ struggles for power, my friend and ethnic studies scholar, Dean Saranillio, asks me why I'm using "Fight the Power" and "My Philosophy." I tell him that I want to use music that raises awareness and can move people to action. The next day, he comes back and drops off the Blue Scholars' self-titled album and *The Long March*. In my headphones, Geo is arguing that Hip Hop wasn't dead it was just "malnourished and underfed."

Right around the same time, in a conversation about Filipin@ American cultural production and performance, my friend and legal scholar Kim Chanbonpin strongly suggests that I listen to Native Guns' *Barrel Men*. She's convinced that the album would help reignite my love for a politically conscious Hip Hop. By the end of the first track, I was (re)initiated into Hip Hop's emancipatory potential. Then on "Said It," Kiwi spits a verse that convinces me that I had found Filipin@ prophets of rage and that the rap that I loved in my youth was definitely NOT dead, but it was now underground and explicit in connecting art and activism:

> *Whether we rhyming or we marching in another rally*
> *From Seattle to the Bay down to southern Cali*
> *Isang mahal sa lahat ng mga kabataan*
> *Ngayon ay lumalaban para sa ating bayan*
> *Back home to overseas, where we be*
> *Three bullets in the belly, Geo, Bam, and Kiwi*
> *We're like practice and theory*
> *Put it together to get the message more clearly*
> *More than merely rapping this is activism*
> *To unite the blind and give 'em back their vision*

The "raptivism" espoused in the song, the operationalization of practice and theory, or praxis, suggesting that Hip Hop could be used as a tool for social justice was particularly appealing to me as an Ethnic Studies scholar and director of a college access program that worked with middle school and high school students in a low-income neighborhood in urban Honolulu. And even more, learning about Bambu's work with Kabataang Maka-Bayan (KmB), Geo's work with AnakBayan Seattle, and Kiwi's work with BAYAN-USA pointed to the performance of a praxis-oriented Filipin@ American Hip Hop, where socially and politically conscious rappers were also actively engaged in community organizing, not just rhyming about it. This is a Filipin@ American rap that does consciousness-raising through music with rappers who are active agents in social justice work.

It's November 2010. It's early afternoon and there are about 175 high school students gathered in the library at Farrington High School, one of the largest public schools in Hawai'i—the student population is about 2,500. The overwhelming majority of the students at the high school are Filipina/o, Samoan, and Hawaiian (these three groups comprise roughly 90% of the student population). The students are waiting for Bambu, Geo, and Kiwi who just finished a lunchtime performance at the school's amphitheater (along with Creed Chameleon, Seph One, K-Luv, and Big Mox) as part of the Shirt The Kids activities. The students seem excited and anxious. I don't think they know what to expect from these Filipino rappers from the continent. When the rappers ask them who in their families and group of friends have gone to college, the students are tentative and I hear muted whispers. They ask about college recruiters coming to their campus. I hear hushed murmurs. They ask about military recruiters on their campus. The students mutter more audibly. They ask about the prison that's a few blocks away. The students are visibly involved and more boisterous. They ask them about their relationships to other students, their teachers, and the administration. The students are fully engaged. Bambu, Geo, and Kiwi share their life stories, talk about their educational experiences, and spit some a cappella rhymes. In this short time, they are able to talk with the students about educational equity, opportunity, and access, college aspirations, and school (racial) climate in ways that I couldn't during the 8 years I worked with this high school and the feeder middle schools. After the workshop, as we're leaving the high school parking lot, there is a small group of young high school-aged Filipino boys hanging out by their tricked-out car, blasting the Blue Scholars' "HI-808." I know these boys are manipulated by the "HI-808" funk but I'm hopeful that they are also inspired by the political messages in the song. (See "Mahalo" on Prometheus Brown and Bambu's album, *Walk into a Bar*, for the song version of this episode.)

Earlier that January, I began teaching my "Filipino Americans" course through rap, though not just by interspersing a song here and there in between reading chapters of Carlos Bulosan's *America Is in the Heart* but I made the music the central part of the curriculum. Following Akom's "Critical Hip Hop Pedagogy," I firmly believe in the emancipatory potential of Hip Hop (see Akom's essay, "Critical Hip Hop Pedagogy as a Form of Liberatory Praxis," and Morrell's "Toward a Critical Pedagogy of Popular Culture: Literacy Development Among Urban Youth"). Music has the power to move us, by not solely giving us something to dance to, but also as a medium for creative and sociopolitical expression. The music my students listen to (the class focuses on songs by Native Guns, Blue Scholars, Bambu, Kiwi, Rocky Rivera, Hopie, Power Struggle, Deep Foundation, Creed Chameleon, and Ruby Ibarra) urges them to expand their reasoning, to be active and critical thinkers, to be reflexive and self-reflective, to examine and understand their own personal and family experiences, and to evaluate past and contemporary societal problems. In a sense, through the music I ask my students to "know history" and to "know self" (as popularized and Inc/orporated by PNOY Apparel) in order to situate their own personal experiences in broader social, cultural, political, and economic contexts.

But as Bambu has cautioned my students, "Music, by itself, is not revolution." In order for Hip Hop to be a liberatory praxis, it cannot be only a mental or intellectual exercise; it also needs to address action. This praxis-oriented rap is very similar to Ethnic Studies' foundational activist stance that insisted that academics actively engage the communities we study as well as where we live, work, play, and do our social justice work. In reading/analyzing the words, soundscapes, and worlds in the music, I encourage my students to critique social inequality and the structures, processes, relations, and discourses of power while being politically active and engaged in their communities (both local and global). In this way, to "know history" and to "know self" pivots on a reconstitution of knowledge/power, which can serve as bases for community formation and political involvement, and an opportunity to speak to power and challenge the established sociopolitical order. Hip Hop, as a liberatory art form and practice, can help us both imagine AND enact a better future.

CAN HIP HOP BE POLITICAL?

By Lily Prijoles

IMAGINE
Political forums
turning into 4 ones
of the Hip Hop elements
Forming into the branches of the government.
In the Legislative branch,
Imagine the writers of your Constitution
Coming straight from the concrete nation.
Shaking this feathered krylon can
Holding it their Just hands
Taking on legislative stands …
Sprayin'
Proclamations fanned and dried
in order to get Results
positive and appealing
To be admired by many in this land.
And all Hail to the legendary hero
Who held a metaphoric can
A stitch, a needle, a thread
A Flag upon allegiance
Which I pledge
For this rebel Betsy Ross' recognizable tag.
3 stripes placed upon this Rag

And all hands are pumped in the air
is more than just a salute
They're pumped in the air
for support Of a more lyrical branch
The branch of the Executive,
The office of the President …

I will not tell a lie
I shall not tell a lie
I CAN NOT tell a LIE
Proclaimed the I
in the middle of the MC
spoken into an M-I-C
a MIC
No longer an I campaign
Imagine,
An MC battle instead of a debate
Nothing written and no speech writers
Just a brain attached to a reciter
Honesty flowing
Freestyling off the dome …
"I got the mic in my hand …"
And that's a common quote
This verbal exchanges
Changes YESs to NOs
And sometimes from
… MAYBE SOs
Popularity gained by mixtapes made
And the result in the end is …
The most positive argument Wins
… but not without Judgment
The Judicial Branch is next

Imagine
bangin' a diamond tipped Gavel
And the justice system being unraveled
Conducting a trial by 12
With the heat of wax
Oppressed by the heightened tax
Of the price of these stacks
(which will be overturned in a couple weeks)
Sworn in by the flair and the scratch
Represented by a vibratic Crab

Governing the ears with Blues Breaks Beats
Appointed a Duck as his right-hand man
And a Hamster to his Left
Taking on non-biased stands
Juggling the
Wa-ways and
the m-m-means for
Pu-PU-public c-c-com-pre-hen-SION
The head nod is an understatement
The heads bob for understand-ment
Passing out mixtapes and cds
Like they were verdicts
And all those posers and fakers of Hip Hop
Will be served as convicts

Now have we forgotten the most important branch
The branch from which the 3 others had branched off from
The "invisible" branch

It is the People Branch
Represented by
The breaker, the dancer
Grabbing inspiration from the 3 others
We the People
Take action
Moving to a soul-filled inspiration
We take 90-degree turns
On a hand
Perpendicular to this Land
Helicopter spins, twists, barrel rolls, to a. . . .
POSE
To An uprock and a t-flair
Legs up in the air for a . . .
FREEZE
The response received is
FREE-dom
It's FREE opinions
FREE movement
FREE minds,
Minds imagine the population
Protected by the governmental
Rhyme and beat
The Beat in which we march and move our feet

The Beat that cultivates our future
By inspiring our speech
Imagining always victory and never defeat
Imagining that,
The mission for this nation was to
never imagine
But to just be
HIP HOP

CLASS IS IN SESSION

HIP HOP IN THE CLASSROOM

By Nate Nevado

It was 1993. The Golden Era of Hip Hop was in full swing. My cousin and I were waiting patiently for our very first performance at my high school's annual Black Student Union (BSU) Talent Showcase. One performer after another went on stage and did their thing, leaving the audience, primarily African Americans, in a frenzy. We were the only non-African Americans competing in the showcase. We didn't know what to expect when it was our turn to take the stage. My heart was racing and I was starting to get lightheaded. We grabbed our mics and …

Wait. Let me backtrack for a moment. Let me provide some quick context on my family background. I was raised in a strict Filipino household. My dad was in the Navy and my mom was a Licensed Vocational Nurse (LVN). I am the oldest of four so the expectations on me to be a great role model to my siblings were very high. My parents, particularly my dad, wanted me to become a civil engineer. He was pushing me to go to UCLA, Harvard University, or the US Naval Academy. He ran a very tight ship so anyone who went against what he thought or suggested would catch a bad one. So I would do what an obedient son would do and that was to go to school, go home, and study. But little did he know I was doing things other than solving algebraic formulas and writing PIE paragraphs.

Throughout high school, I dabbled in most of the elements of hip hop. I would bomb walls late at night, bust b-boy moves at a church social event, and drop freestyles in the back of English class. I was never good at working the turntables so I admired DJs from afar. Emceeing came natural to me. It was also the most accessible element. I can rhyme anywhere from school hallways, bathrooms, house parties, to street corners. I would have stacks of TDK cassette tapes with recorded instrumentals on them such as Smif-N-Wesson's "Bucktown" and Black Moon's "I Got Cha Open."

Then came the BSU Talent Showcase. All of my friends wanted to me to compete but I told them that I'd think about it. In all honesty, I didn't want them to witness me getting slaughtered or booed off the stage. So, I signed up without any of my friends knowing about it. To feel a little better, I asked my cousin from Vallejo to join me.

That led to my demise, or so I thought. My cousin asked his dad if he could drop him off at my place for the showcase. Of course, his dad called my dad and next thing I know, my dad barged into my room demanding an explanation. I eventually explained to him what it was all about and I practically begged him to let me compete. After a lot of going back and forth, he finally agreed to bring my cousin and me to the talent showcase under a couple of conditions. One, he wanted to be there to watch us, and two, that I would give up this "rapping thing." I knew at that moment that my dad was preparing for an "I told you so" moment but I didn't care because I just wanted to perform.

Now fast forward. We grabbed our mics and the beat dropped. My adrenaline was overflowing and as I saw people getting up and waving their hands in the air, my confidence instantaneously grew. Each crew was allowed to do one song for the showcase but we ended up doing three songs because the crowd wanted more. It was one of the most exhilarating moments of my life to be able to move the crowd with our lyrics and beats. We won first place and took home the trophy and $75. I went to my dad to see his reaction but with a stone-cold face, he said, "Let's go home. Now!" On the ride back home, all three of us sat in awkward silence. I wanted to share with my cousin how dope it felt to rock the mic but was too afraid of what my dad would say. We finally got to the house and my dad finally spoke. He asked me, "What will I do with this 'rapping thing'?" "What kind of job can you get out of it?" "What do you learn?" Nothing! He bombarded me with all of these questions that I didn't have the chance to process them to give him clear answers. So I said nothing.

Oh, how I wish I could go back in time to answer those questions. In 2003, I entered the Master's Program in Counseling at San Francisco State University. In our professions, we are constantly reminded of meeting our clients and students where they're at. Being able to effectively assess certain populations will allow us to provide concrete services to help promote positive change. My graduate advisor challenged us to start thinking about programs that we can develop in the future that will help certain groups of people. My specialization in my graduate program was working with college students. My advisor asked me what kind of program I was interested in creating. I told him that I wanted to create a program that can educate and empower our youth and students to become agents of change through hip hop. My advisor gave me a look, a look that was so eerily similar to that of my dad's. He asked me, "What learning outcomes can result from using hip hop?" In the most diplomatic way, he recommended that I should think about it more. However, this time I was not going to say nothing. I told him that I would find a way to make this happen.

In 2007, it happened. A group of about 20 students, faculty advisors, and I had a great discussion about the state of hip hop. It was apparent to most of them that hip hop portrayed in the media through radio and TV didn't provide the true essence of what hip hop is really all about. They were very interested in the rich culture and history of it. They also wanted to explore ways in how it can be used as an educational tool in our classrooms and communities.

Hip hop is an integral part of American culture as evidenced through music, product commercialization, television, and fashion. Unfortunately, hip hop has a bad "rap," due primarily to what is heard and marketed on the radio. The most popular hip hop songs are described as "misogynist, sexist, and violent." What most people do not understand, particularly those who are opposed of the idea of having hip hop used in education, is that "the media powers, who regulate what sells and gets airtime on the radio, are those of dominant culture folks who have their own agendas that have nothing to do with the uplifting of our youth."[1] We cannot blame opposition on their perception of hip hop but we can educate the positive influences and impact of the usage of hip hop in the classrooms. Colleges and universities such as San Francisco State University, UC Berkeley, and George Mason

---

1   Greene, Camilla. "*Connections: The Journal of the National School Reform Faculty*, Connecticut, 2006.

University have implemented programs using hip hop as another tool to use in their classes. This enables the ability for educators to "talk their language." It is all about meeting students where they're at. There is a strong disconnect between what we, as educators, see as important for our students to succeed, as opposed to the needs of our students. "The state of American education legitimizes some ways of knowledge while marginalizing others. It is modeled on white middle-class logic as its referent which silences subordinate voices and disavows those life experiences that do not fit the mold."[2] Standardized education is often mismatched with the community's students' experiences. The use of hip hop as an educational tool takes on a culturally responsive pedagogical approach that favors the student-centered approach. Hip hop is a powerful tool that can be used to teach English, algebra, economics, and chemistry. This allows students to improve on their reading comprehension, think critically, problem solve and reason, and develop literacy skills.

Take rap battles, for example. I've engaged in quite a few rap battles. Battle rap is a form of lyricism in which competitors would rap against each other to come up with the best rhymes. The more personal and relevant your rhymes were, the better. I've literally asked folks about a rapper I was going against so I can load up on some "lyrical ammo" I can use during our battle. You had to think critically and in the moment to ensure yourself a chance to win the battle. If you lose, you learn from it, and try again. As I battled more, I began to read more to obtain more content and found that my literary skills began to flourish. I made it an effort to learn a new word to add to my vocabulary. An English class didn't teach me that. Hip hop did.

By utilizing alternative pedagogical approaches such as hip hop, it reaches out to the youth and students by providing them with a space for emancipating learning experiences. This validates one's experiences and furthers their investment in educating and empowering themselves through the importance of higher education.

So with that said, Rock The School Bells was born in 2007. I reflected on the night that my dad asked me those questions. I realize now that even if I'd answer his questions with the knowledge that I have regarding hip hop education, he would probably not understand. He knows what he knows based on what he's seen and read. If you are a civil engineer, you are successful. If you are a lawyer or doctor, you are successful. There is not enough proven literature for him to view to make that connection to hip hop. My dad is one of many who represent a community of people who have not been given the opportunity to understand the value of hip hop in education and personal development. For the last 5 years, Rock The School Bells has provided that for our youth, students, and our communities at large.

I recently logged onto Facebook to do my usual promotion of Rock The School Bells. As I was creating messages and tagging people, a notification popped up on my screen. Someone had posted a comment on one of my links. It was my dad. Not only did he like my link, he also commented, "I am proud of you son." For the first time in a very long time, I felt validated for the work that I do using hip hop as a tool to promote social change in our communities.

Growing up as a Filipino American, it was a challenging task to balance both assimilating into an American culture and maintaining my own Filipino cultural traditions and values. So, to answer the question posed by my dad and my graduate advisor, I've learned that hip hop allowed me to have a voice to express my triumphs and struggles. I've learned that it is important to learn about different cultures first rather than fall victim to misconceptions. Lastly, I've learned through hip hop the importance of education and sustainability. I may have helped start Rock The School Bells, but it is our youth and students who will take the torch to educate and empower our next generation of leaders. They say that "hip hop is movement" because it was meant to move.

---

2   Giroux, Henry, Colin Lankshear, Peter McLaren, and Michael Peters. *Counternarratives: Cultural Studies and Critical Pedagogies in Postmodern Spaces*. New York and London: Routledge Press, 1996.

CROSSING THE COLOR LINES

FILIPINO AMERICAN ALLIANCES THROUGH ACTIVISM AND HIP HOP

By Kevin Nadal

O ne of my personal claims to fame is that I have proudly represented various parts of the United States—from the West Coast, to the East Coast, and for a short stint even the Midwest. While I grew up in a large Filipino American community in the San Francisco Bay Area, I found myself moving to different parts of the country, primarily for my academic education, but secretly because of my desire for adventure, new experiences, and the chance to meet people from all walks of life. So whether I was living in California or Michigan or my permanent residence in New York City, I always thrived on the opportunity to grow personally, professionally, and spiritually. And in time, I learned that the people I've met in these places and the experiences that would ensue would be my real education. The life-changing lessons I would learn the most from would not be in a lecture hall or classroom, but rather in the communities that I would be involved with.

Before I begin, it may be necessary to share a little bit about my life as a way of providing a context for which I write this narrative. I am a second-generation Filipino American, born and raised in the United States; I am the youngest of three boys who grew up in a two-parent, immigrant, working- to middle-class home. Life in the Nadal house was always a mix of Pilipino and American cultures, which could be exemplified best by the foods we ate—the family dinner with sticky white rice and KFC, a lunch bag with a peanut butter and jelly sandwich and a *lumpia* wrapped in foil, and even the Thanksgiving dinner with a turkey in the middle surrounded by *pancit* (Filipino noodles) and *dinuguan* (blood pork stew) on either side.

I spent my teenage years in the nineties—a decade when the fashion was supposedly better than the eighties but in retrospect was probably worse. The haircuts on the boys in my family ranged from flat tops with lines to a slicked-back pompadour, while the girls sprayed Aqua Net to shape their 6-inch bangs into a perfect fan formation. The local radio stations blasted slogans like "Knowledge Is Power" and "No Color Lines" as we recovered from Rodney King and the L.A. Riots. We pegged our pants in our pre-teens with safety pins, and we wore baggy overalls a year or so later. Our cross-color jeans were bright and in every shade—from orange to purple to forest green. And we listened to everything from MC Hammer to Eazy E, from Michel'le to J.J. Fad, and we even were lucky enough to bob our heads to Biggie and Tupac while they were alive.

The Catholic elementary school I attended was mixed, with fifty percent Filipino American and a sizable number of Latinos (primarily Mexican Americans). The college I attended was more than half Asian American, yet it was also one where Filipinos were always separated from Asians on demographic population reports.

I was always actively involved in the Filipino American community in formal and informal ways. My parents belonged to a typical association that was usually defined by extravagant galas where the kids would roam around the hotel and avoid getting in trouble. I was embarrassed when my parents took us to Filipino community events, but I was happy to go to the same events with my *barkada* (group of friends). I learned how to dance *tinikling*, *singkil*, *pandango sa ilaw*, and other cultural dances. I joined our Filipino student organizations in both high school and college, and I became president of both.

Throughout my youth, the majority of my closest friends and social circles was Filipino American, with an emphasis on the American. I bonded mostly with other second-generation Filipino Americans whose parents all had thick, yet decipherable accents. At the same time, I always had at least 2 or 3 best friends who were Black or Latino, and I always felt comfortable and welcomed in both Black and Latino spaces. In high school, I attended all the Black Student Union events; in college, I was an honorary member of MEChA (the Chicano student activist organization). I was extremely proud of being Filipino American in all ways, yet I always found myself aligning closely with the "other brown folks." And while I had a few close Chinese and Japanese friends, I never felt as comfortable within their communities.

As I moved around the country, I seemed to notice similar trends. When I lived in Michigan, I observed all of the Filipino male students joining the historically Latino fraternity instead of an Asian American one. When I moved to New York, my Latino students would often refer to Filipinos as the "Spanish Asians," while my Black students would call them the "Black Asians." I was easily included in conversations with African Americans and Latinos about race, while many of my Chinese, Japanese, or Korean friends and colleagues reported that they often had to justify that they were people "of color." And just about anywhere in the country, it was common for Black men to nod their heads in a friendly gesture in passing, or for African American women to ask me which parent of mine was Black.

As I transformed from a kid who merely showed up to Filipino events for food, to a student activist who learned about racism and oppression, and to an adult who has managed to integrate social justice, Filipino American, and LGBTQ issues into my career, I've always wondered why Filipino Americans had experiences that were otherwise unique to other Asian American groups. Why were there so many allegiances between Filipino Americans, Latinos, and African Americans? Was it because of skin color? Was it because of bonds from colonialism or racism? Was it because of social class? Was it because of hip hop? And was it just something that I perceived or was this actually a trend across the country?

PNOY Apparel, a Filipino clothing company in San Diego, California, has a phrase that they often use as their motto: "No history, no self. Know history, know self." Thus, it is important to take a look back at the history of the Filipino and Filipino American people in order for me to answer these questions. It is necessary to not just look at the experiences of Filipino Americans in the US today, but also at the history of the motherland.

The Philippines was the only country in the world that was colonized by both Spain and the United States. Prior to colonization, indigenous Philippines could be described as a group of separate islands southeast of mainland China and west of the Pacific Islands where the inhabitants were mostly animistic or Muslim. But after almost 400 years of Spanish oppression, the Philippines became a predominantly Catholic country. Consequently, they acquired many Spanish cultural values (e.g., *machismo*, or male dominance), Spanish traditions (e.g., having "debuts," or coming-of-age celebrations for girls), Spanish surnames (e.g., Mercado, De La Cruz, or Santos), and even Spanish-language influences (e.g., Spanish nouns like "pan" for bread and "leche" for milk)—all of which are also present in Latino communities today. Perhaps Filipino Americans feel connected with Latinos because of their similar Catholic religious traditions, cultural values, and colonial history. Perhaps Filipino Americans feel alliances with Latinos because they have Spanish last names and other people would mistake them for being Latino. And maybe this connection can be viewed as a positive one (e.g., when Filipino American and Latino organizations work together for social justice issues), but arguably it can be viewed as a negative one (e.g., when a Filipino American has colonial mentality and would rather identify as Latino instead of Filipino). Either way, the connection still existed and appeared to be common.

The history of the Filipino American people in the United States may also provide some insight about Filipino Americans and their allegiances with others. The United Farm Workers (UFW) movement was a formed as a result of Filipino American labor leaders who wanted Filipino and Mexican farmworkers to create a greater alliance and become a stronger force. However, this movement is often noted in American history books as being a Chicano or Mexican American movement and fails to recognize the Filipino American farmworkers who took initiative to unite the two parties. Additionally, because of the smaller number of Filipinos in the UFW, they often felt ignored and relationships dwindled. Cesar Chavez (the UFW president and chief Chicano labor leader) was often praised for guiding the movement, while leaders Larry Itliong and Philip Vera Cruz (who were both Filipino labor leaders and vice presidents of the UFW) were not credited for their work and initiative. Although there were some negative outcomes of this movement, this movement symbolized the first of many allegiances that could (and would) ensue between the two ethnic groups.

Perhaps the sociocultural experiences of Filipino Americans have also connected them to other ethnic minority groups. There have been many studies in psychology and education that have pointed to the fact that Filipino Americans experience similar types of racism as other Asian Americans do (see Nadal, 2011 for a review). For example, it is common for many Asian Americans to be forced to justify where they are from (e.g., being asked "No, where are you *really* from?" after an Asian American tells someone they were born in the US). It is also common for Asian Americans to be told that they speak "good English," even though they were born and raised in the United States. Although Filipinos first landed in the US in 1587, and there are now up to four generations in my own family who have spent their lives on American soil, Filipino Americans (and other Asian Americans) would continually be viewed as perpetual foreigners or aliens in our own land.

Research is also finding that Filipino Americans are often the victims of racism that is similar to African Americans and Latinos. For example, it is common for people of these groups to be treated as if they are inferior (i.e., when someone assumes an African American, Latino, or Filipino American wouldn't be smart, capable, or have money). Some research has found that Filipino American teens reported being less encouraged by their high school counselors and teachers to go to college than Chinese Americans would (Teranishi, 2002). This aligns with literature on teacher bias that argues that teachers often unconsciously discriminate against African American and Latino students and assume inferiority (Downey and Pribest, 2004). Other research has found that Filipino Americans are sometimes assumed to be criminals (e.g., when a store clerk follows a person of color to make sure she or he doesn't steal, or when a police officer pulls a person of color over for no reason; Nadal, Escobar, Prado, David, and Haynes, 2012). Because of this discrimination, Filipino Americans may experience psychological distress that is different than other groups; they experience discrimination involving being treated like an alien, an inferior, and a criminal. And because of this distress, Filipino Americans may experience a variety of mental health problems like depression, anxiety, substance abuse, or low self-esteem (see Nadal, 2011 for a review).

Another factor that contributes to Filipino Americans' unique experiences with race is the discrimination that ensues in the Asian American community. Filipino Americans and Pacific Islanders are the often targets of stereotypes of ethnic jokes promoting inferiority of the two ethnic groups with the Asian/Pacific Islander community (Okamura, 1998). These stereotypes are usually based on the notion that Filipino Americans and Pacific Islanders have lower educational attainment levels and lower socioeconomic statuses, as compared to other East Asian Americans, as well as stereotypes that both groups are uncivilized or criminal. As a result of this discrimination, it is uncommon for Filipino Americans to attain leadership positions within Asian American communities and somewhat unusual for specific Filipino American issues to be discussed in Asian American contexts. For example, many Asian American studies classes fail to include Filipino American topics, despite the fact that Filipino Americans are the largest Asian American population in the US and have prominent populations on college campuses. Because of this invisibility, many Filipino Americans may feel marginalized within the Asian American community and may purposefully separate from pan-Asian organizations (Espiritu, 1992). Sometimes these feelings of marginalization may lead Filipino Americans to identify more as Pacific Islanders, primarily because of physical similarities (e.g., brown skin, flat nose) and experiences of discrimination or invisibility.

Filipino Americans also have health problems that are more similar to African Americans and Latinos than to other Asian American groups (see Nadal, 2011 for a review). Filipino Americans have higher incidents of cardiovascular disease, hypertension, diabetes, gout, and obesity. This trend is often attributed to an unhealthy Filipino diet and lack of exercise. This is a similar explanation given for health problems in African American communities, who may have similar nutritional intakes and lack of physical activity. In terms of nutrition alone, there are many similarities between Filipino Americans and African Americans; both groups enjoy eating fried foods, tend to purchase and cook nontraditional and cheaper meats like pig intestines or oxtail, and tend not to prepare meals with a lot of vegetables.

Similarly, various sociocultural experiences may connect Filipino Americans to other ethnic minority groups. Filipino Americans tend to have higher rates of teen pregnancy and HIV/AIDS than other Asian American groups, with rates that are more similar to African American and Latino populations (Nadal, 2011). Second-generation Filipino Americans attain college degrees less than second-generation East Asian Americans (e.g., Chinese, Japanese, and Korean Americans) and Asian Indian Americans (Nadal, 2011). Substance use, particularly drinking alcohol and tobacco use in men, has been found to be more significant for Filipino American samples (Nadal, 2000). Depression for Filipino Americans is found to be higher for Filipino American populations than the general population (Tompar-Tiu and Sustento-Seneriches, 1995) and suicide has been reported as being highly prevalent with Filipina American adolescent girls (Wolf, 1997). While all of these issues tend to affect Latino and African American communities, a major difference is that very few Americans are familiar with these disparaging trends for Filipino Americans. Because of the Model Minority Myth, Filipino Americans are not receiving the services they deserve and these disparities in physical health, education, and mental health persist.

While there is no clear reason to cite why Filipino Americans experience a range of disparaging problems, it is conceivable that experiences with racism (both interpersonal and institutional) may contribute to their alliance with African Americans and Latinos. Perhaps encountering similar types of discrimination allows African Americans and Latinos to feel more connected to Filipino Americans over other Asian American groups. Perhaps the institutional barriers to education, health care, or political voice may influence the joining of oppressed groups. Perhaps the notion that Filipino Americans have a darker brown skin allows African American and Latino persons to feel more affinity with Filipino Americans. And because of all of these reasons, activism can ensue between all of these groups and a united front could be formed. So although experiencing racism is undoubtedly an unfair and unjust problem in the United States, the bonds that it can create between communities can be viewed as a positive outcome.

It is important to note that these trends are only among a few possible reasons supporting why Filipino Americans may bond with African Americans and Latinos. Other issues like social class, socioeconomic status, neighborhood connections, experiences with gangs, and others may all potentially have an influence on the alliance between the groups. Perhaps the trend that Filipino Americans are more likely to date or marry outside of their ethnic group may also contribute to the phenomenon. Filipino American women are more likely to date African American men than any other Asian group is, and there has been an increase of Mexipinos (biracial Mexican/Filipino individuals) and other multiracial Filipino Americans in the country (Nadal, 2011). However, one of the most prominent reasons why Filipino Americans have become so connected to these communities in the past few decades is because of the participation, visibility, and culture of Filipino Americans in hip hop.

Ever since the 1980s, Filipinos on both the West Coast and East Coast have been a force in most of the elements of hip hop. DJs like DJ QBert and DJ Icy Ice on the West Coast and DJ Neil Armstrong and DJ Kuttin Kandi on the East Coast have been among some of my favorite turntablists of all time. Yet, when I was growing up, I also enjoyed my high school friends who would spin 45s in our garages for our birthdays, or who I'd help carry crates of records or extension cords into clubs, just so that I can say "I'm with the DJ" and not pay a cover.

Emcees and lyricists have been around even before I was a teenager, ranging from the Native Guns and the pre-Fergie Black Eyed Peas, and still persist in the new contemporary sounds of Deep Foundation and Ryan "Hydroponikz" Abugan. But they also existed in the non-competitive free flows that my cousins and I would engage in when we were bored at a family party.

Long before Randy Jackson's *America's Best Dance Crew* existed, there were the best of the best dance teams like Culture Shock and old-school Kaba Modern. But there were also my b-boy friends who always seemed to be spinning on their heads on cardboard boxes in our garages, as well as the aspiring adolescents who created dance routines to the sounds of Bell Biv Devoe, Kool Moe Dee, and Oaktown 357 and performed at every Filipino Association Christmas party or high school talent show. Sometimes these dance groups didn't have access to mixers or other fancy equipment, which was apparent by occasional awkward transitions into the next song. Today that would be unacceptable; back then, it was normal and just added character. As long as the audience couldn't hear their Filipina moms screaming in the background, the performers would be happy.

Even in the spoken word or poetry scene, Filipino Americans have always represented well. There were my favorite pioneers like Faith Santilla, Regie Cabico, Alison de la Cruz, Emily Lawsin, and Two Warriors. But I also enjoyed the endearing and empowering poems of the Filipina teenager struggling in her Pinay identity. I watched the young, gay, college-aged Filipino man use his spoken word piece as a way to come out of the closet to his friends in the audience. I witnessed the educator who used her poetry to teach us about imperialism and social justice, while inevitably using the word *makibaka* at least once (but likely five times). And I was humbled by the young college students in the Midwest who I introduced spoken word to in the early 2000s; I hoped to illustrate to them a way of expressing their raw emotions in what I thought was an artistic way, but I later realized it was the only way many of them would know how.

And maybe that is exactly what hip hop has meant to me and the Filipino American community. It has been a chance for us to have our voices heard. It has been the major form of activism for our generation. It has given us the chance to develop positive Filipina and Filipino role models, in a world that didn't (and still doesn't) allow Filipino Americans to be present in the media in the ways that we deserve. So maybe we didn't see many Pinay or Pinoy hip hop pioneers on television, but we did see them spinning at the club, dancing or emceeing at Friendship Games or Filipino Intercollegiate Networking Dialogue (FIND), or performing at the Nuyorican Poets Café in NYC or Bindlestiff in San Francisco. I may not remember the names of the most prominent Filipino American graffiti artists of my time, but knowing many were Filipino American did (and still does) instill a pride in my culture and in my people.

I grew up in a time where the only images of Filipinos in the media were negative—from a former first lady's excess of shoes to a scandalous little league baseball team to the murderer of Versace. I often wonder how not seeing people who look like you in positive ways has an impact on one's self-esteem. Being consistently invisible onscreen may exacerbate feelings of invisibility in everyday life. And even though Filipino kids today have access to the Jabbawockeez and apl.de.ap on their television sets, I hope they still appreciate the real celebrities—the local hip hop heroes like Bambu, Kiwi, Koba, Geologic, DJ Melissa Corpus, Marie Obaña, Mathilda de Dios, K. Barrett, Kimmy Maniquis, Jonathan "Bionic" Bayani, and Michael "Suitkace" Capito who make waves in their communities every day through their art and their hearts. And just as importantly, I hope that young Filipino kids today strive to become local heroes themselves and pass on that flame to future generations.

One of the greatest gifts that the Filipino American presence in hip hop community has given us was the opportunity to feel connected. We have been able to feel connected by crossing colors and uniting with others outside of our community. We have been able to feel connected to a movement of others who believe similarly to us, and others who use art as a way of expressing that. And most importantly, we have been able to feel connected to each other—across color lines, across social classes, and across the continent.

We have consumed each other's stories through our five major senses: sight, sound, smell, taste, and touch. We have visually witnessed the intricate moves of hip hop dance, as well as the graphic art and design on the walls of our urban (and sometimes suburban) neighborhoods. We have listened in awe to the turntabling sounds from Filipina and Filipino fingers, the vicious voices of spoken word artists, and the mesmerizing lyrics leaving Filipina and Filipino lips. And together as a people, we have even smelled victory and struggle, tasted defeat and empowerment, and been touched in our minds and our hearts.

REFERENCES

Espiritu, Y. L. (1992). *Asian American Panethnicity: Bridging Institutions and Identities*. Philadelphia: Temple University Press.

Downey, D. B. and Pribesh, S. (2004). "When Race Matters: Teachers' Evaluations of Students' Classroom Behavior." *Sociology of Education, 77*(4), 267–282.

Nadal, K. L. (2000). "F/Pilipino American Substance Abuse: Sociocultural Factors and Methods of Treatment." *Journal of Alcohol and Drug Education, 46*(2), 26–36.

Nadal, K. L. (2011). *Filipino American Psychology: A Handbook of Theory, Research, and Clinical Practice*. New York: John Wiley & Sons, Inc.

Nadal, K. L., Escobar, K. M., Prado, G., David, E. J. R., and Haynes, K. (2012). "Racial Microaggressions and the Filipino American Experience: Recommendations for Counseling and Development. *Journal of Multicultural Counseling and Development, 40*, 156–173.

Okamura, J. Y. (1998). *Imagining the Filipino American Diaspora: Transnational Relations, Identities, and Communities*. New York: Garland Publishing.

Teranishi, R. T. (2002). "Asian Pacific Americans and Critical Race Theory: An Examination of School Racial Climate." *Equity & Excellence in Education, (35)*2, 144–154.

Tompar-Tiu, A. and Sustento-Seneriches, J. (1995). *Depression and Other Mental Health Issues: The Filipino American Experience*. San Francisco: Jossey Bass Publishers.

Wolf, D.L. (1997). "Family Secrets: Transnational Struggles Among Children of Filipino Immigrants." *Sociological Perspectives, 40*(3), 457–482.

IDENTITY AND RESISTANCE

By Stephen Bischoff

T he prominence of Filipino Americans in hip hop culture has risen since the turn of the 21st century. This rise in prominence has contributed to building pride in identifying as Filipino. Using interview material, this chapter uncovers some of the relationships that might exist between Filipino American identity formation, hip hop culture, and resistance. The Filipino American emcees selected for this chapter have gained significant recognition beyond their local communities and often incorporate "conscious" messages in their artistry and/or community involvement.

For many Filipino American hip hop artists, hip hop culture provides a venue to create "a space of our own." For example, Jojo Gaon, co-founder of isangmahal arts kollective in Seattle, Washington, remarked that part of the development of the organization was to provide a space of expression. Known primarily for spoken word performances and events, isangmahal also showcased other types of creative expression including dance and musical performances. According to co-founder Bobby Gaon, prior to isangmahal's founding in 1997, open mic sessions in the area were predominantly black or white spaces. He stated that:

> there was no safe space for us Filipinos. The venues out there were
> for either Whites or Blacks. Of course, we'd feel more comfort-
> able doing the Black open mic scene. But, then again, it wasn't
> our space. So, we need to create our own space. That's when
> isangmahal arts kollective was born.[1]

isangmahal supported a cultural space and recognized that Filipino Americans have stories to tell and need to express their experiences, especially Filipino American youth. It also suggested that even though Filipino American youth would share spaces with other markedly black spaces, there was still enough interest to have a forum that

---

1   Bobby Gaon, Interview, July 7, 2011.

catered to the Filipino American experience. For Blue Scholars' Geologic, isangmahal arts kollective allowed a comfortable venue for him to express himself without having the feeling of being judged based on his appearance. In addition to Geologic, Angela Dy and Freedom Siyam also contributed to isangmahal's growth. They all recognized the empowerment they gained in learning more about self-expression or from simply having the venue to share pieces about themselves while connecting with other Filipino Americans.

Sharing culture, experiences, and love through isangmahal arts kollective impressed Freedom Siyam. After first seeing performances at a Washington State Filipino American Student Alliance (WSFASA) Conference, Freedom said that being a witness implored him to engage with these people and this type of creativity in some way. He would later attend an isangmahal open mic show. As he attended more and interacted more with participants, Freedom remembers the organization introducing him to new ideas as well as some Filipino Americans being "interested in educating other Filipino Americans about our rich culture."[2] Engaging in Socratic learning through performative art also addressed some of the assimilationist rhetoric and mis/understandings of Filipino and Filipino American history by Filipino American youth. Presenting Filipino American culture through a lens of power in a medium that is both intimate and appealing encouraged the performers and audience to relate through their own understandings of identity. For a population whose history and culture has been co-opted through colonial and neocolonial rhetoric, isangmahal arts kollective helped to validate Filipino American identity and culture.

From her New York base, DJ Kuttin Kandi offered a similar draw to share in ethnic identity with other Filipino Americans. Familiar with the influence of isangmahal, Kuttin Kandi remembers her own experience growing up in New York and attending a dance club that was overwhelmingly Filipino American. She was evidently surprised and excited at the sheer numbers of Filipino Americans whom she would get to interact with at a club called the Village Gate. It drew her to regularly attend and participate with other Filipino American youth. Kuttin Kandi recalled that her Filipino friends who had taken her there didn't realize the impact that sharing ethnic identity and hip hop culture meant to her. In retrospect, Kuttin Kandi says that she would have explained to those friends today that "you just don't understand what this is like for me. To know my own people. We may not be talking about our culture at a party, but just being around my own people. You just don't know what that fucking feels like for me."[3] Going from an imagined community to a more tangible community influenced Kuttin Kandi's identity and political development immensely.

In addition to identity development, hip hop culture can be used as a tool for reaching out to the Filipino American community, especially the youth. When asked if hip hop was important to addressing some of the common struggles for Filipino Americans, Los Angeles-based rapper Bambu quickly agreed and stated that he thought "hip hop is the strongest medium right now to utilize" and that "[w]hen giant corporations jump on it, you know it's powerful." However, Bambu also recognized that hip hop is "not real, [...] concrete change." It can be a "catalyst [to] educate ourselves, [...] activate, and organize." Yet, he states that one "can replace hip hop with anything" since it is a tool. Ultimately for Bambu, hip hop can be used to increase awareness and educate the masses for the purpose of getting others to go out into the community and organize. But, he cautioned that other mediums should be used if they were more appropriate. For now, hip hop culture provides the most relevance and salience for Filipino American youth at this time. As a "culture of resistance" to Jojo Gaon similarly warns that hip hop culture cannot provide that same perspective to youth if they don't have a foundation to view it in that way: "You have to have a good framework of anti-oppression, period. And if not, then it doesn't

---

2   Freedom Siyam, Interview, July 19, 2011.
3   DJ Kuttin Kandi, Interview, September 9, 2011.

work. That's not a good formula."[4] For Jojo, hip hop can be viewed as a *soundtrack* when thinking about how youth can develop an understanding of resistance, a theme based in Filipino American identity development and counter-consciousness, not necessarily within hip hop culture.

The hip hop artists I interviewed pointed out the ways that the occupation and colonization of the Philippines leads Filipino Americans to relate to resistance. E. San Juan Jr. has described the challenge for Filipino American identity by saying that "[b]ecoming Filipino then is a process of dialectical struggle."[5] He goes on to say that the layered understandings for being Filipino American necessarily calls for incorporating the intersections of both Philippine and American societies. As products of these intersections, hip hop artists affirmed the impact it has had on their own identity development. The rapper and community organizer Kiwi pointed out hip hop culture's influence on his own identity-formation process: "When I was first really getting into hip hop, it was like 'I'm hip hop' and I think it just kinda played a role in terms of [...] being a huge part of my identity until I discovered [...] being Filipino."[6] For Kiwi, hip hop culture segued into understanding his ethnic identity as a Filipino. Kiwi explicitly pointed out hip hop's transitional role in his life and the organizing power that he sees in hip hop culture. As someone who felt that "resistance [is] rooted in Filipino identity," Kiwi shows how hip hop culture can provide an inroad to developing Filipino American identity and thus an awareness of resistance.

Similarly, hip hop culture can provide support in resisting various oppressive forces by building self-confidence and rendering voice. Rapper Geologic affirmed that resistance was "absolutely" a theme for Filipino American identity development by going further to state that resistance was part of the "global identity" for Filipinos. With so many Filipinos leaving the Philippines for jobs in other countries that don't match their Filipino education levels, Geologic acknowledged the "undoing" of colonial history today relating the Filipino American and Filipino struggle to the class aspects of labor migration. He references the Filipino diaspora in saying that "we are basically a class of people who have been made to be a labor class for the world."[7] Bonded in struggle and resistance, the Filipino diaspora can relate to one another with histories traced to the Philippines. Rocky Rivera stated that "resistance is the thread that binds us all. All of us Filipinos is that. We're tired. You know, we've been resisting for so long."[8] In struggling against oppression for so long, Rocky sees Filipino Americans who desire to embody model minority stereotypes as people who really "want to be included." Although she claims that she doesn't want to speak for them, Rocky Rivera also feels that Filipinos striving for these types of inclusions are misled in still believing that the "American Dream" exists for them and is attainable. Due to the backwards understandings of meritocracy in the U.S., the struggle for communities of color has become an individual one. Hardships that are part of the everyday experience for Filipino Americans with low socioeconomic statuses have gotten normalized and believed to be challenges that one must go through in order to reach any aspects of the "American Dream." Rocky Rivera recalled her own realization when she "finally understood that it wasn't my fault and it wasn't my parents' fault and it was something that happened way before me [...] that's when I was able to resist in the right way." It is telling that Rocky alludes to distinct types of resistance since those Filipino Americans pursuing the so-called American Dream could be envisioning themselves resisting. Rocky's own consciousness of Filipino history and its relationship to her material conditions allowed her to realize how she could be more effective in resisting. If hip hop culture stimulates and promotes a deeper connection to Filipino history, a historical materialist framework

---

4   Jojo Gaon, Interview, July 18, 2011.
5   San Juan Jr., *Toward Filipino Self-Determination: Beyond Transnational Globalization*, 156.
6   Kiwi Illafonte, Interview, October 14, 2011.
7   George Quibuyen, Interview, July 7, 2011.
8   Rocky Rivera, Interview, October 24, 2011.

within Filipino American youth could be promoted. Nurturing ideologies of resistance plays an important part in the lives of Filipino American youth with responses of resistance varying in methodology.

Angela Dy referenced a similar challenge that she saw within Filipino Americans who choose an assimilationist path. To those taking that path, Angela saw them as possibly feeling that they are resisting in their own individual way. She continues on to say that the assimilationist path "perpetuates oppression" by reproducing internalized oppression. Adding to Geologic's references to socioeconomic class and the global Filipino work force, Angela also suggested that class connections to Filipino Americans affect their acclimation to resistance when she stated: "… I feel that working class youth's material conditions inform them of the need for resistance early on, though it may not be named as such […] and the internalized oppression manifests itself in different ways in different socioeconomic settings."9 Her clarification suggests that Filipino Americans who go through their ethnic identity process can be acclimated to resistance. However, Filipino Americans in lower socioeconomic circumstances may be more motivated to resist oppression given their financial circumstances. With the majority of Filipino Americans coming from poorer communities, it would then suggest that the majority of Filipino Americans would be inclined to learn about and resist oppression during their identity development. Overwhelmingly, participants saw resistance as a necessary part of Filipino American identity development, built on years of colonization and oppression in the Philippines. Although many first-generation Filipino American immigrants want their offspring to assimilate to avoid the "othering" that the U.S. has promoted so well, the yearning to learn and understand Filipino cultural symbols, language, and lineage remains. The use of hip hop culture as a tool to inspire Filipino American ethnic identity development, a deeper sense of critical consciousness, and ultimately resistance makes it an important factor in Filipino American decolonization.

---

9   Angela Dy, Interview, August 5, 2011.

LOVE AND JUSTICE

HOW HIP HOP SAVED ME

By Kiwi Illafonte

1.

I grew up pretty confused about who I was. Not just my Filipino identity, but where I belonged, period. I was being tugged in different directions, whether it was my homies on the block, my family, or my classmates. It was Los Angeles, it was the 80s, and everything seemed pretty black or white, and there wasn't much in between.

Because she was single and working full-time, my mother decided to enroll me in summer camp at the Wilshire YMCA. It was fun, I made hella friends, and had crushes on many camp counselors. This was where I first encountered what we now call hip hop. I remember hearing some uptempo electronic-sounding music (most likely Herbie Hancock's "Rockit") coming from the gym. I walked in and saw one of the homies Mike (his full name was Michael Jackson; we always used to tease him about it) on the floor spinning on his back, his body wrapped tight like a ball. Then he jumped back up, did this move where it looked like he was walking forward but moving backward, then he flipped back onto the floor spinning, this time on his head. I was completely mesmerized.

"What's Mike doing?" I asked my buddy Kamau.

"Aww Jack, you ain't never heard of breakin?" he exclaimed, while attempting to mimic some of Mike's moves (but not quite as well).

I had no idea what Kamau was talking about, but for the first time in my young life, I finally came across something that spoke to me. And to think I never even became much of a dancer.

2.

I knew that I wanted to express myself through hip hop, but as an introverted, shy little boy, rap was the furthest thing from my mind. Not to mention rap wasn't as developed back then. So of course after seeing Mike at the Wilshire Y do his thing, I decided to give breakdancing a try. And I tried and I tried and I tried (for several years actually) until I realized that my physical abilities had a ceiling somewhere between backspins and windmills. Quite simply, while I had rhythm, I just wasn't acrobatic like my other b-boy homies.

So sometime around middle school, I got into graf writing. Now here was something I was a little more talented in, which didn't require me risking a broken neck. I got my hands on that famous *Subway Art* book, and studied it like an aerosol geek. Some of my friends in the neighborhood were also into writing, and formed this crew NBC, "Never Been Caught." Talk about a political statement right there. I eventually joined NBC and we went wild all over (what is now known as) Koreatown and Hollywood. We would go out at crazy hours, like meeting up at 5am and tagging for a couple hours on the way to school. Sometimes I'd go out by myself with a marker and hit up every lightpost and phone booth within a half-mile radius of my crib, just to mark my territory. Some of my funniest experiences getting chased happened during this time, like when the husky security guard at the laundromat around the corner saw us tagging up a wall in the parking lot. He gave chase and we ran like hell, only to realize he'd given up about a quarter of a block into the run.

Not too long after that, my luck ran out when me and a couple homies tagged up Bancroft Middle School. A couple P.E. teachers (who were clearly more athletic than the laundromat security dude) chased us down with the quickness, and we were cold busted. After being passed on to the police, I ended up being interrogated by some asshole Pinoy detective with my mom in the room crying and everything. And well, let's just say I had to find a different acronym for "NBC."

So then DJing came along. And when it comes to DJs, one might argue that Filipinos are practically genetically made for this form of hip hop expression. But unfortunately for me, I was limited economically with the kind of equipment I could afford to buy. I had a couple DJ homies who would let me mess with their turntables, but eventually that wore off. One of them even told me I couldn't come over anymore. I was heated! So I'd practice scratching on my mom's janky stereo system with the built-in turntable on top. I'd use the phono/tape select buttons interchangeably as the transformer. I thought that was pretty impressive for such an unofficial setup. In my heart, I felt like I was destined to DJ. But unless I could make a couple thousand bucks magically appear, that DJ career was not about to happen. I had to figure something else out.

3.

By middle school practically all my friends went from skateboarding to gang banging. A couple of my friends had older brothers who were part of the neighborhood Filipino gang, and they wanted us to start the next generation. And with not much else to do, and because the streets were getting a little grimy and it didn't hurt to have backup, we all eventually became a part of it.

I was pretty hesitant to join, but it was hard to ignore my circle of friends all starting to wear pompadours and baggy pants, smoking cigarettes and cruising around the 'hood. And it wasn't like I could just all of a sudden stop hanging out with them. I mean, we all grew up together. So naturally, at some point I found myself in someone's living room getting initiated, curled up on the floor with five homies punching and kicking me for 60 seconds. I actually didn't even consent to it, and to this day my friends still feel bad for that happening. But whatever, what was done was done. I was in.

The one really crucial thing about this gang was that it was the first time I was around anything explicitly and proudly labeled as Filipino. Our gang included both immigrant and American-born Pinoys (not to mention cats of other ethnicities), and our racial identity was one of the main things that united us. We also incorporated "Filipino" ways of expressing ourselves, whether it was using certain terminologies and accents, or our style. I remember hella wanting to learn Tagalog so I could relate with my first-generation immigrant homeboys through language. For the first time, even though it was just scratching the surface, I was proud to be Pinoy. I was proud to belong to something.

There was a part of gang life that was innocent and adventurous: meeting girls, stealing cars, hanging out, and experimenting with drugs and alcohol. Then there was the part I wasn't too fond of: the violence. There came a point where the war between our rivals was so hot that I used to do windsprints home after school. The tension left all of us with our heads on a swivel, anticipating that car coming around the corner with a bunch of heads who were looking to come at us. Thankfully, with the exception of a few cases, most of us walked away from it just fine. A few ended up in juvie (Juvenile Hall) and/or the federal pen. And a couple unlucky ones, like my close friend Russell, along with some other homies, ended up dead. These were the times when we had to grow up quick, not sure about what it meant to grieve or to heal.

The first (full) rap I wrote was in response to this violence. I don't remember how it went anymore, but I remember writing it after I heard Boogie Down Productions' "Stop the Violence." That song resonated with my conflicting feelings about the gang life, and I honestly believe that the process of hearing that song, and responding to it with my own rap, was perhaps the most lifesaving moment of my adolescence. That song literally saved my life.

4.

By the time I was transitioning between middle school and high school, hip hop was in its own transition, going from what many were calling a phase to, in my opinion, a significant cultural and political phenomenon in the history of black people in America. The music went from mostly party music to proclamations of black pride. Songs like Public Enemy's "Fight the Power," Paris' "The Devil Made Me Do It," and even NWA's "Fuck the Police" made critical thinking and "knowledge of self" something of value as opposed to some grade school requirement. I learned much of my black history from those hip hop songs.

This was somewhat of a rebirth of my hip hop identity. I wasn't quite sure what it was, but I was drawn to this music—these messages—in a life-changing, transformative way. Later on I realized that I related to hip hop because those stories that KRS ONE and Chuck D and Ice Cube were telling were experiences that my own community shared; struggles and feelings of inferiority and frustration as people of color in America. And I was starving for something to feel proud of.

So, with no access (at the time) to anything Filipino, I gravitated towards blackness. Like, I literally wanted to be black. I was young, and didn't yet have any analysis of what cultural appropriation was. I just knew that I identified with the desire to question and rebel. I identified with my homies being fucked with by the police. I identified with the violence and murder of young men from my community at the hands of other young men from my community. I was exhausted from it, and this music provided a soundscape for that experience.

5.

So I didn't have the athleticism to dance, didn't want to get busted again for tagging, and couldn't afford to be a DJ. Well, what else was left to do but rap? It was the cheapest and most accessible way for me to express myself. Now I didn't have the desire, swag, or confidence that most "emcees" seemed to have. But I learned fairly quick that I wasn't too bad with the pen and paper. Though I didn't do too well grade-wise in English class, my teachers would always comment on how I was a "special" writer, and I'd like to think that skill translated over into writing raps. At first I did a good job mimicking my favorite rappers, who at the time had lower, more booming voices. But that didn't sound right, so eventually I settled into my own, scratchy high-pitched voice. And that's the voice I've stuck with (to varying degrees) to this day.

Emceeing put me in a position to experience and express myself through hip hop in perhaps the most powerful way: through words. In addition, I had to earn everything I worked for. On top of that there were only a handful of Pinoy rappers back then, so that made it extra challenging. My very first show, a hip hop showcase in Carson, I got booed. Hard. I learned quick that it was going to take much more than my writing wit to earn respect. I was determined. But where was I to go?

6.

While chillin at a friend's house party, I found myself spittin bars to a small crowd of folks. One of those folks was this dude Wendell Pascual, who along with this other cat Jose Buktaw aka DJ Dwenz, were scheming to start up a hip hop open mic called Foundation FunKollective. The only other open mic in L.A. was the renowned Project Blowed, but at that time—and in my opinion rightfully so—it was difficult for anyone who 1) wasn't Black and 2) didn't rap like Micah 9 to get love there. So Foundation ended up being like an alternative to Project Blowed. My first time going was like a rebirth: b-boys busting moves, DJs spinning, graffers exchanging blackbooks, and of course, rappers passing the mic.

Reluctantly, I navigated my way into the middle, and watched as heads dropped lyric after lyric into the cypher, literally building energy with each line. And while there was a little anxiety about having to prove myself, I almost felt like I was being ushered into the space by these total strangers, curious as to what this short Filipino kid was going to add to the space. And after what seemed like an eternity, the mic came to me. And closed my eyes and spit. And finally, I felt like I belonged. And as nervous as I was, I knew this was my calling.

7.

Foundation became a great space and community for myself and others to work on their craft. There were a number of Filipinos who showed up regularly, including Apl of Black Eyed Peas, Immortal Fader Fyters (IF2), and the homie Jern Eye from Lunar Heights. Some of these regulars were organized as part of the Foundation FunKollective to take ownership of its vision and operations. It really embodied one of Bambaataa's original hip hop mantras: "Peace, Unity, and Having Fun." I got to connect and collaborate with other emcees, learn about the tools and processes of making music, and my overall hip hop identity was nurtured. My skills as a lyricist and emcee began to grow.

But while this was a positive space for me, there was something missing. While my techniques were getting tighter, I didn't have much direction content-wise. I knew the world was fucked up and things needed to change, but I didn't really have a deep analysis around things like oppression and liberation. So ultimately I never felt satisfied with what I was writing because it wasn't really going anywhere; if anything it was regurgitating the same old messaging.

Then I met Faith Santilla. She started coming around to Foundation open mics and became regular at some point. She graduated from Hamilton High and was classmates/close friends with some of the Living Legends crew (such as MURS, Scarab, and Eligh), so she knew way more about underground L.A. hip hop than I did. I think I grew as a fan of hip hop because of her broad taste in music. We had a protracted process of attraction (and acknowledgment of attraction), but eventually after some awkward discussions we ended up dating.

In addition to all the hip hop knowledge, Faith was also involved in this Filipino youth and student organization in Los Angeles called KPK (Kilusan ng Progresibong Kabataan or Movement of Progressive Youth). That was somewhat of a mouthful so eventually the name changed to League of Filipino Students (after the organization in the Philippines of the same name). Faith brought me into KPK. Now mind you, this kind of Filipino organizing—one that connected the struggle of Filipinos in the U.S. to the struggle in the Philippines—was still not quite developed. So what I walked into, as someone who never attended college, was this group of all university students and/or graduates discussing things like imperialism and capitalism. While I was excited and curious, I was also lost and confused because the information and language was more than I could handle. But I stuck with it, mostly because of Faith, who kept pushing me and advocated for my participation.

As part of this process, I was able to participate in an exposure trip to the Philippines in the summer of 1998. Here I was finally exposed to all the conditions that I learned about (or more accurately, was confused about) such as feudalism and bureaucratic capitalism. I got to integrate with various communities—from peasants to students to indigenous folks to workers—and learn about how imperialism was impacting them firsthand. It was then that I realized that the "movement" as we know it was bigger than my own experience, that there are global roots to our struggle, and that our liberation wherever the diaspora has taken us is connected to the liberation of our kababayans back in our homeland.

It was after this trip that I dedicated myself to this movement, the movement for National Democracy in the Philippines.

8.

Upon returning from that first exposure trip, my writing began to change. My political consciousness had transformed, and my raps had no choice but to reflect that. At first my stuff was maybe a little TOO hit-you-over-the-head militant; probably typical of someone who'd finally woken up from their ignorance and discovered reality. At some point it leveled off to being a little more creatively political, in a way that was a little more accessible to more people. It was at this point that I began my transformation from simply an open mic emcee to an actual songwriter, and the themes of my music finally began to have structure and depth. It was time for me to be a recording artist.

By this point I was employed and could finally afford some decent equipment. For creating and recording music, I purchased a Fostex 8-track Reel-to-Reel recorder, a Mackie 16-track mixing board, and my baby, the MPC 2000 sampling drum machine. I feel like I have an appreciation for how music was recorded back in the day because modern computer-operated software like ProTools makes it easy for just about anyone to record music.

The MPC 2000 was the heart of my bedroom studio. Apl actually taught me how to use that bad boy. I became pretty tight with the Black Eyed Peas for a brief period, right before they got signed by Interscope. After that I knew things would change, and I didn't have any interest to be a part of all that. It's crazy to see how far they've gotten today, with the Super Bowl halftime shows and the commercials and everything. And to think these were my homies, who I was around pretty often, whether they were in the studio, or doing shows, or navigating the business of music as young artists. As interesting as it was, I realized pretty early on that that wasn't how I wanted to go about my business. Not to mention I didn't want to hoo-ride on their success. My politics ultimately was what guided me as an artist, as well as the actual craft of emceeing and lyricism.

So with my old-ass recording equipment, I teamed up with my buddy DJ KidWIK (from Immortal Fader Fyters and Ozomatli) to form the crew Vice Versa, and we created our first and only project, "The Concrete EP." This was on some lyrical turntablist sonic experimentalism, with a little Filipino political twist. But not long after the EP came out, KidWIK got STOLEN from me to be Ozomatli's tour DJ. I mean, I was a scrubby little rapper kid, so who was I to object to my boy traveling around the world playing music and shit? So alas, I was left to gigging around with my little portable DAT player (think of it as the great-grandparent of the iPod). But what do you know, I end up getting hella love, and more requests to perform. I think part of it was that I was one of a few Filipino cats out there rhyming, and objectively speaking, I was probably the only one coming with any political shit, talking about anything Filipino for that matter. The content is what created opportunities for me to perform at college campuses for Filipino events, and gave me my first taste of being a consistent performing artist.

9.

Eventually I moved to the Bay. The Bay was different from L.A. in that there was, what I would consider, a more concentrated and thriving Filipino cultural scene. So literally as soon as I settled in, I was getting show requests. I was getting exposed to spaces such as Bindlestiff Studios in San Francisco. I'd see club flyers where some legendary Pinoy DJs would be spinning. Shit, I'd see DJ Qbert kicking it at the Serramonte Mall.

Needless to say, I got hella love when I moved to the Bay. And I ain't really did shit yet. But eventually I began the process for creating my first solo album, and *Writes of Passage: Portraits of a Son Rising* came out in 2003.

This album had a little bit of L.A. and a little of the Bay in it. The biggest influence had to do with being involved in anti-sexism men's work as part of my day job at this youth non-profit health agency called HIFY (Health Initiatives For Youth). I was their publications coordinator and at some point, became the lead editor of a book called *A Young Man's Survival Guide*. Part of creating this book was interviewing and getting contributions from different folks who worked with young men, and one of the groups I came across was an organization called MOVE (Men Overcoming Violence), which worked primarily with perpetrators of domestic violence. A Pinoy was their Interim Executive Director at the time, this guy by the name of Allan Silva. He became one of my biggest mentors. Anyways, MOVE's approach was pretty profound at the time, to actually have men identify why sexism and patriarchy are systems of oppression that not only negatively impact women, but also themselves as men. It created a space for them to reflect on their male shit and identify how to reverse and eliminate those sexist behaviors and language in their lives. It taught them how to be male allies. It was some of these values that I learned about during the creation of this book, and that made me reflect on my own male shit. And while I still had a long way to go to truly become an ally, I was moved enough to incorporate a lot of these values in the creation of this album, not to mention my own personal development to this day.

10.

Shortly after I moved to the Bay, I started hearing about this new Pinoy emcee who started coming around spots in L.A., a cat by the name of Bambu. And after hearing about each other online, we finally met at a community event in L.A. where both of us were performing. I peeped his set and dug what I saw. We started following one another on Asian Ave (think of it as the great-grand uncle of Facebook), and not long after that, I did a guest verse on one of the songs of his *Self Untitled* (2002) album. It was pretty clear that there was some chemistry there, so we ended up doing more work together, namely doing a few shows that we called "The Native Guns Tour." Next thing you know, we start working on more music together, decide to join forces, and kept the tour name as our group name. Say hello to the Native Guns.

So the Guns started doing more shows and building a following. We did a few performances at UC Berkeley where the sound guy was this skinny Chinese dude named Phatrick. He was also one of the lead members of Cal's Students for Hip Hop. At one of the shows, he actually approached Bam about being our DJ, which Bam politely declined. Apparently all the hot DJs were forming a huge line to be our DJ! (Not)

Eventually, after some folks recommended him, I got Phatrick to DJ for my solo shows. He turned out to be the perfect DJ: talented, organized, and most importantly, opinionated. I needed someone who was going to bring ideas to the table. He spoke up and pushed back. He was working out great for me so I brought up the idea of him DJing for the Guns. And although Bam was hesitant, we gave Phatty a shot, and the rest is history. Native Guns was complete.

The Native Guns, in my honest opinion, was perhaps one of the more important cultural formations for our generation of Filipino-Americans. Our solo projects, while quite powerful in their own respect, didn't quite match the impact of our music as a collective. Here you have two outspoken, brown and tattooed Filipino males, going hard on the government, on police, and on global oppression. We expressed our Pinoy pride from a political gangster perspective—that looked beyond lumpia, the tinikling, and Pacquiao—and stretched deeper into the root causes of our people's suffering. We couldn't play it safe. We didn't really have a choice.

Working with Bam was great because dude was a workhorse. Which really pushed me to step up my writing and knock out songs. It also helped that he had a pretty good ear for music. He was great with things like writing choruses, which I sucked at before working with him. Our first project, *The Stray Bullets Mixtape* (2004), was put together in literally one week, maybe two, tops. Eventually we figured out a routine for creating songs even though I lived in the Bay and he was all the way in L.A. And before you knew it, we released our second project *Barrel Men* (2006). Honestly I wasn't really totally satisfied with the album, but something about it was definitive. I think some things just needed to be said, and we picked a perfect time to rap about it. Not long after that, we released *The Stray Bullets Mixtape Volume 2* (2007), which really propelled us into notoriety. Phatrick had a big hand in putting that one together. Phatty was perhaps the perfect bridge between me and Bam, especially when we butted heads, which happened often.

One of the times we were put to the test was when Apl, who'd begun gaining his own popularity because of the "Bebot" song, approached Native Guns about possibly being on a new label he was creating, Jeepney Music. There was a part of us that saw it as a great opportunity to expand our reach, yet there was another part of us that was skeptical because of what we might have to give up as far as our musical and political integrity. Sure enough, things came to a head when we were asked to do a cameo on a remix of the "Bebot" song, which would feature us, Roscoe Umali, and Nump Trump. At first, we thought it would be cool because the original song was actually a proclamation of Filipino pride, so we thought maybe it would be an extension of that. But what the remix became was more of a song directed towards hollering at women. Okay then, fine. We could try to work with that. So Bam and I do a back-and-forth style verse that more or less celebrated Pinays in what we felt was a respectful and empowering way. We felt okay about it. But let's just say that, when the rest of the song was recorded, the remainder of the lyrics were not too different from a lot of the rap music you hear out there: objectifying and misogynist. This put us in somewhat of a tough position because these were not the values we represented, but this was also an opportunity for us. We actually had some hard debates about whether or not to back out. I was pretty firm that I could not, in good conscience, be on that song. In the end, we decided to not be included in the project, which I'm guessing rubbed the label the wrong way, because we didn't really hear much from them after that.

Another point of conflict within Native Guns was our politics. I was pretty entrenched in the work of BAYAN-USA, an alliance of organizations doing work in the Filipino community in the U.S. Bam, for a while, wasn't really part of any organizations, but eventually joined KMB (Kabataan Maka-Bayan), which worked with Filipino youth in Los Angeles. Long story short, there was some funk between those organizations, which would sometimes affect the dynamic between me and Bam, even though neither of us was directly involved in whatever went down. It was a weird position to be in, especially since we were reaching a point where we were really close to blowing up. But that tension, on top of our own internal issues around our musical direction and so forth, ended up being factors in our eventual split in 2007.

Overall, however, I'd say the experience with Native Guns was a good one. We made some pretty damn great music, got to perform all over the country (as well as Canada), and spread our message. And Bam and Phatrick, those are two of my closest friends up to this day. I'm most appreciative of that.

11.
After Native Guns, let's just say I sort of fell off. Musically, at least. I put out *The Summer Exposure Mixtape* (2007), which was actually pretty nice, and after that it's been mostly half-finished songs and projects.

There was the *Sounds of a New Hope* (2009) documentary that chronicled my trip to the Philippines in 2007, which was important because it was the first time they had ever incorporated hip hop into a community exposure trip. I visited gangsters/rappers from two areas in Caloocan City to build with them through music. I actually incorporated workshop material from the hip hop workshops I was helping facilitate in San Francisco at the Filipino Community Center. And that particular trip became a model for future exposure trips where hip hop was incorporated.

But alas, I got back from the Philippines, and my music declined. And as that happened, my political work began to increase. I became more involved locally with the San Francisco Committee for Human Rights in the Philippines (SF-CHRP) and eventually became the Deputy Secretary General of BAYAN-USA. I tried not to neglect my music, but naturally it had to take a bit of a back seat. I think I needed that though. I needed to step up as an organizer and put into practice all the things I was talking about in my music. So for three years, I grinded through the organizing work. And while I don't think I'll win any awards for best Deputy Secretary, I was able to contribute more significantly than I ever had in the past, and I walked away with a stronger perspective on organizing and a sharper analysis when it came to my politics.

12.

It's 2013. And in the last couple years, the music has picked up. Specifically, with my band Bandung 55. What started out as a few local Filipino organizers jamming eventually became a full-on musical collective. And as of this writing, we've been at it for about a year and a half. And it's been a blessing. We all share similar musical AND political objectives. Our songs and themes are intentional. We have a song about immigrant workers. We have another song that was influenced by the Occupy Movement. We are united in our direction and all play a specific role in getting there.

Looking back on myself and my habits, I realize that my process of making music has always been slow. I think part of it is my own insecurity about my voice and my music, and the perception I imagine people might have of it. Like Erykah Badu once said, "I'm an artist, and I'm sensitive about my shit." Perhaps that comes with the inferiority I felt growing up, as a short, quiet, brown kid in Koreatown. All I know is that, whatever it was, that shit still tends to hinder my freedom and my openness to just create, and to just surrender to however people react to it. I think with Bandung, because there isn't a lot of those pressures attached to it, that anxiety around the perception of my music has been less of an issue. I almost feel like where I am currently as an artist has been the most liberating for me.

My overall reflection of my music and being Filipino, I think I did the best I could with what I had. I was pretty damn lucky to come across some really influential folks along the way who helped guide my music (and my life) somewhere meaningful. And if nothing else, I can at least say I went about it with integrity and respect for hip hop, and with love for my people.

CRITICAL PEDAGOGY AND FILIPINO AMERICAN HIP HOP

ANALYZING AND HONORING THE MIXTAPE—A SONG FOR OURSELVES

By Michael Viola

> *"Culture is said to be to society what a flower is to a plant. What is important about a flower is not just its beauty. A flower is the carrier of the seeds for new plants, the bearer of the future of that species."*[1]
>
> —African Proverb

> *"Chris lijima embodies the title of cultural worker. His music did not come from excess or boredom but of necessity."*[2]
>
> —Geologic, Filipino American hip hop artist

C ultural production is always united with other dynamic social sources as a site of constant struggle between those who want to transform society and those who want to maintain its basic features.[3] Therefore, culture must be understood both in its own terms and as a part of larger social and class forces of society. For historically racialized groups in the United States, such as Filipino Americans, culture is a product of a people's history written upon the pages of repression and resistance. According to Teresa Ebert and Mas'ud Zavarzadeh in their book, *Class in Culture*, during times of economic crisis culture can cloud the material contradictions inherent within the system of production.[4] They explain how a "cultural turn" has propagated

---

1   Ngugi Wa Thiong'o, *Moving the Centre: The Struggle for Cultural Freedoms*. Oxford: James Currey Ltd., 1993, pg. 57.
2   *A Song for Ourselves: The Mixtape* downloaded at: http://massmovementtv.blogspot.com/2009/02/song-for-ourselves-mixtape.html (accessed on March 10, 2009).
3   For an important analysis in the struggle over education in the Philippines see Renato Constantino's "The Miseducation of the Filipino" published in *Vestiges of War*, edited by Shaw and Francia, 2002.
4   Ebert, T. L. and M. U. b. u. Zavarzadeh. *Class in Culture*. Boulder: Paradigm Publishers, 2008.

numerous research projects to highlight matters of difference, identity, and social construction as radical avenues of inquiry, yet such projects have either explained away or sidestepped the injustices of capitalist exploitation. In other words, Ebert and Zavarzadeh maintain that a cultural critique divorced from an analysis of class relations and political economy can be utilized to safeguard an inherently exploitative system that has set in motion a multitude of unjust social oppressions. Their analysis is important to consider in this contemporary moment as the power and status of the transnational ruling class grows uncertain with the failed attempts to remedy the inherent contradictions of a capitalist system. To be sure, culture wars cannot be trivialized as a distraction from class politics. However, the organic link between cultural struggles and the struggles to roll back the consolidation of ruling class power demands theoretical and practical exploration.

Ever since the 1970s, global capitalism and the United States' role as global hegemon have experienced a prolonged crisis arising from systemic overproduction.[5] The social system of capitalism has been unable to secure new areas for sustainable productive investment at home, which among other things (e.g., financial speculation) has led the ruling class to turn to market expansion abroad. The short-term remedy to expand capital accumulation in the Middle East and Third World countries has resulted in great material, ideological, and most importantly, human costs. Historically, greater profit and exploitation of workers have been accomplished through various means such as technological advances that have served the interests of profiteering as opposed to human need. As a result, a global working class has been greatly deskilled and impoverished. Furthermore, structural adjustment programs have forced greater trade and investment liberalization on neocolonies such as the Philippines to exploit their labor, to plunder their raw materials, and to control their local economies. In the 1990s, unsatisfied with the extraction of massive economic surplus generated from the debt burdens of the Third World, the benefactors of neoliberal globalization turned to a strategy of "accumulation by dispossession." Through cannibalistic processes that geographer David Harvey explores in his various works, public utilities (e.g., water) and social services (e.g., education) were turned into sinister opportunities for privatization and profit. The economic dispossession of entire populations further constricted opportunities for investments that in turn exacerbated the glut of finance capital. According to the report "On the Global Economic and Financial Crisis" prepared by the Ibon Foundation in the Philippines:

> By the 1990s imperialism increasingly relied on getting its profits
> from purely financial schemes disconnected from any productive
> activity. Parasitic capital took advantage of advances in information
> and communications technology not just to facilitate its global pro-
> duction networks but also to fashion complex financial instruments
> for creating profits outside of any actual productive activity.

Within the United States we are now bearing witness to the barbarism of neoliberal policies of human and environmental extraction that have been systematically imposed upon by (neo)colonized countries of the Global South. In the Philippines such a system has resulted in such widespread unemployment and poverty that 80% of its population earns no more than 2 dollars a day.[6]

How can cultural production within the Filipino diaspora intersect with critical pedagogy enabling us to not only teach against but also transform structures of inequality, racism, and global exploitation? Drawing upon the

---

5   Harvey, David. *A Brief History of Neoliberalism*. Oxford and New York: Oxford University Press, 2005.
6   San Juan, E. *In the Wake of Terror: Class, Race, Nation, Ethnicity in the Postmodern World*. Lanham: Lexington Books.

mixtape produced for the Chris Iijima documentary, *A Song for Ourselves*, I maintain that various forms of cultural production with the Asian American movement has served as an important pedagogical and political tool to not only elucidate but also transform the material contradictions of our society. I analyze a mixtape featuring a number of important Filipino American hip hop artists and activists who commemorate the radical cultural politics of Chris Iijima, whose own music invited listeners to forward an *internationalist* project for justice.

Exploring Filipino American cultural production considered together with a critical analysis of global political economy can help clarify how the unity of people's thought and action (praxis) can exist in two conflicting forms. If people only engage in the social relations into which they are born, assuming that these practices are natural and unchanging, then their praxis will serve to reproduce the extant relations and conditions. On the other hand, people can struggle to see past the widespread forms of cultural production that naturalize the status quo while they also struggle to create a culture rooted in democracy and genuine equality. It is with this dialectical understanding that a culture can develop to truthfully reflect a complex and relational world, so that it may be understood but more importantly, be made anew.

The documentary by the emerging filmmaker Tadashi Nakamura beautifully explores the dialogue between Iijima's music (together with Joanne Nobuko Miyamoto and William "Charlie" Chin who formed the group called Yellow Pearl) and the Asian American movement of the late 1960s and early 1970s. Through valuable interview footage taken before his tragic death, Iijima explains that his music and the Asian American movement were not driven by the politics of identity but by the politics of human struggle. He explains, "I think what is sad for me is that so many Asian American studies types have reduced the Asian American movement and Asian American history to proving that you are Asian and being proud of your ethnicity...That's such a distortion of what it was really about, which was your world outlook and what you believed about what being Asian meant in terms of politics, in terms of culture, and how you saw the world in a progressive, humanist way."[7]

The documentary's mixtape, produced and compiled by DJ Phatrick, begins with the contributing artists (Kiwi and Bambu, both formerly of Native Guns, and Geologic of Blue Scholars) reflecting on Iijima's contributions to the project for cultural, political, and economic freedom. Bambu explains, "Chris Iijima was the soundtrack for the early generation of Asian American freedom fighters. In that spirit I'm hoping to carry on that tradition." Kiwi further adds, "this film is so important for our community because Chris Iijima's legacy is something that we really need to share especially with this generation in these important times." Geologic explains, "Chris Iijima embodies the title of cultural worker. His music did not come from excess or boredom but of necessity."[8] Geologic's sentiment is clearly demonstrated in the Iijima's famous song, "We Are the Children," which is utilized as the musical backdrop for the contemporary reflections. It was during the height of this song's popularity that public outrage over the imperial atrocities of the Vietnam War were reverberating throughout Southeast Asia and the consciousness of Asian American students, women, workers, and artists were unlocked to the palatable ideas of radical social transformation. Iijima's music makes important historical links for an Asian American population dispossessed, racialized, and internally colonized:

> We are the children of the migrant worker.
> We are the offspring of the concentration camp.
> Sons and daughters of the railroad builders.
> Leave their stamp on America.[9]

---

7   *A Song for Ourselves: The Mixtape.*
8   ibid.
9   ibid.

Pushing against the "politics of identity" that was also beginning to emerge from this time period, Iijima refused to disconnect his music of struggle from the unfinished tasks of colonized and subaltern Asian populations fighting for freedom and emancipation in their respective homelands:

> We are the cousins of the freedom fighter,
> brothers and sisters all around the world.
> We are a part of the Third World people,
> Who will leave their stamp on America.[10]

Whether through folksongs or hip hop, music in the Asian American movement has contributed greatly to a culture based not on assimilation and nativism but on resistance and transformation. In the early 1970s, Chris Iijima, Nobuko Miyamoto, and "Charlie" Chin traveled throughout the United States articulating an Asian American identity that was, in Iijima's own words, "originally meant to be a means to an end rather than an end in itself. It was as much a mechanism to identify with one another as it was to identify with the struggles of others, whether African Americans or Asians overseas. It was less a marker of what one was and more a marker of what one believed."[11] In 1973, the trio recorded their album *A Grain of Sand: Music for the Struggle by Asians in America*, which was widely recognized as the soundtrack for progressive Asian Americans in New York, Los Angeles, Honolulu, San Francisco, and Chicago. Today, the album is widely recognized as a classic and even sold in the gift shop of the Smithsonian Institution. However, unlike the present moment where many progressive Asian Americans are unable to articulate what they are trying to "progress" towards, Chris Iijima along with Nobuko Miyamoto are clear and resolute in their political vision. In the artist statement for their album they are clear to explain that their music is a humble extension of the movement and a political project "to communicate our ideas so that we all may struggle together more effectively for the final defeat of capitalism, racism and sexism and the building of a socialist state."

Informed by revolutionary Third World and nationalist writings the cultural politics articulated by Iijima's musical formation, *A Grain of Sand* was not restricted to the Asian American experience alone. Through their music, they struggled for a transformative cultural consciousness that was rooted in a liberated people, free from domination. Their music dialectically linked culture to the inalienable right of every people to carry the burden and the promise of creating their own histories. The song, "Somos Asiaticos" performed entirely in Spanish was inspired by the struggle of Latinos in the Upper West Side of New York City. "Jonathan Jackson" was written in honor of a seventeen-year-old man who was killed by authorities for trying to free his older brother and Black Panther Party member, George Jackson, who was sentenced for one year to life for stealing $70. Many activists from this time period viewed George and Jonathan Jackson as black martyrs killed by an oppressive and racist prison industry.[12] Furthermore, the song, "Warriors of the Rainbow" was inspired by Native Americans organizing for housing rights in Chicago. This particular piece is based on an indigenous legend that "change would be brought about with the coming together of warriors of all colors of the rainbow." Therefore, the entire album is a product of dialogue that Chris Iijima and his colleagues had with workers, students, activists, and families struggling to overcome racial

---

10   ibid.
11   "Remembering Chris Iijima: Early political singer and songwriter died December 31" by Phil Takitsu Nash http://www.imdiversity.com/Villages/Asian/arts_culture_media/nash_chris_iijima_0206.asp.
12   In the United States today, this prison industrial complex incarcerates more of its citizenry than any other country with more than 1 in 100 adults currently locked behind bars. Such statistics are even more appalling when one considers the racial makeup of our nation's prison population and the disproportionate number of young, black and Latino males confined behind bars.

oppression and class exploitation. Paulo Freire recognized dialogue as a central tool for social transformation. In his famous book, *Pedagogy of the Oppressed*, Freire states,

> [T]he more radical the person is, the more fully he or she enters into reality so that, knowing it better, he or she can transform it. This individual is not afraid to confront, to listen, to see the world unveiled. This person is not afraid to meet the people or to enter into a dialogue with them. This person does not consider himself or herself the proprietor of history of all people, or the liberator of the oppressed; but he or she does commit himself or herself, within history, to fight at their side."[13]

The album *A Grain of Sand* is a musical testimony to Freire's idea of dialogue as a practice for freedom. They explain,

> We believe artists should engage in political struggle outside the realm of "Art" so that whatever is created is from a broad perspective and not from a limited aspect of the struggle. We owe our music to the movement and the struggles of all oppressed people. Without them our music is irrelevant. Without them—without you—we have nothing to sing about.

Through dialogue with the racialized and internally colonized peoples of the United States, their music participated in projects of struggle to articulate and confront the injustices of the world so that such realities could be transformed. Through their music they expressed an understanding that such a historic task was the responsibility of the society's most marginalized created under historic conditions and complexities that arise out of race, gender, and ethnic relations that are all intimately linked with class formations. It is to this diverse population they sing:

> You are the music
> You are the song
> You are the ones
> To whom the future belongs.

Chris Iijima dedicated his life embodying the famous maxim of the time: "to serve the people" not only as a cultural worker but also as an educator, lawyer, and father. On December 31, 2005, at the age of 57, Iijima passed away. However, his legacy continues to inspire artists struggling to foster cultures grounded in the ideals of freedom and genuine democracy.

---

13   Paulo Freire, *Pedagogy of the Oppressed*. New York: Continuum, 1990.

Filipino American hip hop artists such as Bambu, Geologic, and Kiwi (to name only a few) have provided the soundtrack to the social movements of the present.[14] The mixtape *A Song for Ourselves* demonstrates hip hop's potential as a transformative pedagogical site for social critique. One of the key contributors to the mix tape is Filipino American hip hop artist Jack De Jesus whose emcee name is Kiwi. In the mix tape Kiwi reflects:

> *The story of Chris Iijima is important in that [he] is one of the few examples we have of what it truly means to be a cultural activist, where your art or in this case your music, is guided by love. Not some kind of romantic love but love for the people, love for humanity and justice.*

In the song "Cause," written and performed by Kiwi, he raps:

> *From Seattle to the Bay to Los Angeles,*
> *Most of us got no choice but to hang with this.*
> *[We] Got nothing to lose, got no reason to fail,*
> *Blood gripping every generation, leaving a trail.*
> *Cheap labor politicians putting people for sale.*
> *Why is the neighborhood hot? Because we're living in hell.*
> *Fast food, t.v. got us all under a spell.*
> *People under the illusion that we're living it well.*

Through his music, Kiwi confronts the contradictions impacting our nation's youth. In the same song Kiwi rhymes:

> *Why do you think we're even here to begin with?*
> *Cause, the white man stole it from the Indians.*
> *We're so blind that we still get played.*
> *Still conditioned till this day, to still think like a slave.*
> *Why you think it cost so much for college?*
> *But at the liquor store a 40 ounce cost a dollar?*
> *Cause, we so blind that we still get played.*
> *Still thinking if we pray that we going to get saved.*

One of the greatest contributions of the mixtape *A Song for Ourselves* is its internationalist standpoint. As the track titled "Gaza 2 Oakland" suggests, hip hop artists can also be transformative cultural workers speaking in solidarity with the marginalized and oppressed worldwide who are utilizing all within their means to transform their surroundings of imposed violence and state terrorism. Kiwi proclaims, "Whether we in Palestine, whether it's

---

14   See: Porfilio, B. & Viola, M. *Hip Hop(e): The Cultural Practice and Critical Pedagogy of International Hip-Hop*. New York: Peter Lang Publishing, 2012; Viola, M. (2006). "Hip-Hop and Critical Revolutionary Pedagogy: Blue Scholarship to Challenge 'The Miseducation of the Filipino.'" *Journal for Critical Education Policy Studies*, Volume 4, Number 2 http://www.jceps.com/index.php?pageID=article&articleID=71; and Viola, M. (2006). "Filipino American Hip-Hop and Class Consciousness: Renewing the Spirit of Carlos Bulosan." *Monthly Review Zine*. http://mrzine.monthlyreview.org/viola150406.html.

for Oscar Grant…We shall no longer be no victims of no circumstance. We going to take down this fucking system, we the worker ants." Kiwi's lyrics are not expressions of blind activism or verbalism. Here, Paulo Freire's words are important to remember, "When a word is deprived of its dimension of action, reflection automatically suffers as well; and the word is change into idle chatter, into verbalism."[15] Freire continues,

> … denunciation is impossible without a commitment to transform,
> and there is no transformation without action. On the other hand,
> if action is emphasized exclusively to the detriment of reflection,
> the word is converted into activism. The latter—action for action's
> sake—negates the true praxis and makes dialogue impossible.[16]

Kiwi's lyrics are informed by his praxis as a community organizer in San Francisco and as a member of the Committee for Human Rights in the Philippines. In 2007 Kiwi, along with Geologic (also of BAYAN-USA), traveled throughout the United States for the successful "Stop the Killings" tour to speak out against the human rights violations in the Philippines and through their music articulate that the internationalism and radical Asian American movement of the late 1960s and early 1970s has not seen its conclusion.[17] In the song "Gaza 2 Oakland," Kiwi rhymes,

> "Give em more than a simple flow.
> This moment is critical…
> Sunshine shinin in the distance I can see it glow.
> I'm trying to sprinkle on some love tryin to see it grow.
> To see it all come together so the people know…
> … We building a movement for something so beautiful.
> Something that's musical, critically lyrical.

The contributors of the mixtape *A Song for Ourselves* are inspired by a people's struggle and informed by revolutionary theory. In the same song, Kiwi names the theorists who inform his own revolutionary cultural practice:

> I've got the fire of my people up inside my heart.
> Light up the spark, when I hit that Marx, Lenin, and Mao.
> Bless you with a different style that is hotter than Mindanao.
> Livin[g] in the here and now.
> My folks are doing things.
> We not relying on no president to bring a change.
> I'm not goin[g] on stage only to entertain.

---

15   Freire, *Pedagogy of the Oppressed*, pg. 87.
16   ibid, pg. 88.
17   BAYAN-USA serves as a democratic clearinghouse of information pertaining to the national democratic movement in the Philippines. Its members consist of diverse sectors such as youth, artists, women, and labor. However, regardless of sector, the various organizations are united in an anti-imperialist perspective and take the position that the conditions for genuine democracy, peace, and cultural survival for global Filipinos will only be made possible with the defeat of foreign hegemony in the Philippine homeland.

Kiwi, Geologic, and Bambu's music is not only a reflection of the world but it is also a tool to recreate it. In the process of creating social transformation, Filipino scholar E. San Juan highlights the need for "organic intellectuals who will integrate themselves with the producing classes—workers, peasants, women, middle strata, the majority of citizens—to establish the basis for a more egalitarian, just, and independent [Philippine] nation."[18] Through such integrations—also known as educational exposure trips—one gains a critical standpoint of neoliberal globalization not provided by corporate media and mainstream academic textbooks. The documentary of Kiwi's summer integration in the summer of 2007 entitled *Sounds of a New Hope* by filmmaker Eric Tandoc provides exemplary firsthand account and analysis of an exposure trip and how hip hop was utilized as an organizing tool for "conscientizacao" (to use Freire's term). Integrating with people used as fodder in the Imperialist lab called the Philippines, Kiwi was able to engage in genuine dialogue with people not only more insightful but also more motivated to change the circumstances of their exploitation. In his song "Cause," Kiwi wonderfully articulates how transformative dialogue is a historic process of struggle:

> *I took my shit and went back to the lab.*
> *Got the formula correct and went back to the Ave.*
> *All my sisters, all my brothers all doing the math.*
> *All building this movement, while we're moving our ass.*
> *Why do you think I do this shit to begin with?*
> *Cause, we've got a legacy of resistance.*
> *Cause, Lapu Lapu did it back in the day.*
> *Chopped off Magellan's head, with a swing of his blade.*
> *Why do you think our people still go hungry?*
> *If we so prosperous what happened to all the money?*
> *Cause, we so blind that we still get played.*
> *We had to sell ourselves just so that we could get paid.*

Integrations such as the one Kiwi conducted are important because they enable a deeper perception of the social, political, and economic contractions set in motion by U.S. imperialism. The everyday violence of neoliberal globalization is not a perspective from which, however well intentioned one may be, an individual can attain a clear picture from a position within the United States. Since ruling groups have material interests in blinding the general public of their plunder and through an international division of labor, it is only through struggle that people can see the underside of the social relations in which all are forced to participate.

The album *A Grain of Sand* and the mixtape *A Song for Ourselves* are products of social movement formations. While both musical forms and the social movements they were involved with are cultural confrontations to neoliberal globalization at different epochs, what unites their songs is an astute understanding that United States imperialism can link the racialized and immigrant experiences of this country to the subjugated peoples of the Third World. The unique synthesis and diverse compilation of songs that I did not speak to in this paper, such as Bambu's "When Will the Time Come?," Blue Scholars' "Back Home," and Chris Iijima's "Vietnamese Lament," articulate important messages of hope and human emancipation. Furthermore, through the medium of hip hop, present-day cultural activists continue the important pedagogical lesson that genuine Asian American empowerment and agency in the era of global capitalism depends not solely upon the successes of local struggles

---

18   E. San Juan, *In the Wake of Terror*, pg. 24.

in the U.S. but also on the victories for popular democratic sovereignty and global justice in locales such as the Philippines as well as other regions of the world. Latin American poet Eduardo Galeano explains this point much more eloquently, "to the extent that the [U.S.] system finds itself threatened by the relentless growth of unemployment, poverty, and the resultant social and political tensions, room for pretense and good manners shrinks in the outskirts of the world, the system reveals its true face."[19]

Cabral's analysis of culture reminds us that "culture, as the fruit of history, reflects at all times the material and spiritual reality of the society."[20] At present, our social relations are not based on mutual exchange but in the quest for profit and power. Hip hop culture certainly reflects this image of society. However, hip hop, like all other forms of cultural production, can present an alternative image of possibility. Just like in languages and literature, the hip hop music compiled in the mixtape *A Song for Ourselves* borrows from various sources to create new sounds and articulations. The listener hears a synthesis taken from hip hop excerpts, documentary interviews of Chris Iijima, Nobuko Miyamoto, and Charlie Chin, along with recognizable hooks from Marvin Gaye and M.I.A. Through this practice, the mixtape serves as the cultural antithesis to the practice of American cultural imperialism. Thus, instead of appropriating and stealing from various cultures of the world, Filipino American hip hop can offer a window to a new culture still struggling to be born. Such a culture is not grounded in the quest for profit and power but rather a global realization of respect, equality, justice, and human need.

---

19   Eduardo Galeano, *Days and Nights of Love and War,* New York: Monthly Review Press, 2000, p. 170.
20   Cabral, A. "Partido Africano da Independência da Guiné e Cabo Verde." *Unity and Struggle: Speeches and Writings*. London: Heinemann Educational Books Ltd, 1980, pg. 149.

VII.

PESOS AND CENTS: SURVIVING INDUSTRIES

PERFORMING TO SURVIVE

ACCEPTING TRUTHS AND FINDING PURPOSE

By DJ Kuttin Kandi

in grade school
sat silent
at the back of the class
denied I was Filipino
when someone like me asked
time seems to travel fast
but I cant forget the
heroin needles in the play yards
or the broken bottle caps
and the rusty monkey bars
in high school I wore polo tees,
Hilfiger jeans
Grand Puba had me
searchin the means
used to rack clothes
to keep my style fresh
with everyone in Hillcrest
class clown
always depressed
wore the pants baggy
cause I wanted to hide my body
ashamed to be the real me
even to my own family

while
my mom fought
to keep my father alive
lost our home
sis and i
tried to survive
so many times
ive tried to take my life
but now
I look back today
And I think I wanna take a ride
—excerpt from "Blue and Red," DJ Kuttin Kandi

I was never allowed to tell anyone that my family had a side business on the weekends where we were street food vendors. To our knowledge, our family were the first to sell Pilipina/o food at all the street fairs and festivals in New York City. My father was an amazing cook and starting a food vendor business seemed like a good idea to generate extra income to our home. Our food specialty was an ukoy (okoy) dish, often known as the "Filipino shrimp fritter." However, in order to make it more accessible to folks who may not be able to eat shrimp, my parents made it vegetarian and used only vegetable oil to fry them. My parents cooked it in front of everyone in giant woks because it was warm and fresh, plus it attracted the crowd to our food booth, which essentially brought more customers. My parents used "marketing strategies" and renamed the ukoy to an Americanized name calling them, "Bean Sprout Pancakes." We also sold other Pilipino and Asian foods like Pork Barbecue, Lo Mein, Fried Rice, and creative inventions like "Potato Frills" and "Apple Fritters." My sister was only 8 years old and I was 10 when we were learning customer service skills to help our parents sell our food at all the street festivals. We worked every Saturday and Sunday starting as early as 5:00 am for set-up and at times we didn't get home until past 12:00 am. We worked at all kinds of street fairs and block parties from small to large such as the Puerto Rican Independence Day Festival, July 4th, Pride Festival, Richmond County Fair, Philippine Independence Day Festival, West 4th Block Parties, Brazilian Festival, and more. Although the street fairs were on weekends my family (which also included my grandparents) spent our time earlier in the week prepping the food such as grocery shopping, cutting the meats and vegetables, stocking our fridges, picking up needed equipment like gas tanks and dry ice, and loading our van. My parents held onto this business for over 12 years but sadly in 1993 we ended our ukoy journey. Due to the price increase of vendor booths/spaces at the street fairs and food vendors flooding the scene, it no longer made sense to continue the business.

It was sad to see our family business come to an end. It brought a lot of pride to my hard-working family. Although there were a lot of struggles such as physical labor, days we made no sales, and financial losses, it was still a successful business. I don't know if my parents ever realized this but they made an impact in many different communities by introducing Pilipina/o food and culture to many people. They also made long-lasting friendships and learned how to become members in these communities. This made a huge impact on my life. It also taught me about hard work and that survival was not just about "making money" but about building community.

By the same token, I could understand why it was time to put our ukoy to rest. After years of hard work and hours upon hours of bending our backs and standing under the hot sun or sometimes in harsh cold weather, my family was beat. My mother was worn down and my father was just about to receive news that he had a tumor, his second cancer since having survived pancreatic cancer in 1985.

Prior to being food vendors, our parents co-owned a little Pilipina/o store in New Jersey City with some friends, but the store often got robbed and they quickly closed it down. I believe the reasons that my parents kept our ukoy business low-key from anyone outside of our family was to protect us from being hurt or losing our business once again. While I always understood these reasons, this was just another thing added to our family secrecy.

My parents never told us that we were a struggling family. They never spoke to my sister and me about our financial debt. Instead they bought us Barbie dolls to keep us happy, took us on road trips to Hershey Park and Disney World. They did the best they could with what they thought was the right thing to do, which was to keep us safe from not carrying the burden of knowing about our struggles. But we were a struggling family who depended so much on credit cards to get by. My mother was the one with the college degree and the stable job who worked her way up as a creditor in a direct marketing firm. So there was a lot of pressure on my mother's back to carry the whole family. My father worked as a part-time banquet waiter and heavily depended on tips and extra hours to get us through the week. On top of this, our parents were supporting 26 of my mother's family members who came from the Philippines to live with us in our old home in Queens. Even with all of these apparent struggles, my parents hid from us our financial woes. As a young teenager still trying to figure out who I was in the world, coupled with my selfish adolescent ways, I was oblivious to how real our problems were and how close we were to losing our home.

My mother went on a mission, traveling the country to try to save my father's life. My father underwent chemotherapy and proton-beam surgery, along with other methods to treat his cancer. Two years later my father died and my mother was left alone with over $80,000 in medical debt along with years of credit card debt. As if things couldn't get any worse, my mother's company where she loyally worked for over 22 years filed for bankruptcy. She was without a job. In less than 2 years, we lost our home.

> i could show you what it means to be in poverty
> where half a slice of bread is worth a strong arm robbery
> rubber slippers fuck the jordans on your feet,
> smack a politician sample the slap into a beat
> —"Rent Money," Bambu feat. Rocky Rivera

As a child who grew up with a lot of family secrecy and was kept "safe" from knowing the realities of our struggles, I learned to live with lies and live with shame. I learned to mask my pain and made up lies to my friends to cover them all up. I did all this to make everyone believe that "everything was okay" and that everything was perfect. While my family had their own valid reasons of not bringing *hiya*—family shame—it created a lot of silencing and did more damage than it did any good for me. But it also taught me how to survive through those lies by making up childhood fantasies. I often used those fantasies to escape the sexual abuse and other forms of violence I was experiencing growing up. Through the fantasies of pretending I was rich or that I was a secret rock star, I became a performer.

Throughout all of the struggles I only had Hip Hop to lean on. After losing a father and a home, and living with the instabilities of lies, Hip Hop seemed to be the only stable thing in my life. Hip Hop seemed to have never left me. When I was in despair, I had a turntable that was donated to me to learn. I also had a blackbook to practice my throwies and tags, and I had my friend/little brother DJ FatFingaz to beatbox for me whenever I felt like tryin to kick an old-school flow. Any way that I could perform, I performed.

When I performed, I survived. I got through another day. I lived.

> We livin this til the day that we die
> Survival of the fit only the strong survive
> —"Survival of the Fittest," Mobb Deep

While there is much I can say that I disagree with about my upbringing, I find purpose in my story. I still find value in my family who have shaped me to be the person I am today. Learning from my parents' work ethics and their own techniques of survival is what got me through a music industry that can sometimes be so brutal.

When the age of Serato came to life for the DJ to start transitioning into mixing MP3s, I wasn't quite ready to cross over to using digital music in my DJ sets. I was still that same 19-year-old girl, back in 1995, but wearing a "Save Vinyl" t-shirt. It was hard for me to let go of what was tradition to me. *Vinyl was tradition! Hip Hop was all about tradition!* But I also knew that the industry was all about the hustle and if I wanted to make a living out of doing something I loved, I had to keep up and be open to the new technology. The reality of our worlds was changing, where our favorite Hip Hop record stores were closing and fame came from instant hits on YouTube. I wasn't one to conform but it also didn't mean I had to be one or the other. I decided to keep a good majority of my vinyl and spin those on occasion. As for the MP3s, I plugged in my laptop and I still performed.

> what would it be/could it be/should it be like/we like
> living in a dream/might/be a better woman if i had a better chance
> if i had a circumstance/well fat chance/this is the hand/that we're
> dealt with
> (nah) no money, no wealth
>
> —"It's Beautiful," Hope Spitshard ft. LuckyIAm

It was hard to catch up with everyone while trying to maintain my authenticity and keep up with my politics. It didn't matter that I had gained international fame and respect; gigs don't always come by that easily when you're a big womyn Hip Hop Pilipina Activist. *Note the intersections of my identities.* Over the years, I was able to navigate in the intersections of what many (not all) call "Underground Hip Hop" while tapping into the more mainstream Hip Hop industry, as long as it didn't contradict my beliefs. However, word does get around when you go up against institutions and radio stations like Hot 97 and Emmis Communications. In 2005, I co-founded R.E.A.C.Hip-Hop (Representing Education, Activism & Community through Hip-Hop) and we protested Hot 97/Emmis Communications for their "Tsunami Parody" song along with a long list of other racist and sexist injustices over the years. Protesting companies in the same industry that I work in can be a pretty gutsy move that puts me in a toxic environment. It placed me in a position where I wasn't just going up against a corporation, but also DJ colleagues who I looked up to and worked with over the years. Don't get me wrong—to this day I do not regret raising my voice and bringing together the Hip Hop community against a radio station that continued to perpetuate multiple oppressions. At the same time, it was pretty much after this campaign where I started rethinking my career and reflecting on newer ways of performing that would serve the people more.

*we aim to make about as much change as a penny/they keep us
drugged up/
the news keep us very scary/i know change is very necessary/
especially when i see more liquor stores than libraries*
—"Exact Change," Bambu

Eventually, I moved out to the West Coast with my new partner, which made things even more difficult in my music career. However, at this point, I thought I was ready to let go of the industry. I was getting more and more frustrated with the "hustle" and saddened by the friends I had helped "come up" in the business but did nothing to return the love. I was also getting emotionally drained by the lookism and fat-phobia that I faced within the industry because I was a large Pinay womyn of color who didn't fit into their standards of size and image. Around this time, I was also hurt by the divisions in our activist communities. I was hurt even more by my own share of perpetuating these divisions. I was at a point where I just wanted to return to the love of the music. I just wanted to perform and not get caught up in the "hustle" for the "hustle" was a different kind of performance. It was a performance that no longer served me (and perhaps never did). Instead it was about "keeping up" when all I wanted to do was just "be."

Many years ago, my best friend Brian Buño questioned my ever-so-busy lifestyle. He said, *"Candice, why do you always have to be on the 'go'? Why do you always have to work so hard? Why can't you just be?"*

I barely remember how I responded but I know it must have been at least real witty and probably real eloquent too. Nonetheless, I tried to shake it out of my head and continued to carry on with my busy life. However, as the years went on, I'd often go back and replay this conversation with my best friend, chuckling at the questions he asked me. I would chuckle because I always thought them to be preposterous. Who would have thought that today I would finally understand what he was trying to say to me?

In April 2012, I was admitted to Sharp Chula Vista Hospital with an irregular heartbeat, chest pains, and breathlessness. I was diagnosed with atrial fibrillation. On the third morning of my hospital stay when I was to be released, I woke up with my cardiologists and nurses around my bedside informing me that my heart had paused for 7 seconds along with two 4-second pauses thereafter. Two days later I had heart surgery and had a pacemaker implanted inside me.

I was lying on that hospital bed crying, doing the "poor me" of *"how did i let myself get to this point?"* But then a spark of light came to me like Lupe Fiasco's "The Show Goes On" blasting out of an old humble 1980s Volkswagen Rabbit. I thought I can continue feeling sorry for myself or I can (re)claim myself and do something to change my life.

"As an activist over the past 18 years of my life, I spent so much of my time forgetting about me. While I do acknowledge the work I did do to take care of me, I also know I would still be so unbalanced. Well not anymore, there needs to be a balance. I need to be more well-balanced. Prior to my recent heart episode, many people from doctors to therapists to friends and family have worked with me on my health journey. Yet, time and time again, I kept pushing myself to the edge and eventually I fell."
—"Notes from a Revolutionary Patient: Oppression is Trauma," Kuttin Kandi

I spent a majority of my life overworking. From the DJ gigs that got me home at 5:00 am to the workshops I was doing at a college to the rallies I was co-organizing to the full-time job I had with my high school students to the all-nighter meetings; I was constantly performing. Because of this I burnt out and my heart told me so. It caught my attention, right on time, before I could have been struck with something far worse, which could have led to my death.

I knew that it was finally time to temporarily put aside all the amazing things that I loved doing and to simply focus on only taking care of me. While my DJing and my activist work were my forms of therapy, they were also tools I didn't know how to balance. They were also used to keep me busy and distracted. They were another way to perform, another way to not face my inner truths, struggles, and emotions. I translate my busy performing lifestyle as my mode to survive. Not paying attention to me and my body was another self-sabotage and slow suicide method for me. My survival performance were my ways of quieting down the times I heard my mother say, "You're famous, but when are you going to make a living?" or the countless times I had to cover up both the physical and emotional scars of my life.

It was time to stop performing or rather find newer ways to perform. So, this past year has been a performance of a lifetime. It's a performance that speaks my loud painful truths, a performance that gets me in touch with my bare soul and reconnects me with my body. It taps into the heart of who I truly am, leaving me naked and vulnerable to all the wounds I've been avoiding for so long. It inspires me to be okay with my imperfections and let go of all that stored-up hurt. The performance is so real that it is no longer a "performance." It is a masterpiece, a canvas that I can sip tea to and pause at while wondering what it all means.

The pause has been too beautiful like the old pause tapes I used to make before I became a DJ. But the pause doesn't stop here. The pause continues even as I slowly welcome back my passions into my life again, including performing. And honestly, I really don't know what I want to do with the rest of my life anymore. When you survive death, it changes you. I no longer care about "keeping up" or "catching up." Of course, it isn't easy. Like anyone else, I still want to plan my life. However, the difference today is that I am learning to simply "be" just as my old best friend once asked me to do so long ago.

It's funny because every so often I'd run into someone who would tell me they miss the old me and want to see me battle again or rock shows and tours like I used to. While I am flattered that people love what I used to do and my role in the music industry, I am learning that who I am now is just as relevant as who I was when I first started competing in DJ battles. I'm proud of how much I've accomplished over the years, especially so because I've also been through my own times of struggle. But I'd like to believe that what I do at this moment also contributes to not just Hip Hop but also to the world. And it doesn't have to be through competition, spoken word, or community organizing. Being simply just me is enough. I've come to finally accept things like my family realized it was time to let go of our ukoy business. Perhaps it is time for me to let go of always having to be "DJ Kuttin Kandi."

Because this is not about me. It is about finding purpose even in struggle, enjoying the hiss from that old crispy record, and "finding the cloud through the rain," for even the cloud carries substance and that hiss holds meaning. This is what those two turntables have been all about since day one.

I am more in tune with the music than I have ever been before. I am finally "in the now." Being in the present has me not clinging to the past or worrying about the future. I am no longer in constant "performance survival mode" but more so at peace with my past and hopeful for tomorrow. It's like "dropping it on the one" when I first put that needle to the groove. It has me finding stability simply by closing my eyes and listening to all that static. I am finally "here." Being "here" has me finding gratitude in all that life has to offer and able to welcome even all the pain that may come. It has me leaping into the sun with my arms spread open saying, "surprise me." It has me fully letting go and letting whatever may come my way be the songs of my life.

"Pain is inevitable, suffering is an option"—haruki murakami

RAP OUT LOUD

By Rocky Rivera

If you asked me five years ago why I started emceeing, I would have said "Because I wanted to be heard." And if you asked me 10 years ago, I would have said, "Because FUCK this SHIT." And if you asked me 15 years ago, I wouldn't have believed you. Who grows up and wants to be a Female MC? Surely that's a set-up for failure, one that promises nothing but headaches and heartbreak. But I knew that it was never my dream to "make it" as a "rap star." In fact, I thought it was beneath me. I, Krishtine T. de Leon, wanted to become a writer.

The youngest of three girls, I was used to being thrust into the spotlight. We danced in hip hop groups for most of my childhood, performing at youth center talent shows, restaurants—my dad's ship once—pretty much any place with a sound system and room to russian kick. One time, my eldest sister said "You should do a rap." I looked at her and said "Pfffft ... yeah right!" But there was the tiniest feeling in the depths of my consciousness that said, *Okay. Maybe. Someday. Just not now.*

My story isn't too different from many immigrant Filipinos. Besides my "unusual" name (as Ms. Hayes, my 1st grade teacher called it) and growing up without the influence of the Roman Catholic Church (more on that later), my upbringing was the classic narrative of many who came to this country from the Philippines: Dad in the Navy; Mom, a nurse. It was my Dad's side that came to shape my identity here, all Americanized, all married to white men, even my gay uncles. My entire Mom's side is still in the Philippines to this day, a chasm never bridged between continents or alternate realities. I knew of them through Kodak film and air mail handwritten letters. Soon, I no longer knew them, just pictures with messages scrawled on the back. I lost my native tongue. I never looked back.

My father was a bibliophile who forced my middle sister and me to share rooms so that he could convert the fourth bedroom into a library. He used to invite the door-to-door encyclopedia salesmen inside to eat dinner with us and read stories with me on their lap. He was also notoriously cheap, so I never had cable or video games, just books and lots of free time to read while my sisters were in their rebellious teens and barely home.

I read through much of the trauma of my young life. I read when my family was fighting just outside my door and had to place my book down and tell them to shut the hell up. I was named after my dad's favorite author, Indian philosopher J. Krishnamurti, whose last words were something like "Follow no one, not even me." It was my dad who valued knowledge over education, independence over conformity, philosophy over religion. Little did he know what would become of his youngest daughter, who learned early that being smart would be her way out. But mostly it manifested as being a smart-ass and having absolutely no respect for authority. I was already a rapper in the making.

It wasn't until senior year that writing became more than just a hobby. My teachers praised my writing and scribbled in the margins words of encouragement that I never heard before. "Go to college! Be a professor! Your writing is amazing!" Surely they were lying to me. My school wasn't exactly the pinnacle of learning; I was merely a kid who read more than the rest of an underachieving and underserved student population. But once again, it was that niggling feeling that told me to believe them, just a little. Maybe they were right? I wasn't sure. There were always reasons to disqualify myself, to say that I could never be good enough, but I went to a four-year university anyway, despite planning to end my public school legacy with a stint at City College. I went to SF State at the age of 17 years and found myself in a whole different world, one that I never knew existed within city limits. And once again, I left another world behind and many of my peers as well. This was another opportunity to be reborn as who I could be, not who I thought I was. The freedom was almost unbearable.

You can say that my timing was perfect because there was a renaissance blooming and I was smack in the midst of it. On a whim, I signed up for Asian American Studies and found myself engaged like never before. I mean, fuck all my other classes—I failed at Ancient Myths, barely passed The Art of Comedy, copied my cousin's homework in Pre-Calculus, and bombed in Biology. But Ethnic Studies stoked that feeling inside of me once again that I was finding harder and harder to ignore. Under Dr. Phil Gonzales, Dr. Dan Begonia, and Dr. Allyson Tintiangco-Cubales, I found myself gazing upon an archetype that I had never actually seen in person: The Filipina/o Scholar. Scratch that, The Revolutionary Filipina/o Scholar. One who protested as a student during the Ethnic Studies Strike of 1968 and came to teach the very class that they fought for. One who taught me about kapwa, kasamas and kulintang. One who was the youngest Pinay PhD I had ever seen. All who showed me a side of my history that was not passive, not fatalistic and forgiving.

I became empowered to push myself a little harder and to open my consciousness wider until it hurt to hear anything else that wasn't feeding me in the same way. I knew she was calling me again and I had to listen. It stirred in me faith in a religion-less upbringing. It became the thing that eventually would hold all my pieces together, when everything else was coming apart at the seams.

I never was an "undeclared" freshman—I always knew Journalism would be my major . But as I moved away from Ethnic Studies, I found myself stifled by the colorless assignments of J-school. I also grew more and more conscious of the economic gap between myself and most of the Filipinos I encountered in college. They weren't "like me"; they weren't even from San Francisco. They had cars at sixteen. Their parents paid for their lodging and filled their fridge with Costco frozen food. They listened to Black Star, dead prez, and Sublime. They rolled hella deep to church together. I had to learn "Our Father" from my best friend the first night I slept over on a Saturday and had to go to church with her. I wasn't like them and I never wanted to be. I heard people saying that I "tried to act black" and it always boggled my mind because everyone—Samoans, Mexicans, even White people from the 'hood—they all sounded like me. We didn't sound black, we sounded poor. So naturally, everything the assimilated Filipino did, I did not. They drove rice rockets, I wanted a muscle car. They had long, straight hair down to their ass-crack. I had kinky, ferocious hair that I braided into knots. They ate with a fork and spoon. I ate with my hands. They did spoken word. So I wanted to rap.

And when I learned that the Filipino identity could be so much more than a dichotomy of Asian-ness versus American-ness, my heart swelled and my throat closed up, like I was holding myself back. It was never about Hip Hop or breaking down barriers, it was about me speaking my truth despite what people might think, because although I'd like to think that I never gave a damn, I truly did, and that's why it took me so long to get in the studio. I was too busy making excuses about how and why that could never happen. So I immersed myself in music in other ways, listening to local artists and putting them on that pedestal that I could never reach on my own. I've always rooted for the underdog, and that was certainly the case in the Bay Area, where we've had glory but never the kind that sticks around to acknowledge you in the face.

I put my passion into elevating local artists like San Quinn, Messy Marv, and E-40. I pitched a story in Magazine Writing class about the local rap scene and how many of our local artists, such as Cougnut and Mr. Cee from RBL Posse, were killed before they had their "big break," and I thought this the reason for our stalled success in the music industry. But it was less than a month later that I received word from a friend in that same class who called to bring me some bad news. "Hey girl, did you hear about Mac Dre? Your story!," she yelled. On November 1st, 2004, Andre "Mac Dre" Hicks was gunned down in Kansas City and suddenly, this unfortunate circumstance became the momentum of a whole movement that I became forever intertwined with. It was exciting to be in the right place with the right connections and the local music industry welcomed me with open arms. It was only right to honor Mac Dre by hearing their stories about him and seeing beef between artists put temporarily on hold by this tragic occurrence of *another* fallen Bay Area hero. The Bay truly came together for a purpose: to continue what Mac Dre couldn't and finally put The Bay on once and for all. I wanted in.

Soon, I was the Editor-in-Chief of a local magazine start-up called *Ruckus*, and we were doing what no other magazine had done: putting Bay Area artists on the cover of every issue and bringing to life a culture that has always eluded the mainstream. Inside its pages were articles like "Anatomy of a Thizz Face" and illustrated hyphy versions of "The Busy World of Richard Scarry." We were not only reporting on an unseen culture, we were creating it. Along the way I interviewed every single Bay Area Hip Hop legend and other mainstream artists who came through to our local radio stations. And though *Ruckus* and I parted ways only one year after its debut, I was accepted as a contestant on a reality series in New York that documented young journalists competing for a coveted position as a *Rolling Stone* Contributing Editor. It was sheer will that got me there, and love for the underdog.

I eventually won the show and the contract and came back to California more homesick than ever. What do you tell someone who accomplishes their ten-year plan one month out of J-school? Winning that show on national television in front of my peers and especially in front of my critics (every wannabe writer applied for the show and either rooted for me, or hated me intensely for stealing their chance) gave me the respect that I wanted, the clips that none of my classmates could have, and a reality show before reality shows became the norm. But it never gave me freedom to tell my own story, even if I was the one writing it for others. That was really it: I was tired of writing about other people. I wanted to write for and about myself, because all the success at a young age only made me feel more isolated and confused.

I came home and collected my royalty checks every month for a year, the most money I had seen in my lifetime. While I cashed those checks, the journalism industry came crumbling down around me, almost as if I looted the joint on an insider tip. The Internet strikes again. I saw what it did to the record industry firsthand, couriers from labels hand-delivering releases to my door with "This copy is for Krishtine de Leon" dubbed over the entirety of it. So I used the extra money to get my final clips in for *The Source* before I decided to put my writing to a halt, at least in the journalistic sense. I never liked speaking in an "institutional voice," and that's precisely what happened after my show. I could never have the freedom of what I did over at *Ruckus* again. Even my blog entries were pored over and scrutinized with a microscope. I took a lot of my anger about the hate I received online and the misrepresentation of my image on the show and I started creating an alter ego that could turn all that ugliness into beauty, and soon after, Rocky Rivera was born.

Taken from the protagonist out of Jessica Hagedorn's novel, *Gangster of Love*, she represented the truth, undiluted, unbridled, and unheard. She became the freedom that I never imagined, the ability to channel something I had only begun to respect and control. And though I stopped writing in my childhood diary, stopped writing stories for magazines and biographies for musicians, she became my muse—so I never really stopped writing at all. I just put it to a beat and said it out loud. And the more I spoke her to life, the more she made sense as a real thing, a tangible object.

In many ways, my story was common. In some ways, it is exceptional. But this time, I became the author of it, embodied it, and stepped off the paper to become a practitioner. In doing that, she gave life to me as much as I to her. And it is still only one story of many. I just had to learn to listen, after all.

"PUT YOUR HAND UP IF YOU'VE NEVER SEEN A FILIPINO DUDE RAP"

By Geologic aka Prometheus Brown

A BAD RAP

It's 1987 somewhere in Waipahu. I am seven years old at a wedding and I'm dressed in slacks, a dress shirt, and a pair of Adidas. The rented-out gymnasium is laid out from front to back like almost every big party I've been to: a food table laid out buffet style; tables and seats for eating and chilling; a dance floor that's too big; and, at the very end of the room, a DJ behind a table standing between two large speakers flanked by his pompadour-and-rat-tailed mobile DJ crew.

I remember thinking they were the coolest Filipinos I've ever seen. I had been to many other Filipino parties with DJs but these dudes aren't playing music from their living room speakers or using two tape decks. They have turntables and their own sound and lighting system. A banner hangs on the wall behind them repping their mobile DJ company name, probably something like "fresh" or "fusion" or something else that begins with "f." They play all the '80s pop stuff all wedding DJs should play, but they're also playing a bunch of rap. I emulate the older kids' breakdance moves when they aren't looking. The DJ plays Run-DMC's "My Adidas," and I'm like "hey, I'm wearing those!"

This isn't one of those "when I fell in love with hip-hop" moments. It's simply one of hundreds of moments I remember, out of many more I've forgotten, where hip-hop happened to be the soundtrack of my upbringing. For many Filipino kids who grew up in 1980s America, we didn't fall in love with hip-hop, but we fell in love while hip-hop surrounded us. Before *YO! MTV Raps* and *The Source* magazine and weekly rap radio shows, it was at the big Filipino party—debuts, weddings, graduations, christenings, birthdays—that hip-hop music ingrained itself into my musical DNA.

It wasn't until later that I even knew hip-hop was called hip-hop. I got into it because all my friends and cousins were into it and we all got a rush out of listening to music with curse words. In 3rd grade I started trading cassette tapes with classmates. I discovered Too $hort, N.W.A., even local joke rap like 2 Local Boiz. In 4th grade I got suspended when my teacher caught me pulling out a copy of 2 Live Crew's "Me So Horny" cassette maxi-single from my backpack during class. I was sent to the principal's office, where the vice principal lectured me on why *all* rap is bad, and he made me write a one-page handwritten essay regurgitating everything he just said as if I'd start believing it if I was forced to write it. Then they called my Ilocano parents to come get me.

I remember thinking, wow, I've never seen old people react like this to music before. They were trippin' like someone stole something from them or insulted their family. Because of music. And not even music they were familiar with, but music that someone else told them was bad. That's when I really turned it up and listened to every rap record I could. I knew that whole "rap is bad" propaganda was bullshit because I was actually learning things from these songs that I wasn't learning in a classroom. Black History, police brutality, all the stuff Ronald Reagan's administration was doing that wasn't on the news. While they were saying rap was violent, I was listening to rappers unite against violence on "Self Destruction" and "We're All in the Same Gang." While they were saying rap was misogynistic, I was listening to 2Pac's "Keep Ya Head Up."

"I'M NOT FILIPINO, I'M HIP-HOP"

Aunties and Uncles would rib us young Filipino hip-hop heads saying things like "kasdia nangisit," (which roughly translates to "like a Black") or yelling "yo, yo, yo" at us when we walked past the mah-jong table. Sometimes they'd make us rap for their entertainment. My first audience was cousins, aunties, and uncles and my first performed raps were some MC Hammer song I still know all the words to. It was playful mocking combined with old prejudices multiplied by all the bad things they heard about rap from news or church. Of course, the kids in the community who did white people stuff like study classical music or listen to rock never got accosted for "trying to be white."

They didn't realize that the white people we were supposed to emulate treated us like shit while the black people we were supposed to avoid were cool to us. Or, just cooler. So when people ask if I've faced any prejudice or detractors being Filipino and trying to rap, I say yes; but primarily from the racists in my own community. Maybe that's why I never really tripped when I heard it from non-Filipinos. I had already heard the worst before I ever rapped outside of my neighborhood. I never heard anything ignorant stuff like that from my parents, but their sentiments weren't that far off.

First-generation-in-America parents and their second-generation-in-America children both experience America for the first time at the same time. Except us kids got to navigate our assimilation gradually while our parents arrived here with the idea that whatever white people were doing, we gotta do too if we want to be successful in America. And for many of them, hating on rap was part of that program. I'm lucky that I had parents who, while they weren't thrilled about my enthusiasm for rap, never openly discouraged or disparaged it. Pops, in fact, was a music head with a decent cassette and vinyl collection and enjoyed rap as long as it didn't have the word "fuck" in it ("shit" was ok, though). Looking back, pops and I were doing the same thing: he was assimilating into his US military guy world and I was assimilating into west coast '80s baby America. He did it with sports and becoming Republican, I did it with video games, comic books, and rap music.

Young Filipino hip-hop heads used to say shit like "I'm not Filipino, I'm hip-hop." By the mid-1990s, Filipino DJs and b-boys started getting shine while us aspiring Filipino rappers cheered them on, at the same time wondering when it was our turn. As I attended more hip-hop events through high school and college, I'd run into people, even other Filipinos, who would assume I was a DJ or a b-boy and would give me that look when I told them I rapped. At one point, I even said "fuck it, if Filipino dudes are only allowed to be DJs, and I'm too fat to windmill, then I'll just be a DJ." So I did, but after realizing how big a chunk it was taking out of the little money I made bagging groceries for tips, I gave it up (there are 100s of copies of DJ Geologic mixtapes floating around Bremerton).

So I became one of those "I'm not Filipino, I'm hip-hop" guys. I don't think I ever said it out loud, but I heard it from other Filipinos and I didn't disagree with them. It was a marker that told us that our assimilation project was over. That we weren't outsiders, but part of the circle, even if it meant concealing our ethnic identity. No, *especially* if we concealed our ethnic identity. Maybe it was some shame about being Filipino that motivated some to distance themselves from their community. Others grew up around mostly non-Filipinos and had trouble trying to relate to other Filipinos. I'm sure many were giving a middle finger to all the people in our community who said we were trying to be Black. All those things played a role in it for me to some degree, but for me I didn't want to be seen as Filipino because most people, including many Filipinos, believed Filipinos weren't supposed to rap.

RAPPING ABOUT BEING FILIPINO

By my sophomore year at the University of Washington, I was entering rap battles and traveling to other cities doing spoken word gigs with *isangmahal arts kollective* and solo rap stuff as "Geologic." Most of these events were curated by an emerging network of other Asian Pacific-Islander artists who were doing similar things (open mics, conferences, concerts) in different cities, and the internet kicked this network into another gear. Many of the initial connections were made at the very first API Spoken Word & Poetry Summit in July 2001, hosted in Seattle. Before 2000, the only Filipino rappers I knew about were Mastaplann, Apl.de.Ap from Black Eyed Peas with his thick-ass accent, and a handful of dudes from around the way, none of whom actually put out a record. By 2002, I was making songs and rocking shows alongside Filipino rappers from the east coast, midwest, and west coast.

The year was 2001. In November of that year, I was at San Francisco State University. I had just gotten done finishing a solo set of spacey quasi-nationalistic poetry, went outside, smoked a joint, and walked back inside to hear a song start with these two bars:

"I love this underground rap shit / I love my mom's thick Filipino accent"

I didn't know who was rapping, but I looked up and saw a short brown brother *rocking it*. His name was Kiwi, backed by DJ Owl Boogie, and he was rapping about being Filipino to Filipinos who were responding to his calls, putting their hands up, and laughing at his jokes. At this point, I had already seen dudes rap about being Filipino but suck at rapping, and a few good Filipino rappers rap about everything but being Filipino. But seeing and hearing Kiwi rock was a revelation: it's possible to rap about being yourself *and* rap well.

Up until this point, I wasn't rejecting or embracing being Filipino—like rap music at a wedding, it was just there. I was part of FASA at UW and joined a Filipino-centric arts collective and my group of friends were mostly Filipino cats I went to high school with. But most of them weren't really trying to branch outside of their organizations or cliques, while I was never fully comfortable there. So I started getting into battle rapping.

Being the only Filipino dude, or maybe one of 2 or 3 Asian dudes, in an organized rap battle in the early 2000s was some crazy shit. I had proven myself at parties, schoolyards, and outside of rap shows, where at least a handful of other Filipino dudes would have my back if it got racial. But it was different repping for your community in front of a crowd of people who think Asian stereotypes are actually funny. I look back and cringe sometimes at it but I'm grateful for having gone through it. As my guy Gabriel Teodros reminded me, the battle circuit was "steel sharpening steel": a proving ground where you had to get your skills up to par to be respected. I fused that cutthroat experience with the nurturing, judgment-free-zone experiences of spoken word spaces and open-mics. Particularly *isangmahal*, which was Filipino-centric but open to anybody who wanted to be a part of it. There,

I was exposed to cool militants, organizers, teachers, and students who did the opposite of what battle rappers do: embrace who you already are. I had always felt a dissonance between investing so much time equally either battling or collaborating, being insulted or being encouraged, told my people weren't shit and hearing that we have a long history of struggle. But it was moments like hearing Kiwi rap live for the first time that helped bridge the parts inside of me that hadn't been connected yet.

BEING FILIPINO AND RAPPING

Whenever I'd go on tour with Blue Scholars, I would do a survey of the crowd while I'm on stage. In between songs, I will ask of these mostly white crowds: "put your hand up if you've never seen a Filipino dude rap." In cities I've never been to, it's always more than half the crowd, and, in many instances, such as Portland, Maine, or Des Moines, Iowa, or Burlington, Vermont, virtually everyone in the building had their hand up. But in the last couple years alone, I've found myself asking this question less as more crowds began to not put their hands up. It makes sense as now, there are thousands of Filipinos rapping in America, and many of them are rapping well. It's crazy to hear some of them tell me that I was somehow influential in their decision to pursue rapping. A lot of them, even if I didn't know them personally, I would still be a big fan of. Some of them I am a big fan of and haven't met yet. Some of them I was a big fan of until I met them. All of us descend from colonized people, and all of us are doing a little bit of decolonization through our raps.

Every Filipino rapper has had a conversation with someone about lumpia. Or experienced the awkwardness of having the one thing someone says to you when you tell them you're Filipino is that they once dated a Filipina like it's some kind of 'hood pass. Many of us have arrived at soundcheck for our shows and have had the soundman assume that we're the DJ. At the same time, we're putting out records and videos and touring like we never have before. And even in places where 90% of the crowd doesn't look like me, there's always a brown cheering section somewhere in the building. Sometimes, like in LA, the Bay Area, or New York, they'll be all up in the front with flags and "makibaka! huwag matakot!" chants. My favorite shows of all, though, besides in my hometown of Seattle, happen where almost everyone in the crowd looks like me, in Hawai'i.

Once, while on tour with Hieroglyphics in 2008, we had a stop in Nashville. On the night of the Country Music Awards. After the show, I'm in a conversation with a white kid who's grilling me about being Filipino: where are my parents from? do I speak Tagalog? what's my favorite food? Great, I'm thinking to myself, another white boy just discovering Filipinos and he wants me to be his cultural navigator. Right as I'm about to cut the conversation short, he reveals that his mom is Filipina and he grew up in the Philippines. That tonight was the first night he'd ever seen a Filipino guy rap and it made him proud. Then he started speaking Tagalog so fast I couldn't understand it. Few moments have humbled me and resonated me like that one. It reminded me that what I do can fill a cultural void for some Filipino kid that I once had myself, and also that I'm far from having this whole ethnicity thing figured out.

"YOU NEED TO DEFINE YOUR SUCCESS THE WAY YOU WANT IT"

By DJ Neil Armstrong and Mark R. Villegas

ON 5TH PLATOON AND THE TURNTABLIST SCENE

5th Platoon is my DJ crew in New York City. We started in late 1996. We used to actually be called 1st Platoon when we first came out. And then, no one really complained but it was a little arrogant of us to call ourselves 1st Platoon so we changed it to 5th Platoon. It was supposed to represent the five boroughs of New York. Our whole point at the time was to kill the battle scene, so we took a military name.

Honestly, the turntablist scene is pretty much dead. A good comparison would be jazz. Jazz is still around of course, but it's not what it once was. Jazz was the premiere black music art form. Nowadays, everyone wants to be a rapper, everybody wants to be a singer, but nobody wants to play the trombone, nobody wants to play jazz flute. That just doesn't happen these days. Turntablism is kind of the same thing. You have your rock star DJs now. Back in the day, that really didn't exist. If anything, everyone wanted to be a turntablist. Even if you were an established DJ, you wanted to learn how to scratch, you wanted to kind of be like Roc Raida. But these days, people want to be like Steve Aoki. Or Skrillex, you know, he's more of a producer, but he often gets billed as a DJ. Or Deadmaus, or people like that. So it's different now.

I'm not saddened by it. It still exists, it's just not mainstream, it's not popular. When I started to DJ, my whole life was just scratching and that whole aspect. But it's different now. I do more parties and it's kind of more a different thing. It really depends how you want to put it. I'm not the type to be upset about it. It's a natural progression, unfortunately. *Real* turntablism comes out of hip hop and honestly hip hop is in a screwed-up place right now.

ON MIXTAPES

I started making mixtapes at one point and I guess people really liked what I was doing. I didn't really transition per se. There was a point where I started getting interested in making *a* mixtape in particular and it ended up propelling everything else that happened and I guess I just got known for it. Nothing was done on purpose. At that time I was still a turntablist kid but I was utilizing my turntablist skills to do something else and I just kind of lucked out I guess.

The first mixtape I did was called *Original*. And it was an original sample mixtape so I would just go back and forth between the original sample and whoever sampled it. So Edie Brickell and the New Bohemians and Brand Nubian. At the time, underground hip hop was still in fashion. If you were an underground hip hop kid you had more props than if you listened to like the equivalent to 2 Chainz would be today. I did that mixtape back in 2001. So that was a little over ten years ago. That was my first one and my favorite mixtape that I did.

ON JAY-Z

The *DNA of the Blueprint* I did as a kind of homage to my time working with Jay. So I was on tour with Jay from 2008 to 2009. I stopped DJing for him around 2010 when he started doing the *Blueprint 3* USA world tour. So I did it kind of like a thank you for Jay for giving me the opportunity to rock with him. Up to that point, I hadn't really did a mixtape that was geared towards a "normal," pop, hip hop audience. Like I said, I was more of an underground hip hop DJ and this one had more mass appeal. It was all music from the *Blueprint* albums, so *Blueprint 1*, *Blueprint 2*, *Blueprint 3* with the original samples. It kind of told a story about Jay.

He found me. I never knew before I started DJing for him that he needed a DJ to tour with him for the Mary J. Blige tour and my name came up from a girl named Vashtie Kola. She kind of told him, "You need to work with this guy named Neil." And that was that, the beginning of everything. Vashtie used to work with him at Def Jam. She was kind of like a "downtown *it* girl."

I did a bunch of stuff with Jay from that point. We did the Glastonbury Festival, we did a bunch of stuff for Obama. I'm the first hip hop DJ to perform for the inauguration of a U.S. president. Madison Square Garden. Pick something, I've done something.

OUT OF THE ASIAN SCENE

One of the secrets is, in my opinion, when you start to take this stance that you are an Asian artist, you only cater to Asian art, Asian venues, it's like preaching to the choir. People are already converted. If you're preaching to the choir they already know to love Jesus. You're not doing anything, you're not gaining any market, you're not doing anything new, you're not preaching to new people.

Especially since, to a large extent, there is an appropriation of a culture. Especially if you're not American. You're not from an urban area. You're appropriating essentially what is seen on TV, what you think is happening on a record or whatever. You know, why would an outside artist ever look at you except as an imitator?

But if you take a stance, like, "No, I'm not an Asian DJ. I'm a *DJ*. I'm not an Asian producer. I'm a *producer*. I'm not an Asian MC. I'm an *MC*." You know, people will see you in that light. You can have a wider audience. You can talk to a larger group of people.

It helps though, because when I first started to get paid there would be Asian—you know Harvard used to ask me to talk about being an Asian person in the industry or things like that. I remember doing a show in I think Connecticut. That show was us [5th Platoon], it was Jin, and Far East Movement. And there were probably like a hundred people in the room at most. That's another prime example of a group [Far East Movement] that broke out of a mold. Far East Movement back in the day, they were closer to a group like the Pharcyde. They rapped a certain way, they had a certain whatever. But, that appeal is not mass appeal. They had to figure out the right group to go to, and they ended up doing a sound similar to Black Eyed Peas. I guess "party rock" is the term they use. So they changed up their sound a little bit and they literally went from playing with me in a room full of one hundred Asian people to—God, the last time I talk[ed to] them I asked, "What is the biggest show you ever did?" And they were like, "60,000 people." You need to basically widen your audience especially if you are Asian and you're trying to do urban stuff. If you stay in a box, you're always going to be in that box.

All the Asian guys that used to bring us up to do gigs, that's the choir. They wanted us, in particular, at that time period—people used to describe my crew as the East Coast Skratch Piklz. Mountain Brothers was really big. We were kind of the representatives of Asians in pop culture. It's a little different now. There was no John Cho. There was no Harold and Kumar at the time. It was different back then. So we were kind of that representative element. Even today, any DJ crew who is worth their grain of salt treats the 5th Platoon and the members of my crew a lot of respect because we were doing stuff that today people can't do. That was our role at the time, to be like role models for in particular Asians who didn't have much of a voice in American pop culture.

BEING ROLE MODELS

I'd like to say I read an article about Nina Simone. I guess she wasn't the biggest advocate of pushing for civil rights. That really wasn't her thing. I'd like to think it was an article in *The Fader* and she was on the cover [*The Fader*, Issue 38, May/June 2006]. I'm almost positive it said something like, "Ok, I'm already black. What else do you want me to fuckin do?" You know, essentially that. It's like, "How else can I prove this to you. I'm black. I'm the one whose face is in front of everybody. There's nothing else I need to do. I don't have to talk about it, I don't have to march. I don't have to do any of that shit. I do what I do, and I'm affecting more change than all the hollerin that anyone can do because I'm in people's faces showing them my talent and my love." I'm extending what it said, but essentially that's what it was. She was like, "Why are you complaining? I'm in people's faces. I do what I do, I don't have to do anything else."

I'm definitely of that opinion. There's a lot of poetry art forms where—I think at a certain point the whole "street poetry," you know, Def Jam poetry slam stuff—I think a lot of Asian kids in particular got into that because it was something—you know you don't have to be a great rapper. You know a really good rapper has everything—charisma, vocal sense, style. A lot of Asian kids—that's not—you know right now, Asian kids are probably the fuckin—it's like Urkel. Urkel back in the day was not so stylish. But today, that's what all the hipsters are wearing. Back in the day, Asians were quieter, passive, all that crap. So when a lot of the street poets came out, it resonated with a lot of Asian folks. Some people did it really good, some people were really successful doing it. But then, there was definitely a faction where it really seemed like a lot of these people were just whining. For almost no reason. I know some guys who used to be poets who used to get paid. I'd be like, "Yo, I got black friends. I got white friends. I got Asian friends who have to drive a bus to get paid. And you are literally just talking to get paid. How the hell can you complain about anything?"

So when it came in particular to my art form, I definitely was not—you know, I don't think anyone can call me an activist. Anybody who knows me personally, I was never really into that. I would always use my sister as an example. I bet you money a lot of people would have called her kind of "white-washed" for a lack of a better term, a "twinkie," blah blah. I don't think she ever had an Asian boyfriend as far as I know. But you know what? My sister was a judge. She was a lawyer. She worked for the state. And every day, someone saw her face in a position of power. So she don't have to holler. She never has to say, "Well, look at me, I'm Asian." She just did it. So I'll always look at her and be like, "That's an example of someone who just does it." So for me, it was kind of the same thing.

I'm not trying to downplay the need. Everything is needed at a certain point. Someone has to speak out for the stuff that doesn't get spoken out for. But, my job for me was always like, "I'm going to be the best DJ. I'm gonna show people it doesn't matter what color you are." And I'm not gonna shove it in people's faces. And I think that was kind of instrumental in people kind of being like, "You know what? Neil is kind of a real dude. He's not really out for some personal gain. He doesn't need to prove himself. It's his skills, his love of the art form, his love for the culture. That's enough. Here's an Asian face. Here's someone who looks different. We're going to accept him because he's proven himself."

I think it's unfortunate for some people when they start yelling too loud, they get lost. It gets lost. Instead of doing something, you just yell something. Sometimes that gets lost. If you look universally, across the board, it's kind of like that for people who have been successful. Like Chad Hugo. He's not really like that. He produces music. That's it. He didn't say, "I'm only going to produce for Asian artists." Or, "I'm only going to do shows for Asian people." Lord knows how many hits the Neptunes has. That's because he's just doing his job as a music producer that happens to be Asian, not the other way around. Apl.de.ap, unless he talks about it, that's not the person you realize. It's later on you realize, "Oh shit, oh he's Filipino."

I think in our culture, for being American, you have to meet people halfway. That's a better way to get people to be like, "Oh shoot, this other culture is the shit. I want to learn about it. Let me try Filipino food. Let me do this. Let me do that." Forcing it upon people can get you ridiculed or people just won't understand. It's that whole adage of, "You can catch more bees with honey." That's the kind of attitude I took when it came to people understanding that I am a Filipino American.

ON "SUCCESS"

Even "conscious," "normal" hip hop is not mass marketable these days. Nobody wants to hear about doing good shit. Everybody wants to hear about getting drunk, and good kush, and alcohol. This is not that time period. Who knows? Who knows what's going to happen in the future? There is a market. There has been some successful—you know, Bambu. A lot of people know him, not just Asian people. He is a respected artist on the West Coast. But to make a viable living with that type of rap? Even black artists, even white artists are not doing that—making "conscious" rap and making money. That's just not happening. It's not the time period right now.

You need to define your success the way that you want it. If your success is that you get to do what you do, do what you love every day—you know I'm not the richest DJ out there. I'm not the most successful. Paris Hilton who can't DJ to save her life has made more money than I'll ever make as a DJ. She does shit. She does absolutely nothing. She just takes up space, from what I understand. That's her job in life is to take up space. She's made more money DJing than I'll probably ever will. Ok, am I successful compared to her? Not financially. But, in every single other way—go ahead and try to argue with me and say that I'm not successful.

BUILDING SKILLS, BUILDING CONNECTIONS

LESSONS ON THE BUSINESS OF DJING

By DJ Icy Ice

My story begins in the late 80s in the City of Carson just 20 minutes from downtown LA; a multi-cultural, suburban town in the South Bay. Carson at that time was a good snapshot of urban America, dominated by minorities (primarily African Americans, Latinos, Samoans, and Filipinos). It was a rough city where gangs, fights, drugs, and shootings were the norm, but at the same time, my hometown was also known for its great high school football tradition and award-winning music program. Even though it was rough growing up in Carson, there was a huge sense of pride and community. Us "urban kids" relished the fact that we were consistently champions year in and year out through football and music. The clash of experiences from growing up in Carson helped serve me well in dealing with different types of people and different types of situations later in life.

Fortunately, I was raised by two loving, hardworking parents who put heavy emphasis on going to school and becoming a professional doctor, lawyer, or engineer. But when I got introduced to Hip Hop, my life took a completely different turn. My first exposure to Hip Hop was back in elementary school through break dancing. Then, in junior high I was introduced to DJing. Although I played instruments as a kid, such as the violin, all the different saxophones, and a little piano, I instantly fell in love with the turntable! From that point on, I did whatever I could to become a DJ. I went to friends' houses to just play on turntables. I worked a number of small jobs and did chores for dad to work towards buying my first pair of turntables.

I put in countless hours of practice to learn the basics. I saved my lunch money and wouldn't eat just so I could buy records. I stole milk crates from liquor stores and supermarkets to store my records. I learned to link up with guys who had more money than me (from their parents) to buy DJ equipment so we could DJ parties. But there were three things that helped me most in accelerating my growth as a DJ. One was having a group like Unique Technique in Carson to show me how it was done. Another was having DJ crews like the Knights of the Turntable and the legendary DJ Joe Cooley come DJ for my junior high school dances. Third was listening to DJs on the radio, like Mix Masters Tony G, Julio G, Alladin, and Joe Cooley, who were in the mix every week on a small AM radio station called 1580 KDAY.

By the time I was 15 years old I was DJing my local school dances, birthday parties, and even weddings. But a turning point for me in my aspiration to become a DJ was when I attended my first Filipino dance club party at the Hyatt Regency in downtown LA put on by Spectrum Entertainment. I was blown away by the concert-style sound and lighting DJ set-up with the most talented Filipino DJs I had seen at that point. DJ Curse and DJ What of Public Image from Cerritos were killing it on four turntables. Soon after, I met DJ Rhettmatic from Double Platinum. I saw my future, and I had to become like them! From that point on, I kept practicing and building up my skills as a DJ. Once I was known as an up-and-coming DJ in the area, some friends from church introduced me to Jimmy Corpus, who was the head of Spectrum. They were the promotion group responsible for throwing the biggest Filipino parties in LA.

Shortly after, I joined Spectrum and through Jimmy I got my first hands-on education in the world of promoting parties. Up to this point, my focus had been about improving my DJ skills, but through hanging with Jimmy, he taught me more of the business aspects of being a DJ. He taught me how to promote, where to promote, how to talk to people, and ultimately how to study trends in our scene and capitalize on them. I was a sponge, taking in all that knowledge. Jimmy was my first mentor. He schooled me in the business aspects of being a DJ/promoter and taught me well. During this time, the late 80s, Jimmy helped me lay a foundation for what I would be doing as a DJ and gave me a good introduction into how to run business as a DJ company.

A few years later, I left Spectrum and formed a DJ crew called Legend Entertainment with all the homies I grew up with: Alex, Oz, Lloyd, James, Fabio, Gil, and quite a few others. We took what we learned from Jimmy and expanded on it. Other crews at the time, United Kingdom (Curse, Rhettmatic, and DJ What), International Groove (Doug Kanagawa), and Proof Positive (Joel, Troy, and Hideo), were all holding down the Asian scene in LA. But after bringing in David Gonzales into Legend, we really took our crew to new levels. David Gonzales wanted to focus on throwing events and the business side of Legend. Together we eventually became the largest Filipino/Asian promotion crew in the scene and ruled Southern California from the early 90s until the early 2000s. We were doing weekly 18+ and 21+ clubs in LA and Hollywood such as The Source, Mecca, Empire, and doing the biggest fundraising events for all the college-based Filipino groups. But what Legend became known for most was bringing live concerts to our Filipino/Asian scene with groups such as Rodney O and Joe Cooley, Doug E Fresh, Mad Lion, The Pharcyde, The Alkaholiks, The Skratch Piklz, Dru Hill, Destiny's Child, and so many more. We even expanded what we were doing in LA and took it to other California cities from San Diego to San Francisco. Legend Entertainment taught me the nightclub and concert promotions side of the business on a whole other level.

Curse and J-Rocc had ideas of forming a new DJ crew. Shortly after those discussions of forming a new crew, my sister DJ Symphony and I were asked to become members of this new crew called The Beat Junkies. This was a collection of DJs from many other crews forming one super DJ crew. Some of the DJ crews out around at that same time were The Invisibl Skratch Piklz from San Francisco, The X-Men aka The X-Ecutioners from New York, and 5th Platoon from Queens, NY. What made the Beat Junkies unique from the other crews was the diversity of styles we encompassed: battle DJing, team routines, and music production. And, our members were part of legendary Hip Hop groups like Dilated Peoples and The Visionaries. Another unique aspect of the crew was DJing in nightclubs, hosting nightclubs, and DJing on radio for two of the top Hip Hop stations in LA (Power 106 and 92.3 The Beat). The Beat Junkies were diverse in all the different styles and areas of DJing. We recently celebrated our 20-year anniversary as a crew and continue to grow and contribute to the DJ culture to this day. Being part of the Beat Junkies crew made me grow and become better all around in skill as a DJ, which eventually helped me land on LA radio station 92.3 The Beat. This eventually led me to DJing internationally.

During the mid-90s, I met Julio G and Tony G from the KDAY Mixmasters, some of my earliest influences. I invited them to the Legend events we were doing at that time. Julio G came out to Mecca, which we hosted at Prince's Old Nightclub, "Glam Slam." Julio G experienced the Filipino/Asian Scene from Legend Entertainment for the first time and a few of the Beat Junkies on the turntables. Shortly after that, he invited DJ Melo D and myself to do guest spots on 92.3 The Beat with him and Tony G, eventually landing us spots on 92.3 The Beat. I started playing on the weekends, doing the "Old School Lunch Mix" and "John London and the House Party Morning Show." I was fortunate to be part of the station and experience their rise to the #1 Radio Station in Los Angeles. But in the early 2000s, the station got sold and I wound up on 93.5 KDAY (the legendary Hip Hop LA Radio station re-incarnated) and played for the Morning Show on that station as well as the mix shows on the weekends. Around 2007, I jumped at an opportunity to DJ for the radio legend Rick Dees for his morning show "Rick Dees in the Morning" on Movin' 93.9 FM. But unfortunately that station got sold in 2009. I joined Power 106 shortly after Movin' and am still currently part of the Power Mixers. One of the key lessons I learned in radio is that change will happen. You've got to be willing to evolve and grow with the changes. Another lesson I stood by was that the entertainment business is based on relationships. You've got to master the art of creating and maintaining relationships or you will not have much of a future in this business.

In 2000, a lot of my DJ friends were becoming producers or joining or forming Hip Hop bands and groups. I felt more compelled to produce in a different way. Not so much through producing music, but instead producing a retail record store business. So I decided to start a retail store with the help of my parents to secure the capital to open my business. I then recruited experienced help in retail record stores, Mike Jew and C-Los, who were instrumental in opening the Fat Beats Record Store in Los Angeles. This team opened Stacks: The Vinyl Authority, a retail record store located in Cerritos. Stacks quickly became a Hip Hop community center differentiating itself from other stores through the style of in-store artist appearances and hosting workshops. As a company, we didn't exactly invent anything new in the retail record store business, but we always strived to do things a little differently, and in turn, gained the respect of the DJ community. The success of the Cerritos Stacks location gave us the ability to expand the business to open up an online e-commerce website, and two other store locations in San Diego and Ontario. When the recession hit in 2007, and the digital, non-vinyl-based Serato Software was catching fire with the DJ community, I was forced to close the doors of Stacks. Opening up retail stores and online e-commerce sites in essence became my master's education in business. It incorporated what I learned in previous years from dealing with different types of people, running a mobile DJ business, and running nightclub and concert promotions. It also helped me learn a whole new set of skills and knowledge in running a business. By being hands-on with all aspects of my business, I was prepped for the next steps I would take.

After shutting down all my Stacks stores, it took me about six years to recover from losses and get back to stability business-wise. To be honest, it made me rethink and second-guess what I was doing with my DJ career. Other factors that made decisions tougher this time around were I had gotten married and had my first son a few years before Stacks officially closed, so the losses were even harder to bear. But with the help of my wife Heidi, the love and support of my friends and family, and the many lessons learned from running the Stacks retail record stores, I was able to bounce back even stronger.

Nowadays, I primarily run online businesses such as www.TurntableU.com, an online DJ school where you can learn lessons on DJ Skills from the comfort of your own home and on your own time. Another is a subscription-based record pool for DJs, www.ExclusiveGrooves.com, where DJs can come to one spot for music and video content for their sets. We took the Stacks record store brand that we built up and transformed it into a Hip Hop TV show platform called StacksTV, which airs online on www.StacksTV.net, BReal.TV, as well Cable TV on MYX Network nationwide. At the time of this writing, I'm in the process of starting the nation's first video mix show with Power

106, which will bring live video mixing on-air on Power 106 and online at www.Power106.com simultaneously. I'm also helping in creating the DJ curriculum of the first Hip Hop School of Arts in Pomona, CA with legendary b-boy Lil Cesar of the Air Force Crew. As an entrepreneur at heart, I'm constantly looking for opportunities to do business where I see there's a pressing need. And of course, the businesses I have chosen to get into are businesses that revolve around my life's passions: DJing, love of music, and doing positive, progressive projects. Although I chose more of an entrepreneurial path, I do a lot of businesses more as a labor of love. These are not businesses that will make me tons of money, but more or less I do these things to help new or established DJs to learn in new ways. As hard as it is to believe, I do it more for the love than for the money. I also believe because I've done things more for the love than for the money, I've enjoyed the longevity in my career and my business dealings.

Because this is where I am currently in this stage of my career, one of the biggest areas of my life I'd like to give you a glimpse into is the delicate balance between family and career. As of the time of the release of this chapter, I've been blessed richly with my family life, being married to my wife Heidi for the past nine years, and having four sons: seven years, two years, and nine-month-old twins. I wear multiple hats in my family life: husband, daddy, chauffeur, etc., and I enjoy it. Like building a career as a DJ, building and maintaining a healthy family life takes hard work and having the right partner for the journey can't be understated. A partner in life who understands what it is I do, supports my career, and makes sacrifices so I can do what I gotta do to be the DJ/entrepreneur I am today. That's the qualities of the incredible wife I have in Heidi. Not only does she support me in my career goals and ambitions, she pushes and challenges me. At the same time being the backbone of our family, holding down the home front, and being the guiding light for our sons. There's just no way I can do what I do without my wife. I stress the importance of having the right person to have your back. With this line of business, I'm out of town quite often, or busy on the weekends (usually times she's off from work). The challenge of giving time to my wife and boys is very real, let alone being present for family functions and friends' special events (like birthday parties, anniversaries, etc.). It's tough! At the end of the day, having God in the center of our marriage, and working together with Heidi has given me the ability to be able to balance marriage and this crazy DJ career of mine.

Bottom line, with this journey I have been on, it's been all about people. To do all the different things I've done and am currently doing in my career as a DJ, I need to work with and entertain people. To do all the different business projects I work on, it demands working with different teams. To enjoy the fun-filled family life I'm enjoying, it takes working with my wife and kids and all the people who help us with our family. Everything in this journey is about people; it's important to find that connection with everyone. This could be through sharing a bond or an experience to help solidify what you're doing together. I always try to treat everyone positively and with respect. Through the relationships and the passion for music, this is what drives me to keep going!

HOMESTEADY

By Krystilez

T he very first rap song I fell in love with was "Regulate" by Warren G and Nate Dogg. As an elementary school student somewhere around 6th grade, the whistles and the funk just blew my mind. The story about gambling and getting jacked really hit me, as these were things I recall as a young kid in the Hawaiian Homestead in Nanakuli. My friend and I sat there and wrote every single lyric down and practiced while rewinding the cassette single in my stereo for hours. We sat there going back and forth just enjoying singing along to the song. I had heard a bunch of rap songs before like "Supersonic" by J.J. Fad and songs by 2 Live Crew (bass-heavy freestyle music was huge in my community), but nothing hit my heart like the West Coast music that came out during that era.

In elementary school, I had always been surrounded by Hawaiians. Nanakuli Elementary had the highest percentage of Hawaiians per student body, at a whopping 98% (considering the school was built on Hawaiian Homestead land, which means you must have at least the federally mandated 50% Hawaiian blood quantum to own a home there). I was raised by Hawaiians in my neighborhood, and actually believed I was a Hawaiian up until about the 5th grade. It wasn't until I entered intermediate school when I would actually meet a lot of different people, including Filipinos.

In band class, a Filipino friend of mine introduced me to Bone Thugs-N-Harmony. This moment was the start of my absolute obsession with rap music. Not only did their melodic staccato rhythmic raps please my ears, it was their obsession with the dark side that completely enticed my imagination. Talking to the dead, ouija boards, sound effects to accent the scenarios their words were describing drew me in. It wasn't so much about the lives they were portraying, but the creativity behind their stories. It was so different from what I was used to hearing, and I wanted to be that. I wanted to create something different, and tell my story. If these guys could have a kid like me in a small town of Nanakuli rapping about Cleveland, I thought I could reciprocate that somehow and have someone in Cleveland rap about Hawai'i. I already loved writing, and I really wanted to do it, I just never knew how or where to start.

During freshman year of high school, I noticed a little rap group forming in band class who called themselves "Free Floers." The leader was a new kid from another school named Duke King (he lived in Nanakuli, but had gone to another school, Aiea, which was more in tune with non-traditional cultures, such as Hip Hop). I thought they were the coolest kids on the block. They were always passing around the Walkman playing songs they'd recorded, and people were enjoying it. During class they were playing around with freestyles, always joking and having a blast. One day after a band show, I was walking home with my friend and she had told me to wait because Duke lived right near us and we could all walk together. On our way home we talked about Hip Hop and whatnot and he urged me to try to freestyle. He was persistent, making me feel confident enough to burst through my bubble, and when I did my first freestyle, it sucked. But they made me feel like it was okay and that I needed to continue. Duke later invited me to come by his house and record songs on his karaoke machine.

This was my first real introduction to Hip Hop culture. A few of my friends would break dance and were graf writers, and I tried but they weren't my thing. I was instantly drawn to the recording, the music, the descriptions, the storytelling, the emotions, and rhythms. It just felt right to me and I knew this is what I wanted to do with my life. I found a way to tell my story. Soon we had a few performances under our belt and had produced our first cassette mixtape "Homestead Productions Vol. 1" around 1998. We printed 30 copies and sold 20 out of a shop in Ala Moana called Radio Free, which was a non-commercialized radio station that played whatever they wanted. It was a very proud moment for me in high school. From there, I wanted to learn more how to make it bigger, in and out of Hawai'i.

We had a few stints on the radio doing intros for a DJ named Kutmaster Spaz. We made some noise in the Hawai'i Hip Hop scene, but being on the west side and far away from Honolulu, it proved difficult to not only network but get notoriety because we'd have to take a 2-hour bus ride to get to Honolulu every day and we didn't have access to the town-based community at the time. This fueled my anger because I knew I had the skills and something special to share. I learned on the west side how to get myself known in town.

Hip Hop is a very aggressive and competitive style of music, which is the exact opposite of the most successful music coming out of Hawai'i. As opposed to the laid-back acoustic stylings of contemporary Hawaiian and reggae music and its fusion into "Jawaiian" music, Hip Hop mostly had a driving beat. This would prove to be a hard challenge for the local industry to accept such a style of music breaking the norm, and later I learned why. It's the ambiance of Hawai'i that doesn't allow Hip Hop to be accepted in the general public. Hip Hop's birthplace was a concrete jungle, surrounded by buildings upon buildings and urban neighborhoods, whereas here in Hawai'i, we don't have much of that (besides Waikiki). Although it's continuing to grow, it's not in the island's soul to feel these rhythms. We're much more in tune with nature and the earth, which makes the laid-back acoustic stylings more appealing to islanders. It would be hard for most island people to adopt Hip Hop naturally and organically due to the surroundings. But for us, growing up in the poverty-stricken west side of O'ahu, we relate to urban music because it speaks of the pain and struggles that we can identify with: drugs, violence, and all that stuff that rap music glorifies. All I heard was ghetto raps all day, and it consumed much of my youth.

The more I became a rapper, the more I became consumed by the trinity of money, power, and respect. The influence that Hip Hop had on me was unbreakable. I got into street life with all kinds of knowledge I had learned from rap, which gave me a slight advantage in the game because I didn't only hear rap music, I listened, studied, learned, and applied it. I got into battling because I wanted people to respect my skills as a rapper, but more so to prove to myself I was worthy to be among the best.

The competitive nature of Hip Hop had gotten me far, even after battling. In the music industry, I wanted to prove something, so I attacked anyone who was in my way, burning bridges I never intended on crossing, constantly pushing for Hawai'i Hip Hop to be recognized as a respectable genre. During my career, I've attacked (with my music) a national corporate radio company manager and director of programming (Clear Channel), as well as the most-respected music award show in Hawai'i, the Na Hoku Hanohano Awards, all with great success. By success, I mean I influenced proper changes. Anything further would be egotistical.

I was a part of the biggest Hip Hop record label Hawai'i had ever seen, Tiki Entertainment. A well-funded organization, we pumped out the most Hip Hop albums in Hawai'i from one company. I released two projects with them, one with a reformed version of the group that started in my High School known as "The Free Floers" and my first solo project, *The O*, which sold the most units for a Hawai'i Hip Hop album, topping off at almost five thousand copies. Regardless of the internet and underground success, radio wouldn't play *The O* in rotation, so when I saw the opportunity to get into radio and learn the game to help publicize our genre of music, I took it. Unfortunately, when I did get a spot to put artists on, I didn't get the support from the community I had wished for. That told me a lot about Hawai'i Hip Hop in and of itself, and its nature of competition eating itself away.

At this point I changed my game plan. Instead of helping a community of competitive egotistical artists (who you can't be mad at because that's the nature of Hip Hop music), I decided I would instead design a blueprint with my own career. Given that they're already looking at me as competition instead of a leader, they would move when I move, as I move. That to me was the best I could do for the community. Like the old cliché goes, "Give a man fish, he eats for a day. Teach a man how to fish, and he eats for a lifetime."

Being in radio has taught me about not only the music industry, but entertainment in general. On such a large platform, I was able to see how different things made people react in specific ways. As an artist and a writer, I realized the attention span of the general public isn't receptive to complexity, not even in the slightest. With this in mind, I learned how to design entendres that would stimulate someone who heard the words, and someone who listened to the words to satisfy both parties. All the years of freestyling had enabled me to use that as a strength in my personality. Rebuttals I learned from battling became a form of entertainment, flipping whatever someone would say into an entirely different direction. Another thing I gained from radio was the ability to "speak well" and whole-heartedly in front of an audience. It really helped me become comfortable with being myself, and helped me break away from the "aww yeah, I do it for blahzay blah" hype-talk. To top off all of the radio experiences, the most important lesson I learned was from *how* I got the job. I have no college experience, nor any broadcast experience, yet I instantly got a show all because it's who you know.

I've always kept my roots in mind when making my music, and with Hawai'i Hip Hop being such a unique collective of artists who've drawn inspiration from so many different places, it was okay for me to just keep it real and be me, which was a Hawaiian-raised Filipino. Both cultures are very similar, as all islanders are, and get along very well in these islands. To me, a lot of artists in this scene are all looking for identification and acceptance, and what my producer Spoox told me a long time ago, for significance. Colonization has our people missing the very foundations that are in us from when we are raised; we are always looking at mainstream artists for direction more than just inspiration. We have so many strong cultures here, and it's definitely a strength that Hawai'i Hip Hop artists aren't utilizing to their full potential. I was guilty of this as well, but you live and you learn. Again, I'm hoping the blueprint I design will help save them steps, as I, too, am learning along the way.

A few of us local rappers (me, Big Mox, Mic 3, and Osna) who are now known collectively as the group "Angry Locals" formed one complete vibe. We had recorded so many songs together at Osna's studio we decided to start a group and put an album out. Since no one in Hawai'i had seen any mainstream success, even in the local industry, we figured we could take our little niche markets we had individually and throw them all together. We splashed a hint of our cultural backgrounds in there, and voilà, we became an instant success in Hawai'i Hip Hop. We figured since Hawai'i stereotypes Hip Hop as "angry" music, we ran with that name. I had known the brand would do well, because it was a simple enough name for people to recognize, and we vibe well with each other and it shows in our music. We all have different styles individually, and our solo projects each have their own uniqueness to them. As a producer, Osna likes to experiment a lot with different sounds; Mox has a vocalist background, heavy underground Hip Hop roots, and also sings with a jazz band. Mic 3 is the most culturally aware of the group, and very tuned in with his Filipino roots. Together, we brought mainstream awareness to the Hip Hop scene in Hawai'i. We have a great chemistry and have given Hawai'i Hip Hop a little more hope.

More than anything, in my music I try to help people the way Hip Hop music helped me. A lot of the songs I write help me grow as a person and a lot of the songs that inspired me to become an artist or inspire me today let me walk away with something. Whether it be a lesson about life or a different angle to look at something, the very foundation of it all is sharing. That's what Aloha is all about, the give and take, being *pono* (balanced), and throughout my journey thus far with Hip Hop, I've learned that things revolve, and it's your choice to evolve. I'm currently working on a fusion of Hip Hop and reggae with my good friend, mentor, and producer from Tiki Entertainment, Spoox. We feel this is the future sound for Urban Island culture. It comes from our souls as well as the ambiance of our home.

I've laid enough of a foundation in Hawai'i Hip Hop for people to use if they choose to, and I answer questions honestly and informatively. I no longer get angry when people bite me or feel competitive towards me. Hip Hop has given so much to me and that is how I reciprocate. They say Hawai'i is a bunch of crabs in a bucket … well they're not pulling me down, I'm pulling them up. Aloha Forward, Always.

THE WAY OF THE B-BOY

IMMIGRANT DREAMS, INTERNATIONAL SUCCESS

By Jerome "Jeromeskee" Aparis and
Roderick N. Labrador

ON GROWING UP FILIPINO IN THE UNITED STATES

I was born in Ormoc City, in the province of Leyte, in the Philippines. My parents and grandparents were born there as well. Before we moved to Seattle in '85, we went to Texas for about six months then we moved because my dad could not find a job there and we had family in Seattle. We moved to the US to seek a better opportunity and at that time in the Philippines, [during] the Marcos regime, there were a lot of bad things going on. There were killings in my neighborhood so my family wanted to move away from that.

I came here when I was 3 or 4 and when I started going to kindergarten I was having my Tagalog and English mixed up so it was really hard for me to communicate. The doctor told my parents to only speak in English to me. I have two older sisters and an older brother and they all know how to speak fluent Tagalog and Bisaya. But for me, I only understand. I know how to say certain words. I was kinda confused about what language I should speak, but eventually, of course, I spoke English. But part of me, well a lot of me, wished that my parents would have chosen to speak [to me] in English and Tagalog and Bisaya. That kind of shaped my way of speaking and communicating.

Being first-generation, going straight from the Philippines to the US, we weren't that well off. We started from humble beginnings. I would have hand-me-downs from my brother and sisters. I would wear, literally, my sisters' clothing, but they were really hip and cool so they made it all look really fresh, to a point where a lot of the kids at school would ask where I get my clothes but little did they know that it was actually hand-me-downs from my sisters but they just made it look cool. I believe, that in Filipino culture, you make the best of what you have. That was part of my family philosophy: whatever you had, you make the best of it and just own it.

I was pretty much the only Filipino kid in my school, majority was white kids and we had some Mexican kids. There was limited Asian, limited diversity at my school. In elementary, I had to really learn and understand that I was going to be separated but I was smart enough, as a little kid, to mingle and be cool with everybody, no matter their background but to work together and learn from each other.

BECOMING A B-BOY IN SEATTLE

I didn't understand what hip hop was truly about until middle school. I was in seventh grade when my older brother showed me this b-boy move called the indie step. He didn't teach me the simplest step, which is the 2 step, so he was getting frustrated with me. I came from the background of playing sports so I knew movement, but I didn't know rhythm. When he showed me this indie step, that sparked something in me. Then he showed me a VHS tape of all these b-boys. It was Rock Steady Crew, a compilation of 80s and 90s battles and that opened my eyes more. My sisters would go to break battles and tell me how awesome they were. I started doing research, started finding VHS tapes. Back in the day, you couldn't just go on YouTube. You had to go search for it so I would ask my brother, his friends, and my sisters' friends to find videos. When I watched *Beat Street*, the Rock Steady Crew versus the New York City Breakers, that blew my mind. I watched that over and over and over again. And then I went to several places to search for b-boys in White Center in Seattle. I danced there for a while but they all stopped. Then I saw my first break war. I saw Boss Crew and all these crews in that area. I was just really fascinated and blown away by breaking, by b-boying. Boss Crew was pretty much the epitome of breaking at that time. I was just mesmerized by how amazing they were. But little did I know about the pioneers called DVS crew—Fever One, Soul, Sneke, Hughes, Ray One.

We have a really rich legacy in Seattle coming from DVS Crew, who really was outstanding in the art form. Amazing graffiti artists and b-boys. They shaped the whole Seattle scene. They inspired and influenced Massive Monkees. Fever is our local Seattle legend. He's the one who kept on dancing through the 80s. He kept the tradition alive and he learned his fundamentals and technique from Icy Ice of New York City Breakers. Fever later on took me under his wing and was a huge inspiration for Massive Monkees.

There was also Circle of Fire. Old-school cats wouldn't really consider them b-boys back in the day because they infused capoeira, jazz, house dancing. They infused all kinds of dance elements and would enter b-boy competitions but what we appreciated from them was they were open to doing different styles, to doing different movements, and they had the idea of bonding together, living in a house together. We modeled off that honestly. We all moved in together and we also took the idea of being out there, trying different movements and not always staying in the box.

I tried out for my first b-boy crew called Oasis, who practiced in Chinatown. They knew some of my friends in White Center and were recruiting people. You had to battle the crew to get down with them. For two straight weeks before the battle, I trained so hard, 2–3 hours a day, then it came down to me and this other kid, Edenbert. The other guy got in and I was burnt, mad, frustrated, angry. My "cousin" Celistino, who was in Boss Crew, was there and suggested I go to Jefferson Community Center, where his crew and ABC, the younger generation of Boss, practiced.

Jefferson Community Center was a whole different deal. I didn't know anybody there. I had to take two buses from Burien to Chinatown—that took about an hour—and from Chinatown to Jefferson Community Center, which was at Beacon Hill, which took another twenty minutes. Slowly but surely I got to know everybody and then started making noise for myself and I got into ABC. From there, I got into Boss and I was one of the last members. In the Seattle scene in the late 90s, a lot of people were stopping. Boss Crew pretty much stopped except me, Brysen, and Granite Rock. Before we stopped we called ourselves Untouchable Style Monkeys because we wanted to be a whole new entity, a whole different crew. There was another crew who also danced there, called Massive ...

We established Massive Monkees in 1999. We were just little kids who had a vision; we wanted to collaborate and just have fun. We competed and wanted to be the best in Seattle. We had day jobs, and went to school in between. We did whatever we had to do to save up money, fly ourselves out to New York to learn from the pioneers, and to other parts of the east coast and west coast to compete. We didn't really care if we won or lost, we just kept on going. Our big breakthrough was winning the 2004 World B-Boy Championships in London. That was huge for us and from then on, we did a lot of international competitions and we won several world titles, like in Japan, Denmark, different places in Europe and Asia. We just won another world competition called R16 in Korea [in 2012].

AMERICA'S BEST DANCE CREW (SEASON 4)

They wanted us in Season 2. We just did a tour and we were debating to see if we wanted to go on the show. ABDC Season 1 was a hit and successful. But at that same time, we were offered our first big sponsorship from Bic. This was a huge sponsorship deal and they had a stack of papers that we had to agree to. Each [ABDC and Bic] wanted an exclusive agreement. Basically we had to choose one or the other and it was either guaranteed sponsorship or a chance to go on TV. At that time, we were established enough to understand that we didn't have to be desperate. So we chose the company that wanted to sponsor us, which I believe was the right, logical choice at the time. We worked on a hybrid documentary and tutorial called *Way of the Bboy* and we did this whole campaign for the Coosh headset that Bic had created and to drive *Way of the Bboy*.

Later on, ABDC asked us for Season 3 and we were like, "Nah, we're good." Season 4, they wanted us back so we sat down and asked each other, "Why do we want to do this?" What it came down to was we wanted to represent our city, our friends and families, for them to see and witness what we do. We wanted to show that we could adapt to the mainstream idea of breaking, but still do us. Overall, it was a success. We learned a lot about TV [laughs]. A lot about the drama that comes with it. There's a lot that goes down, a lot that happens behind the scenes. We stayed true to ourselves—when they told us to be like somebody or to copy certain moves, we said no. We represented us, our friends and families, and the city of Seattle.

GETTING INTO ROCK STEADY CREW

Fever One was my mentor and influence in breaking. He got into Rock Steady Crew. He moved out to New York in '96–97 and got down with Rock Steady Crew. In '99, I went there, first time in New York. It was an amazing experience. And I entered the Rock Steady Anniversary [Battle] in '99 and I went to the finals. Lost in the finals, but made a lot of noise and met a lot of Rock Steady pioneers and Rock Steady members and they were already looking out and seeing how I would develop over time. Fever One suggested it, Crazy Legs called me up. I had to think about it. And I got down in 2000 and I'm still down. I've seen a lot of transformation in Rock Steady Crew, member-wise. I'm proud to be down with them because I respect the Rocky Steady past, where it is now, and where it's going in the future. I really have a close friendship with Mr. Wiggles, Sugar Pop, and Crazy Legs. All the new-generation cats, I have mad love and respect for them. I still stand strong with Rock Steady even though Massive Monkees is doing their thing. It's an honor to be down with Rock Steady and I take great pleasure in representing Rock Steady. Wherever I go, whatever country I'm in, even if it's a Massive Monkees thing or Jeromeskee thing, it does not matter, I will rep Rock Steady to the fullest.

B-BOYING/B-GIRLING OUTSIDE THE US

Internationally, they get it. Of course, in different countries, it's a little different here and there, what level or degree they look at it as art. But for the most part, they respect it, are amazed by it, and want to be part of it. In any place on the planet, there are always b-boys. What's great about this dance is that it does not judge. You don't have to come from a certain background. Honestly, you can be a businessman by day and then be a b-boy by night. I've seen that over and over again. Kids in the Philippines, they break dance in their *tsinelas*, b-boy in their slippers. As long as there is music and rhythm playing, they're dancing in basketball courts. And nobody is telling them, "You can't do that." They just go about doing it and learning. That's what makes it really beautiful.

When we were in Japan, it was beautiful. When we arrived, I believe there were 7 of us who went and we pretty much got the red-carpet treatment—the Prime Minister of Japan and a whole group of people greeted us. Day one, we had press there and had an opening dinner ceremony where it was Japanese-style and we were specially invited guests. Every single second there we had our personal interpreters. They made us feel really special, every moment was so unique and so powerful. One day, I was judging the whole day and the crew went around in the city. They came back later on that night and we all met up and when we were walking back to our hotel, there were Japanese b-boys about 20 feet [away] and we could hear them saying, "Massive, Monkees. Massive, Monkees." They were doing the chant that we do, but we never taught them. We found out that they learned that through our DVDs. So from a whole different part of the world, these Japanese b-boys, who didn't know how to speak English, were doing our chant. We were just blown away so we ran up to them and started chanting with them. It was a beautiful moment for us.

Wherever you go, their culture, their environment will affect how they break and express themselves. I was teaching a class at a studio [in Japan]. I had high school kids, college kids, and I was teaching toprock and I remember a grandma and grandpa—I'm talking about in their 80s—they're doing my movements. I was teaching 2-3 8 counts, but they were doing it slowly, with nice precision, making it graceful like it was tai chi. They didn't have this preconceived negative notion of breaking or that it's a young, cool, hip thing. They just respected the art form. I was just like, "Wow! A grandma and grandpa doing breaking moves and flowing with it."

The R16 in Korea—it's literally like the NBA Finals. We had media day for the first day—numerous photographers taking pictures of all the crews from different countries. Each crew representative had to sit down, lawn table style, just like how they do on the NBA Finals, and do a press conference. Each representative had to talk about how it felt to be in R16, how it felt to represent your country, and your strategies and tactics. Very professional. It's huge. In Korea, the government, they have three things that they sponsor: archery, taekwondo, and b-boying. That's how significant it is over there.

MARKETING "JEROMESKEE"

There's this idea of the b-boy or as an artist in general, where if you win a big competition or [get to] be on TV, everything else will come to you. I've been asked to do these TV gigs and asked to do other big competitions, like Red Bull BC One finals, but at the end of the day, you gotta hustle, you got to work the system. If I was just competing, I would not be making a living out of this. So I've really expanded. Besides competing, I'm doing power talks, judging and doing appearances in different countries, coaching; I teach at studios, like Cornerstone Studio. I teach and coach about ten times a week. I have a full schedule. Now, I'm getting into informational products. I have an amazing team that does apps, Beautiful Code Factory. I have two apps out right now, Windmills 3SF and

Bboy Step By Step: How to Dance [streetdanceapp.com]. I also have a third app, the Bruce Lee JKD app, where we partnered with Taky, Bruce Lee's best friend and really it's awesome. I got to direct and co-produce the whole app and the commercials, too. I got to really collaborate with talented people. I'm also working on Body Rock Breaking [jeromeskeecoaching.com], which is basically for working professionals and people who have two left feet [laughs] and teaching them how to move and groove, how to have rhythm, and how to learn breaking cool moves in the fastest and safest way. And I'm also doing Breakfit Challenge, which is basically P90X and breaking together, for guys out there who want to learn how to groove and dance and also have a great strengthening, conditioning, and endurance workout. All of the products, the concepts, the philosophies behind them are 17 years in the making. It's about impacting people, serving people, and to really build relationships.

COMMUNITY INVOLVEMENT, LOCALLY AND GLOBALLY

We're doing this b-boy/b-girl league in Seattle called the Massive Break Challenge, which is school versus school, so middle schools will battle different middle schools and high schools will battle different high schools and we wrap up with a grand finale, which is at the Bagley Wright Theatre. The goal is to really inspire kids to take risks, to go out there and feel like a rock star. I wanted to pack out the seats at the professional theater and to really let teachers, friends, and family know how amazing these students are. How much time and dedication [go into it], how professional this art form is. It's been a huge success. We do that each year. It gets bigger and better each year. We just did it recently at the Northwest Folklife Festival.

I've also partnered up with a non-profit group called Arts Corp and another one called Extraordinary Futures, which is a Massive Monkees non-profit going on their second year now. Arts Corp is one of the leading non-profits in the US and I've been with them for 11 years. I'm constantly teaching, but the community work that sticks out to me is when I was in the Philippines. My sister, who lives in the Philippines right now—she was born there but raised here in Seattle—but she went back to the Philippines to dedicate her life to impacting people. She and my uncle, Nep Aparis, who is the Vice-Mayor in Ormoc City, wanted to do something while I was there. My friend Joe, Jorawk of Massive Monkees, and I went to the orphanage center to donate our time. We did a power talk—told the kids that anything is possible, that we believed in them, that we came through struggles, too, how you can overcome them and make things happen. We did a workshop, we danced with them, we vibed out with them. Basically, just spent time with them and really got to know them.

Another moment in the Philippines changed my life forever. My sister does a lot of government work out there and I went to a safe house for trafficked young girls. The safe house was in a hidden location and when I went there, we wanted to find out their fears and needs because I was thinking, "How am I going to incorporate breakdancing into this?" These girls are frightened by men because they've been abused by men. I'm thinking, "How am I going to teach them how to physically do something, since they are physically scared to do things because they have been physically [and sexually] abused, and still empower them?" That was a huge challenge, but the workshop went well. It was successful to a point where we sat down and the staff told me that this was the first time ever where each girl told their story, told me about their struggles, what they went through. Hearing their stories blew my mind. That just fueled me even more, it inspired me. It really affected me, where I know I have to do even more.

AUTHOR BIOS

ALVES, ANNA

Anna Alves is a NYC-born and California-bred writer living in Jersey City, NJ, working on her first novel. Currently, she is a PhD student in American Studies at Rutgers University at Newark. She recently received her MFA in Creative Writing, also from Rutgers-Newark, and also holds a BA in English and History and MA in Asian American Studies from UCLA. A 2006 PEN Center USA Rosenthal Emerging Voices Fellow, her stories have been published in *Amerasia Journal*, *Tilting the Continent: Southeast Asian American Writing*, *Strange Cargo: An Emerging Voices Anthology*, *Kartika Review*, and *Dismantle*, an anthology from Voices of Our Nations Arts. Formerly, as a Ford Foundation Program Associate and consultant, she assisted in projects that generated *Total Chaos: The Art and Aesthetics of Hip-Hop* edited by Jeff Chang and the national report, *Towards a Cultural Community: Identity, Education and Stewardship in Filipino American Performing Arts*.

APARIS, JEROME "JEROMESKEE"

Jerome "Jeromeskee" Aparis is a b-boy from Seattle, WA and represents Massive Monkees, the world-renowned Rock Steady Crew, and Seattle Hip Hop legends DVS Crew (Dropping Vicious Styles). Massive Monkees have won numerous competitions across the globe over the past decade, including the 2004 World B-Boy Championships, the R16 B-Boy Masters World Championship, and they were also featured on MTV's *America's Best Dance Crew*. Jeromeskee has competed in, judged, and won numerous b-boy events throughout the world, including in Europe, Asia, Mexico, Canada, and the U.S. He was featured on *Dancing With The Stars* and was one of the coaches on *MTV's MADE: I Want To Be A B-boy*. He also does work with non-profit organizations, including Extraordinary Futures and he serves as a teaching artist for Arts Corp, a Seattle-based non-profit organization that fosters confidence, creativity, and critical thinking for students.

BAMBU

Bambu, from the city of Los Angeles, has been making his mark on the Hip Hop scene for almost a decade. His first album, "self untitled …" first saw the light of day on the 10-year anniversary of the LA Rebellion of 1992 and the climb has been forward since. Soon after releasing that first LP, Bambu joined fellow Los Angeles emcee, Kiwi and Bay Area transplant DJ Phatrick to create the now-defunct group, Native Guns. After the group disbanded, DJ Phatrick and Bambu continued to do shows around the country and eventually built a reputation as strong live performers. Bambu dropped his follow-up solo album, "… i scream bars for the children …" in 2007 and "… exact change …" in 2008. "… paper cuts …" dropped at the end of February, 2010 and has definitely solidified the emcee as one of Los Angeles' best. He recently released the hard-hitting mixtape with DJ Muggs and the Soul Assassins. His most recent album, "… one rifle per family." debuted in 2012. Bambu has also been involved in community organizing, working with groups like People's C.O.R.E (Community Organization for Reform and Empowerment) and Kabataang maka-Bayan (KmB), or Pro-People Youth, in Los Angeles.

BISCHOFF, STEPHEN

Stephen Bischoff is Associate Director for Multicultural Student Services and Retention Counselor for the Asian American and Pacific Islander Student Center at Washington State University (WSU). Stephen earned his Master's and Doctorate degrees in American Studies as well as his Bachelor's and Master's degrees in Business at WSU. His research interests include Filipino Americans, Hip Hop culture, popular culture, and social justice. He has taught courses through the Critical Culture, Gender and Race Studies (CCGRS) department at WSU that include: Introduction to Comparative Ethnic Studies, Introduction to Asian Pacific American Studies, Race and Racism in U.S. Popular Culture, and Hip Hop Around the Globe. Stephen is committed to serving underrepresented and underserved populations while eager to grow his critical consciousness. He enjoys spending time with his partner Rachel and their two sons, Isaiah and Zion, in addition to keeping up with soccer, basketball, and photography in his free time.

BRIONES, MARTIN

Martine Briones is a producer, writer, artist, and former DJ. He is the founder of SkyHigh Music, a production company specializing in all types of music and multimedia.

BUÑO, BRIAN

Poet, Filmmaker, and Prose Politician. Co-founder of guerrilla::words. Born in Brooklyn, NY—raised in Jamaica, Queens—he has returned to reside once again in B-R-O-O-K-Lyn, the Planet. Began inking dreams as a child, and published in various poetry anthologies starting at the age of twelve. Moved on to playwriting, stageworks, then eventually took on the spotlight to perform poetry and spoken word. Still scribing, currently works in video production, and continually pursuing a film career. Comrade, father, husband, and believer in mankind.

CAJAYON, GENE

Cajayon attended film school at Loyola Marymount University, where he began work on The Debut, his first feature film. A groundbreaking coming-of-age story about a Filipino American family, Cajayon completed The Debut after an arduous 8-year production process.

The Debut's crowd-pleasing success on the film festival circuit inspired Cajayon to launch an ambitious theatrical self-distribution campaign. For 2 years, The Debut's grass roots promotional team traveled to 15 major cities across the United States, promoted the film directly to Asian Pacific American and mainstream communities, and grossed US$1.8 million at the box office. The movie's extraordinary success led to a domestic and international distribution deal with Sony Pictures.

Cajayon is currently developing several feature length screenplays. Glass Street (Sundance Lab finalist) is a multi-cultural crime drama, Saturday Morning Christmas (Tribeca All Access) is a coming-of-age dramedy about a 70's era immigrant family, and Jesus of Shaolin is a horror comedy mash-up.

CALVARIO, ARNEL

Believing in using his talents and resources to promote community outreach, positivity, "respect for all people," artistic expression, and education, Dr. Arnel Calvario has dedicated himself to the CA dance scene since his college days. In 1992, he founded UC Irvine's own Kaba Modern. He was a dancer/choreographer for DVS and Chill Factor and in 1998 he also joined Culture Shock® Los Angeles. He managed the six Kaba Modern dancers from MTV's hit show *America's Best Dance Crew*, Fanny Pak, the Beat Freaks, & Kinjaz and continues to be the advisor for Kaba Kids, Kaba Modern, and Kaba Modern Legacy. Arnel is proud and grateful to currently be the Board President of Culture Shock L.A. and Culture Shock International. He continues to teach dance workshops and judges dance events nationally and internationally. His longstanding dedication to the dance community has been recognized by awards such as his award for "Innovative Leadership" by the National Association of Asian-American Professionals, his induction into the Hall of Fame at the 2011 World of Dance Industry Awards, his televised 2012 Filipino Champion award presented by TFC (the Filipino Channel), and being the recipient of the 2012 Culture Shock International Visionary Leader award. He has also been featured as a guest writer for the *L.A. Times* as a critic for America's Best Dance Crew Season 5 and served as Battle Coordinator for both Hip Hop International World Battle and Urban Street Jam for the past 4 years.

CAMBAY, CHERYL

Cheryl Cambay has been involved in Hip Hop dance for over 25 years. She grew up in Cerritos, CA and is an original Kaba Modern dancer from 1992 to 1997. During her undergraduate studies at University of California, Irvine, she began to perform rap/spoken word. Cheryl was a company dancer in Culture Shock Los Angeles—a nonprofit Hip Hop dance organization promoting dance education from 2003 to 2007. She is a former company director for Future Shock LA (youth dance company under the direction of Culture Shock LA) and was on the Board of Operations as the Marketing Director for CSLA from 2005 to 2011. Cheryl is the current Secretary and sits on the Board of Directors for Culture Shock LA. Cheryl is a Regional Clinical Manager specializing in sales/marketing and has worked in the Addiction/Mental Health field for over 15 years. She currently resides in Long Beach, CA.

CAPITO, MICHAEL "SUITKACE"

Michael "Suitkace" Capito is a b-boy from New York City. He has been dancing since 1999 and is an active member of The Breaks Kru. He is recognized for helping to pioneer the use of contortionism in b-boying. He is the founder of the freestyle dance crew, Part Time Models. He has also danced for the Flying Jalapeño Popper Stick Avengers, Fr3sh Dance Company, and the Hip Hop music group Deep Foundation. He teaches classes to aspiring new b-boys and b-girls. Suitkace currently works as a registered nurse. He is also a Lego photographer.

CASTRO, JOHN MANAL

From San Jose, Caifornia, John Manal Castro is a writer, producer, and sarcastic human being. He received his BA in Film and Television Arts at Cal State University, Long Beach where he wrote and directed the acclaimed short film, "Diary Of A Gangsta Sucka," a biting experimental documentary poking fun at the wannabe gangster phenomenon in suburban Los Angeles. Following graduation, he co-produced and co-wrote The Debut, one of the first American feature films about the Filipino-American experience. In addition to his film work, Castro attended the Culinary School Of The Pacific in Honolulu Hawaii. His experience inspired him to co-produce, write and perform onstage in the Cooking Show With Karimi and Castro, which satirized the complexity of food and political consciousness. He currently lives in Los Angeles.

CHANG, BENJI

Originally hailing from Cerritos, California, DJ UltraMan first immersed himself in Hip Hop culture in middle school and was heavily influenced by the conscious Hip Hop era. Mentored by members of Fascination, Legend, the Beat Junkies, and Empire DJs, he has been involved in record and event promotions, college radio, TV, and sharing stages with acts like the Jurassic 5, Ice Cube, Far East Movement, Native Guns, Dumbfoundead, and OutKast. He represents the Cerritos All-Stars and mETHODOLOGY crew, and has been active in Icon Events, Legend, 21XL, and the eventsco. Aside from DJing, he has traveled throughout the US and Pacific Rim to speak and teach about Hip Hop, education, Asian Americans, and community activism. He has been involved in numerous grassroots organizations in inner-city LA including JUiCE, the M+M Project, and Chinatown Kung Fu & Lion Dance troupe. He earned his PhD in Education at UCLA, currently teaches at Teachers College, Columbia University, and resides in Harlem, New York.

CHANG, JEFF

Jeff Chang is the executive director of the Institute for Diversity in the Arts at Stanford University. Named by the Utne Reader as "One of the 50 Visionaries Who Are Changing Your World," Jeff Chang has been a USA Ford Fellow in Literature and a winner of the North Star News Prize. He is the author of the American Book Award- and Asian American Literary Award-winning, *Can't Stop Won't Stop: A History of the Hip-Hop Generation*, and the editor of "Total Chaos: The Art and Aesthetics of Hip Hop." His latest book is *Who We Be: The Colorization of America* (St. Martin's Press). He is a co-founder of ColorLines, the SoleSides Hip Hop crew, and CultureStr/ke.

CREED CHAMELEON

Creed Chameleon is a Hip Hop artist from Hawai'i and the first underground rapper to be nominated for the Na Hoku Hanohano Awards. Now residing in Arizona, he has repped and helped elevate the Hawai'i Hip Hop scene for over a decade, earning various honors, awards, and valuable experience. The mixed Filipino--descent rapper has often been a promoter's first choice for performing and opening for national Hip Hop artists such as Wu-Tang Clan, Dilated Peoples, Talib Kweli, Too Short, Chino XL, De La Soul, Mos Def, Gym Class Heroes, Living Legends, Aceyalone, Abstract Rude, Myka 9, Digable Planets, The Grouch, Murs, Scarub, Eligh, Atmosphere, Aesop Rock, El-P, Brother Ali, Nas, Souls of Mischief, Slum Village, Typical Cats, and he even performed at the first-ever Rock the Bells Hawaii Festival in 2007. In 2009, he had the opportunity to be one of the exclusive performers to jump on the OOF! inter-island tour with Blue Scholars and Bambu. In summer 2010, Creed toured Southern California to support his album, *The Ultimatum*, which gained highly acclaimed reviews from local artists and fans. In 2011 and 2012, Creed joined forces with Big Island and Los Angeles natives Analog Dive to push "LA Got Aloha," a Hip Hop movement to build bridges between LA and HI artists in order to spread the "aloha spirit" through artistic media on an international level. Just recently, Creed was invited on the Vans Warped Tour 2012 performing on the Bring It Back stage in selected cities alongside Flip The Bird CEO and artist Tassho Pearce.

CUSTODIO, CINDY L.

Cindy L. Custodio brings eleven years of experience as a legal researcher and assistant court clerk manager for an attorney's service to Parker Waichman. Since joining the firm, she has worked in the Nursing Home Litigation Unit and assists our nursing home attorneys working cases from beginning to end, including preparation of legal documents including complaints, motions, discovery demands and responses, bills of particulars, as well as Surrogate's Court filings. Ms. Custodio holds a Bachelor of Arts in Government from John Jay College as well as a Paralegal Certificate from Queens College and was awarded an Outstanding Academic Achievement Award from Westlaw. Aside from her life in law, she is a wife and a mother to 3-½ year old twin boys. She loves music and supports her family, friends, and community.

DE MIRA, MARIO "NOMI"

At the age of 21, Nomi packed his bags and left his hometown of St. Paul, MN, for Brooklyn, NY. His band at the time, the Oddjobs, was set on becoming the biggest thing out of Brooklyn since the Beastie Boys. For three years, they toured the continental US, couch-crashing and crashing tour vans. After the disbanding of Oddjobs, Nomi found himself in San Francisco, CA in 2004. Nomi became involved at the Filipino Community Center (FCC) in 2005. Together with rapper/activists Kiwi and Pele, Nomi began to teach Hip Hop workshops to youth at the (FCC). Nomi's experience as a worker organizer and advocate has had a big influence on his music. His last record *Remittances* (2010, Beatrock Music) was a dedication to the millions of Filipino migrant workers around the world. Nomi continues to do Hip Hop writing workshops, and views art and culture as a media tool in advancing progressive causes in continuing the fight for social justice.

DEEP FOUNDATION

Deep Foundation, consisting of three emcees representing Queens and New Jersey, remains a benchmark in socially relevant hip hop. With lyrics based on their lives and personal experiences, CeeJay, ILL Poe, and Mugshot have given voice to an underrepresented Filipino American demographic and seek to imbue their compatriots, both young and old, with a renewed sense of cultural pride. Deep Foundation has brought its boom-bap era influenced hip-hop to domestic and international audiences since 2002. With the release of their debut album, *The First Draft,* and groundbreaking music videos for "Children of the Sun" and "Sleep," Deep Foundation has captured the hearts and imaginations of fans worldwide. In addition to their musical success, the media has also taken note of their drive and originality, having been featured in *Filipinas Magazine*, the cover of *FOKAL Magazine*, *The Philippine Daily Inquirer*, The Myx Channel, PBS, The Filipino Channel, Spike TV and HBO. They have released a brand new EP entitled *Deep Foundation & Hydroponikz present Generation ILL* which is available on iTunes and CD Baby.

DEHAVEN, CHRISTINA

Christina is a member of the Producers Guild of America. She works as a production manager, line producer, co-producer, and producer on numerous short films, features, documentaries, commercials, and music videos, including for the Grammy Award-winning group, The Black Eyed Peas. Earlier in her career, Christina participated in the production of *The Debut*, serving as assistant to director Gene Cajayon. Short films she produced have played the festival circuit, including Sundance, Tribeca, and SXSW, and one that aired on HBO called Smell of Coffee. She has also co-produced two feature length documentaries, including *My Uncle Berns*, which also aired on HBO and 761st. She most recently completed production as supervising producer on Season 2 of *In Between Men*, a web-based TV series.

DJ DELINGER

Born in Brooklyn, NY, Delinger started DJing when he was twelve years old listening to his brother DJ Kuya D in the basement in Queens. He formed Kuya Tribe in NY and moved to VA shortly after. He has been spinning for 19 years, repping Kuya Tribe all over VA and across the country.

DJ ICY ICE

As an original member of the World Famous Beat Junkies, DJ Icy Ice has amassed a resume that includes nearly two decades of performing on the world's biggest stages. Icy Ice's artistry has been showcased at the largest music festivals, hottest club venues, and celebrity private parties throughout the US, Australia, China, Canada, Dubai, Europe, Japan, Mexico, the Philippines, Sri Lanka, and more. He has also been the exclusive party DJ for Manny Pacquiao, The Black Eyed Peas, and Kanye West, as well as for the Grammy Awards, American Music Awards, the Sundance Film Festival, NBA All-Star Games, The Democratic National Convention After Party, The Magic Convention, SEMA, LA Fashion Week, X-Games, and hundreds of other corporate and private events. Icy Ice is universal across the DJ spectrum, spinning as a DJ and Video Mixer for LA's top-rated radio station, Power 106, to hosting music TV shows, to appearing in movies, to owning multiple retail shops and the music websites StacksTV.net, ExclusiveGrooves.com, and TurntableU.com. Icy Ice is currently featured as a DJ doing mixes for Wave 891 in Manila. His mixes are also heard weekly by tens of millions throughout the US and the Philippines via syndication on Superadio. For the past several years, Icy Ice has been expanding the exposure of "Visual Turntablism" through a variety of high-profile online platforms and can be seen live every Tuesday at StacksTV.net and BReal.TV (Cypress Hill's online channel). Icy Ice's accomplishments include spinning for acclaimed radio stations such as KKBT 92.3 The Beat, 93.5 KDAY, Divine Forces Radio on 90.7 KPFK, and Movin 93.9 FM with Rick Dees in the Morning. Icy Ice has been the resident DJ for Guerilla Union's "Rock The Bells" Music Festivals and toured as the DJ for legendary Hip Hop artist KRS-One.

DJ KUTTIN KANDI

Candice L. Custodio-Tan, known as DJ Kuttin Kandi, born and raised Queens, NY, is widely regarded as one of the most accomplished female DJs in the world. She is also a Writer, Spoken Word Poet, Theater Performer, Educator, Hip Hop Feminist, and Community Organizer. She is a member of DJ team champions 5th Platoon, co-founder and DJ for the all-female Hip Hop group Anomolies, co-founder of the famed NY monthly open mic nights "Guerrilla Words," and co-founder of the coalition R.E.A.C.Hip-Hop (Representing Education, Activism & Community through Hip Hop). DJing for over 15 years, Kandi competed in over 20 DJ competitions such as ITF and Vibe. She is a *Source* DJ Champion and has been the only female DJ to make it to the DMC USA finals. Kuttin Kandi has been interviewed in numerous magazines and newspapers such as *The Source*, *Vibe*, *Vogue*, *YM*, *Rolling Stone*, The *New York Times*, The *Daily News*, and the *Vibe Hip-Hop Diva's* book. Kandi has performed all around the world with artists such as Bob James, Kool Herc, Afrika Bambaataa, Jay-Z, Gangstar, LL Cool J, Mya, MC Lyte, the Roots, Young Gunz, Dead Prez, Immortal Technique, Black Eyed Peas, Common, Jean Grae, BlackStar, and punk Riot Grrrl group LeTigre, just to name a few. Kandi has been honored and performed at venues such as the Rock and Roll Hall of Fame, Lincoln Center, and Madison Square Garden for WNBA's NY Liberty. She is a known Pop Culture Political Essayist and has written for several anthologies and blogs. She currently resides in Chula Vista, CA where she works at UC San Diego's Women's Center. www.kuttinkandi.net.

DJ KUYA DERRICK

Born in Brooklyn, NY, DJ Kuya D started spinning freestyle at twelve years old. He spun with Queens' finest DJ crews, EPP, IntroBass Productions, and historic collabos with DJ Roli Rho. He now resides in Virginia Beach, running the scene with the almighty Kuya Tribe.

DJ NEIL ARMSTRONG

Born and raised in NYC, DJ Neil Armstrong has literally traveled the world because of his love of Hip Hop. As one of Jay-Z's former tour DJs, he was the first person to represent on the 1s and 2s for an inauguration of a US president in 2008. As a global ambassador for Adidas, he follows in the footsteps of Jam Master Jay, spreading the art and culture and love of Hip Hop and music to the masses.

DJ QBERT

DJ Qbert, or Grandmixer Qbert, is a turntablist and composer. He grew up in the golden age of the San Francisco Bay Area DJ battle scene of the late 1980s. Battling and training in the artform is what sets DJ Qbert apart from the rest. He is relentless in unlocking the sounds and systems of scratching. It is Qbert who is credited for championing the turntable as a musical instrument. He is often referred to as the Jimi Hendrix of the turntables, known to make them sing in complex and unimaginable ways. He has invented the most scratching techniques and musical innovations of any DJ in history. Qbert is credited for being a world ambassador of the DJ as a musician and turning the turntable into a respected musical instrument. A former DMC World Champion and DMC Hall of Fame inductee, DJ Qbert has developed some of the most important works that have shaped the Hip Hop and Electronic music landscape—from the 1994 release of *Demolition Pumpkin Squeeze Musik*, hailed by *Source* magazine as the best mixtape of all time, to his innovations with his very own skratch records that set the stage for DJs to rebuild all their elements ready to manipulate through custom-created vinyl. He created a DJ group to play pieces of his turntable band, giving rise to the Invisibl Skratch Piklz. In 1998, he released his album, *Wave Twisters*, accompanied by an animated film that syncs with the music, which was drawn by legendary San Francisco artist Dug-1. DJ Qbert is also featured in Doug Pray's film, *Scratch*, and was part of Apple Inc's "Switch" ad campaign. His inventions for Vestax hold as today's blueprints for turntablism, he was also first to break ground for DJs in the gaming industry with his work with EA Sports, and he is a co-founder of Thud Rumble, a media management company.

DOCUYANAN, LEO

Leo Docuyanan was born in Guam and raised in Southeast San Diego, CA. He is self-taught and concentrates on portraiture of artists in the greater Bay Area Hip Hop community. He has exhibited work in San Francisco, Los Angeles, San Diego, and New York. He is a lover of carne asada and medium-format film. View his work at www.leodocuyanan.com.

ESCLAMADO, LEO

Leo Esclamado is a 2nd-generation Filipino American from Jacksonville, Florida. In Jax, he was part of the b-boy crews Nex Level and the Isotonic Mangos. Inspired by the Fil-Am and Hip Hop scene in Duval, he attended University of Florida, where he worked with the Hip Hop Collective to host Soul Cypher, an event that celebrated the Florida Hip Hop scene, from 2003 to 2005. He has been involved in immigrant rights and community development and organizing for over seven years. Currently, he is a community organizer working with newly arrived Filipino families and undocumented youth through TIGRA—Transnational Institute for Grassroots Research Action based in Oakland, California and Manila, Philippines. Leo has a Master's in Social Work from the University of Michigan. He will always be a student of Hip Hop dance and culture.

EVANGELISTA, JONATHAN "TOOK"

Jonathan "TOOK" Evangelista was born in the Philippines and immigrated to the U.S. with his entire family when he was 3 years old. While he grew up in the inner-city of Los Angeles, Hip Hop naturally became one of his greater interests in life—not that inner-cities and Hip Hop were things that only existed together per se, but because Hip Hop spoke to the things he encountered growing up (the drugs, the violence, the "vandalism," the struggles) and became much more of a foundation for his thought and, later, his photography. While attending a community college in Santa Monica, CA, and after completing much of the photography curriculum to figure out what he wanted to do in life, he realized that photography was the one thing he thoroughly enjoyed and appreciated. In 2004, he relocated to Honolulu and, ultimately, he married his love for Hip Hop with his love for photography and became one of the few photographers to document the local Hawai'i Hip Hop scene. He now works with various groups/organizations in the planning and organization of events within the street culture. Beyond that, he has started to elevate his photography to "fine art" and is currently completing several works for exhibit.

FRANCISCO, JOHN "LIL' JOHN"

Lil' John Francisco was born In Vallejo, CA and raised in Oakland and Alameda, CA. He has been involved in Hip Hop since it made its way to the West Coast in the early 1980s. He was a member of Roc On Creation, an early b-boy crew out of Alameda, CA. He is a member of TDK (Those Damn Kids/Teach Dem Kulture) Graff/Hip Hop crew out of Oakland, CA. He is raising his children and preserving REAL, True Hip Hop that involves the four main pillars of Hip Hop: Writing/Art, DJing, MCing, and B-boying. He continues to keep the spirit and legacy of his brother, Mike "Dream" Francisco, alive. DREAM One TDK TMC FC TFP KTD. The Destiny Kontinues ...

FRANCISCO, MIKE "DREAM" (BIO EXCERPT WRITTEN BY SPIE ONE)

Michael Francisco, better known to the world simply as "Dream," was tragically murdered on the night of February 17, 2000. Oakland's twelfth homicide that year claimed one of the West Coast's premiere graffiti artists. Dream started writing in 1983 and soon became recognized as one of the San Francisco Bay's stylistic innovators. Dream understood that art should not just be nice to look at but needs to be used as a weapon of defense against oppressive injustice. He organized and participated in very controversial gallery installations, such as "No Justice, No Peace—Word from the Underground" (1993) and "Amerikan Terrorism—Shadows on the Global Street" (1995). Along with taking a stand against police violence, nuclear proliferation, colonialism, and cigarette companies, which target people of color, he produced artwork in defense of Mumia Abu-Jamal and against corporate takeovers of peoples' institutions. With firm pride in his Pinoy roots, Dream embraced other cultures as well. He built bridges between the Black and Asian/Pacific Islander communities.

GEOLOGIC, AKA PROMETHEUS BROWN

Prometheus Brown, aka Geologic, aka Geo Quibuyen, is a Cali-born, Hawai'i-raised, Seattle-based rapper with a camera. He attended the University of Washington, where he met Sabzi to form the acclaimed Seattle Hip Hop duo Blue Scholars in 2002. In 2010, he started the Rappers W/ Cameras vanity project (parties, photozines, blog) with Thig Nat of The Physics. In 2011, he teamed with long-time collaborator Bambu to form the supergroup The Bar, and officially joined the Beatrock Music roster. Geo has toured all over North America, being the first Filipino rapper to rap in front of many crowds, which he asked, "How many of you are seeing a Filipino dude rap for the very first time?" Geo abandoned a struggling but budding writing career to pursue music, having written for UrbanEarth.com, *URB* magazine, and being the Urban Music reviewer for the *UW Daily*. He resumed his dormant desire to write, launching Prometheusbrown.com as a film blog in 2008 and contributing to online publications such as *Racialicious* and IMDb.com. He has contributed op-ed pieces for *Al-Jazeera* and *The Seattle Times*, for which he wrote an editorial rap on gun violence that was nominated for a 2012 Online Journalism Award. Currently, Geo is the Seattle Town Hall artist-in-residence, and in spring 2013, returned to UW to complete his BAs in History and American Ethnic Studies.

GINELSA, PATRICIO

Patricio Ginelsa is originally from Daly City, CA, where his passion for filmmaking developed while creating video movies with his neighborhood at the age of 13. After receiving his BA in cinema production at the University of Southern California, Patricio became the Associate Producer of the award-winning film *The Debut* and assisted in its two-year-long theatrical self-distribution tour, leading to a home video deal with Columbia Tri-Star.

Inspired by the grassroots nature of that campaign, Patricio teamed up with A.J. Calomay of Xylophone Films to form a community-based process of filmmaking starting with the completion of the feature-length video *Lumpia* (2003 Hawaii International Film Festival, 2004 Toronto ReelWorld), which received a rave review from *Variety*, calling it a movie that takes "low budget to new heights … and should be shown in high school media classes across the continent."

Ginelsa's emphasis on storytelling and community collaboration can be seen in the multiple music videos he's directed for various independent artists. He wrote and directed three music videos for the Grammy-Award winning group The Black Eyed Peas, "The Apl Song" (2004) and two versions of "Bebot" (2006), one of which was lauded with the California Preservation Foundation Presidents Award for its focus on Stockton's Little Manila District. Other awards include Best Music Video for his Native Guns "Champion" video at the 2007 San Diego Asian Film Festival and for Bambu's "Ceooka & Rooks" at the 2009 Chicago International Hip Hop Film Festival.

Under his production company Kid Heroes Productions, Patricio continues to develop his passion projects while maintaining his day job and somewhat of a normal life.

HOPIE

Hopie is not your average rapper. Really. First, she independently released her debut album, *The Diamond Dame*, in July 2008, immediately garnering national attention and a nomination for URB's Next 1000. Then, Hopie did a 180 and took a short hiatus to earn her doctorate from U.C. Hastings, emerging only to release two music videos and a t-shirt series with Adapt Clothing, and to perform at Paid Dues in April 2010. As the ink on her law degree dried, Hopie returned to the music scene with an eclectic body of work, including *Dulce Vita* released in 2011 and *Raw Gems* in 2012. In 2013, she released *Sugar Water*. The pint-sized, tattooed academic has always carved her own, decisively rebellious, path. To distract from realities of her rocky start in Manila, and a difficult, short-lived childhood in San Francisco, Hopie dove headfirst into music. To date, Hopie is self-taught or classically trained in violin, voice, music composition, spoken word, drums, and guitar. Still, Hopie's primary allegiance remains far from the ivory towers of music theory, lying markedly in experimentation with rap. In fact, Hopie's brand of Hip Hop is anything but sullen or conventional.

HORTILLAS, JASON

Jason "Encite" Hortillas is a writer, event organizer, and emcee. Presently he is the Marketing Director for Freebase America. He was the host and general manager for New York City artist showcase Guerrilla Words from 2002 to 2007. Encite later worked as a consultant for Kanye West and 50 Cent producer, Illmind. As an emcee, Encite has worked with Deep Foundation and Skyzoo, opened up for groups like Little Brother and served as an event host for clients like DMC and Scion. Behind the pen, Jason contributed for music media sites like The Smoking Section and Vapors. He now resides in New Jersey with wife Diana and son Dillan.

JAVIER, ZAR

Zar Javier was born in Iloilo, Philippines and raised by loving parents, Remedios and Nonito Jamindang, in San Diego, CA. He attended San Diego State University and graduated with a BS in Information Decision Systems and a minor in Computer Science. He founded PNOY Apparel in 1999 and serves as Creative Director and CEO. PNOY Apparel is a cultural clothing company that highlights Philippine and Filipino American history and focuses on the "Know History" ideology. Zar also started Shirt The Kids in 2008, a charity campaign that provided "Sammy The Sunshine" tees to impoverished children across the Philippines. Today, the "Know History" ideology continues through a new sub brand, Kampeon, (which uses the Tagalog word for "champion"). Kampeon broadens PNOY Apparel's design and consumer demographic as well as philanthropic duties internationally.

KIWI ILLAFONTE

Kiwi Illafonte is a community organizer and cultural worker based in Oakland, CA (by way of Los Angeles). He is one-third of the renowned Filipino American rap group Native Guns and his solo work includes *The Summer Exposure Mixtape* and *Writes of Passage: Portraits of a Son Rising*. He also served as the Deputy Secretary General of BAYAN-USA, a national alliance of groups organizing for the rights and welfare of Filipinos both in the Philippines and the US, and was the subject of the documentary film, "Sounds of a New Hope." Kiwi is currently creating and performing new music with his live band Bandung 55, and works as a Health Educator at a high school clinic in Hayward, CA.

KNOWA LAZARUS

Cedric Bonjoc aka Knowa Lazarus is half of the music group Q-York. Born and raised in Queens, NY, he recently migrated to the Philippines. He is a husband, a father, a believer, and a dreamer. Live life with purpose and passion and anything is possible!

KRYSTILEZ

Krystilez is an emcee from Hawai'i. This critically acclaimed and highly controversial artist also hosts a popular nightly radio show on 102.7 da BOMB. With countless solo projects under his belt, he is also 1/4 of the Hawai'i rap supergroup, Angry Locals, whose albums include *Aloha From Hawaii*, *Shaka to da Neck Mixtape*, *The Los Wages Tour*, and *Locals Only*. His solo projects include *The Greatest HI* (featuring The Free Floers), *The O*, and *The Pho Curry Mixtape*. Widely known for his witty lines and his true-to-Hawai'i content in his lyrics and style, "Steezy" is the definition of an "Urban Island Artist." His most popular song to date, "Bloodline," remains a staple and anthem among the many generations of fighters and defenders of Hawai'i. "Love I Get," from his latest release, *The Huliau Mixtape*, marked his first song in radio rotation as he moves towards a sound that will mix Urban Island Culture with the mainstream.

LABRADOR, RODERICK N.

Dr. Roderick N. Labrador is an Assistant Professor of Ethnic Studies at the University of Hawai'i at Mānoa. His research and community work focuses on race, ethnicity, class, culture, language, migration, education, Hip Hop, and cultural production in Hawai'i, the US, and the Philippines. He is a 1.5-generation Filipino American—he was born in the Philippines and immigrated to the U.S. during elementary school, growing up in southeast San Diego. He has lived in Honolulu for nearly 20 years and for the past several years, "Professor Rod" has worked with promoters and businesses like ESSA, FOES, Curators of Hip Hop, The Got Rice? Show, Gumz/Workhouse, In4mation, and About The Goods to organize local Hip Hop shows and events, including Shirt The Kids—Honolulu. He also hosts "Inside the Ethnic Studies Studio" where he and his students conduct interviews, workshops, and forums with local, national, and international Hip Hop artists.

LAZARUS, KNOWA

Cedric Bonjoc aka Knowa Lazarus is half of the music group Q-York. Born and raised in Queens, NY, he recently migrated to the Philippines. He is a husband, a father, a believer, and a dreamer. Live life with purpose and passion and anything is possible!

MABALON, DAWN

Dawn Bohulano Mabalon, PhD, is a third generation Pinay born in Stockton, California and an associate professor of history at San Francisco State University, where she teaches courses in US history, US empire in the Philippines, American food history, and race and ethnicity. She received her BA in history and an MA in Asian American Studies from UCLA, and a PhD in history from Stanford University. With Lakan de Leon and Jonathan Ramos, she directed the documentary *Beats, Rhymes and Resistance: Pilipinos and Hip Hop in LA* (2000). Her poetry, essays, and articles have been published in *maganda* and *Filipinas* and in the books and anthologies *Tomorrow's Memories: The Diary of Angeles Monrayo* (2004), *Coming Home to a Landscape: Writings by Filipinas* (2004), *Pinay Power: Pilipina Peminist Theory* (2006), and *Positively No Filipinos Allowed* (2006). She is the co-author of *Filipinos in Stockton* (Arcadia, 2008), co-editor of *Filipinos in San Francisco*

(Arcadia, 2010), and author of *Little Manila Is in the Heart: The Making of the Filipina/o American Community in Stockton, California* (Duke University Press, 2013). She is a founding board member of the Little Manila Foundation in Stockton, California, which works to preserve the Little Manila Historic Site; a National Scholar on the board of trustees of the Filipino American National Historical Society; and president of the board of Pin@y Educational Partnerships. She has been engaged in Hip Hop Pinayism with her BFF sistafriend Allyson for more than 20 years.

MALAYA LP

Born in Manila and raised in Los Angeles, Malaya LP, aka Paisley, has resided on O'ahu since age 20 and has been woven into the Honolulu music scene since 1997. At 22, she went to New York City to attend conservatory. Back on O'ahu, she released her first project called *Memoirs of the Tempo* in 2007 with Tempo Valley, a group that played an integral role in the Honolulu music scene. After the dissolution of that group, Paisley continued her musical journey with Seph One composing and performing together as freelance artists and both returned to the University of Hawai'i at Mānoa to complete their degrees, with Paisley earning a Bachelor's in Anthropology. She has also been the lead vocalist for a number of experimental and jazz ensembles in Honolulu, which most recently includes Subtonic Orchestra and the acoustic trio TR3ES. She is a musical mentor for Hawai'i youth through the Mana Maoli Music Collective and is an active supporter/advocate in the areas of gender violence awareness/prevention, homeless and immigrant communities, and issues concerning food sovereignty and cultural preservation. Her recent work also includes serving as a Bilingual Pilipina Advocate for survivors of domestic violence on the island of O'ahu. Malaya LP has a few collaborations in the works, including an upcoming music project featuring some of the finest producers from the Pacific and a theme song for an upcoming web series.

MANABAT, CORINNE

Corinne is a Filipina American filmmaker and hip hop head (as a b-girl and lyricist), born and raised from the forgotten borough of Staten Island. Currently, she is co-producer of the tentatively titled *What Happened to Danny?*, a feature documentary on the death of 19 year-old Pvt. Danny Chen and a community's inspirational fight for justice. Her latest work, "Why We Rise," is a documentary short about three brave, young New Yorkers who reveal what it's like to grow up without having legal immigration status. As a media educator, Corinne has been involved with Global Action Project, Third World Newsreel, Tribeca Film Institute, and Maysles Institute.

MANILA RYCE

Manila Ryce was born and raised in the South Bay of Los Angeles, CA and has a BFA in Illustration with emphasis in Animation. He has worked in electoral politics for Dennis Kucinich and Ralph Nader, and currently works at a local level with progressive and revolutionary organizations in Southern California. Manila believes that all artists are morally obligated to address real issues with their exposure, and thus focuses on social justice issues—often using humor as his lubricant. Manila's other hobbies include sleeping, resting, dozing, hibernating, crashing, passing out, nodding off, reposing, slumbering, snoozing, and taking the occasional nap. When writing a bio, he also enjoys referring to himself in the third person.

MARTIN, AARON "WOES"

Aaron "Woes" Martin was born on O'ahu, but spent most of his childhood between Southern California and Nevada, returning to Hawai'i for high school. In 1998 a devastating, near-death car accident inspired him to leave the islands once again, this time to Seattle, Washington. Invigorated by the change and the new environment, the city, and being indoors, he started experimenting with various art media and discovered a flourishing art movement in the US continent. Refueled and inspired, he returned to Hawai'i. Aaron had his first exhibitions in Hawai'i in 2002 and since then, he has shown his work in galleries along the West and East Coasts as well as for many traveling exhibits in the United States, London, Berlin, Japan, Hong Kong, Singapore, Indonesia, the Philippines, Thailand, Australia, and New Zealand. Aaron is also well known in the designer toy world for his iconic characters done in 3D form, from resin collectible figures to vinyl toys. He is regularly posted up at Comic-Con in San Diego and New York. In 2011, Aaron started Army of Snipers, an international collective of artists who range from street artists, videographers, photographers, painters, sculptors, musicians, and graphic designers. AOS uses its global network to connect with each other, expand its fan base, and to experience art life on a broader spectrum.

NADAL, KEVIN

Dr. Kevin Leo Yabut Nadal is an award-winning professor, psychologist, performer, activist, and author who received his doctorate in counseling psychology from Columbia University in New York City. Currently, he is an Associate Professor of Psychology at John Jay College of Criminal Justice, City University of New York, where he is also the Deputy Director of the Forensic Mental Health Counseling Program. He has published over 60 works on multicultural issues in the fields of psychology and education, including *Filipino American Psychology: A Handbook of Theory, Research, and Clinical Practice* (Wiley, 2011), *Women and Mental Disorders* (Praeger, 2011), and *That's So Gay! Microaggressions and the Lesbian, Gay, Bisexual, and Transgender Community* (American Psychological Association, 2013). A California-bred New Yorker, he was once named one of *People* magazine's hottest bachelors, and he has been featured on Fox News, The Filipino Channel, PBS, The Weather Channel, The History Channel, and HGTV.

NEVADO, NATE

Nate Nevado is a counselor and teacher at Skyline College for the last eight years. He is the founder and coordinator of Rock The School Bells (RTSB), a Hip Hop Educational Conference that aims to empower and educate students about the importance of higher education, career exploration, healthy lifestyles, and social change within their communities through Hip Hop. As a result of the successful work of RTSB, Skyline College will be opening the new Center of Hip Hop Arts, Scholarship, and Education (CHASE) in the fall of 2013. This center will provide Hip Hop educational resources and best practices and pedagogies for students and faculty. He has been a student of Hip Hop since the early 90s as part of a Bay Area emcee crew called the Lyrical Assassins as well as a part of a b-boy crew called the Sub-City Rockers. Every now and then, he'll dust off the mics during class and rock some verses for his students, reminding them that in Hip Hop, we are always students.

PRIJOLES, LILY

In between vandalizing driveways with washable chalk and winning the Mira Mesa HopScotching championship in '04, Lily Prijoles has been working on her Master's in Community Representing for over 10 years. She received her Bachelor's from Academy of Art University in San Francisco, studying filmmaking and Puzzle Fighter and joining PAPA (Pinoy and Pinay artists). Lily is a proud former volunteer of the prestigious Bindlestiff Studios, where her internationally renowned group 8th WONDER was formed, turning her into an actual performer of Bindlestiff Studios. She later joined a band of gypsy/renegade filmmakers pushing a movie called *The Debut*. She later joined her *Debut* pals who started Kid Heroes Productions/Xylophone films, turning her into a proud "utos-utos" girl/production worker. Currently, Lily finds herself back in her childhood neighborhood of Mira Mesa in San Diego, "serving the people" combo meals at Filipino Food & Bakery and starting a ruckus with KAMP, Kuya Ate Mentorship Program.

RAMIREZ, JOSEPH

Joseph Allen Ruanto-Ramirez is a Katutubo American of Aeta, Igorot, Lipi, and Moro descent, and Ilokano. He received his BA in Ethnic Studies from the University of California, San Diego and his MA in Sociological Practice from CSU San Marcos. He currently works at UC San Diego's Cross-Cultural Center and works for the Vice Chancellor for Equity, Diversity, and Inclusion. His focus of research looks at Katutubo American experiences in Philippine America and the ethno-racial project in the modern Philippine nation-state. He also looks at youth culture in relations to race and ethnicity, gender and sexuality, technology, and the politics of "(re)imagining" and "remembering." His activism revolves around indigenous politics and rights and being critical of Pilipina/o American performativity of indigenous identities and cultures.

REGIS-LU, ETHEL

Ethel Regis-Lu is a doctoral candidate in the Department of Ethnic Studies at UC Berkeley. Her dissertation, tentatively titled, "Mediating Diaspora: Transnational 'Ethnic' Media and the Global Filipino," investigates how state projects and media produced in and outside the Philippines shape the identities and experiences of Filipino diasporans. Her work examines the notion of "Global Filipino" by analyzing television programs on The Filipino Channel (TFC) and gleaning insight from interviews with media producers and Filipino American audiences. Lu has worked in areas of public health research and education, including at the San Diego Comprehensive Research Center in Health Disparities, where she co-authored "A Conceptual Model for Faculty Development in Academic Medicine: The Underrepresented Minority Faculty Experience" in the *Journal for the National Medical Association* (Sept/Oct 2011 Education issue). Lu currently works as the Teaching Assistant Coordinator for the Culture, Art, and Technology writing program at the University of California, San Diego.

ROB NASTY

For the past 20 years, Rob Nasty has been a champion uprocker and established b-boy from the San Francisco Bay Area. He has made personal pilgrimages to Brooklyn, NYC and learned from the best of the best at this style of dance. A seasoned veteran in all forms of "rocking," Rob Nasty is leading the next generation of dancers into the "New Rock Era" and is dedicated to spreading "Rock Dance Culture" around the world!

ROCKY RIVERA

Rocky Rivera is an accomplished journalist-turned-emcee whose editorials appeared in *XXL*, *The Source* and *Rolling Stone* magazine before she decided to pursue an artist's life. Trading her Moleskines for microphones, she's dropped three musical projects since 2008, *Married to the Hustle Mixtape*, the self-titled album, *Rocky Rivera* (2010), and *POP KILLER MXTP* (2011). Her second album, *Gangster of Love*, is dropping in the fall 2013 on Beatrock Music. In 2012, Rocky became the only female artist at the VIBE HOUSE's Respect The West Showcase at the SXSW Festival, sharing the stage with West Coast favorites such as Nipsey Hussle, Strong Arm Steady, Snoop Dogg, and Kendrick Lamar. In the past, she's opened up for diverse artists such as Zion-I, Macklemore, Blue Scholars, Pac Div, and Dead Prez. Rocky continues to headline up and down the West Coast with her crew performing her signature blend of thought-provoking lyrics and bass-rattling rhymes. For more info, go to www.rockyrivera.com.

SAPIGAO, JANICE

Janice Lobo Sapigao is a Pinay poet and writer born and raised in San Jose, CA. She is a community organizer, Voices of Our Nation (VONA) alumna, radio show co-host of paperjam on TropMag.com, and co-founder of the Sunday Jump, an open mic in Los Angeles' Historic Filipinotown. She enjoys playing with stuffed animals, drinking green tea, running, and cooking.

SEPH ONE

Known as Seph One on O'ahu airwaves, the emcee/host/radio DJ for HI-Level Funkshun on KTUH 90.3 FM, has been a representative of Hip Hop Arts in Hawai'i for nearly two decades. Born in Washington, DC and raised in parts of the US and Europe, he has been a resident of Hawai'i for most of his life. He released his first project with Hip Hop collective Triangular Prizm in 2001 and has been blessed to open up for the likes of Pharcyde, Living Legends, Mos Def, Talib Kweli, and De La Soul, as well as sharing the stage with the Wu-Tang Clan, Bone Thugs-N-Harmony, and Supernatural for Rock the Bells in 2007. Near the end of a derailed project with the band Tempo Valley, he developed a close friendship with Paisley, the featured vocalist of the group, with whom he also recorded multiple tracks. After a sudden break from the band, the two pursued the enlightenment of their minds through education, with Seph One completing a Bachelor's degree in Ethnic Studies. Music now moves the two through community outreach projects and grassroots organizing. By day, he coordinates community engagement projects as a male advocate and role model for mobilizing men in the movement to end gender violence. He has traveled across the islands providing training and education, attending various conferences and workshops to raise awareness around domestic-violence issues. He has been featured in several albums with fellow emcees, including Hunger Pains, Mo Illa Pillaz, and the Mana Maoli Music Collective. Seph One is a conscious living and breathing sound wave surfer; you might catch him surfing a sound wave at a cypher near you.

SIYAM, FREEDOM ALLAH

Freedom Self-Born Allah Siyam hails from Rainier Valley of Seattle, the 98118. Free has four degrees from four different institutions of higher learning that rest on a foundation of 120 degrees of knowledge, wisdom, and understanding of the Five Percent. The Northwest Filipino American Student Alliance, isangmahal arts kollective, and Omega Phi Omega Fraternity were important to Freedom as a student. As founding member of Anakbayan Seattle, the Philippine U.S. Solidarity Organization, BAYAN-USA, and the International League of People's Struggle, US chapter, Freedom imagines another world possible, where the ruling classes are reeducated and the people dictate policies that ensure a more egalitarian world. Free got 12 jewels and has 12 years' experience as an educator in different capacities—as a classroom teacher, dean of students, assistant principal, and member of the adjunct faculty. In 2006 Freedom was the target of annoying interrogation by the *Federales*. His only crime is being Filipino in America.

STELLBURG, RIANA "RUDIFIED"

Riana "Rudified" Stellburg is an avid music lover born and raised in Hawai'i. She is Haolepino in the 808. Stellburg received her Bachelor's degree in Photojournalism from Hawai'i Pacific University in 2012. In 2008, she was introduced to the underground Hip Hop scene and was in love. Stellburg then received an internship with the publication *Contrast* magazine. There she wrote her first magazine article on the Hawai'i Hip Hop group Monarx. Later, the Star-Advertiser's *Honolulu Pulse* hired her as the youngest freelance photojournalist and her first published article featured Odd Future. She has photographed national and international music icons of all genres, such as Earth, Wind, and Fire, Dead Prez, and Murs. In 2012, she coordinated and fundraised for 808SPEAKERBOX, a showcase featuring local Hip Hop acts. Currently, Stellburg is the manager for About The Goods, a local Hip Hop shop. Stellburg also is a DJ and has opened up for various local and national Hip Hop acts, including Bambu and Geologic.

TINTIANGCO-CUBALES, ALLYSON

Born and raised in the San Francisco Bay Area, Dr. Allyson Tintiangco-Cubales is an Associate Professor in the College of Ethnic Studies at San Francisco State University. She is also an affiliated faculty member in the doctorate program for Educational Leadership in SFSU's School of Education and the current coordinator of the Master's program in Asian American Studies. Tintiangco-Cubales has published several books and a wide array of articles that focus on the development of ethnic studies curriculum and community-responsive pedagogy. Her research focuses on urban youth, community studies, critical performance pedagogy, motherscholaring, and Pinayism, a concept that she coined in 1995. She is also currently writing about Babaylan pedagogy and her life as a community-engaged motherscholar-of-color. Amongst her many projects, she has led initiatives that have forwarded Youth Participatory Action Research (YPAR) and Teacher Participatory Action Research (TPAR), which she developed in 2010. Since 2007, she has served as a consultant with the San Francisco Unified School District on the development of ethnic studies curriculum for high school students. In addition to her responsibilities as a faculty member at SFSU, Tintiangco-Cubales is the founder and director of Pin@y Educational Partnerships (PEP), an ethnic studies educational pipeline that creates partnerships and projects that work toward social justice. Along with her work on campus and in the community, she teaches a variety of courses including Filipina/o American

Literature and Culture, where she uses Hip Hop as text. For almost twenty years, she's been collaborating on many projects—from creative to academic—with her bestie, Dr. Dawn Mabalon, but for real, it all began with Hip Hop and spoken word in the 90s!

VILLEGAS, MARK R.

Mark R. Villegas is a poet, filmmaker, blogger, and PhD candidate in Culture and Theory at the University of California, Irvine. He is a navy brat who grew up in Yokosuka, Japan; Pascagoula, Mississippi; Long Beach, California; and Jacksonville, Florida. His films *Hip Hop Mestizaje*, (2007), *Lyrical Empire: Hip Hop in Metro Manila* (2010), and *Global Pinay Style* (2011) have been screened in classrooms and at film festivals around the world and can be viewed online.

VIOLA, MICHAEL

Michael Viola is core faculty in the liberal arts program at Antioch University Seattle. His research fields include critical pedagogy, transnational social movements, radical cultural production, and critical theories of race. He is currently working on a book project exploring the contributions of Filipina/o American activism to social theory and global social movements.

WANG, OLIVER

Oliver Wang is an associate professor of sociology at CSU, Long Beach. He is author of *Legions of Boom: Filipino American Mobile Disc Jockey Crews of the San Francisco Bay Area* (Duke University Press) and has also published essays on Asian American MCs, retro-soul music, and the social geography of fusion taco trucks. He writes regularly on arts, music, and culture for NPR and KCET's *Artbound*, as well as his own audioblog, Soul-Sides.com. He's been an active radio/club DJ since 1993 and now does weddings and private events.

ZANOTTI, MILAN

Milan Zanotti is not new to the industry. A former Christian rapper who decided that the life of ministry and religion was a contradiction to her spritiual views and how she REALLY felt about herself, she left the ministry and Christian rap to do broadcast radio for 102.5 KDON. From there, she met some people who "wanted to sign her and make her famous," though what they wanted was not in line with what Milan wanted for her future. She left them and became a renegade. On her own, she collaborated and worked with the other OUT artists like LASTO and FoxxJazell and has done some songs with other rappers and artists outside of OUT music. With her hard and gangsta delivery, she seems to throw in a little twist with her sexy and seductive lyrics. Not only does Milan rap about money, sex, and diamonds, but she rhymes about her life and troubled past. Milan was NOT always MILAN. She is a transgender WOMAN who came from a broken home. Her mother had her at a very young age and her father was incarcerated and never around. When Milan was younger, she had to fend for herself a lot because her mother met a new man, who was very verbally and mentally abusive towards Milan; this abuse went on for years. Not only was she battling at home, but she was also struggling at school, where she was picked on, made fun of, and bullied. She became alone, suicidal, and confused about life, so that's when she turned to GOD and music to help release her pain. Now she is working on her debut album and other projects. HUSTLE is in her blood, and through trials and tribulations, she's never given up.

CPSIA information can be obtained at www.ICGtesting.com
Printed in the USA
BVOW10s1830100515

399658BV00007B/157/P